SILENCE AND SIGN LANGUAGE IN MEDIEVAL MONASTICISM

Silence and Sign Language in Medieval Monasticism explores the rationales for religious silence in early medieval abbeys and the use of nonverbal forms of communication among monks when rules of silence forbade them from speaking. After examining the spiritual benefits of personal silence as a form of protection against the perils of sinful discourse in early monastic thought, this work shows how the monks of the abbey of Cluny (founded in 910 in Burgundy) were the first to employ a silent language of meaning-specific hand signs that allowed them to convey precise information without recourse to spoken words. Scott Bruce discusses the linguistic character of the Cluniac sign language, its central role in the training of novices, the precautions taken to prevent its abuse, and the widespread adoption of this custom in other abbeys throughout Europe, which resulted in the creation of regionally specific idioms of this silent language.

SCOTT G. BRUCE is Assistant Professor of Medieval History at the University of Colorado at Boulder.

Cambridge Studies in Medieval Life and Thought
Fourth Series

General Editor:

ROSAMOND MCKITTERICK
Professor of Medieval History, University of Cambridge, and Fellow of Sidney Sussex College

Advisory Editors:

CHRISTINE CARPENTER
Professor of Medieval English History, University of Cambridge, and Fellow of New Hall

JONATHAN SHEPARD

The series Cambridge Studies in Medieval Life and Thought was inaugurated by G. G. Coulton in 1921; Professor Rosamond McKitterick now acts as General Editor of the Fourth Series, with Professor Christine Carpenter and Dr Jonathan Shepard as Advisory Editors. The series brings together outstanding work by medieval scholars over a wide range of human endeavour extending from political economy to the history of ideas.

For a list of recent titles in the series, see end of book.

SILENCE AND SIGN LANGUAGE IN MEDIEVAL MONASTICISM

The Cluniac Tradition c. 900–1200

SCOTT G. BRUCE

CAMBRIDGE
UNIVERSITY PRESS

CAMBRIDGE UNIVERSITY PRESS

Cambridge, New York, Melbourne, Madrid, Cape Town, Singapore, São Paulo

Cambridge University Press
The Edinburgh Building, Cambridge CB2 8RU, UK

Published in the United States of America by Cambridge University Press, New York

www.cambridge.org
Information on this title: www.cambridge.org/9780521860802

First published 2007

Printed in the United Kingdom at the University Press, Cambridge

A catalogue record for this publication is available from the British Library

Library of Congress Cataloging-in-Publication Data
Bruce, Scott G. (Scott Gordon), 1967–
Silence and sign language in medieval monasticism: the Cluniac
tradition *c.* 900–1200 / Scott G. Bruce.
p. cm. – (Cambridge studies in medieval life and thought ; v4th ser., 68)
Includes bibliographical references and index.
ISBN-13: 978-0-521-86080-2 (hardback)
ISBN-10: 0-521-86080-6 (hardback)
1. Cluny (Benedictine abbey)   2. Monastic and religious life – France – Cluny – History – Middle
Ages, 600–1500.   3. Silence – Religious aspects – Christianity.   4. Solitude – Religious
aspects – Christianity.   5. Sign language – France – Cluny.   I. Title.
BX2615.C63B78   2007
419'.1–dc22   2007013266

ISBN 978-0-521-86080-2 hardback

for Anne and Mira,
share this with me

Fast gleichen sie einander alle;
in Gottes Gärten schweigen sie,
   wie viele, viele Intervalle
in seiner Macht und Melodie

Rainer Maria Rilke, Die Engel (1902)

CONTENTS

TABLES

ACKNOWLEDGMENTS

This book has grown in the telling and with it my debts to the individuals and institutions that have sustained and supported me from its inception to the present. It began as an idea suggested by Richard C. Hoffmann, one of many inspired professors who introduced me to medieval studies when I was an undergraduate at York University in Toronto. Those who know Rich know how much this project owes to his relentless inquiry into all things fishy. As a dissertation, it benefited much from the generous insights of my teachers at Princeton University. Giles Constable, my advisor and oft-times fencing partner, shared his unrivalled knowledge of Cluniac history and provided a model of professional integrity. In our many epee bouts over the years, I only beat him once. He knows why. Peter Brown encouraged a long view of late antique monasticism and did the most to inform my thinking about Christian asceticism. His support and example were invaluable for the completion of the dissertation. Early on in this project William Chester Jordan helped me to disentangle the thorny prose of the Cluniac sign lexicon. Since then he has posed difficult questions and dispensed words of wisdom, both in the quiet of his office and in the welcoming din of the Annex. He even delivered the "moolah" on time. For that and so much else, I owe him thanks. Along the way, many learned individuals read parts of the manuscript or shared their expertise with me. My thanks to: Susan Boynton, Isabelle Cochelin, Stephen Epstein, John Fleming, Jason Glenn, Bruce Holsinger, Drew Jones, Dominique Iogna-Prat, Gert Melville and Barbara Rosenwein. Parts of this book have already appeared in print in various guises: "The Tongue is a Fire: The Discipline of Silence in Early Medieval Monasticism (400–1100)," in *The Hands of the Tongue: Essays on Deviant Speech*, ed. Edwin Craun (Kalamazoo, 2007), pp. 3–32; "Monastic Sign Language in the Cluniac Customaries," in *From Dead of Night to End of Day: The Medieval Customs of Cluny / Du coeur de la nuit à la fin du jour: Les coutumes clunisiennes au moyen âge*, ed. Susan Boynton and Isabelle Cochelin, Disciplina monastica III (Turnhout, 2005), pp. 273–286; "The Origins of Cistercian Sign

Acknowledgments

Language," *Cîteaux: Commentarii Cistercienses* 52 (2001): 193–209; and "Lurking with Spiritual Intent: A Note on the Origin and Functions of the Monastic Roundsman (*Circator*)," *Revue bénédictine* 109 (1999): 75–89. I owe the editors and anonymous readers of these journals and collections my thanks for helping me to shape and nuance many of the ideas presented here. I would also like to acknowledge with gratitude the audiences who listened to conference papers and public lectures on the topics treated in this book, specifically those at Boston University, Harvard Divinity School, Technische Universität Dresden, the University of California at Santa Cruz, Westfälische Wilhelms-Universität Münster and Williams College.

I was very fortunate to research and write the dissertation that became this book under the protective wing of a generous institution. A Graduate Fellowship from Princeton University supported me for many years of coursework and composition. Grants from the Department of History, the Group for the Study of Late Antiquity, the Association of Princeton Graduate Alumni and the Council on Regional Studies allowed me to spend summers in Europe, where I consulted manuscript sources and visited monastic sites. With a Charlotte W. Newcombe Doctoral Dissertation Fellowship from the Woodrow Wilson Foundation (1999/2000), I was able to finish the dissertation *and* pay the rent on the rambling attic apartment we had on Witherspoon Street. Since then, I have enjoyed the support of a research assistantship in the School of Historical Studies at the Institute for Advanced Study in Princeton (2000/2001), a Friedrich Solmsen Postdoctoral Fellowship at the Institute for Research in the Humanities at the University of Wisconsin (2001/2002) and finished the lion's share of the revisions of the book as a Visiting Scholar at the Medieval Institute at the University of Notre Dame (2004/2005). I am especially grateful to Paul Cobb, Drew Jones, Tom Noble and Janneke Raaijmakers for making me feel so at home in South Bend.

Many of the merits of the book in its final form are due to the critical acumen of my editors, Jonathan Shepard and Rosamond McKitterick, who were exceedingly generous with their comments on the manuscript and very patient with me when circumstances delayed its completion. My thanks as well to those members of the editorial and production staff at Cambridge University Press who facilitated the creation of the book. I am also grateful to two students, Brianna Depperschmidt and Troy Tice, whose keen eyes caught several errors in the typescript.

Equally important are the friends and family who have supported me with their loving presence despite the distances that sometimes separate us. These friends have been family: Lisa Bailey, Paul Cobb, James Cunningham, Jason Glenn, Peter Low, Molly Polk, Suman Seth, Edith Sheffer, Aminda Smith and Susannah Strang. For their part, my wife's

Acknowledgments

family has given me a tremendous gift: they invited me home and with them I found a home. My warm thanks to Lucy Lester, George Dalin and T. William (Billy) Lester in Hyde Park; and to Eric, Audrey, Bob, Matthew and Maurine Lester in Saint Joseph and Sawyer. My professional vocation has taken me far afield from the old neighborhood in Scarborough, where I grew up, but my own family never lets me forget where I started. My siblings are the best of friends: Steve (Satch) Bruce, Lynn (Lynnless) Dickinson and Paul (Dickie) Dickinson. Our brother Stewart left us long before this work began, but we remember him still. My beloved parents, Bev and Gord, taught me everything I know about hard work and its rewards. They embraced this project with the kind of indulgence that most families show their youngest child, but they did not hide their eagerness to see the work done. I regret that my father did not live to hold the book in his hands, but I am comforted by the fact that he would have been proud of it. One of the many admirable qualities of my father was his inability to hide the pride that he took in the accomplishments of his children. He and my mother are the heroes of my life.

Even with all of this support, the book may not have been completed at all without the love and encouragement of Anne. She has taken time from her own research to read chapter drafts and to tame my turgid prose; on long walks and on many phone calls from Troyes, she has helped me find my way through a labyrinth of textual and conceptual difficulties; and every day that I have been graced with her presence she has reminded me that a life spent toiling in the word mines beside her is the best kind of life there is. This work is dedicated to her.

SGB
Vic's Expresso & News
Boulder, Colorado
26 June 2007

Note on Latin words and biblical citations

Several of the words for signified objects that appear in the monastic sign lexicons of the Middle Ages are not attested in any other source from the period (Tables 1 and 3–5). While it is reasonable to deduce the general meaning of some of these terms (*rufeolae*, for instance, are clearly a special kind of bread), others resist a reliable translation without further corroboration of their meaning (for example, *navetum, verves, cigara* and *burciolum*). When in doubt, I have left the original Latin term untranslated.

The biblical citations in this book refer to the Vulgate, which follows the numbering of the Psalms found in the Septuagint rather than the original Hebrew.

ABBREVIATIONS

AASS	*Acta sanctorum quotquot toto orbe coluntur*, ed. Jean Bolland *et al.* (Antwerp, 1643–)
Bernard	Bernard of Cluny, *Ordo Cluniacensis sive Consuetudines*, ed. M. Herrgott, in *Vetus Disciplina Monastica* (Paris, 1726; repr. Siegburg, 1999), pp. 136–364 (cited by book, chapter and page number)
BHL	*Bibliotheca hagiographica latina antiquae et mediae aetatis*, 2 vols. (Brussels, 1898–1901) with supplemental volumes published in 1911 and 1986 (cited by *BHL* number)
BN	Bibliothèque nationale, Paris
Canterbury	The Canterbury Sign Lexicon (individual signs cited by number)
CCCM	*Corpus christianorum: Continuatio medievalis* (Turnhout, 1966–)
CCM	*Corpus consuetudinum monasticarum* (Siegburg, 1963–)
CCSL	*Corpus christianorum: Series latina* (Turnhout, 1963–)
Cluny	The Cluniac Sign Lexicon (individual signs cited by number)
CSEL	*Corpus scriptorum ecclesiasticorum latinorum* (Vienna, 1866–)
DHGE	*Dictionnaire d'historie et de géographie ecclésiastiques* (Paris, 1912–)
Dictionnaire de spiritualité	*Dictionnaire de spiritualité, ascétique et mystique doctrine et histoire* (Paris, 1922–)
Fleury	The Fleury Sign Lexicon (individual signs cited by number)
Hirsau	The Hirsau Sign Lexicon (individual signs cited by number)
MGH SRG	*Monumenta Germaniae Historica: Scriptores rerum Germanicarum in usum scholarum separatim editi* (Hanover and Berlin, 1871–)
MGH SS	*Monumenta Germaniae Historica inde ab anno christi quingentesimo usque ad annum millesimum et quingentesimum: Scriptores in folio*, 32 vols. (Hanover and Leipzig, 1826–1934)
PL	*Patrologia cursus completus: Series latina*, ed. Jacques-Paul Migne, 221 vols. (Paris, 1844–1888)

List of abbreviations

RB	*Regula Benedicti*, ed. Adalbert de Vogüé, in *La règle de saint Benoît*, 7 vols., *SC* CLXXXI–CLXXXVII (Paris, 1971–1972)
RM	*Regula magistri*, ed. Adalbert de Vogüé, in *La règle de Maître*, 3 vols., *SC* CV–CVII (Paris, 1964–1965)
SC	*Sources chrétiennes* (Paris, 1941–)
Statuta	*Statuta Petri Venerabilis abbatis Cluniacensis*, ed. Giles Constable, *CCM* VI (Siegburg, 1975), pp. 19–106
Ulrich	Ulrich of Zell, *Consuetudines Cluniacensis*, *PL* CXLIX, cols. 643–779 (cited by book, chapter and column number)
William	William of Hirsau, *Constitutiones Hirsaugienses*, *PL* CL, cols. 923–1146 (cited by book, chapter and column number)

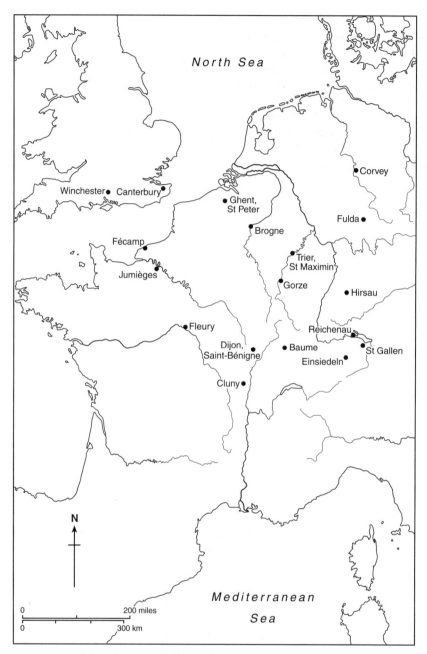

North Sea

Winchester ● Canterbury ●

Fécamp ●

Jumièges ●

Fleury ●

● Ghent,
St Peter

● Brogne

● Trier,
St Maximin

● Gorze

Dijon,
Saint-Bénigne

Cluny ●

● Baume

● Corvey

Fulda ●

● Hirsau

Reichenau

● St Gallen

Einsiedeln ●

N

0   200 miles
0   300 km

Mediterranean
Sea

Monastic centres in the tenth and early eleventh centuries

INTRODUCTION: THE DORMANT LANGUAGE

"Every angel is terrifying." The sentiment of this line from Rainer Maria Rilke's poem *The First Elegy* (1912) seems as cold and distant as starlight.[1] It contrasts markedly with the sympathetic and comforting images that late modern people usually evoke when they think about the messengers of God. Over the past century, one of the most understated achievements of western culture has been the successful domestication of these immortal beings of light. While Rilke could still imagine that any contact with angels would consume him in their "overwhelming existence" (*stärkeres Dasein*), the notion that their beauty is the beginning of terror has lost its meaning in the cultural vocabulary of the west.[2] With softened gazes, these celestial beings now accompany us through the paces of our mundane lives, sigh along with us at our troubles, and offer up to us as comfort a longer, more balanced, perspective on the anxieties that attend our mortal condition. Even the most sublime articulations of this image, like Wim Wenders' celebrated film *Der Himmel über Berlin* (1986), subvert Rilke's hierarchy in ways that ensnare angels in our own narcissistic preoccupations.

Despite the gulf of centuries that separate them, Rilke's depiction of angels as remote and untamable agents of God that inspired sincere awe and fear in those mortals fortunate (or unfortunate) enough to encounter them had much in common with the sensibilities of the early medieval monks who are the subject of this book. Angels in the Middle Ages had little tolerance for human frailties. Take this anecdote told by an eleventh-century chronicler. According to Ralph Glaber, a certain monk at the

---

[1] Rainer Maria Rilke, *Die erste Elegie*, line 7: "Der jener Engel ist schrecklich." ed. Rilke Archiv with Ruth Sieber-Rilke, in *Sämtliche Werke*, 7 vols. (1955–1997), vol. I, p. 685.

[2] *Ibid.*, lines 1–6: "Wer, wenn ich schriee, hörte mich denn aus der Engel / Ordnungen? und gesetzt selbst, es nähme / einer mich plötzlich ans Herz: ich verginge von seinem / stärkeren Dasein. Denn das Schöne ist nichts / als des Schrecklichen Anfang, den wir noch grade ertragen, / und wir bewundern es so, weil es gelassen verschmäht, / uns zu zerstören."

church of St. Germain in Auxerre habitually spat and dribbled while praying at the altar of Mary. His unseemly conduct in such a holy place prompted a terrifying rebuke from an angel, who appeared to him in a vision as a man dressed in white garments. "Why do you shower me with spittle?" the angel asked in annoyance. "As you see, it is I who receive your prayers and bear them to the sight of the most merciful judge!" Upon waking, the monk was beside himself with fear and vowed to exercise more rigorous control over his comportment when he prayed. He strongly encouraged his brethren to do likewise.[3]

As this episode makes clear, the visitation of an angel evoked reverential awe and more than a touch of trepidation in early medieval viewers, who valued and feared these immortal beings precisely because they were favored to enjoy the eternal presence of God. So great was the allure of their privileged place in the celestial hierarchy that monks and other religious specialists in the Christian tradition attempted to model their behavior on the unearthly characteristics of angels. By renouncing the transient satisfactions of the world and cultivating in cloistered seclusion the unchanging qualities of their angelic exemplars, early medieval monks conformed their lives as far as possible to emulate their counterparts in heaven in the hope of meriting a place among the ranks of the Christian elect at the end of time.[4]

It is a central argument of this book that the brethren of Cluny, an abbey founded in 910 in Burgundy, developed this monk–angel analogy to a degree that was unprecedented in the monastic tradition. The active promotion of this ideal and the terms by which they defined and pursued it account for Cluny's rapid rise to prominence in the late tenth and eleventh centuries. Undistinguished at the time of its foundation, this monastery achieved its reputation for sanctity in no small part because the ideal of angelic conduct fostered by its monks led contemporaries to believe that their prayers had an unrivalled efficacy among the heavenly host in whose image they modeled their lives. Building the ideals of

---

[3] Rodulphus Glaber, *Historiarum libri quinque* 5.1.7: "Apparuit ei stans iuxta altare quidam candidis indumentis circumdatus, preferens in manibus pannum candidissimum, atque in huiusmodi erumpebat uerba: 'Cur me' inquiens 'sputis propriis uerberando inlinis? Nam ego, ut cernis, suscipio munus tuarum orationum, deferens illud ad conspectum misericordissimi iudicis.' Qua uisione correptus, frater ille et sese continuit, et certeros ut se, in quantum ualerent, in sacris locis continerent ammonere curauit." ed. and trans. John France, in *Rodulphus Glaber: The Five Books of Histories and the Life of St. William* (Oxford, 1989), p. 224.

[4] Useful starting points on this topic include Suso Frank, *ΑΓΓΕΛΙΚΟΣ ΒΙΟΣ: Begriffsanalytische und begriffsgeschichtliche Untersuchung zum "engelgleichen Leben" im frühen Mönchtum* (Munster, 1964); and Conrad Leyser, "Angels, Monks, and Demons in the Early Medieval West," in *Belief and Culture in the Middle Ages: Studies Presented to Henry Mayr-Harting*, ed. Richard Gameson and Henrietta Leyser (Oxford, 2001), pp. 9–22.

their community on the foundation of this program of celestial discipline, the abbots of Cluny eventually rose to positions of great influence in European society.[5]

Cluniac monks imagined angels in terms of three fundamental qualities, the emulation of which became central to their monastic vocation. The first of these was sexual purity. The monks of Cluny preserved their chastity by denying their desire for carnal pleasure and by cleansing their minds of sinful fantasies. The second was the celebration of an elaborate and protracted psalmody, that is, the intonation of biblical psalms sung in praise of God. Gathered together in their church, the brethren of Cluny directed their voices to heaven in imitation of the celestial chorus that glorified God throughout time. The third expression of angelic mimesis fostered by the Cluniacs was also the most innovative and contentious: the cultivation of a profound and reverential silence. Many early monastic communities encouraged the regulation of speech as a precaution to prevent negligent monks from indulging in gossip and other sins of the tongue that corroded their communal way of life. The monks of Cluny were different. They were the first to understand the discipline of silence as a powerful and admirable virtue in its own right. The collective denial of the will to speak rivaled the celebration of the divine office as a unifying practice that actualized in their community the dwelling place of the angels in heaven. This new way of thinking about silence was not universally welcomed by their contemporaries, however. In the early tenth century, the Cluniacs roused indignation among other ascetics, who claimed that they introduced unprecedented novelties at the expense of age-old traditions governing the cultivation of silence in cloistered communities. They responded to these criticisms by defending their custom of silence with biblical authority as a virtue sanctioned in the Old and New Testaments and witnessed by the saints of Christian antiquity. In doing so, the monks of Cluny articulated a new ideology of Christian asceticism that married the glorification of silence to the ideal of an angelic life realized in mortal bodies.

The refashioning of religious ideals that elevated the practice of silence to the highest constellation of Christian virtues confronted the Cluniacs with an unexpected challenge. In cloistered communities that sometimes numbered hundreds of monks, the cultivation of a strict and reverential silence conflicted with the fact that some form of communication was

---

[5] The early history of the Cluniacs and the development of their ascetic ideals are discussed at length in Chapter 1, pp. 15–28, below. For an eleventh-century example of the influence wielded by an abbot of Cluny at the highest level of secular affairs, see Joseph H. Lynch, "Hugh I of Cluny's Sponsorship of Henry IV: Its Context and Consequences," *Speculum* 60 (1985): 800–826.

necessary for the operation of the abbey and the orchestration of its rituals. Rather than relinquish their ideal of silence as an essential virtue, the monks of Cluny created a silent language of hand signs that enabled them to express their needs without recourse to any verbal exchange. Sources for the internal life of Cluniac abbeys in the tenth and eleventh centuries provide considerable insight into the character of this import- ant, but seldom imagined, aspect of medieval monastic discipline. These texts also allow us to make inferences about the parameters of this little known custom and the context of its use.

The replacement of spoken words with silent signs raises the same questions today as it did for these monks a millennium ago. Since they were instructed to avoid the perils of human discourse, how could cloistered individuals condone the use of a silent form of information exchange like a sign language that seemed to provide them with the means to evade their precepts against speaking? More to the point, what prevented otherwise silent monks from sinning through the garrulous use of their hands? While monastic signs were introduced to safeguard the brethren of Cluny from sinful utterances as they pursued their ascetic program of angelic imitation, it was clear to them that this custom threatened to provide negligent individuals with a ready outlet for the expression of idle or indulgent thoughts. As we will see, these concerns shaped the linguistic character of the Cluniac sign system and influenced the mechanisms of observance and control that were intended to curb its misuse in the monastery.

This book sets out to explain the relationship between silence and sign language and the role of these customs in the realization of the angelic ideals fostered in the Cluniac tradition from the founding of the great Burgundian abbey in 910 to the end of the twelfth century, by which time the custom of using signs in place of speech had become widespread in religious communities throughout western Europe. In recent decades, the near ubiquitous concern for the preservation of silence in medieval religious houses has drawn the attention of several scholars, although none of them has directed attention toward the centrality of silence in the ascetic program fostered at Cluny.[6] The same cannot be said of the custom of sign language. This seemingly esoteric practice has attracted very little attention, even from experts in the history of Christian asceti- cism. In the early eighteenth century, Edmond Martène reproduced the

---

[6] Ambrose G. Wathan, *Silence: The Meaning of Silence in the Rule of Saint Benedict* (Washington, DC, 1973) remains a reliable guide to the study of this topic and covers a broader range of material than its title implies. See also Paul F. Gehl, "*Competens Silentium*: Varieties of Monastic Silence in the Medieval West," *Viator* 18 (1987): 125–160.

earliest sources for monastic sign language in his monumental work on the historical significance of liturgical texts from the Middle Ages, but the impact of his efforts was minimal.[7] The small handful of historians who have explored the topic since Martène's time have done so with varying degrees of intellectual investment.[8] The marginalization of this practice was only offset by its exotic appeal, which assured it an anecdotal role in general histories of medieval monasticism, where it was often presented in disparaging or comical terms.[9] The appearance in 1981 and 1989 of critical editions of the most important Latin lexicons of Cluniac and Cistercian sign-forms has failed to recuperate the image of this practice.[10] As a result, a comprehensive account of the origin and functions of monastic sign language and its relation to the discipline of silence at Cluny has never been written.

The lack of scholarly attention to Cluniac sign language is especially surprising given the recent interest that historians of medieval art, vernacular literature and political performance have shown in deciphering the meaning of gestures in the premodern period. Many studies have attempted to isolate and identify visual and narrative depictions of physical actions that express emotional states and social relationships among medieval people, from private acts, like pointing and winking, to public rituals, like the clasping of hands that cemented oaths of fealty or the posture of submission expected of a supplicant. Working with the presumption that the meaning of premodern gestures is unintelligible to modern readers, historians have attempted to reconstruct their social

---

[7] Edmond Martène, *De antiquis monachorum ritibus libri quinque* 5.18: "De locutione per signa," in *De antiquis ecclesiae ritibus libri*, 4 vols., 2nd edn (Antwerp, 1736; repr. Hildesheim, 1967–1969), vol. IV, cols. 826a–837a.

[8] See, for example, Louis Gougaud, "Le langage des silencieux," *Revue Mabillon* 19 (1929): 93–100; Gérard van Rijnberk, *Le langage par signes chez les moines* (Amsterdam, 1953); Eric Buyssens, "Le langage par gestes chez les moines," *Revue de l'Institut de Sociologie* 29 (1954): 537–545; and Paul Gerhard Schmidt, "*Ars loquendi et ars tacendi*: Zur monastischen Zeichensprache des Mittelalters," *Berichte zur Wissenschaftsgeschichte* 4 (1981): 13–19.

[9] G. G. Coulton, *Five Centuries of Religion*, 4 vols. (Cambridge, 1923–1950), vol. I, pp. 87–88; Eileen Power, *Medieval People* (Boston and New York, 1924), p. 67, where she remarked that "[t]he sort of dumb pandemonium which went on at Eglentyne's dinner table must often have been more mirth-provoking than speech"; Joan Evans, *Monastic Life at Cluny, 910–1157* (London, 1931), pp. 88–89, who called it "a strange monastic language" (p. 89); and C. H. Lawrence, *Medieval Monasticism: Forms of Religious Life in Western Europe in the Middle Ages*, 2nd edn (London and New York, 1989), pp. 118–119. For the best general treatment of this custom, reflective of the new prestige afforded to monastic customaries as historical sources, see Anselme Davril and Eric Palazzo, *La vie des moines au temps des grandes abbayes, Xe–XIIIe siècles* (Paris, 2000), pp. 89–93.

[10] Walter Jarecki, *Signa Loquendi: Die cluniacensischen Signa-Listen eingeleitet und herausgegeben* (Baden-Baden, 1981); and Walter Jarecki, "Die 'Ars signorum Cisterciensium' im Rahmen der metrischen Signa-Listen," *Revue bénédictine* 99 (1989): 329–399. See also the comprehensive reviews of Jarecki's book by Giles Constable in *Mittellateinisches Jahrbuch* 18 (1983): 331–333; and by Kassius Hallinger in *Zeitschrift für Kirchengeschichte* 44 (1983): 145–150.

and political context in order to determine what they communicated to a medieval audience. The goal of their collective project is to decode the meaning of the vast repertoire of expressive motions and postures employed during the Middle Ages.[11] Monastic signs have generally fallen outside of the purview of this historiography because, unlike the social and political gestures depicted in medieval art, literature and narrative sources, their meaning is readily available in descriptive lexicons of sign-forms that Cluniac monks composed to aid in the instruction of their use.[12] The only work of scholarship in this field that treats monastic sign language at all is Jean-Claude Schmitt's wide-ranging *La raison des gestes dans l'occident médiéval*, published in 1990.[13] Cluniac signs fit uneasily, however, into Schmitt's general thesis, which locates a renewed emphasis on the relationship between bodily control and monastic discipline in a twelfth-century treatise on the instruction of novices composed by Hugh of Saint Victor.[14] To be sure, Hugh presented his readers with a vivid taxonomy of physical gestures and the moral traits encoded by them, but as this book aims to demonstrate, the explicit relationship between comportment and personal virtue expressed by Hugh and his contemporaries was already an implicit characteristic of monastic sign language in the tenth century. In this regard, the turning point that Schmitt locates in the twelfth century probably had more to do with the new vocabulary with which prelates ordered and communicated their ideas than with changes in the moral presumptions that guided the physical behavior of common monks. With this information in hand, the present study is quite different in its aim and scope from other scholarly treatments of medieval gesture. Since the meaning of individual monastic signs is expressly transparent, this work sets out to explain the Cluniac rationale for creating a silent language of hand signs and examines how these signs functioned as a vehicle for communication within the material context of the abbey and the moral context of religious discipline.

As an historical phenomenon, the silent language of the Cluniacs was a living system, a dynamic process of visual communication that relied on

---

[11] The literature on these topics is vast, but there is a convenient bibliography in *New Approaches to Medieval Communication*, ed. Marco Mostert (Turnhout, 1999), pp. 219–221. Recent studies of importance on aspects of medieval gesture include: Jean-Claude Schmitt, *La raison des gestes dans l'occident médiéval* (Paris, 1990); Geoffrey Koziol, *Begging Pardon and Favor: Ritual and Political Order in Early Medieval France* (Ithaca and London, 1992); *Gesture in Medieval Drama and Art*, ed. C. Davidson (Kalamazoo, 2001); and J. A. Burrow, *Gestures and Looks in Medieval Narrative* (Cambridge, 2002).

[12] On the Cluniac sign lexicon, see Chapter 2, pp. 63–66, below.

[13] Schmitt, *La raison des gestes*, pp. 253–257.

[14] *Ibid.*, pp. 173–205. This treatise is discussed in the context of canonical views of silence in Chapter 5, p. 156, below.

the studied movement and learned perception of its participants. It is now a dormant language.[15] Knowledge of it does not derive from lived experience or pictorial representations, but rather from descriptions of individual sign-forms and oblique references to their use preserved in medieval saints' lives, exempla collections, personal letters and especially monastic customaries.[16] Monastic customaries were compilations of legislation that provided detailed information about the customs observed in cloistered communities, such as liturgical ceremonies, the duties of officials and the training of novices, including their instruction in sign language.[17] Some scholars have cast doubt on the reliability of this genre as an historical source, expressing concern that the contents of customaries represented the normative ideals of monastic legislators rather than the lived experiences of individual monks.[18] This statement of caution is well founded with respect to customaries imposed on religious communities explicitly to introduce new observances following a period of reform, but it ignores the possibility that this genre could serve other purposes. In fact, many customaries written in the tenth and eleventh centuries were directive or descriptive in function.[19] Directive customaries were written for internal use to affirm existing customs during times of crisis or transition, while descriptive customaries were composed to

[15] Some present-day monastic communities, particularly those in the Trappist tradition, still employ sign languages and thereby forge a link between their current practices and those of their predecessors. In fact, most of these modern monastic sign systems bear little resemblance to their medieval antecedents. See Robert A. Barakat, *Cistercian Sign Language* (Kalamazoo, 1975); and Suzanne Quay, "Signs of Silence: Two Examples of Trappist Sign Language in the Far East," *Cîteaux: Commentarii Cistercienses* 52 (2001): 211–230.

[16] The present study relies exclusively on textual evidence. Although medieval sculpture and manuscript illumination are richly populated with gesturing figures, I have been unable to find convincing depictions of the use of monastic sign language among them. For a catalogue of illustrative gestures in medieval art, see François Garnier, *Le langage de l'image au moyen âge*, 2 vols. (Paris, 1982). Kirk Ambrose has recently shown, however, that awareness of this custom can inform art historians in their understanding of gestures in Romanesque sculpture created for a monastic milieu. See Ambrose, "A Visual Pun at Vézelay: Gesture and Meaning on a Capital Representing the Fall of Man," *Traditio* 55 (2000): 105–123; and, more generally, Ambrose, *The Nave Sculpture of Vézelay: The Art of Monastic Viewing* (Toronto, 2006).

[17] On the character of the Cluniac customaries and their value as historical sources, see the articles collected in *From Dead of Night to End of Day: The Medieval Customs of Cluny / Du cœur de la nuit à la fin du jour: Les coutumes clunisiennes au moyen âge*, ed. Susan Boynton and Isabelle Cochelin (Leiden, 2005).

[18] See, for example, Kassius Hallinger, "*Consuetudo*: Begriff, Formen, Forschungsgeschichte, Inhalt," in *Untersuchungen zu Kloster und Stift* (Göttingen, 1980), pp. 140–166, who stressed their prescriptive character ("Verpflichtungscharakter") in response to interpretations that treated them primarily as descriptive documents; and Lin Donnat, "Les coutumiers monastiques: une nouvelle entreprise et un territoire nouveau," *Revue Mabillon* n.s. 3 (1992): 5–21, esp. pp. 14–16.

[19] Anselme Davril has employed the terms "directive" and "descriptive" as part of a useful system of taxonomy that categorizes examples of this genre by their readership and function. See Davril, "Coutumiers directifs et coutumiers descriptifs: D'Ulrich à Bernard de Cluny," in *From Dead of Night to End of Day*, ed. Boynton and Cochelin, pp. 23–28.

provide information about the traditions of one religious community for the benefit of another without otherwise implying an obligation for their adoption. Directive and descriptive customaries were thus primarily commemorative and indicative in character and therefore reflect more clearly the actual customs observed in early medieval abbeys, thereby providing remarkable insight into the daily lives of their inhabitants.

Despite their value as historical sources, several factors have conspired to keep monastic customaries at a distance from the concerns of current scholarship. Accessibility to reliable editions has certainly hindered research. Until recently, most monastic customaries were either unedited or available only in rare (and often faulty) transcriptions from the seventeenth and eighteenth centuries.[20] The series *Corpus consuetudinum monasticarum* (1963–present), devoted to the publication of critical editions of monastic legislation from the Middle Ages, has rehabilitated the genre somewhat by making more of these texts available to an academic readership.[21] The impact of this endeavor has been most apparent in Europe. Over the past two decades, scholars working in Germany and other countries have formed the vanguard of an historiography on monastic orders and their legislative traditions that has brought the customaries to the center of wide-ranging discussions of literacy and the role of documents in the service of religious reform.[22] In contrast, historians of medieval monasticism in North America have been occupied primarily, although not exclusively, with the study of gender construction and the social meaning of charters.[23] While several scholars in the United States

[20] Further on these early editions, see Marc Saurette, "Excavating and Renovating Ancient Texts: Seventeenth- and Eighteenth-Century Editions of Bernard of Cluny's *Consuetudines* and Early-Modern Monastic Scholarship," in *From Dead of Night to End of Day*, ed. Boynton and Cochelin, pp. 85–107.

[21] On the achievements of the series to 1991 and plans for future editions, see Pius Engelbert, "Bericht über den Stand des *Corpus Consuetudinum Monasticarum* (*CCM*)," *Studien und Mitteilungen zur Geschichte des Benediktinerordens und seiner Zweige* 102 (1991): 19–24.

[22] See, for example, Joachim Wollasch, "Reformmönchtum und Schriftlichkeit," *Frühmittelalterliche Studien* 26 (1992): 274–286; Klaus Schreiner, "Verschriftlichung als Faktor monastischer Reform: Funktionen von Schriftlichkeit im Ordenswesen des hohen und späten Mittelalters," in *Pragmatische Schriftlichkeit im Mittelalter: Erscheinungsformen und Entwicklungsstufen*, ed. Hagen Keller, Klaus Grubmüller and Nikolaus Staubach (Munich, 1992), pp. 37–75; Florent Cygler, Gert Melville and Jörg Oberste, "Aspekte zur Verbindung von Organisation und Schriftlichkeit im Ordenswesen: Ein Vergleich zwischen den Zisterziensern und Cluniazensern des 12./13. Jahrhunderts," in *Viva Vox und Ratio Scripta: Mündliche und schriftliche Kommunikationsformen im Mönchtum des Mittelalters*, ed. Clemens Kasper and Klaus Schreiner (Münster, 1997), pp. 157–176. Important studies of the customaries by Gerd Zimmermann and Dominique Iogna-Prat fall outside the scope of this tradition. My indebtedness to the scholarship of these two pioneering monastic historians will be apparent throughout the book.

[23] Barbara Rosenwein, "Views from Afar: North American Perspectives on Medieval Monasticism," in *Dove va la storiografia monastica in Europa? Temi e metodi di ricerca per lo studio della vita monastica e regolare in età medievale alle soglie del terzo millennio*, ed. Giancarlo Andenna (Milan, 2001), pp. 67–84.

and Canada have made the Cluniac customaries the focus of their research, they have not pursued their work collectively with the thematic coherence that is so apparent in contemporary European scholarship.[24]

The present study of silence and sign language at Cluny takes as its focus the customaries written at the great Burgundian abbey in the late eleventh century.[25] Books of customs composed by the monks Bernard and Ulrich offer the most detailed evidence for the practice of silence among the Cluniacs and the character of the sign language that they employed in place of speech.[26] There is considerable overlap in the content of the customaries of Bernard and Ulrich, which has complicated our understanding of their relationship to one another. In an influential article published in 1959, Kassius Hallinger argued that Ulrich's customary was dependent on that of Bernard.[27] In his view, Bernard composed his work in two books around 1074. Ulrich used this text as a model, but systematized its contents and reorganized them into three books around 1083. Hallinger then inferred that Bernard wrote a second redaction of his customary shortly thereafter (*c.* 1084–1086) as a way of explaining the parts of his text not found in Ulrich's work. Joachim Wollasch has challenged this thesis by arguing that the customaries of Bernard and Ulrich were independent compositions.[28] Claiming that there is no manuscript evidence for the two recensions of Bernard's work proposed by Hallinger, Wollasch argued that the textual parallels between the customaries were more likely the result of the authors' use of the same pool of available resources around the same time. He has offered a

---

[24] For a recent sampling of approaches to the Cluniac customaries by North American scholars representing several disciplines, see the articles by Susan Boynton, Scott G. Bruce, Jennifer A. Harris, Carolyn Marino Malone, Frederick S. Paxton, Diane J. Reilly and Marc Saurette, in *From Dead of Night to End of Day*, ed. Boynton and Cochelin.

[25] For the best introductions to the Cluniac customaries, with exhaustive references to earlier literature, see Isabelle Cochelin, "Evolution des coutumiers monastiques dessinée à partir de l'étude de Bernard," and Gert Melville, "Action, Text and Validity: On Re-Examining Cluny's *Consuetudines* and Statutes," in *From Dead of Night to End of Day*, ed. Boynton and Cochelin, pp. 29–66 and 67–83.

[26] I have relied on the standard editions of these texts throughout the book: Bernard of Cluny, *Ordo Cluniacensis sive Consuetudines*, ed. M. Herrgott, in *Vetus Disciplina Monastica* (Paris, 1726; repr. Siegburg, 1999), pp. 136–364 (cited hereafter as "Bernard" followed by book, chapter and page number); and Ulrich of Zell, *Consuetudines Cluniacensis*, PL CXLIX, cols. 643–779 (cited hereafter as "Ulrich" followed by book, chapter and column number). For a diplomatic edition of Bernard's customary based on MS BN, Latin 13875, see *The Cluniac Customary of Bernard / Le coutumier clunisien de Bernard*, ed. and trans. Susan Boynton and Isabelle Cochelin, forthcoming. Critical editions of both customaries are in preparation by Laurentius Schlieker and Isabelle Cochelin for *CCM*.

[27] Kassius Hallinger, "Klunys Bräuche zur Zeit Hugos des Grossen (1049–1109)," *Zeitschrift der Savigny-Stiftung für Rechtsgeschichte: Kanonistische Abteilung* 45 (1959): 99–140.

[28] Joachim Wollasch, "Zur Verschriftlichung der klösterlichen Lebensgewohnheiten unter Abt Hugo von Cluny," *Frühmittelalterliche Studien* 27 (1993): 317–349.

conservative – and now generally accepted – redating of the customaries to 1078 or shortly thereafter (Bernard) and 1079–1084 (Ulrich).[29]

The enterprise of recognizing and recovering references to monastic sign language and its use in legal and narrative sources from Cluny and elsewhere presents a number of interpretative challenges for the historian. Medieval authors drew from a wide range of words and phrases to describe this silent language, but their inconsistency often makes it difficult to ascertain whether they were referring specifically to monastic signs or generally to conventional gestures that were not part of a recognized sign system. Allusions to the use of monastic sign language appeared in a number of near synonymous Latin guises, sometimes in the work of a single author. The most common word for an individual hand sign was *signum* ("sign"). Less common was *nutus* (literally "nod," but usually employed in its widest sense as "indicator"). Anglo-Saxon authors at the turn of the first millennium called monastic signs *indicia* in Latin and *tacn* in Old English (both words carry the broad meaning of "sign" or "indicator"). One tenth-century Cluniac author referred to them uniquely as *notae* ("marks" or "characters"). Verbs and phrases for the act of making monastic signs included *significare, signo petere, signo facere, per signa insinuari, indiciis indicare* and *nutibus ostendere*. Even the most frequent and transparent Latin word for sign (*signum*) must be treated with caution, however, because monastic authors used it to indicate all manner of signals and cues, like the striking of wooden tablets and the tolling of bells, as well as the silent motions of fingers and hands. Fortunately, in most instances, the context of the word or phrase provides a reliable measure of its meaning.

The semantic challenges attendant with the study of this practice are not limited to the medieval evidence. This book employs the term "sign language" as a generic designation for the system of meaning-specific gestures employed by the brethren of Cluny and their imitators from the tenth century onwards. Some will undoubtedly question the appropriateness of this choice of terminology. Most people associate "sign language" with the mode of visual-kinetic communication commonly used by deaf people.[30] In North America, this term is usually identified with American Sign Language (ASL). The practice of deaf people using signs

---

[29] I am persuaded by Wollasch's conclusions and employ them in this study, but he does not have the final word on the issue. The validity of his findings has recently been questioned by Isabelle Cochelin, who has suggested subverting the traditional primacy of Bernard's customary in favor of Ulrich. See Cochelin, "Evolution des coutumiers monastiques," pp. 29–30, n. 3. A definitive resolution to this issue must await the appearance of critical editions of the two customaries in question (see n. 26, above).

[30] Harlan Lane, *When the Mind Hears: A History of the Deaf* (New York, 1984); and Oliver Sacks, *Seeing Voices: A Journey into the World of the Deaf* (New York, 1989).

has existed in some American communities since the seventeenth century, when hereditary deafness among the earliest settlers on Martha's Vineyard necessitated the use of a sign system. This local idiom of silent communication eventually exerted a profound influence on the sign language developed at the American Asylum for the Deaf in Hartford, Connecticut, in the early nineteenth century, which in turn contributed to the development of ASL.[31]

The application of the term "sign language" to a medieval practice may seem anachronistic, especially since monks did not use their hand signs to overcome impairments in hearing or speaking. Moreover, as scholars of deaf education have correctly pointed out, monastic signs lacked many fundamental linguistic principles like grammar and syntax and therefore, by strict definition, did not constitute a true language in the modern sense of the word.[32] While the term "sign language" may not be a precise definition of the linguistic character of monastic signs, it does convey with accuracy the medieval understanding of their function in the abbey. Monastic authors referred to them specifically as "signs for speaking" (*signa loquendi*), that is, as a visual–manual surrogate for verbal discourse. While monastic signs did not have the expressive potential of spoken languages (for reasons discussed in Chapter 2, below), they nonetheless served as a functional replacement for speech. Moreover, the term "sign language" has a much wider semantic range in modern parlance than some linguistic historians would care to admit. The term has been readily applied to sublinguistic systems of meaning-specific gestures used among hearing people who are unable to communicate due to excessive noise in modern industrial settings or because of the precepts attendant with their religious beliefs.[33] With careful qualification, it is equally

[31] Nora Ellen Groce, *Everyone Here Spoke Sign Language: Hereditary Deafness on Martha's Vineyard* (Cambridge, MA, 1985).
[32] See, for example, Lois Bragg, "Visual-Kinetic Communication in Europe Before 1600: A Survey of Sign Lexicons and Finger Alphabets Prior to the Rise of Deaf Education," *Journal of Deaf Studies and Deaf Education* 2 (1997): 1–25, esp. p. 2, where she defines languages as "natural communication systems that (1) have both a lexicon and a grammar, (2) are capable of expressing any thought on any subject, (3) are learned by at least some infants during the normal language-acquisition-threshold age, and (4) are living, growing, changing systems." See also Susan Plann, "Pedro Ponce de Leon: Myth and Reality," in *Deaf History Unveiled: Interpretations from the New Scholarship*, ed. J. V. Van Cleve (Washington, DC, 1993), pp. 1–12, at p. 11, n. 17.
[33] On the use of "sign language" in a Canadian lumber mill, where the noise of machinery prevented oral communication, see Martin Meissner and Stuart B. Philpott, "The Sign Language of Sawmill Workers in British Columbia," *Sign Language Studies* 9 (1975): 291–308. Likewise, the members of the ill-fated Movement for the Restoration of the Ten Commandments of God in Uganda allegedly used a "sign language" as part of their religious discipline. See Henri E. Cauvin, "Fateful Meeting Led to Founding of Cult in Uganda," *New York Times*, 27 March 2000, p. A3. Neither of these systems would meet Bragg's definition of language (see n. 32, above).

appropriate as a designation for the medieval sign system under consideration in this study.

This book begins by examining the benefits and boundaries of the discipline of silence among the Cluniacs and the central role played by this custom in their ascetic program of angelic mimesis (Chapter 1: Uttering No Human Sound). Although rudimentary signs found use in some ancient abbeys, the glorification of silence at Cluny created the institutional context for the development of an elaborate system of meaning-specific hand signs that allowed the brethren to communicate their needs and to receive instruction and reprimand without recourse to speech. Chapter 2 (The Training of the Hand) analyzes an eleventh-century sign lexicon from Cluny to make inferences about the linguistic character of this silent language and the qualities of the imagination that created it. Chapter 3 (A Silent Commerce of Signs) compares this extraordinary document with the Cluniac customaries of Bernard and Ulrich to reconstruct the specific functions of monastic signs and their range of application in the abbey. The utility of this custom was not lost on other cloistered communities, whose abbots strived to imitate many of the traditions that earned the monks of Cluny a reputation for sanctity. The spread of monastic sign language in the tenth and eleventh centuries to religious houses outside of Burgundy and the modifications made to adapt it to local needs different from those at Cluny are the subjects of Chapter 4 (Transmission and Adaptation), which emphasizes the adaptability of this custom as a key attribute to its widespread appeal. The final chapter of the book (Chapter 5: Continuity and Criticism) carries this analysis of the dissemination of Cluniac sign-forms into the twelfth century. Despite differing opinions about the utility of the spoken word, the new religious orders of this period maintained a remarkable continuity with early monastic thinkers with respect to their attitude toward silence. Consequently, they recognized the utility of borrowing the practice of sign language from the Cluniacs to safeguard this virtue in their abbeys and hermitages. In fact, the adoption of this custom was so widespread that by the year 1200 the use of hand signs in place of spoken words had become a recognized feature of the monastic vocation in religious communities throughout northern Europe. The conclusion to the book considers the possibility that the earliest attempts to teach deaf children to speak in sixteenth-century Spanish abbeys tapped into sensibilities that were informed by the rich cultural tradition of nonverbal communication that had existed in Benedictine abbeys since the tenth century.

Chapter 1

UTTERING NO HUMAN SOUND

Early medieval abbeys were alive with sound. The glorification of God through the celebration of the divine office was the primary activity of cloistered men and women, who intoned the psalms for the benefit of their souls and for the spiritual well-being of the entire Christian community. Like heavenly bees in their hives, monks were not silent in their industry. Their lips were always busy with the buzzing of prayer and praise.[1] Yet in this sonorous environment, monks also esteemed the cultivation of silence as a saving virtue. Apart from their participation in devotional activities like the divine office, it was often forbidden for them to utter a sound. Silence emerged as an important aspect of monastic conduct in the earliest days of Christian asceticism, the first principle of which was the renunciation of the world in anticipation of the Last Judgment. As the great monastic historian Jean Leclercq observed: "All forms of asceticism – mortification, chastity, obedience, poverty – derive from this first idea of the total renunciation of everything that is not from God and to prepare for the total adherence, in the glory to come, of the soul and body of the redeemed to the one all-sufficient God."[2] Monastic silence did not entail the complete suppression of human speech, however, as the term implies in its modern sense. Rather, it involved the regulation of the desire to utter words that were harmful to the disciplined development of the individual monk and the prayerful purpose of the entire *coenobium*. In accordance with this, early medieval monks were instructed to renounce any spoken words that mired their thoughts in the world and distracted their attention from God. Rules of personal conduct

---

[1] Many medieval authors compared monks and bees. For examples from early monastic texts, see Corbinian Gindele, "Bienen-, Waben- und Honigvergleiche in der frühen monastischen Literatur," *Regulae Benedicti Studia* 6/7 (1981): 1–26; and Anna Taylor, "Just Like a Mother Bee: Reading and Writing *Vitae metricae* around the Year 1000," *Viator* 36 (2005): 119–148.

[2] Jean Leclercq, *The Life of Perfection: Points of View on the Essence of the Religious State*, trans. Leonard J. Doyle (Collegeville, MN, 1961), p. 27.

and literary models of virtuous behavior written for cloistered communities in this period shared a general concern with the avoidance of sinful words. As a result, the denial of the will to speak became known in the early Middle Ages as an essential characteristic of monastic discipline, defined here as the practices through which individuals formed and directed their moral disposition in the pursuit of Christian virtue.[3]

Despite widespread esteem for the cultivation of silence in most cenobitic communities, the translation of this discipline into practice became an issue of serious contention in the early tenth century, when the abbots of the monastery of Cluny (founded in 910 in central Burgundy) espoused a much more rigorous and comprehensive ideal of this custom than their predecessors and contemporaries. Freighting the abnegation of the desire to speak with new moral and eschatological expectations, the brethren of Cluny amplified traditional precepts against talking to such an extent that they were accused of innovation and novelty. The Cluniac response to these criticisms articulated an understanding of the discipline of silence that would exert a powerful influence in the monastic world for centuries to come. In their effort to emulate the conduct of the angelic host in heaven, the monks of Cluny fostered a celestial silence in their abbey that foreshadowed their participation in the eternal glorification of God at the end of time. Their detractors considered this marriage of symbolic association and embodied experience to be an unprecedented and therefore dangerous reinterpretation of received tradition. While the measures taken to foster silence in most other religious houses were largely precautions to prevent monks from indulging in the pleasure of human discourse and thereby eroding the integrity of personal discipline in their communities, the early Cluniacs espoused an ideal of silence that was both positive and actualizing. At Cluny, the avoidance of speech not only protected monks from sins of the tongue, but also directed and shaped their behavior to make it consonant with that of the angels, whose ranks they hoped to join in the life to come.[4] This cultivated affinity with immortal beings of light lent the spiritual enterprise of the Cluniacs an awesome efficacy in the eyes

---

[3] I am indebted throughout this study to Talal Asad's discussion of monastic discipline in *Genealogies of Religion: Discipline and Reasons of Power in Christianity and Islam* (Baltimore and London, 1993), pp. 125–167 (Chapter 4: On Discipline and Humility in Medieval Christian Monasticism), esp. pp. 135–139.

[4] In thinking about this process of mimetic actualization among the monks of Cluny, I have benefited from reading Clifford Geertz's study of public exhibitions of political power in nineteenth-century Bali, where he observed: "The state ceremonials of classical Bali were metaphysical theatre: theatre designed to express a view of the ultimate nature of reality and, at the same time, to shape the existing conditions of life to be consonant with that reality; that is, theatre to present an ontology and, by presenting it, to make it happen – make it actual." See Geertz, *Negara: The Theatre State in Nineteenth-Century Bali* (Princeton, 1980), p. 104; quoted in Asad, *Genealogies of Religion*, p. 133.

of their patrons, even as it challenged traditional expectations of monastic conduct in tenth-century Europe.

The contribution of the early Cluniacs to the understanding of monastic silence as a foreshadowing of the angelic life has not been fully appreciated by historians of medieval monastic culture. The abbey of Cluny was famous in the Middle Ages – and is best remembered today – for the lavish splendor and daunting length of its liturgical services, the singing of which seemed to occupy the brethrens' every waking hour. While historians have drawn the analogy between the continuous celebration of the divine office at Cluny and the angelic chorus that sings eternal praises to the majesty of God, the discipline of silence, which governed the utterances of the monks when they were not intoning the psalms, played an equally vital role in reifying the great Burgundian abbey as an image of the world to come. By examining the evidence for this custom at Cluny from its founding in 910 to the height of its renown during the abbacy of Hugh the Great (1049–1109), this chapter shows how the abbots of Cluny deployed the cultivation of silence to present their community as a conduit between the mortal and angelic realms and how the aggressive promotion of the centrality of this custom in the angel–monk analogy marked a significant – and for some, jarring and unacceptable – departure from received tradition. To contextualize the innovative approach to silence pursued by the brethren of Cluny, the chapter compares their way of life to those customs fostered in early medieval monasticism from the desert hermits of the fourth century to the Carolingian reform of religious life and its legacy in the ninth century. In this analysis of Cluniac self-representation, it is important to recognize that ideals of religious conduct often met with resistance from the very monks whose lives were shaped and governed by them. With this in mind, the chapter concludes with a consideration of the strategies employed by the abbots of Cluny and other contemporary monasteries to encourage and enforce the discipline of silence in their communities.

COELESTIS DISCIPLINA

The abbey of Cluny has cast a long shadow on modern perceptions of monastic culture in the tenth and eleventh centuries.[5] Founded by Duke

---

[5] Recent historiographical overviews criticize the tendency of historians to present Cluny as a static, paradigmatic religious institution and emphasize the distinctiveness of various stages of the abbey's history, particularly the tenth century. See Barbara Rosenwein, *Rhinoceros Bound: Cluny in the Tenth Century* (Philadelphia, 1982), pp. 3–29; and Giles Constable, "Cluny in the Monastic World of the Tenth Century," in *Il secolo di ferro: Mito e realtà del secolo X (Spoleto, 19–25 aprile 1990)*, Settimane di

William I of Aquitaine on the site of a Burgundian villa bequeathed to him in 893 by his sister Ava, herself an abbess (*abbatissa*), the community was originally small in number and modest in endowment.[6] Writing in the 1040s, when vocations at Cluny rose into the hundreds and gifts from lay patrons increased significantly, Ralph Glaber reminded his readers of the abbey's humble beginnings, when it boasted only twelve monks and fifteen holdings of land.[7] In many respects, tenth-century Cluny was indistinguishable from other late Carolingian monasteries.[8] In his foundation charter, Duke William granted the monks immunity from lay and episcopal interference in the election of abbots and forbade the unlawful seizure and alienation of the abbey's properties. He also recommended that the brethren adhere to the precepts of the *Rule of Benedict*, the celebrated sixth-century handbook for the organization and operation of monastic foundations.[9] The duke entrusted the apostles Peter and Paul and their earthly representative the pope with the care and protection of the community. As Constance Bouchard and others have shown, there was nothing novel about the terms of Cluny's rights of immunity, its adoption of Benedict's teachings or its dependence on the papacy. The *Rule of Benedict* had become widespread by the year 900 in the wake of the religious reforms sponsored a century earlier by Abbot Benedict of Aniane and Emperor Louis the Pious (r. 814–840) to standardize monastic observances in the Frankish heartlands. Although the decrees of the

studio del Centro italiano di studi sull'alto medioevo 38 (Spoleto, 1991), pp. 391–437, repr. in Constable, *Cluny from the Tenth to the Twelfth Centuries: Further Studies* (Aldershot, 2000), no. I. The most comprehensive history of Cluny from its foundation to the twelfth century remains Joachim Wollasch, *Cluny, Licht der Welt: Aufstieg und Niedergang der klösterlichen Gemeinschaft* (Düsseldorf and Zürich, 1996).

[6] For Ava's donation of the villa to William and the duke's foundation charter for the abbey, see *Recueil des chartes de l'abbaye de Cluny*, ed. Auguste Bernard and Alexandre Bruel, 6 vols. (Paris, 1876–1903), vol. I, pp. 61 (no. 53) and 124–128 (no. 112), respectively. On the discrepancies concerning the date of the foundation charter (909 or 910), see Constable, "Cluny in the Monastic World of the Tenth Century," p. 401, n. 35.

[7] Rodulphus Glaber, *Historiarum libri quinque* 3.5.18, ed. John France, in *Rodulphus Glaber: The Five Books of Histories and the Life of St. William* (Oxford, 1989), p. 124. Although Glaber was a resident at Cluny for a relatively short time (c. 1030–1035), he gathered much of the material for his *Histories* there. See John France, "Rodulphus Glaber and the Cluniacs," *Journal of Ecclesiastical History* 39 (1988): 497–508.

[8] For what follows, see Constance B. Bouchard, "Merovingian, Carolingian and Cluniac Monasticism: Reform and Renewal in Burgundy," *Journal of Ecclesiastical History* 41 (1990): 365–388, at pp. 371–373; and Constable, "Cluny in the Monastic World of the Tenth Century."

[9] The date of the *Rule of Benedict* (*RB*) and its relationship to the anonymous *Rule of the Master* (*RM*) have inspired some debate in recent years. See Marilyn Dunn, "Mastering Benedict: Monastic Rules and Their Authors in the Early Medieval West," *English Historical Review* 105 (1990): 567–594; Adalbert de Vogüé, "The Master and St. Benedict: A Reply to Marilyn Dunn," *English Historical Review* 107 (1992): 95–103; and Marilyn Dunn, "The Master and St. Benedict: A Rejoinder," *English Historical Review* 107 (1992): 104–111. I am most persuaded by the traditional dating of the work to the sixth century.

Aachen councils of 816 and 817 succeeded in establishing the *Rule of Benedict* as the authoritative guide for cloistered communities throughout the Frankish realms, the reformers did not achieve their objective of enforcing a uniform interpretation of its precepts.[10] Moreover, decades earlier in the mid-ninth century, other religious houses in Burgundy, including the convent of St. Martin in Nevers and the abbey of Vézelay, had been granted assurances of immunity and protection similar to those enjoyed by Cluny.

What distinguished Cluny most from its tenth-century counterparts was the commitment of its earliest abbots to a monastic *ordo*, a specific idiom of spiritual life recommended in the community's foundation charter.[11] Duke William charged the brethren to pray assiduously for the remembrance of him, his family members and retainers, as well as for the state of the Christian religion. In doing so, he encouraged them specifically "to seek and desire with full commitment and inner order the heavenly way of life."[12] Intercessory prayer for the benefit of Christian souls was a long-established monastic custom by this time, harkening back at least a century to the reign of Louis the Pious, when monks offered their prayers for the health and success of the emperor and his sons and for the stability of his kingdom.[13] Where Duke William's foundation charter differed so markedly from its precedents in the monastic tradition was the explicitness of the stake its author had in the moral disposition of those responsible for the industry of prayer. Duke William directed the monks of Cluny to conduct their daily lives in emulation of the angels, immortal beings of light that praised God eternally in heaven. What he had in mind by this statement in practical terms was not communicated in the charter. It was left to the abbots of Cluny to decide how to foster and enforce in their fledgling community a program of virtuous conduct consonant with the duke's ideal.

---

[10] Josef Semmler, "Benedictus II: Una regula, una consuetudo," in *Benedictine Culture, 750–1050*, ed. W. Lourdaux and D. Verhelst (Leuven, 1983), pp. 1–49.

[11] On this sense of the term *ordo*, see J. Hourlier, "Cluny et la notion d'ordre religieux," in *À Cluny, Congrès scientifique: Fêtes et cérémonies liturgiques en l'honneur des saints Abbés Odo et Odilon*, ed. Société des amis de Cluny (Dijon, 1950), pp. 219–226.

[12] *Charta qua Vuillelmus, comes et dux, fundat monasterium cluniacense* (no. 112): "Ita duntaxat ut ibi venerabilie oracionis domicilium votis ac subplicationibus fideliter frequentetur, conversatioque celestis omni desideratio et ardore intimo perquiratur et expetatur, sedule quoque oraciones, postulationes atque obsecrationes Domino dirigantur, tam pro me quam pro omnibus, sicut eorum memoria superius digesta est." *Recueil des chartes de l'abbaye de Cluny*, ed. Bernard and Bruel, vol. I, pp. 125–126.

[13] The *Notitia de servitio monasteriorum*, composed in 828, delineated the services demanded from imperial abbeys by the crown, including the provision of revenues and produce as gifts (*dona*), men from their lands for military service (*militia*) and prayers (*orationes pro salute imperatoris vel filiorum eius et stabilite imperii*). See the edition of P. Becker in *CCM* I (Siegburg, 1963), pp. 493–499.

Information about the daily life of the early Cluniacs under the direction of their first abbots is not abundant when compared with the wealth of detail about the community provided by the eleventh-century customaries of Bernard and Ulrich (discussed below). Nonetheless, sources attributed to Odo, the second abbot of Cluny (925–942), are replete with suggestions that he followed Duke William's injunction to direct his brethren to live in consonance with their angelic counterparts. Odo was the most prolific of Cluny's early abbots.[14] Before pursuing a cloistered life, he served as a canon at St. Martin's cathedral in Tours, where he composed an epitome of Gregory the Great's *Exposition on the Book of Job*.[15] Around 910, he left Tours in search of a more authentic form of religious vocation, which he soon discovered in Burgundy at the abbey of Baume-les-Moines. Little is known about the details of monastic life at Baume-les-Moines in the tenth century apart from the evidence provided by the *Life of Odo* composed shortly after the abbot's death in 942 by his disciple John of Salerno.[16] Situated at the confluence of the rivers Seille and Dard in the Jura, the community had been founded in the sixth century during the wave of ascetic enthusiasm that followed the Irish monk Columbanus and his protégés through Gaul.[17] The abbey eventually fell into decline until the year 904, when it was restored by Abbot Berno (d. 927). A few years later, in 910, Duke William asked Berno to direct his new monastic foundation at Cluny approximately 70 kilometers to the southwest of Baume-les-Moines in the wooded hills near Mâcon. The close relationship between Cluny and Baume-les-Moines in this period is well

---

[14] One of the fullest treatments of Odo's literary work remains Max Manitius, *Geschichte der lateinischen Literatur des Mittelalters*, 3 vols. (Munich, 1911–1931), vol. II, pp. 20–27. See also Franz Brunhölzl, *Geschichte der lateinischen Literatur des Mittelalters*, 2 vols. to date (Munich, 1975–), vol. II, pp. 202–210 and 585–586.

[15] Odo of Cluny, *Epitome moralium sancti Gregorii in Job*, PL CXXXIII, cols. 105–512. The identification of this work as Odo's remains open to debate. For an attempt to link Odo to another medieval epitome of Gregory's *Moralia*, see Gabriella Braga, "Problemi di autenticà per Oddone di Cluny: l'Epitome dei 'Moralia' di Gregorio Magno," *Studi Medievali* 18 (1977): 45–145.

[16] On the career of John of Salerno and the composition of the *Vita Odonis*, see Ernst Sackur, *Die Cluniacenser in ihrer kirchlichen und allgemeingeschichtlichen Wirksamkeit bis zur Mitte des elften Jahrhunderts*, 2 vols. (Halle an der Saale, 1892), vol. I, pp. 359–363; Girolamo Arnaldi, "Il biografo 'romano' di Oddone di Cluny," *Bulletino dell'Istituto Storico Italiano per il Medioevo e Archivio Muratoriano* 71 (1959): 19–37; and Helmut Richter, *Die Persönlichkeitsdarstellung in cluniazensischen Abtsviten* (Erlangen, 1972), pp. 23 and 26–65. On the *dossier hagiographique* of Odo of Cluny, see Dominique Iogna-Prat, "Panorama de l'hagiographie abbatiale clunisienne (v. 940–v. 1140)," in *Manuscrits hagiographiques et travail des hagiographes*, ed. Martin Heinzelmann (Sigmaringen, 1992), pp. 77–118, at pp. 81–87, repr. in Iogna-Prat, *Etudes clunisiennes* (Paris, 2002), pp. 35–73.

[17] Bernard Proust, "Essai historique sur les origines de l'abbaye de Baume-les-Moines," *Mémoires de la Société d'Emulation du Jura* (1871–1872): 23–132; and L. H. Cottineau, *Répertoire topo-bibliographique des abbayes et prieurés*, 2 vols. (Mâcon, 1939), vol. I, cols. 283–284, s.v. Baume-les-Messieurs.

attested.[18] Berno was the abbot of both houses and five other local monasteries as well (Massay, Déols, Gigny, Mouthier-en-Bresse and the cell of St. Lothian).[19] While there were no formal bonds of institutional association between these communities, there seems to have been some uniformity of practice during Berno's tenure as abbot. The *Life of Odo* clearly implied that the brethren of Cluny and Berno's other abbeys observed the same customs as those upheld at Baume-les-Moines.[20] Odo succeeded his mentor as abbot of Baume-les-Moines and Cluny in 925. Despite the demands of his office, he remained an effusive and energetic author, composing works of hagiography, sermons and moral treatises in prose and verse.[21] Taken together, this dossier of sources allows us to infer the principles of the monastic ideal espoused by Odo during his abbacy.

The sustained effort of literary and legislative activity of eleventh-century Cluniacs produced many texts that cast light on the durability of Odo's monastic ideal and its realization in the daily lives of the brethren. Odo's successors as abbot of Cluny – Aymard (942–954) and Maiolus (954–994) – expressed themselves in actions rather than words. Maiolus in particular was a tireless diplomat, power broker and advocate of monastic reform who traveled continuously throughout his abbacy.[22] Although he wrote very little, Maiolus actively fostered the Cluniac scriptorium, which emerged in the late tenth century as an important center of text production.[23] It was during his abbacy that monks of Cluny committed to parchment the earliest collections of their liturgical

---

[18] For a summary of the tenth-century evidence, see Giles Constable, "Baume and Cluny in the Twelfth Century," in *Tradition and Change: Essays in Honour of Marjorie Chibnall*, ed. Diana Greenway, Christopher Holdsworth and Jane Sayers (Cambridge, 1985), pp. 35–61, at pp. 36–39; repr. in Constable, *Cluny from the Tenth to the Twelfth Centuries*, no. VIII.

[19] See Berno, *Testamentum, PL* CXXXIII, cols. 853–858. Further on Berno's will and the context of its composition, see Wollasch, *Cluny, Licht der Welt*, pp. 30–36.

[20] See John of Salerno, *Vita Odonis* 1.23, where John attributed the following words to Odo: "Ipse enim pater Euticus institutor fuit harum consuetudinum, quae hactenus in nostris monasteriis habentur." *PL* CXXXIII, col. 54a.

[21] For a catalogue of Odo's literary work, consult the authorities cited in n. 14, above.

[22] On Maiolus and his influence, see Dominique Iogna-Prat, *Agni Immaculati: Recherches sur les sources hagiographiques relatives à saint Maieul de Cluny (954–994)* (Paris, 1988); Dominique Iogna-Prat and Barbara Rosenwein, *Saint Maïeul, Cluny et la Provence: Expansion d'une abbaye à l'aube du moyen âge* (Mane, Haute Provence, 1994); *Saint Mayeul et son temps: Actes du congrès international de Valensole, 2–14 mai 1994* (Dignes-les-Bains, 1997); and *San Maiolo e le influenze Cluniacensi nell'Italia del Nord: Atti del Convegno Internationale nel Millenario di San Maiolo (994–1994) Pavia-Novara, 23–24 settembre 1994*, ed. Ettore Cau and Aldo A. Settia (Como, 1998).

[23] On the activity of scribes during the abbacy of Maiolus, see Monique-Cécile Garand, "Copistes de Cluny au temps de saint Maieul (948–994)," *Bibliothèque de l'Ecole des Chartes* 136 (1978): 5–36. Further on the Cluniac scriptorium, see Jean-Pierre Aniel, "Le scriptorium de Cluny au Xe et XIe siècles," in *Le gouvernement d'Hugues de Semur à Cluny* (Mâcon, 1990), pp. 265–281; and Sébastien Barret, "Cluny et son scriptorium (Xe–XIIe siècles)," in *Cluny ou la puissance des moines: Histoire de l'abbaye et de son ordre, 910–1790* (Dijon, 2001), pp. 48–53.

customs.[24] These were the first steps toward the grand literary enterprises that occupied the brethren throughout the long abbacies of Odilo (994–1049) and Hugh the Great (1049–1109). The eleventh century witnessed the flourishing of abbatial hagiography at Cluny directed toward the commemoration of the virtues and miracles of their heroic tenth-century leaders, Odo and Maiolus.[25] This was also a period of active consolidation and self-conscious organization for the community. Under Hugh the Great, the monks collected hundreds of charters into massive cartularies and codified over a century of received tradition in great volumes of customary law.[26] The monastic ideals enshrined in the eleventh-century accounts of the lives of Cluniac saints and the contemporary record of disciplinary standards recorded in the customaries of Bernard and Ulrich are resonant with the ascetic principles fostered a century earlier by Odo and his contemporaries.

Although the favorable comparison of monks and angels was an old one by the tenth century, Odo of Cluny and his followers were the first to emphasize this similitude repeatedly and emphatically as a defining aspect of their religious vocation and as a rationale for their rigorous standards of personal asceticism, the first principles of which were the avoidance of sexual intercourse, the celebration of continuous praises to God and the cultivation of an expectant, all-embracing silence.[27] For Odo, monastic life at Cluny was nothing less than the conduct of angels embodied in human practice (*coelestis disciplina*).[28] The saints were those who perfected in this life the otherworldly demeanor of the heavenly host. Odo embraced this ideal in his own life to set an example for his brethren; his biographer described him as equal parts angel and mortal (*angelicus videlicet et humanus*).[29] By the eleventh century, this appellation was being applied to the Cluniac community as a whole. Peter Damian addressed Hugh the Great as an archangel

[24] *Consuetudines Cluniacensium antiquiores cum redactionibus derivatis*, ed. Kassius Hallinger, *CCM* VII.2 (Siegburg, 1983).
[25] Iogna-Prat, "Panorama de l'hagiographie abbatiale clunisienne (v. 940–v. 1140)."
[26] For editions of the charters relevant to the history of Cluny, see *Recueil des chartes de l'abbaye de Cluny*, ed. Bernard and Bruel; and *Les plus anciens documents originaux de l'abbaye de Cluny*, ed. Hartmut Atsma, Sébastien Barret and Jean Vezin, 2 vols. (Turnhout, 1997–2000). Further on the compilation of Cluny's charters in the eleventh century, see Dominique Iogna-Prat, "La confection des cartulaires et l'historiographie à Cluny (XIe–XIIe siècles)," in *Les cartulaires: Actes de la table ronde organisée par l'Ecole nationale des chartes, Paris 5–7 septembre 1991*, ed. Olivier Guyotjeannin, Laurent Morelle and Michel Parisse (Paris, 1993), pp. 27–44. On the customaries of Bernard and Ulrich, see the Introduction, pp. 9–10, above.
[27] On the comparison of monks and angels in medieval sources, see Leclercq, *The Life of Perfection*, pp. 15–42.
[28] Odo of Cluny, *Sermo 3* (*De sancto Benedicto abbate*), *PL* CXXXIII, col. 722a. I have borrowed the phrase "embodied in human practice" from Asad, *Genealogies of Religion*, p. 137.
[29] John of Salerno, *Vita Odonis* 2.5, *PL* CXXXIII, col. 63c.

of monks who fostered a celestial life among his followers.[30] Close identification with the angels was an effective means of self-promotion in Cluniac thought, but it also enunciated a way of life that had serious eschatological consequences for the brethren. Odo defined them succinctly in his *Life of Count Gerald of Aurillac*: "If monks are perfect, they are like the blessed angels, but if they return to the desire of the world they are rightly compared to apostate angels, who by their apostasy did not keep to their home."[31] Living in the perfect likeness of God's immortal servants, the brethren of Cluny could expect to join their company at the end of time. If any Cluniac monk abandoned this way of life, however, he would be cast down into the darkness like the rebel angels to await the Last Judgment.

The fear of sexual desire and the spiritual dangers associated with it were a common feature of the moral landscape of early medieval monasticism, but the monks of Cluny stood out among their contemporaries by expressing a pronounced concern for the avoidance of carnal longings as they pursued their ideal of achieving the likeness of angels on earth.[32] During his abbacy, Odo composed in Latin verse a spiritual meditation comprising 5,755 lines known as the *Occupatio*.[33] This long poem was intended to provide its monastic audience with an object of moral and intellectual rumination that would simultaneously encourage the reader to cultivate traditional virtues and distract him from the encroachment of sinful thoughts. Dread at the possibility of same-sex desire in the cloister was an overwhelming preoccupation of the poet. According to Christopher A. Jones, who has examined Odo's poem in the context of monastic reform, the *Occupatio* "treats the sin of Sodom at a depth possibly unequalled by any other text between John Chrysostom in the late fourth century and Peter Damian in the mid-eleventh."[34] The abbot's poetic

---

[30] Peter Damian, *Epistola* 6.4, *PL* CXLIV, col. 374ab.

[31] Odo of Cluny, *Vita Geraldi* 2.8: "Si, inquit, monachi perfecti sunt, beatis angelis assimilantur; sin vero ad saeculum desiderium revertuntur, apostaticis angelis, qui suum domicilium non servaverunt, per suam utique apostasiam, jure comparantur." *PL* CXXXIII, col. 675b; trans. Gerard Sitwell, in *Soldiers of Christ: Saints and Saints' Lives from Late Antiquity and the Early Middle Ages*, ed. Thomas F. X. Noble and Thomas Head (University Park, PA, 1995), p. 331.

[32] For a convenient overview of the importance of chastity in the early monastic tradition, with reference to earlier literature, see Albrecht Diem, *Das monastische Experiment: Die Rolle der Keuschheit bei der Entstehung des westlichen Klosterwesens* (Münster, 2005). On chastity in the Cluniac tradition, see Dominique Iogna-Prat, "Continence et virginité dans la conception clunisienne de l'ordre du monde autour de l'an mil," in *Académie des Inscriptions et Belles-Lettres: Comptes rendus*, 1985 (Paris, 1985), pp. 127–146.

[33] Odo of Cluny, *Occupatio*, ed. Anton Swoboda (Leipzig, 1900). Studies of this poem are rare owing to the obscurity of its language. For a subtle treatment of this difficult text, see Christopher A. Jones, "Monastic Identity and Sodomitic Danger in the *Occupatio* by Odo of Cluny," *Speculum* 82 (2007): 1–53.

[34] Jones, "Monastic Identity and Sodomitic Danger," p. 4.

admonitions about the dangers of homosexual longing included a strong promotion of the cultivation of celibacy in pursuit of the angelic life:

Connected by a particular bond to Him who was born of a virgin, they take care to keep what is precious distinct from what is vile. From heaven above they have been called the Lord's own voice in as much as they worthily imitate the angelic hosts on high, namely by leading, while still in their physical bodies, the life of the angels. There is nothing I can say that does full justice to the virtue of such men.[35]

John of Salerno's *Life of Odo* gave voice to similar concerns about the protection of chastity in the cloister. Odo himself was accused of grave misconduct in the chapter meeting when he took a child oblate to the latrine in the middle of the night, believing that a burning lantern hung nearby would suffice to ensure the innocence of his intention when in fact he should have awoken a third party to accompany them.[36] Likewise, the customaries of Bernard and Ulrich instructed monks to guard their modesty in any circumstance that could incite sexual thoughts. Strict rules of conduct surrounded them as they dressed and undressed in the dormitory to prevent a glimpse of their naked bodies from kindling desire in their brethren.[37] A program of sacred reading and regulated comportment helped the monks of Cluny to avoid opportunities for the arousal of same-sex desire by populating their minds with sacred words and by directing their behavior so that they lived in consonance with their angelic ideal.

In emulation of the heavenly host, the Cluniacs contemplated the divine presence continuously through carefully orchestrated rituals of corporate and private prayer.[38] The decades around the turn of the first millennium saw a marked increase in the length and complexity of liturgical ceremonies at Cluny and other abbeys in its orbit of influence.[39] The duration of the day and night offices varied considerably with the season, but they were especially long during Lent. There is every indication, however, that the monks considered the extent of the liturgy to be

---

[35] Odo of Cluny, *Occupatio*, lines 545–550: "Virgineae proli quodam quasi federe iuncti / Diuidere a uili preciosum sunt studiosi. / Qui uelut os domini sunt celitus inde uocati, / Qui merito angelicis simulantur in axe cateruis, / Scilicet angelicam quod agunt in corpore uitam. / Nil plene dignum uirtute fatemur eorum." ed. Swoboda, pp. 164–165. I am most grateful to Drew Jones for his assistance with this translation.

[36] John of Salerno, *Vita Odonis* 33, PL CXXXIII, col. 57c.

[37] On the rules of comportment for dressing and undressing at eleventh-century Cluny, see Chapter 3, pp. 85–86, below.

[38] Further on the divine office at Cluny and the role of sign language in the orchestration of liturgical services, see Chapter 3, pp. 87–88, below.

[39] Kassius Hallinger, "Das Phänomen der liturgischen Steigerungen Klunys (10./11. Jh.)," in *Studia historico-ecclesiastica: Festgabe für Prof. Luchesius G. Spätling O. F. M.*, ed. Isaac Vázquez (Rome, 1977), pp. 183–236, with references to earlier literature.

important and necessary for the fulfillment of their holy purpose. The customary of Ulrich reported that the senior brethren of Cluny censured a monk in the chapter meeting for curtailing the reading of a lesson during the divine office.[40] This sentiment changed in the twelfth century, when Abbot Peter the Venerable (1122–1156) made several attempts to shorten the liturgy because the monks found it burdensome.[41] But eleventh-century authors saw fit to praise the masses at Cluny and compare them favorably with the work of angels.[42] The long vigils of the Cluniacs allegedly had the power to free the souls of the sinful dead from the demons that tormented them.[43] Individual monks could be relentless in their personal prayers as well. The holiest of them recited the psalms without rest, their mouths moving so incessantly that they seemed to chew upon the sacred words.[44] The monk Jotsald claimed that Odilo, the fifth abbot of Cluny, even sung the psalms in his sleep.[45] The text of the psalter evoked the realm of heaven so strongly that its recitation could even elevate a pious layman to the ranks of the angels. When the saintly Count Gerald of Aurillac intoned the psalms, Odo described him as uttering no human sound (*nil mortale sonans*).[46] This phrase resonated with associations related to divine speech from classical antiquity. The abbot of Cluny borrowed the words from Virgil's *Aeneid*, where the poet had deployed them to characterize the prophetic utterance of the Delphic

---

[40] Ulrich 1.1, col. 645a.

[41] See, for example, *Statuta* 1, 14, 31, 65 and 67, pp. 40–42, 52–53, 66, 96 and 98. On the liturgical reforms of Peter the Venerable, see Robert Folz, "Pierre le Vénérable et la liturgie," in *Pierre Abélard – Pierre le Vénérable: Les courants philosophiques, littéraires et artistiques en occident au milieu du XII siècle (Abbaye de Cluny, 2 au 9 juillet 1972)* (Paris, 1975), pp. 143–161.

[42] Rodulphus Glaber, *Historiarum libri quinque* 5.1.13: "Erat siquidem, ut ipsi prospeximus, mos illius cenobii a prima diei aurora useque in horam prandii propter fratrum copiam continua missarum celebratio; que uidelicet tam digne pureque ac reuerenter fiebat ut magis angelica quam humana exibitio putabatur." ed. France, p. 236.

[43] See Jotsaldus, *Vita Odilonis* 2.15, ed. Johannes Staub, in *Iotsald von Saint-Claude, Vita des Abtes Odilo von Cluny, MGH SRG LXVIII* (Hanover, 1999), pp. 218–220; and Rodulphus Glaber, *Historiarum libri quinque* 5.1.13, ed. France, pp. 234–237. Further on intercessory prayer at Cluny in this period, see Dominique Iogna-Prat, "Les morts dans la compatibilité céleste des moines clunisiens autour l'an mil," in *Religion et culture autour de l'an mil: Royaume capétien et Lotharingie*, ed. Dominique Iogna-Prat and Jean-Charles Picard (Paris, 1990), pp. 55–69; English trans.: "The Dead in the Celestial Bookkeeping of the Cluniac Monks Around the Year 1000," in *Debating the Middle Ages*, ed. Lester Little and Barbara Rosenwein (Oxford, 1998), pp. 340–362.

[44] See, for example, John of Salerno, *Vita Odonis* 2.5: "Semper psallens cogebat nos psallere secum." *PL* CXXXIII, cols. 63d–64a; and Peter the Venerable, *De miraculis libri duos* 1.20: "Os sine requie sacra verba ruminans." ed. D. Bouthillier, *CCCM LXXXIII* (Turnhout, 1988), p. 61. For other examples of monastic *ruminatio*, see Jean Leclercq, *Etudes sur le vocabulaire monastique du moyen âge*, Studia Anselmiana 48 (Rome, 1961), pp. 134–138.

[45] Jotsaldus, *Vita Odilonis* 1.5, ed. Staub, pp. 154–155.

[46] Odo of Cluny, *Vita Geraldi* 1.11: "Dixerat haec, et psalterium a capite, nil mortale sonans, cum eisdem percucurrit." *PL* CXXXIII, col. 650b.

oracle as she spoke with the voice of Apollo.[47] Like the seer of Delphi, the monks of Cluny channeled holy words from on high and thereby participated with the angels as they sung eternal praises to God.

While the preservation of celibacy and the promotion of continuous prayer have received due attention from scholars as ascetic principles important to the monks of Cluny and their contemporaries, the discipline of silence has been overlooked as an essential component of the Cluniac program of angelic mimesis. The earliest abbots of Cluny were unwavering in their conviction that the abnegation of the will to speak was vital for the realization of Duke William's ideal that the brethren embrace the "heavenly way of life."[48] Little is known about the monastic principles fostered by Berno, the founding abbot of Cluny, but the custom of silence was among the five virtues extolled in his last will and testament, the only document that provides a firsthand glimpse of the religious practices he valued most.[49] The ideals of Berno's successors were much more transparent. The comparative abundance of hagiographical and legislative sources that extol the virtues of the abbots of Cluny and flesh out the lived principles of their brethren in the tenth and eleventh centuries are unanimous as to the centrality of the discipline of silence in the ascetic program of angelic imitation fostered among the Cluniacs, beginning with the abbacy of Odo.

The regulation of speech had an eschatological significance that was central to the worldview of the second abbot of Cluny. In his own writings, Odo exhorted his readers to avoid human discourse in pursuit of celestial lives of inner order and moral purity in expectation of the Second Coming.[50] Precepts against speaking enforced at tenth-century Cluny to achieve this ideal were allegedly so strict that contemporaries accused the brethren of distorting the *Rule of Benedict* and dismissed Cluniac customs as modern novelties.[51] Odo's hagiographer, John of

---

[47] Virgil, *Aeneid* 6.49–51: "maiorque videri / nec mortale sonans, adflata est numine quando / iam propiore dei."
[48] On Count William's mandate to the monks of Cluny, see n. 12, above.
[49] Berno, *Testamentum*, *PL* CXXXIII, col. 857a.
[50] Generally on Odo's monastic ideals, see Jean Leclercq, "L'idéal monastique de saint Odon d'après ses oeuvres," in *A Cluny*, ed. Société des Amis de Cluny, pp. 227–232; Kassius Hallinger, "Zur geistigen Welt der Anfänge Klunys," *Deutsches Archiv für Erforschung des Mittelalters* 10 (1954): 417–445; Raffaello Morghen, "Riforma monastica et spiritualità cluniacense," in *Spiritualità Cluniacense: Convegni del Centro di Studi sulla spiritualità medievale, 1958* (Todi, 1960), pp. 33–56; and Rosenwein, *Rhinoceros Bound*. There are revised English translations of the articles by Hallinger and Morghen in *Cluniac Monasticism in the Central Middle Ages*, ed. Noreen Hunt (Hamden, CT, 1971), pp. 11–28 and 29–55, respectively.
[51] John of Salerno, *Vita Odonis* 2.12, *PL* CXXXIII, col. 68b: "Diximus ista de antiquis vatibus, ut nullus arbitretur hoc silentium modernis temporibus fuisse inventum, sicut quidam male suspicantes fatentur."

Salerno, responded to these criticisms in his account of the abbot's saintly life. According to the *Life of Odo*, it was the denial of the will to speak that set the Cluniacs apart from other ascetics of their time.[52] No Cluniac monk ever spoke at unsuitable hours, that is, when the *Rule of Benedict* forbade talking altogether. No conversation was permitted on those days when the brethren celebrated a twelve-lesson office. During the week-long octaves of Christmas and Easter, complete silence reigned day and night throughout the entire abbey.[53] Against the claims of unnamed detractors that these prohibitions were unprecedented and therefore unwelcome in the monastic tradition, John made the case for their hallowed antiquity by compiling a genealogy of sacred silence that stretched from the Hebrew prophets to the monks of Cluny.[54] Since ancient times, John maintained, prophets had proclaimed with divine authority that silence accompanied hope, strength and goodness (Isa. 30.15 and Lam. 3.26–28). King David himself had sung its benefits in a psalm favored by early monastic authors: "I said: 'I will guard my ways that I may not sin with my tongue. I will bridle my mouth, so long as the wicked are against me'" (Ps. 38.1).[55] Likewise, Christ was known to have retreated to a mountain to pass entire nights alone in silent prayer (Matt. 14.22–23; Mark 6.45–46; Luke 6.12 and 21.36–37; and John 8.1–2). The desert fathers imitated Christ in turn by mortifying their tongues in the wilderness. Far from inventing new and unheralded customs, John argued that the brethren of Cluny were the direct heirs of a rich tradition of sacred silence passed down to them from the Hebrew prophets and the Gospels through the example of early Christian hermits like Paul, Anthony, Hilarion, John Cassian and Benedict himself.[56]

Throughout the *Life of Odo*, the consequences of idle speech were expressed in an uncompromising tone. Without silence, John maintained, the monastic life was fruitless and barren. When a monk lost his

---

[52] *Ibid.* 1.32: "Est et alius inter eos taciturnitatis modus." *PL* CXXXIII, col. 57a. Although John was describing the customs of Baume-les-Moines, where Odo made his profession, it is likely that these descriptions reflected contemporary practice at Cluny as well, because Berno was the abbot of both houses. See nn. 19–20, above.

[53] *Ibid.* 1.32, *PL* CXXXIII, col. 57ab.

[54] For what follows, see *Ibid.* 2.12–13, *PL* CXXXIII, cols. 68a–69a.

[55] "Dixi custodiam vias meas ne peccem in lingua mea custodiam os meum silentio donec est impius contra me." On the use of this psalm in the *Rule of Benedict*, see p. 35, below.

[56] This passage reminds us that Gregory the Great's portrait of Benedict as a hermit in the tradition of Anthony and other desert fathers remained a potent symbol in the early medieval imagination. Further on this point, see John Howe, "St. Benedict the Hermit as a Model for Italian Sanctity: Some Hagiographical Witnesses," *American Benedictine Review* 55 (2004): 42–54.

ability to bridle his speech, whatever he believed that he could do virtuously or well would come to nothing, according to the teaching of the desert fathers.[57] John populated his narrative with exemplary monks who cultivated silence when others would have been tempted to speak. A disciple of Odo preferred to lose a horse to a thief, rather than raise the alarm during the night, when talking was forbidden.[58] Another monk who had received instructions from St. Benedict in a dream duly waited for the period of silence to end before he informed his brethren what the saint had said.[59] Two monks captured by Norsemen refused to speak, even when threatened with death.[60] Bound and beaten, they remained silent in imitation of Christ, as he was prefigured in the book of Isaiah: "Like a lamb that is led to the slaughter and like a sheep that before its shearers is dumb, so he opened not his mouth" (Isa. 53.7). John encouraged his readers to consider how reprehensible it would be for monks to transgress the tenets of the *Rule of Benedict* by breaking their silence when they acted of their own free will. Their conduct, he assured them, would be compared with that of the captive monks by God at the Last Judgment. He left his audience to consider the terrible consequences of this comparison.[61]

The books of customs codified at Cluny in the late eleventh century suggest that the brethren of Cluny actualized Odo's ideals about the cultivation of silence in the monastery. According to the customary of Bernard, conversation was prohibited in the church, the dormitory, the refectory and the kitchens. Talking at night was also strictly forbidden. In addition, no one was allowed to speak anywhere in the abbey during the celebration of the divine office, a communal activity that took place during most hours of the day and intermittently throughout the night as well. The monk in charge of the infirmary was the only exception to this rule. If he had the need, he could speak to the sick monks when they gathered for their common meal.[62] Ulrich of Zell rehearsed the list of traditional places in the abbey where monks were never allowed to talk in the customary that he compiled for the brethren of Hirsau, but his readers were already familiar with these long-established customs and desired to know more about the times when speech was permissible. Ulrich explained that there were only two periods set aside for supervised conversation at Cluny: first after the prayers that followed the chapter meeting and again in the

---

[57] John of Salerno, *Vita Odonis* 2.11, PL CXXXIII, col. 67a.
[58] *Ibid.* 2.10, PL CXXXIII, col. 66cd. [59] *Ibid.* 3.11, PL CXXXIII, col. 83a.
[60] *Ibid.* 2.12, PL CXXXIII, col. 67b. [61] *Ibid.* 2.12–13, PL CXXXIII, cols. 68a–69a.
[62] Bernard 1.74.33, p. 273: "In omnibus officinis monasterii, quae intra castelli circuitum sunt, nemo unquam fratrum loquitur, dum regularis hora canitur, excepto infirmario, cui concessum est loqui, nonnisi de ipsa necessitate, ad illam horam ad quam infirmi comedunt."

afternoon after the office of Sext.[63] The length of these recesses is unknown, but Ulrich cautioned his readers to keep them very brief (*brevissimus*).[64] Such opportunities for speech were becoming increasingly rare in any case, for by the late eleventh century the amplification of the liturgy threatened to smother even these venues for sanctioned discourse. As Ulrich noted in his customary: "Quite often before all of the monks can take their places in the cloister and one of the brethren can utter a single word, the bell for Vespers is rung and that is the end of talking."[65] Moreover, the heightened ritual of feast days and the reverence expected during important liturgical seasons often cancelled out these times altogether. During the vigil of Pentecost, the monks lost their hour of speaking in the afternoon.[66] On Mondays, Wednesdays and Fridays in Lent, and throughout the week-long octaves of Christmas and Easter, no one was allowed to speak in any precinct of the abbey.[67]

The silence of the Cluniacs was both expectant and anticipatory. Avoiding all human discourse, the brethren conformed their behavior to an ideal of angelic conduct that actualized in this life their future participation in the heavenly chorus. John of Salerno justified the reverential silence instituted by Odo during the octaves of Christmas and Easter in direct reference to this eschatological anticipation. Although it was difficult for the human will to endure, this earthly silence was very brief compared to what it signified: the eternal silence to come.[68] This custom, first expressed in the *Life of Odo* and articulated over a century later as a lived principle in the customary of Bernard, was the echo of a precept of Gregory the Great (d. 604) in his *Exposition on the Book of Job*, an epitome of which appeared in a twelfth-century library catalogue from Cluny under Odo's name.[69] In this work, Pope Gregory taught that God

---

[63] Ulrich 1.12, col. 658d.   [64] Ulrich 1.40, col. 686a.

[65] Ulrich 1.18, col. 668c: "Saepius namque priusquam omnes in claustro consideant, et aliquis fratrum vel unum verbum faciat, pulsatur signum ad vesperas, et ecce ibi finis loquendi."

[66] Ulrich 1.23, col. 671b.

[67] Bernard 2.20, pp. 323–324. Cf. John of Salerno, *Vita Odonis* 1.32, PL CXXXIII, col. 57ab.

[68] John of Salerno, *Vita Odonis* 1.32: "Octava enim Natalis Domini et ejus Resurrectionis summum silentium die noctuque fiebat in illis. Brevissimum quippe istud, illud significare fatebantur aeternum silentium." PL CXXXIII, col. 57ab. For the suggestion that eschatological strains in Odo's writings reflect a concern for the approach of the first millennium, see Johannes Fried, "Endzeiterwartung um die Jahrtausendwende," *Deutsches Archiv für Erforschung des Mittelalters* 45 (1989): 385–473, at pp. 413–414; translated into English (without footnotes) as "Awaiting the End of Time Around the Turn of the Year 1000," in *The Apocalyptic Year 1000: Religious Expectation and Social Change, 950–1050*, ed. Richard Landes, Andrew Gow and David C. Van Meter (Oxford, 2003), pp. 17–63, at pp. 32–33.

[69] John of Salerno, *Vita Odonis* 1.32, PL CXXXIII, col. 57ab; and Bernard 2.20, pp. 323–324. Generally on Gregory the Great's influence on Odo's thought, see J. Laporte, "Saint Odon, disciple de saint Grégoire le grand," in *A Cluny*, ed. Société des Amis de Cluny, pp. 138–143. For the inference that Gregory's work informed the monks of Cluny in their practice of silence, see

could not communicate the divine majesty directly to the frailness of human faculties in this life, but used instead the voices of his apostles and preachers. After the resurrection of the elect at the end of time, there would be no need for God to communicate through spoken words because His Word would fill everyone and penetrate their minds with the power of its innermost light.[70] The strict silence of the Cluniacs foreshadowed their participation in the experience of the silent omnipresence of God.

Following the celestial ideal suggested in their foundation charter by Duke William of Aquitaine, the abbots of Cluny introduced an innovative understanding of the custom of silence. John of Salerno's *Life of Odo* mounted an eloquent defense of this principle at Cluny, but his work is only one voice in a debate about authority, tradition and the threat of innovation in the cloister that took place in the early tenth century. The strictness of the precepts against speaking enforced among the Cluniacs offended others who perceived their customs as a threat to received traditions. In fact, the Cluniac contribution to the understanding of monastic silence cannot be fully appreciated without taking account of the centuries-old ideals and lived traditions associated with this custom that Odo's adversaries were so eager to defend. Like so many other aspects of Christian asceticism, monastic silence and the customs surrounding it trace their origins to the Egyptian desert in late antiquity.

SET A WATCHMAN TO MY MOUTH

The earliest monastic authors were not effusive cataloguers of sins of the tongue. Evidence for their attitudes toward idle conversation is relatively scant, especially when compared with the rich and ordered taxonomies of harmful speech and its consequences that survive in scholastic and pastoral literature from the later Middle Ages.[71] Nonetheless, currents of concern for the dangers of careless words are clearly discernible in many monastic

---

Hallinger, "Zur geistigen Welt der Anfänge Klunys," pp. 427–429 (*Cluniac Monasticism in the Central Middle Ages*, ed. Hunt, pp. 39–41). Further on Odo's epitome of Gregory's work, the authenticity of which has been doubted, see n. 15, above.

[70] Gregory the Great, *Moralium libri* 30.4.17, *PL* LXXVI, col. 533ab. On prophecy and the speech of God in Gregory's thought, see Conrad Leyser, *Authority and Asceticism from Augustine to Gregory the Great* (Oxford, 2000), pp. 177–185.

[71] Carla Casagrande and Silvana Vecchio, *Les péchés de la langue: Discipline et éthique de la parole dans la culture médiévale*, trans. Philippe Baillet (Paris, 1991); Edwin D. Craun, *Lies, Slander, and Obscenity in Medieval English Literature: Pastoral Rhetoric and the Deviant Speaker* (Cambridge, 1997); and Sandy Bardsley, *Venomous Tongues: Speech and Gender in Late Medieval England* (Philadelphia, 2006).

sources written between the fourth and sixth centuries.[72] They are especially prevalent in normative rules of conduct, like the sixth-century *Rule of Benedict*, which became the most influential touchstone of monastic legislation in the Middle Ages.[73] The authors of these rules lived with a strong sense of history and tradition. For them the instruments of monastic virtue were preserved in a body of literature by and about the ancient monks of the eastern deserts, particularly the *Sayings of the Desert Fathers* and the *Rule of Saint Basil*.[74] Among these works were translations of Greek texts on monastic life as well as original compositions of displaced eastern ascetics, like John Cassian (d. *c.* 432/435), who wrote for Latin-speaking audiences. The words and deeds of the earliest hermits provided templates of discipline and practice for the abbeys of early medieval Italy and Gaul.

The first Christian monks led harsh lives of self-deprivation and devotion on the fringes of urban societies throughout Egypt and the Near East in late antiquity.[75] The desert, the measureless setting of their struggles, was an ambivalent image in early monastic literature. It was depicted both as a flowering paradise inhabited by angels and as a

---

[72] Ambrose G. Wathan, *Silence: The Meaning of Silence in the Rule of Saint Benedict* (Washington, DC, 1973); Adalbert de Vogüé, *La règle de saint Benoît: Commentaire historique et critique (Parties I–III)*, SC CLXXXIV (Paris, 1971), pp. 227–280; Peter Fuchs, "Die Weltflucht der Mönche: Anmerkungen zur Funktion des monastisch-asketischen Schweigens," *Zeitschrift für Soziologie* 15 (1986): 393–405; repr. in *Reden und Schweigen*, ed. Niklas Luhmann and Peter Fuchs (Frankfurt, 1989), pp. 21–45; and Leyser, *Authority and Asceticism*, esp. pp. 95–98.

[73] Further on the *Rule of Benedict*, see n. 9, above. For a complete list of the earliest surviving monastic rules from Gaul and Italy, see Adalbert de Vogüé, *Les règles monastiques anciennes (400–700)* (Turnhout, 1985), pp. 53–60.

[74] *RB* 73.4–6, pp. 672–674: "Aut quis liber sanctorum catholicorum Patrum hoc non resonat ut recto cursu perueniamus ad creatorem nostrum? Necnon et Collationes Patrum et Instituta et Vitas eorum, sed et Regula sancti Patris Basilii, quid aliud sunt nisi bene uiuentium et oboedientium monachorum instrumenta uirtutum?" On the reception of Basil of Caesarea's work in western abbeys, see Adalbert de Vogüé, "Influence de sainte Basile sur le monachisme d'occident," *Revue bénédictine* 113 (2003): 5–17. More generally on the transmission of eastern ascetic ideals to the west in this period, see R. Lorenz, "Die Anfänge des abendländischen Mönchtums im 4. Jahrhundert," *Zeitschrift für Kirchengeschichte* 77 (1966): 1–61.

[75] Derwas J. Chitty, *The Desert a City: An Introduction to the Study of Egyptian and Palestinian Monasticism Under the Christian Empire* (Oxford, 1966); Philip Rousseau, *Ascetics, Authority, and the Church in the Age of Jerome and Cassian* (Oxford, 1978); and by the same author, *Pachomius: The Making of a Community in Fourth-Century Egypt* (Berkeley, Los Angeles and London, 1985); Peter Brown, *The Body and Society: Men, Women and Sexual Renunciation in Early Christianity* (New York, 1988), esp. pp. 213–240; Douglas Burton-Christie, *The Word in the Desert: Scripture and the Quest for Holiness in Early Christian Monasticism* (New York and Oxford, 1993), esp. pp. 76–103 and 134–177; Graham Gould, *The Desert Fathers on Monastic Community* (Oxford, 1993); James E. Goehring, *Ascetics, Society, and the Desert: Studies in Early Egyptian Monasticism* (Harrisburg, PA, 1999); Marilyn Dunn, *The Emergence of Monasticism: From the Desert Fathers to the Early Middle Ages* (Oxford, 2000), pp. 1–81; and Adalbert de Vogüé, *Regards sur le monachisme des premiers siècles: Recueil d'articles*, Studia Anselmiana 130 (Rome, 2000).

sweltering landscape of terrifying vastness, abounding in monstrous creatures.[76] For the monks themselves, the desert was a crucible of discipline, where they tempered their carnal passions through sexual abstinence, extreme fasts, sleepless nights and ceaseless prayers. The aim of their devotion was intensely personal. Through rigorous mortification, the desert fathers strove to strip away all vestiges of their individual will and surrender themselves completely to God. They sought nothing less than a return to the condition of Adam in the Garden of Eden, before his willful disobedience caused the Fall of Man. In the words of Peter Brown: "Once they had faced out the terrible risks involved in remaining human in a nonhuman environment, the men of the desert were thought capable of recovering, in the hushed silence of that dead landscape, a touch of the unimaginable glory of Adam's first state."[77]

The "hushed silence of that dead landscape" was broken routinely by the voices of hermits. Verbal exchange was an essential feature of the relationship between ascetic masters and their disciples. The desert was home to many great old men, spiritual fathers whose purity of heart lent their words an unassailable authority.[78] These men attracted a steady stream of aspirants and visitors, who clamored to hear their advice: "Abba, speak a word to me."[79] The *Sayings of the Desert Fathers* depicted with extraordinary vividness a series of intimate and anxious consultations between masters and disciples about the doubts that assailed aspiring monks in the desert: "How should we live? Why is my heart hard and why do I not fear God? Tell me, what must I do to be saved?"[80] The responses of the desert fathers provided their listeners with spiritual direction, but they also reinforced the norms and behavior-patterns of the community of disciples. Taken together, first as an oral tradition and later as a body of texts, these sayings created a

---

[76] For examples of these images in the writings of Jerome and other early monastic authors, see Antoine Guillaumont, "La conception du désert chez les moines d'Egypte," *Revue de l'Histoire des Religions* 188 (1975): 3–21; Patricia Cox Miller, "Jerome's Centaur: A Hyper-Icon of the Desert," *Journal of Early Christian Studies* 4 (1996): 209–233; and James E. Goehring, "The Dark Side of the Landscape: Ideology and Power in the Christian Myth of the Desert," *Journal of Medieval and Early Modern Studies* 33 (2003): 437–451.

[77] Brown, *Body and Society*, p. 220.

[78] Rousseau, *Ascetics, Authority, and the Church*, pp. 19–32; Burton-Christie, *The Word in the Desert*, pp. 76–103; and Gould, *The Desert Fathers on Monastic Community*, pp. 26–87.

[79] *Vitae patrum* 5.3.2, 5.3.25 and 5.6.12: "Dic mihi aliquod verbum." *PL* LXXIII, cols. 860c, 864b and 890d; trans. Benedicta Ward, *The Desert Fathers: Sayings of the Early Christian Monks* (New York, 2003), pp. 12, 17 and 56.

[80] *Vitae patrum* 5.1.13, 5.3.22 and 5.14.2: "Quomodo debet homo conversari? Unde est, abba, cor meum durum et non timeo dominum? Dic mihi, quid faciam ut salvari possim." *PL* LXXIII, cols. 856c, 864a and 947d; trans. Ward, *Desert Fathers*, pp. 5, 17 and 140.

shared context of moral understanding for the correct practice of ascetic discipline.[81]

Not all verbal utterances were beneficial, however; some threatened the integrity of monastic communities and the souls of their inhabitants. Early rules of conduct for cloistered men and women made a sharp distinction between words used for holy purposes, like the instruction of disciples and the praise of God, and those that were useless and potentially harmful.[82] Generally speaking, idle words were those that did not pertain to the edification of the faith.[83] The sins of slander and murmuring merited special attention in early monastic literature. Slander was perilous for monks because it countermanded the teachings of Christ on one of the most important commandments: to love your neighbor as yourself (Matt. 22.36–40). Envious disparagement pitted the brethren against one another and created discord within the community.[84] In the words of one desert father: "It is better to eat meat and to drink wine, than to eat the flesh of the brothers in slander."[85] Preachers in early medieval Gaul also warned their monastic audiences that such talk eroded the spiritual benefits of their vocation.[86] Monks who spoke evil of others were especially vulnerable to the "poisoned blades of their own tongues."[87] Slanderous words wounded the object of their malice as well. According to Bishop Valerian of Cimiez (d. *c.* 460), the tongue had an evil

---

[81] Burton-Christie, *The Word in the Desert*, pp. 150–177; and Maud Gleason, "Visiting and News: Gossip and Reputation Management in the Desert," *Journal of Early Christian Studies* 6 (1998): 501–521, at pp. 502–503.

[82] See, for example, Basil of Caesarea, *Regula* 40 and 86, ed. K. Zelzer, *CSEL* LXXXVI (Vienna, 1986), pp. 85–86 and 165–166; Augustine, *Ordo monasterii* 5 and 9, ed. George Lawless, in *Augustine of Hippo and His Monastic Rule* (Oxford, 1987), pp. 74 and 76; *Regula orientalis* 17.9 and 17.16, ed. Adalbert de Vogüé, in *Les règles des saints pères*, 2 vols., *SC* CCXCVII–CCXCVIII (Paris, 1982), vol. II, p. 472; *RM* 9.51, vol. I, p. 416; *RB* 4.53 and 6.8, pp. 460 and 472; and Columbanus, *Regula monachorum* 2, ed. G. S. M. Walker, in *Sancti Columbani Opera* (Dublin, 1957), p. 124.

[83] Basil of Caesarea, *Regula* 40, ed. Zelzer, pp. 85–86.

[84] Burton-Christie, *The Word in the Desert*, pp. 138–143; and Gould, *The Desert Fathers on Monastic Community*, pp. 121–123.

[85] Hyperechius, *Sentences* 4, cited by Gould, *The Desert Fathers on Monastic Community*, p. 121.

[86] *Homilia* 39 (*Ad monachos* 4): "Quid enim prodest afflictio corporalis, si linguam nequitiis et obtrectationibus polluamus?" ed. John Leroy and Fr. Glorie, in *Eusebius "Gallicanus": Collectio Homiliarum*, 3 vols., *CCCM* CI (Turnhout, 1970–1971), vol. II, pp. 459–460. For an important study of this frequently overlooked sermon collection, see Lisa K. Bailey, "Preaching and Pastoral Care in Late Antique Gaul: The Eusebius Gallicanus Sermon Collection" (Ph.D. dissertation, Princeton University, 2004).

[87] *Homilia* 40.6 (*Ad monachos* 5): "Hic sumus, et tuti non sumus. Aut enim cordis cogitationibus uariis et improbis atque inhonestis agitamur aut uenenatis linguae gladiis uulneramur, pro minimis et paruissimis rebus scandalizantes." ed. Leroy and Glorie, in *Eusebius "Gallicanus": Collectio Homiliarum*, vol. II, p. 480. Early medieval warnings about the dangers of monastic slander were not limited to Gaul. See David McDougall and Ian McDougall, "Evil Tongues: A Previously Unedited Old English Sermon," *Anglo-Saxon England* 26 (1997): 209–229.

all its own: the power to pierce the secret recesses of the human heart. Once inflicted, these wounds lasted a lifetime. Only death could free the stricken organ from the spite of evil speech.[88]

Unlike slander, which eroded lateral relationships in the abbey, the sin of murmuring was an act of disobedience, an expression of discontent against one's superiors that undermined the vertical hierarchy of the monastic community. Many ancient rulings advised monks to complete their assigned tasks without verbal complaint of this kind.[89] Murmurers should live in fear of Paul's foreboding advice to the Christian community at Corinth (1 Cor. 10.10): "Do not grumble, as some of them did and perished at the hands of the Destroyer."[90] Like the ancient Hebrews who murmured against Moses and Aaron in the wilderness (Num. 14.1–37), rebellious and disgruntled monks made their complaint in the hearing of the Lord and risked kindling the fire of divine wrath. If some among the people of God perished in the desert because of the sin of murmuring, asked Alcuin of York (d. 804), how much more deserving of punishment is a cloistered monk, if he does not fear to sow evil grumblings in his mind?[91]

Early monastic authors also condemned the unbridled expression of foolish mirth.[92] There was no place for laughter in the tortured landscape

---

[88] Valerian of Cimiez, *Homilia* 5.2–3: "Singulare autem malum est lingua ... Enumerari non potest quantis sit lingua jaculis accincta verborum, quibus satis promptum est etiam quae sunt animae secretiora percutere. Quamcumque autem aures injuriam suscipiunt illico ad cordis secreta transmittunt: ubi si semel introierit, sine mortis exitu non recedit." *PL* LII, cols. 706c and 707c. Further on Valerian, see Jean-Pierre Weiss, "Le statut du prédicateur et les instruments de la prédication dans la Provence du Ve siècle," in *La parole du prédicateur, Ve–XVe siècle* (Nice, 1997), pp. 23–47.

[89] See, for example, Augustine, *Ordo monasterii* 5, ed. Lawless, p. 74; *Statuta Patrum* 26, ed. Adalbert de Vogüé, in *Les règles des saints pères*, vol. I, p. 278; *RM* 2.44 and 5.7, vol. I, pp. 368 and 378; and *RB* 35.13, p. 568. Cloistered women were also warned against the sin of murmuring. See Caesarius, *Regula virginum* 17.1–2, ed. Joël Courreau and Adalbert de Vogüé, in *Césaire d'Arles: Oeuvres monastiques*, 2 vols., SC CCCXLV and CCXCVIII (Paris, 1988–1994), vol. I, p. 192.

[90] *Regula sanctorum patrum* 3.13: "Timere debent illud dictum terribile: Nolite murmurare, sicut quidam eorum murmurauerunt et ab exterminatore perierunt." ed. Adalbert de Vogüé, in *Les règles des saints pères*, vol. I, p. 194.

[91] Alcuin, *Epistola* 168: "Si aliqui ex populo Dei in heremo propter murmurationis perierunt peccatum, quanto magis monachus monasterii spiritali plectatur vindicta, si murmurationis malo mentem inolescere non metuit?" *MGH Epistolae* IV, ed. Ernest Dümmler (Munich, 1978), p. 276.

[92] Basilius Steidle, "Das Lachen im alten Mönchtum," *Benediktinische Monatsschrift* 20 (1938): 271–280; Pedro Max Alexander, "La prohibición de la risa en la Regula Benedicti: Intento de explicación e interpretación," *Regulae Benedicti Studia* 5 (1976): 225–284; G. Schmitz, "*Quod rident homo, plurandum est*: Der Unwert des Lachen im monastische geprägten Vorstellungen der spätantike und des frühen Mittelalters," in *Stadtverfassung, Verfassungsstaat, Pressepolitik: Festschrift E. Naujoks*, ed. F. Quarthal and W. Setzler (Sigmaringen, 1980), pp. 3–15; Irven M. Resnick, "*Risus monasticus*: Laughter and Medieval Monastic Culture," *Revue bénédictine* 97 (1987): 90–100; and Jacques Le Goff, "Le rire dans les règles monastiques du haut moyen âge," in *Haut moyen âge: Culture, éducation et société. Etudes offertes à Pierre Riché*, ed. Claude Lepelley *et al.* (Nanterre, 1990), pp. 93–103.

of the desert. The great old men despaired to hear their disciples express levity. Upon overhearing someone laugh, a hermit was said to ask in an ominous tone: "We have to render an account of our whole life before heaven and earth and you can laugh?"[93] The saints of early monasticism were ever mindful of the terrible reckoning of sinful words and deeds that confronted every soul at the end of time.[94] Their constant reflection on the Last Judgment meant that the spirit of penitence followed them like a shadow.[95] It was more fitting for the desert hermits to weep in this world and thereby earn laughter in the world to come (Luke 6.21). Some of their western emulators, like Bishop Martin of Tours (d. 397), were never seen to laugh.[96] On the whole, however, Latin authors tempered the harsh penitential spirit of the desert with respect to the expression of mirth. Their rulings tended to treat laughter like any other verbal utterance: it only became a sinful and dangerous practice when it was excessive and disruptive.[97]

Like an embankment that wards off a destructive tide, the cultivation of silence deflected the dangerous erosion of sinful words. Early medieval precepts on monastic conduct promoted silence at all times.[98] Rulings for cloistered communities forbade talking specifically in the church, the refectory and the dormitory. Personal conversation was strictly prohibited in the church because the celebration of the divine office demanded the full attention of monks.[99] Even brethren who came there to pray in solitude were encouraged to do so in silence, esteeming tears and the

---

[93] *Vitae patrum* 5.3.23: "Vidit senex quemdam ridentem, et dicit ei: Coram coeli et terrae Domino rationem totius vitae nostrae reddituri sumus, et tu rides?" *PL* LXXIII, col. 864b; trans. Ward, *Desert Fathers*, p. 17.

[94] *Vitae patrum* 5.11.10, *PL* LXXIII, col. 934b.   [95] *Vitae patrum* 5.3.24, *PL* LXXIII, col. 864b.

[96] Sulpicius Severus, *Vita sancti Martini* 27: "Nemo umquam illum vidit iratum, nemo commotum, nemo maerentem, nemo ridentem." ed. Jacques Fontaine, in *Sulpice Sévère: Vie de saint Martin*, 3 vols., *SC* CXXXIII–CXXXV (Paris, 1967–1969), vol. I, p. 314. Sulpicius' *Life of Martin* exerted a strong influence on ideals of saintly comportment throughout the early medieval period. See Barbara H. Rosenwein, "St. Odo's St. Martin: The Uses of a Model," *Journal of Medieval History* 4 (1978): 317–331; and Julia M. H. Smith, "The Problem of Female Sanctity in Carolingian Europe, c. 780–920," *Past and Present* 146 (1995): 3–37, at pp. 14–16.

[97] See, for example, John Cassian, *De coenobiorum institutis* 12.27.6: "risus leuis ac fatuus, effrenata atque indisciplinata cordis elatio," ed. Jean-Claude Guy, in *Jean Cassien: Institutions cénobitiques*, *SC* CIX (Paris, 1965), p. 492; *RM* 9.51, vol. I, p. 416; *RB* 4.53–54, 6.8, 7.59–60, pp. 460, 472 and 486–488; Defensor of Ligugé, *Liber scintillarum* 2.55, ed. H. M. Rochais, 2 vols., *SC* LXXVII and LXXXVI (Paris, 1961–1962), vol. II, pp. 142–146; Columbanus, *Regula coenobialis fratrum* 4, ed. G. S. M. Walker, in *Sancti Columbani Opera* (Dublin, 1957), p. 148; Donatus, *Regula ad virgines* 17, ed. Adalbert de Vogüé, in "La règle de Donat pour l'abbesse Gauthstrude," *Benedictina* 25 (1978): 219–313, at p. 262; *Regula Pauli et Stephani* 37, ed. J. M. Villanova, in *Regula Pauli et Stephani: Edició crítica i comentari* (Montserrat, 1959), pp. 122–123.

[98] *RB* 42.1, p. 584: "Omni tempore silentium debent studere monachi, maxime tamen nocturnis horis."

[99] John Cassian reported this practice among the monks of Egypt in *De coenobiorum institutis* 2.10.1, ed. Guy, p. 74. See also *Statuta Patrum* 39, ed. de Vogüé, in *Les règles des saints pères*, vol. I, p. 282.

fervor of the heart over a clamorous voice.[100] Garrulous monks distracted the devout from their attentive worship. Likewise, personal silence in the refectory ensured that the brethren applied their minds to the lessons of the texts read aloud during meals.[101] Bishop Aurelian of Arles (d. 551) instructed monks to attend to the reader without conversing so that they could be nourished outwardly by the food and inwardly by the word of God.[102] Lastly, talking at night was always expressly forbidden as well.[103] The fifth-century *Rule of the Master* discouraged its readers from speaking once they had completed Compline, the last office of the day. They were instructed to keep so profound a silence throughout the night that no one would believe that any monks were in the abbey at all.[104] In the seventh century, a monk named Waldebert advised the cloistered women of Faremoutiers not to sleep facing each other in the same bed because it may incite the desire to talk together in the dark.[105] As this example shows, the shared proximity of cloistered life presented inevitable problems to a community imperiled by the content of unregulated conversation.

Early medieval hagiographers made clear to their monastic audiences the dreadful consequences of idle speech. In the *Life of Benedict*, Pope Gregory the Great related how the holy abbot warned two religious women to curb their tongues and refrain from unguarded conversation under threat of excommunication. A few days later, both women died without changing their ways and were buried in the church. So powerful and binding was Benedict's admonition that, during the celebration of the mass, whenever the deacon called out "Whoever is not in communion, let him leave this place," the dead women rose from their tombs and shambled from the church.[106] An offering to God from the saint restored the women's souls to communion, but the message of the episode was

---

[100] *RB* 52.1–4, p. 610.
[101] The custom of silence *ad mensam* was first attested in Egyptian monasteries as well: John Cassian, *De coenobiorum institutis* 4.17, ed. Guy, p. 144. See also *RB* 38.5, p. 574: "Et summum fiat silentium, ut nullius musitatio uel uox nisi solius legentis ibi audiatur."
[102] Aurelianus, *Regula ad monachos* 49, *PL* LXVIII, col. 393a. The same rule applied to cloistered women. See Caesarius, *Regula virginum* 18.2: "Sedentes ad mensam taceant, et animum lectioni intendant." ed. Courreau and de Vogüé, vol. I, p. 192.
[103] See, for example, *Regula orientalis* 44: "Nemo alteri loquatur in tenebris." ed. de Vogüé, in *Les règles des saints pères*, vol. II, p. 494.
[104] *RM* 30.12–13, vol. II, p. 164.
[105] Waldebertus, *Regula ad virgines* 14, *PL* LXXXVIII, col. 1065b.
[106] Gregory the Great, *Libri dialogorum* 2.23.1–4, ed. Adalbert de Vogüé, in *Grégoire le Grand: Dialogues*, 3 vols., *SC* CCLI, CCLX and CCLXV (Paris, 1978–1980), vol. II, pp. 204–208. Excommunication was usually reserved as punishment for chronic lapses in discipline. See *RB* 23, p. 542.

plain to Gregory's audience: sins of the tongue had the power to exclude Christians from the community of the faithful, both in this life and in the life to come. When speech was pregnant with danger, silence offered the greatest protection.

The discipline of silence was more than a safeguard against the perils of wayward speech; it was also a positive practice in its own right. In the vastness of the desert, where spoken words could resound with unearthly force, the early hermits taught that the cultivation of silence was essential both as a means of achieving a heightened awareness of the presence of God and as a necessary preparation for the utterance of good and useful words.[107] The hermit Agathon allegedly kept a stone in his mouth for three years to learn how to remain silent.[108] The reward for such diligence was enlightened discernment: "If the soul keeps far away from all discourse and words, the Spirit of God will come to her and she who was barren will be fruitful."[109] Consequently, hermits were not hasty to answer the questions of their disciples. It was not uncommon for them to sit in silence for many days, ignoring the pleas of their followers until the spirit moved them to speak.[110]

Monastic rules from Gaul and Italy emphasized that the abnegation of the desire to converse was a virtue intimately related to humility and obedience. Cassian warned that the sin of pride clouded monastic discernment with respect to the tongue.[111] Individuals who were puffed up with self-importance were usually far too eager to engage in idle conversation and only seemed to cultivate silence when nursing rancorous thoughts about others. Monks of this kind were no friends of silence (*nec umquam taciturnitatis amica*). The sixth-century *Rule of Benedict* devoted an entire chapter to the moral benefits of this virtue (Chapter 6: *De taciturnitate*), commencing with verses from the Book of Psalms that united silence and humility: "I have set a watchman to my mouth. I was mute and was humbled and I remained silent from good things" (Ps. 38.2–3).[112] Silence was also an expression of obedience, a virtue closely related to

---

[107] Burton-Christie, *The Word in the Desert*, pp. 146–150; and Heinrich Holze, "Schweigen und Gotteserfahrung bei den ägyptischen Mönchsvätern," *Erbe und Auftrag* 69 (1993): 314–321.

[108] *Vitae patrum* 5.4.7, *PL* LXXIII, col. 865b.

[109] *Apophthegmata Patrum* (Poemen 18), ed. Jean-Claude Guy, in *Recherches sur la tradition grecque des Apophthegmata Patrum* (Brussels, 1962), p. 31; trans. Burton-Christie, *The Word in the Desert*, p. 147.

[110] See, for example, *Apophthegmata Patrum* (De abbate Pambo 2), in *Patrologia cursus completus: Series graeca*, ed. J. P. Migne, 161 vols. (Paris, 1857–1903), vol. LXV, col. 368cd.

[111] For what follows, see John Cassian, *De coenobiorum institutis* 12.27, ed. Guy, pp. 488–492.

[112] *RB* 6.1, p. 470: "Posui ori meo custodiam. Obmutui et humiliatus sum et silui a bonis." According to the rule, monks achieved the ninth step of humility when they remained silent and spoke only when asked a question (*RB* 7.56, p. 486).

humility.[113] Early medieval monks emulated the example of Christ, who was obedient unto death. Through fear of hell or in expectation of eternal life, they hastened to obey the command of a superior as though it was a command from God.[114] The *Rule of Benedict* enjoined them never to speak without permission:

Therefore, because of the grave importance of silence, let the permission to speak be granted only rarely to observant disciples, even though it be for good and holy and edifying words, because it is written: "In speaking profusely you will not escape sin" (Prov. 10.19). And elsewhere: "Death and life are in the power of the tongue" (Prov. 18.21).[115]

Monks were required to seek permission to speak from a superior with the utmost humility and respectful submission.[116] This privilege was granted only to individuals who could be trusted to shun worldly topics and temper their words with modesty and restraint.[117] Important monastic officials, like the abbot, the cellarer and the porter, were also allowed to converse in accordance with the demands of their offices.[118] Without permission to speak, however, the obedient monk was expected to remain silent.

In the economy of personal salvation that characterized early monasticism, the discipline of silence had a dual function: it safeguarded the monk's soul from the perils of sinful speech and it fostered the virtues of humility and obedience. It would be misleading to conclude, however, that the earliest monks abandoned the need for speaking altogether. From Egypt to Gaul, the spoken word was the medium of divine service, humble teaching and official duties. The tongue was always a dangerous instrument, liable at any time to succumb to the pleasures of idle conversation and immoderate laughter, but the discerning monk knew the boundaries of its proper use. In the words of Bishop Valerian of Cimiez:

---

[113] Prompt obedience was the first step of humility (*RB* 5.1 and 7.10–30, pp. 464 and 474–480). Further on monastic obedience, see Jean Leclercq, "Religious Obedience According to the Rule of Benedict," *American Benedictine Review* 16 (1965): 183–193; Adalbert de Vogüé, "Obéissance et autorité dans le monachisme ancien jusqu'à Saint Benoît," in *Imaginer la théologie catholique: Permanence et transformations de la foi en attendant Jésus-Christ: Mélanges offerts à Ghislain Lafont*, ed. Jeremy Driscoll, Studia Anselmiana 129 (Rome, 2000), pp. 565–600; and Stephen M. Hildebrand, "*Oboedientia* and *oboedire* in the Rule of Benedict: A Study of Their Theological and Monastic Meanings," *American Benedictine Review* 52 (2001): 421–436.

[114] *RB* 5.3–4 and 7.34, pp. 464 and 480.

[115] *RB* 6.3–6, p. 470: "Ergo, quamuis de bonis et sanctis et aedificationum eloquiis, perfectis discipulis, propter taciturnitatis gravitatem rara loquendi concedatur licentia, quia scriptum est: In multiloquio non effugies peccatum. Et alibi: Mors et vita in manibus linguae."

[116] *RB* 6.7, pp. 470–472.

[117] See, for example, Caesarius, *Regula virginum* 19.1–5, ed. Courreau and de Vogüé, vol. I, pp. 192–194; and *RB* 6.7, 7.60, 22.8, 42.11 and 47.4, pp. 470–472, 486–488, 542, 586 and 598.

[118] *RB* 2.4–25, 6.6 and 64.2, pp. 442–446, 470 and 648 (abbot); *RB* 31.13–14, p. 558 (cellarer); and *RB* 66.1–4, pp. 658–660 (porter).

"To speak and to remain silent, each is a perfection. The case of each consists in holding to the proper measure of words. Silence is great and speech is great, but the wise man sets a measure upon them both."[119]

THE TONGUE IS A FIRE

In the age of the Carolingians, the internal life of abbeys underwent significant changes that posed direct challenges to traditional standards of personal conduct, including the discipline of silence. By the eighth century, monastic communities had spread and flourished throughout the new kingdoms of the west.[120] Inspired by the hardships of the first hermits, the monks of northern Europe sought the remoteness of impenetrable swamps, high mountain tops and other uninviting locales that recalled the hostile and otherworldly landscape of the desert. Like the early fathers, their goal was personal salvation. They strove for perfection in this world and deliverance in the next through a penitential life dedicated to the praise of God and the cultivation of virtue. Due to a steady increase in monastic vocations throughout this period, many abbeys expanded from modest, quiet settlements to large, bustling communities that resembled small towns.[121] The custom of oblation, the act of consecrating a child to God's service in an abbey, became a common practice by the eighth century and may account for the growth of some monasteries.[122] In places like Fulda, Corbie and Aniane, the liturgical celebration of the brethren competed with the noise of resident artisans and the multitude of servants and livestock necessary to sustain the material needs of expanding religious communities. This new dynamic within the walls of Carolingian abbeys marked a departure from the ideals of seclusion that characterized ancient monasticism and thereby raised concerns about the disruptive effect of idle conversation among the brethren.[123]

---

[119] Valerian, *Homilia* 5.7: "Ita et loqui et tacere perfectio est. Est autem utriusque partis causa verborum tenuisse mensuram. Magnum est tacere, magnum est loqui; sed sapientis est utrumque moderari." *PL* LII, col. 709b; trans. Georges E. Ganss, in *Saint Peter Chrysologus, Selected Sermons and Saint Valerian, Homilies*, The Fathers of the Church 17 (New York, 1953), pp. 334–335 (slightly modified).

[120] The most comprehensive study of monasticism in this period remains Friedrich Prinz, *Frühes Mönchtum in Frankenreich: Kultur und Gesellschaft in Gallien, den Rheinlanden und Bayern am Beispiel der monastischen Entwicklung (4. bis 8. Jahrhundert)*, 2nd edn (Munich, 1988).

[121] On the great numbers of monks reported in Carolingian abbeys, see U. Berlière, "Le nombre des moines dans les anciens monastères," *Revue bénédictine* 41 (1929): 231–261, at pp. 242–243.

[122] Mayke de Jong, *In Samuel's Image: Child Oblation in the Early Medieval West* (Leiden, 1996).

[123] On this point, see Otto Gerhard Oexle, "Les moines d'occident et la vie politique et sociale dans le haut moyen âge," *Revue bénédictine* 103 (1993): 255–272; and Richard E. Sullivan, "What Was Carolingian Monasticism? The Plan of Saint Gall and the History of Monasticism," in *After Rome's Fall: Narrators and Sources of Early Medieval History, Essays Presented to Walter Goffart*, ed. Alexander Callander Murray (Toronto, 1998), pp. 251–287.

At the same time, Carolingian monarchs began to take an active interest in directing religious life in their kingdom in ways that influenced regulations concerning the avoidance of sinful words.[124] There was no uniformity of monastic custom in this period. Every community employed its own amalgam of rulings (*regulae mixtae*) culled from oral tradition and from written customs circulated under the names of great abbots, like Benedict and Columbanus.[125] Carolingian kings and their advisors believed that the military success and spiritual well-being of the political community depended on the prayerful intervention of monks.[126] As a result, in the early ninth century, Emperor Louis the Pious (r. 814–840) undertook a sweeping reform of monastic houses in the Frankish heartlands with the goal of standardizing the customs of the abbeys in his realm. The emperor wanted abbots to promote and enforce a uniform standard of discipline to ensure the efficacy of monastic prayers for the kingdom. Two councils of religious officials convened at the royal palace in Aachen in 816 and 817, where they endorsed the precepts of the *Rule of Benedict* as the model for this unprecedented reform.[127] In the three centuries since its composition, the *Rule of Benedict* had established itself as a trusted and balanced guide for the monastic vocation, but it was only one voice in a chorus of received tradition. Some ancient communities resisted the imperial reform policies and clung tenaciously to their received customs, but many responded by introducing new rules of conduct, including regulations intended to safeguard silence in their cloisters.

Beginning in the eighth century, abbots adopted measures to ensure that the close proximity of secular servants and visitors did not disturb the brethren. Carolingian monks inhabited an enclosed network of rooms and corridors known collectively as the *claustrum*. This precinct comprised the cloister, the dormitory, the refectory, the chapter hall and various service

[124] For the impact of the Carolingians on monastic life, see Josef Semmler, "Karl der Grosse und das fränkische Mönchtum," in *Karl der Grosse: Lebenswerk und Nachleben*, ed. Helmut Beumann et al., 5 vols. (Düsseldorf, 1965–1968), vol. II, pp. 255–289; Josef Semmler, "Pippin III. und die fränkischen Klöster," *Francia* 3 (1975): 88–146; Josef Semmler, "Mönche und Kanoniker im Frankenreich Pippins III. und Karls des Grossen," in *Untersuchungen zu Kloster und Stift* (Göttingen, 1980), pp. 78–111; and Rosamond McKitterick, *The Frankish Kingdoms Under the Carolingians, 751–987* (London and New York, 1983), pp. 106–139.
[125] Gérard Moyse, "Monachisme et réglementation monastique en Gaule avant Benoît d'Aniane," in *Sous la règle de saint Benoît: Structures monastiques et sociétés en France du moyen âge à l'époque moderne* (Geneva, 1982), pp. 3–19.
[126] For what follows, see Mayke de Jong, "Carolingian Monasticism: The Power of Prayer," in *The New Cambridge Medieval History*, Volume II, c. 700–c. 900, ed. Rosamond McKitterick (Cambridge, 1995), pp. 622–653.
[127] On the decrees of the Aachen assemblies and their impact, see Josef Semmler, "Die Beschlüsse des Aachener Konzils im Jahre 816," *Zeitschrift für Kirchengeschichte* 74 (1963): 15–82; and Semmler, "Benedictus II".

chambers.[128] A doorway in the choir of the abbey church provided entry to
the cloister, but access was forbidden to all but the monks. Guesthouses were
built at a distance from the monastic precinct to prevent the activities of
secular guests from distracting the brethren. The so-called *Plan of Saint Gall*,
a ninth-century schematic layout for a large abbey, portrayed separate
hospices for visitors, pilgrims and dignitaries with their retinues, all of
which were well removed from the dormitory of the resident monks.[129]
According to Hildemar of Corbie, a *magister* who gave expository lectures
on the *Rule of Benedict* in Civate around 845, the segregation of monks and
laymen was especially important at night. It was fully expected that laymen
would stay up late talking and laughing and would thereby disturb monks
within hearing range, who should pass the night in silence and prayer.[130]
Nonetheless, despite such precautions, the steady drone of human discourse
surrounded the brethren in their cloister. Large Carolingian abbeys were the
nexus of oral information, where a constant flow of travelers exchanged
news of the outside world. Monks whose duties took them beyond the
monastic precinct were forbidden from speaking about their outings, but
even the best precautions could not prevent them from overhearing
rumours of war and diplomacy, portents and weather, murder and miracles.[131] As a ward against such distractions, Hildemar urged his students to
build a spiritual *claustrum* within themselves and therein protect their souls
from the onslaught of the relentless din that echoed around them.[132]

New rulings on silence also governed personal communication
between the brethren themselves. The earliest Carolingian customaries
reiterated the *Rule of Benedict*'s precepts on the observance of silence in
the refectory, the oratory and the dormitory, but they also gave voice to
new sources of concern.[133] Many attempted to curb wayward speech in

---

[128] On the boundaries of the *claustrum* and the fear of secular intrusion into monastic space, see de Jong, "Carolingian Monasticism," pp. 636–640.
[129] Walter Horn and Ernest Born, *The Plan of Saint Gall: A Study of the Architecture and Economy of and Life in a Paradigmatic Carolingian Monastery*, 3 vols. (Berkeley, Los Angeles and London, 1979), vol. I, pp. 249–253, and vol. II, pp. 139–153. The relationship of the *Plan of Saint Gall* to the reality of ninth-century monasticism remains a matter of debate. For the most recent and comprehensive study of this unique document, see Werner Jacobsen, *Der Klosterplan von St. Gallen und die karolingische Architektur: Entwicklung und Wandel von Form und Bedeutung im fränkischen Kirchenbau zwischen 751 und 840* (Berlin, 1992).
[130] Hildemar, *Expositio regulae sancti Benedicti* 65, ed. Rupert Mittermüller, in *Vita et Regula SS. P. Benedicti una cum Expositio Regulae a Hildemaro tradita* (Regensburg, New York and Cincinnati, 1880), pp. 611–612.
[131] On the prohibition against speaking for monks returning to the abbey, see *RB* 67.5, p. 662; and Hildemar, *Expositio regulae sancti Benedicti* 67, ed. Mittermüller, pp. 612–613.
[132] Hildemar, *Expositio regulae sancti Benedicti* 67, ed. Mittermüller, p. 613.
[133] See, for example, Theodomar, *Epistula ad Theodoricum gloriosum* 24, ed. J. Winandy and K. Hallinger, *CCM* I (Siegburg, 1963), p. 134; and *Ordo Casinensis I* 1, ed. T. Leccisotti, *CCM* I (Siegburg, 1963), p. 101.

situations that had not troubled the sixth-century author of the *Rule*. Carolingian abbots were especially worried about monks who spoke needlessly while they worked, whether inside the monastic precinct or on the grounds of the abbey, so brethren were usually instructed to perform their appointed tasks either in silence or with the singing of psalms.[134] The continuous recitation of the psalter served the same purpose as silence for laboring monks: it occupied their minds with holy words and kept them from engaging in idle conversation. Unlike silent contemplation, however, which was private and knowable only to God, the voices of monks intoning the psalms assured their superiors that their minds were directed toward heaven as they worked. This precept may have been an outgrowth of Ambrose of Milan's claim that the ancient language of the psalms was so transcendent that it was in effect a language of silence.[135] It may have also expressed the influence of the sermons of the sixth-century preacher Caesarius of Arles, who instructed his lay parishoners to ruminate on sacred Scripture to ward off the unwelcome entry of sinful thoughts into their minds.[136] Irrespective of its origins, the continuous recitation of psalms by monks to guarantee the purity of their thoughts while they labored emerged in the ninth century as a common aspect of religious discipline.

Other venues for harmful speech occupied the attention of Carolingian abbots as well. At Corbie, monks required the permission of a superior or the reason of necessity to speak in the warming room when they gathered by the fire in the winter months.[137] The ritual of foot washing also provided an occasion for the brethren to engage in illicit conversation. The *Rule of Benedict* gave no specific directives for conduct during this weekly activity, but Carolingian abbots felt it necessary to restrict personal interaction out of fear that it could dissolve into sinful discourse.[138] The Aachen decrees of 816 and 817 ordered that foot washing be accompanied by the singing of antiphons, but in some ninth-century abbeys it was customary to perform the ritual without uttering a word.[139]

---

[134] See, for example, Ardo, *Vita Benedicti abbatis Anianensis et Indensis* 38, ed. G. Waitz, *MGH SS* XV.1 (Hanover, 1887), p. 216; and Rimbert, *Vita Anskarii* 35: "Inter psalmos autem cantandum frequenter etiam manibus operari solitus erat." ed. G. Waitz, *MGH SRG* LV (Hanover, 1884), p. 68, repr. in *Quellen des 9. und 11. Jahrhunderts zur Geschichte der hamburgischen Kirche und des Reiches* (Darmstadt, 1961), p. 110.

[135] Ambrose, *Enarrationes in XII Psalmos Davidicos*, prol.: "Cum psalmus legitur, ipse sibi est effector silentii. Omnes loquuntur, et nullus obstrepit." *PL* XIV, col. 925b.

[136] Leyser, *Authority and Asceticism*, pp. 95–98.

[137] Hildemar, *Expositio regulae sancti Benedicti* 6, ed. Mittermüller, p. 203.   [138] *RB* 35.9, p. 566.

[139] *Synodi primae decreta authentica* 21, ed. J. Semmler, *CCM* I (Siegburg, 1963), p. 463; *Epistola cum duodecim capitulis quorundam fratrum ad Auvam directa* 10, ed. H. Frank, *CCM* I (Siegburg, 1963), p. 336; and Hildemar, *Expositio regulae sancti Benedicti* 42, ed. Mittermüller, pp. 454–455.

Silence encroached on most aspects of the lives of Carolingian monks. The *Rule of Benedict* encouraged its readers when and where to remain silent, but by the late eighth century a striking inversion had occurred. Speech prohibitions so dominated the daily activities of the brethren that Carolingian abbots felt it necessary for the first time to set aside specific parts of the abbey and certain times of the day for supervised conversation. At Montecassino, the abbot signaled the end of the nocturnal silence by reciting a verse from Scripture. After the morning chapter meeting, the monks typically refrained from speaking throughout the day unless the abbot chose to recite the verse again to give them the opportunity to converse for a brief time in the afternoon before they went off to work.[140] At Corbie, the monks were permitted to gather together for conversation after the unsuitable hours for speaking had passed.[141] Similarly, the religious women addressed in a later recension of the *Memoriale qualiter*, a late Carolingian liturgical customary, were permitted to converse with one another during an interval between the morning chapter meeting and the office of Sext, but only in the cloister or in another place where it was deemed permissible to speak.[142] From this point onward, in many cloistered communities monks could only speak with their fellows for a short period of time under the watchful eyes of their superiors. These rulings further limited and controlled opportunities for idle speech among the brethren. With them, silence gained new territory in the abbeys of Carolingian Europe.

It would be misleading, however, to advance the claim that the discipline of silence played such a dominant role in every articulation of spiritual life in this period. In the eighth century, Archbishop Chrodegang of Metz (d. 766) composed a rule for the canons serving in his cathedral church that promoted silence as a virtue consonant with, but not central to, the ideal of priests pursuing a life in common.[143] An active patron of cenobitic monasticism, Chrodegang was intimate with the *Rule of Benedict*. In the early 750s he endorsed a literal interpretation of its precepts at the abbey of Gorze, which he established in the countryside near Metz. While the archbishop's knowledge of Benedict's work clearly informed his *Rule for Canons*, it did not prevent him from making distinctions between the virtuous principles

---

[140] *Ordo Casinensis I* 6, ed. Leccisotti, *CCM* I, p. 102.
[141] *Consuetudines Corbeienses* (Capitulorum fragmenta 2), ed. J. Semmler, *CCM* I (Siegburg, 1963), p. 418.
[142] *Memoriale qualiter II* 8, ed. C. Morgand, *CCM* I (Siegburg, 1963), pp. 271–272.
[143] For what follows, see M. A. Claussen, *The Reform of the Frankish Church: Chrodegang of Metz and the Regula canonicorum in the Eighth Century* (Cambridge, 2004), esp. pp. 58–113 (on the principles espoused in the *Rule for Canons*) and 114–165 (on its relationship to the *Rule of Benedict*).

appropriate for cathedral clergy and those most fitting for monks. His aim of promoting a new set of regulations specific to the life of canons was twofold: to provide a shared context of personal discipline in which the clergy could free their minds from vice and thereby to prepare them to preach this change of heart as a model for the reform and renewal of the spiritual life of the laity. For Chrodegang, the sin of pride was the greatest obstacle to the fulfillment of this program of clerical reform. Drawing selectively from the precepts of the *Rule of Benedict* and other early medieval sources for communal life, the archbishop's *Rule for Canons* emphasized repeatedly the importance of humility and obedience as virtues that prevented harmful discord between individuals and protected the integrity of hierarchical relationships, without which the community could not function. While Chrodegang instructed his cathedral canons to remain silent throughout the night to safeguard their tongues from idle speech, this idiom of monastic virtue was clearly ancillary to the studied cultivation of those qualities that prevented the corrosive effects of pride and discord.

Nonetheless, monks were not alone in their efforts to avoid useless and empty words. One of the salient features of Carolingian monasticism was the penetration of its ideals into the highest levels of secular society. During the ninth century, Frankish emperors donning the mantle of kingship shouldered with it the expectation that they would govern their personal will as well as their kingdoms. Books of counsel composed by abbots and church prelates provided rulers with moral compasses for the exercise of imperial justice and mediated to them the monastic value of self-mastery in matters of personal comportment.[144] Works written to promote the reign of Emperor Louis the Pious are the most conspicuous exponents of monastic kingship in this period.[145] An episode in Thegan's account of the emperor's life written in 836 stressed his studious detachment from frivolity in terms reminiscent of contemporary monastic precepts against the expression of unbridled mirth, like those found in the concordance of ancient rules compiled by Abbot Benedict of Aniane and in the commentary on the *Rule of Benedict*

---

[144] Further on the marriage of moral and political ideologies in the Carolingian age, see Hans Hubert Anton, *Fürstenspiegel und Herrscherethos in der Karolingerzeit* (Bonn, 1968); and Michel Rouche, "Miroirs des princes ou miroir du clergé?" in *Committenti e produzione artistico-letteraria nell'alto medioevo occidentale, 4–10 aprile 1991*, Settimane di studio del centro italiano di studi sull'alto medioevo 39, 2 vols. (Spoleto, 1992), vol. I, pp. 341–367.

[145] Thomas F. X. Noble, "The Monastic Ideal as a Model for Empire: The Case of Louis the Pious," *Revue bénédictine* 86 (1976): 235–250; Thomas F. X. Noble, "Louis the Pious and His Piety Reconsidered," *Revue Belge de Philologie et d'Histoire* 58 (1980): 297–316; and Mayke de Jong, "Power and Humility in Carolingian Society: The Public Penance of Louis the Pious," *Early Medieval Europe* 1 (1992): 29–52.

by Smaragdus of St. Mihiel, both of whom had the young emperor's ear.[146] According to Thegan, when actors and jesters delighted his imperial court with their antics, Louis remained unmoved. Even though his entourage showed proper moderation in their laughter, the emperor set himself apart by expressing no emotion at all.[147] His controlled countenance was a public declaration of a mastery of the will that legitimized his right to rule.[148]

The discipline of silence acquired new meanings in the crowded halls of Carolingian abbeys. The *Rule of Benedict* devoted considerable attention to the means of avoiding sinful speech, but the ambiguity of some of its passages puzzled Carolingian commentators. Particularly vexing was its author's tendency to modify the word "silence" (*silentium*) with adjectives like "utmost" (*summum*) and "total" (*omne*).[149] Hildemar of Corbie attempted to reconcile these distinctions for his students. His commentary on the *Rule* thus provides one of the clearest articulations of the character of monastic silence in Carolingian thought. When bolstered by a superlative or totalizing adjective, he explained, the word *silentium* carried the weight of absolute silence. This meaning was context specific, however. It applied only to the refectory, to the oratory at the close of the liturgy and during the time set aside for reading. The latter precept did not imply that monks read silently. Rather, it was intended to dissuade individuals from making any noise that would disrupt the attention (*intentus*) of those listening to books read aloud for their edification (*lectio*) or those reading quietly by themselves (*meditatio*).[150] In all other instances, however, the word *silentium* did not signal a strict prohibition against verbal utterances. The *Rule of Benedict* encouraged the cultivation of silence at all times, and especially at night.[151] According to Hildemar, this precept meant that monks could converse with discretion, but only

---

[146] Benedict of Aniane, *Concordia regularum* 20, *PL* CIII, cols. 861–862; and Smaragdus, *Expositio in regulam sancti Benedicti* 2.7.59, ed. Alfred Spannagel and Pius Engelbert, *CCM* VIII (Siegburg, 1974), p. 188.

[147] Thegan, *Gesta Hludovici imperatoris* 19, ed. E. Tremp, in *Thegan: Täten Kaiser Ludwigs, MGH SRG* LXIV (Hanover, 1995), pp. 200–204.

[148] For a compelling analysis of this episode, see Matthew Innes, "He Never Even Allowed His White Teeth to Be Bared in Laughter: The Politics of Humour in the Carolingian Renaissance," in *Humour, History and Politics in Late Antiquity and the Early Middle Ages*, ed. Guy Halsall (Cambridge, 2002), pp. 131–156.

[149] *RB* 38.5 (*summum fiat silentium*), 48.5 (*cum omni silentio*) and 52.2 (*cum summo silentio*), pp. 574, 600 and 610.

[150] Further on the act of reading in a medieval monastic context, see Mary Carruthers, *The Book of Memory: A Study of Memory in Medieval Culture* (Cambridge, 1990), pp. 170–173.

[151] *RB* 42.1, p. 584: "Omni tempore silentium debent studere monachi, maxime tamen nocturnis horis."

with suppressed voices (*sub silentio*), that is, in whispers.[152] In Carolingian monastic thought, the goal of the discipline of silence was not the complete cessation of human sound, but the fostering of a hushed and reverential tone among the brethren that pervaded every aspect of their cloistered lives.[153]

This expectation challenged even the most stalwart individuals. Hildemar understood the abnegation of the desire to speak freely as a kind of mortification because it was a denial of the will.[154] His contemporary Smaragdus of St. Mihiel stressed the salvific benefits of this discipline in vivid metaphors that underscored the graveness of his concern for sins involving speech. For him, the tongue was a fire that devoured the forest of virtues by speaking badly.[155] Both prohibitive and unifying, silence was among the monks' strongest allies. By moderating discerning speech and preventing sinful utterances, it was the nourisher of virtues and the guardian of souls.[156] It also bound the brethren together in their common purpose. The denial of carnal needs, like the desire to speak, distinguished monks from the rest of humanity. Like the celebration of the liturgy, which underwent a dramatic shift in the eighth century from the ancient practice of a single monk chanting the psalms for the benefit of his silent brethren to choral psalmody involving the participation of the entire monastic community, the cultivation of silence was a shared and harmonious experience in a world of individual and discordant voices.[157] Shrouded in their protecting silence, Carolingian monks transcended the cacophony of earthly sounds that encroached upon their cloister.

---

[152] Hildemar, *Expositio regulae sancti Benedicti* 38: "Hoc enim notandum est, quia, ubi B. Benedictus dicit silentium cum adjectione *summum*, sicuti in hoc loco facit, et ubi dicit *maxime nocturnis horis*, et iterum *nulla sit denique cuiquam loqui licentia*, et ubi dicit cum omni silentio, vult, ut nullatenus loquatur; ubi vero dicit solummodo *silentio* sine adjectione aliqua, de suppressa voce dicit, sicut legitur in evangelio, ubi legitur mortuo Lazaro Martha silentio dixisse Mariae sorori suae: 'Magister adest et vocat te.' Ibi enim, sicut dicit B. Augustinus, silentio de suppressa voce intelligendum est." ed. Mittermüller, p. 424 (see also pp. 453 and 456–457). For the source of this allusion, see Augustine, *In Johannis evangelium tractatus cxxiv* 49.16, ed. D. R. Willems, CCSL XXXVI (Turnhout, 1954), p. 428.

[153] Hildemar, *Expositio regulae sancti Benedicti* 7, ed. Mittermüller, pp. 262–264.

[154] *Ibid.* 43: "Et hoc etiam sciendum est, quia sicut laborat erga voluntatem propriam, ita etiam erga silentium, quia silentium mortificationem significat." ed. Mittermüller, p. 457.

[155] Smaragdus, *Expositio in regulam S. Benedicti* 6.5: "Ignis est lingua, quia virtutum silvam male loquendo devorat." ed. Spannagel, p. 159.

[156] *Ibid.* 6.1: "Nutrix virtutum et custos est animarum." ed. Spannagel, p. 159.

[157] On monastic psalmody in the early medieval period, with an emphasis on the shift from solo to choral singing, see Joseph Dyer, "Monastic Psalmody of the Middle Ages," *Revue bénédictine* 99 (1989): 41–73. Further on the themes of concord and consonance in Carolingian music, see Karl F. Morrison, "Know Thyself: Music in the Carolingian Renaissance," in *Committenti e produzione artistico-letteraria nell'alto medioevo occidentale*, vol. I, pp. 369–483.

Uttering no human sound

While the Aachen assemblies of 816 and 817 succeeded in establishing the *Rule of Benedict* as the authoritative guide for the cloistered life throughout the Frankish realm, the reformers failed to achieve their objective of enforcing a uniform interpretation of its precepts.[158] As Kassius Hallinger has shown, the amplifications to traditional customs against idle speech fostered in Carolingian abbeys and endorsed by Abbot Benedict of Aniane's program of reform had a significant influence on expectations of monastic conduct throughout the ninth and tenth centuries, but there remained considerable variation both in the implementation of this practice and in its understanding.[159] While many religious houses no doubt embraced the reforming decrees of Aachen, there must have been others that resisted the new precepts and clung tenaciously to their traditional customs. The widespread adoption of the *Rule of Benedict* in late Carolingian abbeys was an assurance, however, that the custom of silence retained its currency as a saving virtue in most cloistered communities, irrespective of their response to the imperial reforms. Like their late antique predecessors, the monks of tenth-century Europe cultivated silence as a safeguard against the sins of slander and murmuring and abstained from idle conversation to cultivate the virtues of humility and obedience.

The proper measure of the discipline of silence only became an issue of contention in the early tenth century, when the monks of Cluny and allied communities amplified traditional precepts against speaking to an unprecedented degree and enriched them with positive moral and eschatological associations. In emulation of the heavenly host, the Cluniacs set themselves apart from their contemporaries in their unrivaled effort to actualize in their cloister the eternal silence that would accompany the resurrection of the elect at the end of time. Responding to criticism that the speech restrictions enforced at Cluny were modern novelties alien to the monastic tradition, John of Salerno's *Life of Odo* argued that the cultivation of silence was an ancient idiom of Christian virtue and self-denial as attested by the Hebrew prophets, the earthly ministry of Christ and the heroic mortifications of the desert fathers. For the monks of Cluny, the denial of the desire to speak was an essential characteristic of their deliberate self-fashioning on the model of angelic conduct. Like the eradication of sexual desire and the continuous recitation of praises to God, the cultivation of an all-embracing silence was an important part of their attempt to realize in the frailness of their human bodies the otherworldly attributes of the heavenly host.

---

[158] Semmler, "Benedictus II."
[159] Kassius Hallinger, *Gorze-Kluny: Studien zu den monastischen Lebensformen und Gegensätzen im Hochmittelalter*, Studia Anselmiana 22–25 (Rome, 1950), pp. 925–928.

45

GUARDS AND WARDS

Despite the program of initiation that existed at Cluny and most other abbeys for the indoctrination of new members, there was a recurring fear that monks would succumb to the temptations of idle words and unruly laughter.[160] The abbots of Cluniac monasteries dealt with this problem in several ways. They sometimes made provision for hermits living in their vicinity to take part in the life of the community, thereby providing the brethren with virtuous models of spiritual devotion. The shortcomings of the eremitic life were also instructive to monks, because they reinforced the cenobitic model of communal discipline and complete obedience to a spiritual father. The Cluniacs and their contemporaries also employed mechanisms of observance to discover negligent individuals. Special officials, known as roundsmen (*circatores*), patrolled the abbey to detect and report suspicious conversation overheard among the brethren. Lastly, early medieval abbots often encouraged correct behavior by rousing the eschatological fears of their charges with tales of divine punishment for breaking rules against speaking. These included ghost stories, in which the spirits of dead monks returned to warn the living of impending torments in the afterlife for those who committed sins of the tongue.

From the beginnings of Christian asceticism in the fourth century, hermits represented the pinnacle of Christian devotion and self-sacrifice in early medieval religious practice.[161] These hardy individuals endured austere lives of personal mortification in forests and swamps that recalled the remoteness of the desert where Jesus had fasted and prayed. As Abbot Peter the Venerable assured a recluse named Gilbert in the early 1120s, the narrow caves of hermits earned them the width of heaven.[162] The eremitic vocation was a serious option for devout Christians in the tenth and eleventh centuries. When the young Anselm arrived at Bec in 1059,

---

[160] On the preparation of Cluniac novices for entrance into the community, see Chapter 2, pp. 67–68, below.

[161] On the desert hermits of late antiquity, see pp. 29–31, above. More generally on the eremitic movement in early medieval monasticism, see Jean Leclercq, "L'érémitisme en occident jusqu'à l'an mil," in *L'eremitismo in occidente nei secoli XI e XII: Atti della seconda Settimana internazionale di studio (Mendola, 30 agosto–6 settembre 1962)* (Milan, 1965), pp. 27–44; Giles Constable, "Eremitical Forms of Monastic Life," in *Istituzioni monastiche e istituzioni canonicali in occidente, 1123–1215: Atti della settima Settimana internazionale di studio (Mendola, 28 agosto–3 settembre 1977)* (Milan, 1980), pp. 239–264, repr. in Giles Constable, *Monks, Hermits and Crusaders in Medieval Europe* (London, 1988), no. V; and Henrietta Leyser, *Hermits and the New Monasticism: A Study of Religious Communities in Western Europe 1000–1150* (New York, 1984).

[162] See the introduction to Peter the Venerable's letter to Gilbert (*Epistola* 20): "Dilectissimo atque in Christi uisceribus specialiter amplectendo fratri Gisleberto, frater Petrus humilis Cluniacensium abbas, pro angustia cellae, latitudinem caeli." ed. Giles Constable, in *The Letters of Peter the Venerable*, 2 vols. (Cambridge, MA, 1967), vol. I, pp. 27–41, at p. 27.

he chose between entering a monastery, founding a house for the poor on his family estate and retreating to a hermitage.[163] Even so, those who made the commitment to the solitary life often found their seclusion interrupted by contact with cloistered communities. Around 1075, Abbot Hugh the Great wrote to the hermit Anastasius, urging him to abandon his Alpine cave to join the brethren of Cluny.[164] Anastasius hailed originally from Venice, but his name implies a Greek origin, so his appeal to the Cluniacs may have been linked to his association with the ancient eastern monks whom they held in such esteem. The tireless piety of the solitary impressed the brethren. When they retired to the refectory for their meal, Anastasius lingered in the oratory to pray, content with only bread and water. While the others slept, he kept vigil on bent knees throughout the night.[165] At the coming of Lent, the hermit longed for his solitude and retired to remote places where he mortified his body with severe fasts and genuflections.[166] These virtuous activities inspired emulation in the community. Peter Damian allegedly commented that he saw many Pauls and Anthonys when he visited Cluny. Although they did not dwell in the desert, these monks earned the same reward through their imitation of the famous hermits.[167]

Abbots welcomed solitaries into their communities, but also recognized the dangers of their vocation and used this knowledge to underscore the benefits of cenobitic monasticism. The life of the hermit was more perilous than the life of the monk because it was unregulated. Although they lived in inhospitable and remote places, hermits were rarely alone, for visitors often traveled to their cells to learn from their pious example firsthand. The interactions between hermits and their admirers were a

---

[163] Eadmer, *Vita sancti Anselmi* 1.6, ed. Richard W. Southern (Oxford, 1972), p. 10.
[164] *Vita Anastasii*, PL CXLIX, cols. 423–434, esp. col. 428c: "Cumque per aliquot dies de vita et conversatione Cluniacensium fratrum abbas multum referret, virum Dei monuit, et multum rogavit ut Cluniacum secum adiret, ubi et votum suum complere posset, et exemplum bonae conversationis caeteris fratribus daret." On the career of Anastasius, see M. Arnoux, "Un Vénitien au Mont-Saint-Michel: Anastase, moine, ermite et confesseur († vers 1085)," *Médiévales* 28 (1995): 55–78. On the hermits associated with Cluny in the twelfth century, see Jean Leclercq, "Pierre le Vénérable et l'érémitisme clunisien," in *Petrus Venerabilis 1156–1956*, ed. Giles Constable and James Kritzeck, Studia Anselmiana 40 (Rome, 1956), pp. 99–120; and G. Chachuat, "L'érémitisme à Cluny sous l'abbatiat de Pierre le Vénérable," *Annales de l'académie de Mâcon* 58 (1982): 89–96.
[165] *Vita Anastasii* 4, PL CXLIX, col. 428cd.   [166] *Ibid.* cols. 428d–429a.
[167] *De Gallica Petri Damiani profectione et eius ultramontano itinere* 13: "Veraciter ibi multos reperi Paulos, plurimos vidi Antonios. Qui etsi solitudinis habitationem non incolunt, anachoritarum premium imitatione operum non amittunt." *MGH SS* XXX.2, ed. Gerhard Schwartz and Adolf Hofmeister (Hanover, 1934), pp. 1034–1046, at pp. 1041–1042. For the influence of the model of St. Anthony on medieval monks, see Jean Leclercq, "Saint Antoine dans la tradition monastique médiévale," in *Antonius Magnus Eremita 356–1956: Studia ad antiquum monachismum spectantia*, ed. Basil Steidle, Studia Anselmiana 38 (Rome, 1956), pp. 229–247.

source of constant worry for abbots, because no authority was present to monitor the quality of their traffic with the outside world. Burdened with their solitude, hermits could easily succumb to the temptations of idle conversation. An eleventh-century guide for solitaries instructed its readers to remain silent in their cells out of reverence for God, just as they did in the oratory.[168] In the letter of Peter the Venerable mentioned above, we find him reminding his reader that the higher calling of the hermit carried with it an increased responsibility for proper conduct. The abbot was adamant in his warning to Gilbert to guard the use of his tongue:

> Just as a door opens or closes depending on necessity, thus should the door of your mouth be opened to usefulness or closed to foolish and empty words. It should be opened to the brethren for their edification and closed to the distraction of those voicing spiteful words or grumbling. It should be opened to the encouragement of visiting monks and closed to the talkativeness of the curious. In brief, one should hear or say only useful things. If this is not an option, then the hermit should not disrupt his silence.[169]

The urgency of Peter the Venerable's admonition stemmed from his tenuous control over the situation. The abbot's inability to enforce discipline directly was clearly vexing to him, for he was acutely aware that any negligence on the part of the recluse would be detrimental to the monks who came into contact with him. The letter addressed Gilbert personally, but it was intended for a wider audience as well.[170] The thrust of its message was clear to medieval readers: the temptation of sins involving wayward speech made the hermit's vocation a dangerous pursuit. It was always safer for monks to live together within the walls of a monastery under the watchful eyes of others.

In large cloistered communities like Cluny, abbots attempted to prevent idle conversation and other lapses in discipline with mechanisms of observance. They charged roundsmen (*circatores*) with the duty of patrolling the monastery to discover and report negligences among the brethren.[171] These officials were direct subordinates of the claustral

---

[168] Peter Damian, *De ordine eremitarum* (*Opusculum* 14), PL CXLV, col. 332b.

[169] Peter the Venerable, *Epistola* 20: "Ut sicut ostium necessitate tantum aperitur et clauditur, sic oris tui ostium utilitati aperiatur, nugacitati uel uanitati claudatur. Aperiatur fratribus ad aedificationem, claudatur ad obloquentium uel murmurantium detractionem. Aperiatur ad exhortationem superuenientium religiosorum, claudatur ad uerbositatem curiosorum. Et ut breuiter dicam, aut audiatur aliquid utile aut dicatur, uel si ista non fuerint, silentii censura a solitario non rumpatur." ed. Constable, vol. I, pp. 40–41.

[170] The manuscript tradition of the letter suggests that it was widely read in monastic communities in the later medieval period. See *ibid.* vol. II, p. 70.

[171] For what follows, see Scott G. Bruce, "Lurking with Spiritual Intent: A Note on the Origin and Functions of the Monastic Roundsman (*Circator*)," *Revue bénédictine* 109 (1999): 75–89.

prior. A comparison of their duties with those of their superior illustrates their purpose and effectiveness. At Cluny, the claustral prior made a round of the abbey at the end of every day after Compline.[172] His task was to ensure that the community was secure for the night. He stayed behind after the monks had filed from the church and, lantern in hand, systematically moved through the empty rooms of the abbey until he reached the dormitory. When he was satisfied that everyone was in bed, he too retired. In contrast, the roundsmen followed no predetermined route or timetable. The randomness of their patrols was intended to heighten the fear of detection in negligent monks, as a statement by Ulrich of Zell makes clear: "Let them patrol the entire enclosure not once but many times during the day so that there is neither a place nor a time in which any brother, if he should engage in irregular activity, may be unconcerned by the possibility of detection."[173] A *circator* could appear at any time in any part of the abbey, from the kitchens to the infirmary to the cemetery. Only the presence of the abbot or the prior deterred them, for they were ordered to show discretion and avoid the parts of the monastery where their superiors were known to be.[174]

The thought that a *circator* could appear at any moment from around any corner in the abbey must have been a strong deterrent to potential transgressors, but it did not prevent violations from taking place. The roundsmen were ever on the watch for monks who succumbed to the temptations of sleep or sexual misconduct, but they emerge from monastic legislation primarily as guardians of silence. When a *circator* happened upon some brethren talking, the suspect monks were expected to rise and state whether they had obtained authorization to speak. If not, then they could expect reproach on the following day in the chapter meeting.[175] The roundsmen themselves never passed judgment on negligent individuals. When they encountered monks involved in some breach in discipline, they often passed by in silence, noting all that they had seen and leaving any punitive action to the abbot.[176]

The roving eye of the *circator* was often not enough to deter deviant monks. The abbots of Cluny and their contemporaries also evoked the

---

[172] On the office of the claustral prior at Cluny, see Bernard 1.3, pp. 141–143; and Ulrich 1.6, cols. 740d–741b.

[173] Ulrich 3.7, col. 741c: "Propterea totum claustrum non semel set multoties in die circumeant, ut nec locus sit nec hora in qua frater ullus securus esse possit, si tale quid [contra ordinem] commiserit, non deprehendi et non publicari."

[174] Ulrich 3.7, col. 741c.

[175] Bernard 1.4, p. 144; Ulrich 3.6, col. 741c; William 2.20, cols. 1067b–1068d; and *Decreta Lanfranci: The Monastic Constitutions*, ed. and trans. David Knowles (London, 1951), p. 78.

[176] *Decreta Lanfranci*: "Circumitores vero nec verbo nec signo ei respondeant, se modeste pertranseuntes." ed. Knowles, p. 78. See also Bernard 1.4, p. 144.

fear of the awesome power of heavenly judgment to compel their charges to obey rules of silence. Exemplary tales illustrated the swift and terrible efficacy of divine vengeance against brethren who failed to hold their tongues. The tenth-century *Life of Odo* described the punishment of an angry brother, who had rebuked another monk during the hours of silence. Reminded that it was forbidden for him to speak, the brother could not restrain his rage and yelled: "God did not make me a serpent, so that I should hiss at you, nor did he make me an ox, so that I should bellow, but he made me a man and gave me a tongue so that I might speak!"[177] The negligent brother continued to bark out inappropriate words and showed no regret for his actions when questioned the next day in the chapter meeting. The will of God struck him down for his arrogance and disobedience. First, he lost his voice, the vehicle of his negligence. Three days later he died without ever speaking again.

Dread of purgatorial punishments for sins of the tongue haunted the brethren as well. Ghosts returned to the world of the living to admonish and punish negligent monks or to warn them by their own example of the torments that awaited sinners after death.[178] An early twelfth-century *Life of Hugh the Great* wedded a grave warning for monks to guard their tongues from idle words and unruly laughter with an example of the miraculous efficacy of monastic silence, when it was cultivated by virtuous monks. Durannus, the bishop of Toulouse and a former abbot of Moissac, was allegedly overly fond of mirth. Hugh the Great had warned his friend to change his ways, but Durannus persisted in his error until his death. Soon thereafter a monk of Cluny received a ghostly visitation from the dead bishop. The soul of Durannus was clearly in torment. Foaming at the mouth, the apparition begged the monk to inform Abbot Hugh that he required aid. The abbot picked seven monks to perform a week-long vigil of silence as penance for the dead bishop. The negligence of one of them interrupted the vigil and prompted the return of the ghost, but they tried again and eventually succeeded in freeing Durannus from his

---

[177] John of Salerno, *Vita Odonis* 2.23: "Non enim serpentem me fecit Deus, ut tuo more debeam sibilare, nec bovem ut debeam mugire, sed hominum me fecit, et ut loquar linguam mihi tribuit." *PL* CXXXIII, col. 74a.

[178] Jacques Le Goff, *The Birth of Purgatory*, trans. Arthur Goldhammer (Chicago, 1984), pp. 177–181; Franz Neiske, "Visionen und Totengedenken," *Frühmittelalterliche Studien* 20 (1986): 138–185; and Jean-Claude Schmitt, *Ghosts in the Middle Ages: The Living and the Dead in Medieval Society*, trans. Teresa Lavender Fagan (Chicago, 1998), pp. 59–78. Ghost stories also played a role in prompting monks at Marmoutier and its dependences to carry out their obligations. See Sharon Farmer, *Communities of Saint Martin: Legend and Ritual in Medieval Tours* (Ithaca and London, 1991), pp. 138–146.

wretched condition.[179] This episode illustrated to readers that dire punishment awaited monks who failed to discipline their tongues. It also showed that silence was a potent weapon in the intercessory arsenal of medieval monastic communities.

CONCLUSION

In 1140, after his career had ended in a condemnation for heresy, Peter Abelard retracted his suspect opinions, cast off the cloak of his notoriety and entered the Cluniac priory of St. Marcel in Châlon, where he lived as a monk until his death in 1142.[180] In a letter of consolation sent to Abbess Heloise in 1144, Peter the Venerable portrayed the learned man's last years as a model of monastic discipline. In particular, the abbot praised his discretion when speaking and his pious cultivation of silence:

> He was continuously reading, often at prayer, and always silent, except when a friendly conversation with his fellow monks or a lecture on holy subjects to the community compelled him to speak ... His mind, his tongue, his actions were always cultivating, teaching, and saying holy, philosophical, and learned things.[181]

Peter the Venerable cradled the memory of Abelard in a language of monastic virtue that had resonated throughout western Europe since the fourth century. The discipline of silence did not require early medieval monks to abandon all speech. Rather, it directed them to avoid sinful and idle utterances and to exercise discernment and control when the duties of their office obliged them to converse. Surrounded by the bustle and noise of human society, Carolingian monks learned to cultivate an inner silence to protect their souls from the intrusion of secular words. In the tenth century, the brethren of Cluny amplified traditional rules against speaking in pursuit of an angelic ideal of monastic life that shunned the utterance of human sounds. The severity of their customs drew criticism from their contemporaries and set them apart from other ascetics of their time. The operation of a large abbey like Cluny demanded, however, that the brethren communicate with one another, even when the strictest rules

---

[179] Gilo, *Vita Hugonis* 21, ed. H. E. J. Cowdrey, in "Two Studies in Cluniac History 1049–1126," *Studi Gregoriani* 11 (1978): 5–298, at pp. 90–92. This cautionary tale was repeated in other twelfth-century lives of the abbot. See Hugh, *Vita Hugonis* 24, ed. Cowdrey, in "Two Studies," pp. 133–134; and Raynald, *Vita Hugonis* 18, PL CLIX, col. 901ab.

[180] Michael Clanchy, *Abelard: A Medieval Life* (Oxford, 1997), pp. 288–325.

[181] Peter the Venerable, *Epistola* 115: "Lectio erat ei continua, oratio frequens, silentium iuge, nisi cum aut fratrum familaris collatio, aut ad ipsos in conuentu de diuinis publicus sermo eum loqui urgebant ... Mens eius, lingua eius, opus eius, semper diuina, semper philosophica, semper eruditoria meditabatur, docebat, fatebatur." ed. Constable, vol. I, p. 307.

of silence forbade them from speaking aloud. To this end, the early Cluniacs introduced one of the most original innovations to the medieval monastic tradition: a silent language of hand signs that served as a replacement for speech in their monastery. Through the use of nonverbal signs, the monks were able to express their needs and concerns without abandoning their ideal of cultivating a celestial silence. At the same time, however, they were faced with the dilemma that their speaking hands could become as dangerous a medium for sinful thoughts as any wayward tongue. The origins of the Cluniac sign language and an inquiry into its linguistic character are the subjects of the following chapter.

Chapter 2

THE TRAINING OF THE HAND

Early medieval monks could imagine the ideal community of the faithful. The author of *The Voyage of Saint Brendan*, a tenth-century moral tale about an Irish monk who sailed the uncharted western sea, depicted it far away on a lonely island, a journey of many months from any known land.[1] St. Brendan had been there. The holy man and his entourage had found the island as they sailed in search of the promised land of the saints. On the beach an old abbot greeted them with kisses and, without a word, led them to his monastery. At the gate he made it known with a movement of his hand that silence was the guiding principle of the place. "Guard your mouths from speech," Brendan warned his followers, "lest your foolish words pollute these brothers."[2] The monks who lived on the island never conversed with one another. Instead, their hearts told their abbot all that they needed and he responded by writing on a tablet.[3] "We

---

[1] The date of the composition of the *Navigatio sancti Brendani abbatis* and the identity of its author are contested. Some of the earliest manuscripts of the *Navigatio* were copied in the tenth and eleventh centuries in Lotharingia (modern Lorraine and the Rhine Valley extending northwards to the Low Countries). Carl Selmer inferred from the manuscript tradition that an Irish monk active in this region composed the *Navigatio* in the early tenth century. See Selmer, "The Beginnings of the St. Brendan Legend on the Continent," *Catholic Historical Review* 29 (1943): 169–176; and Selmer, "Israel, ein unbekannter Schotte des 10. Jahrhunderts," *Studien und Mitteilungen zur Geschichte des Benediktiner-Ordens und seiner Zweige* 62 (1949–1950): 69–86. More recently, David Dumville has argued that the *Navigatio* was the product of the late eighth century. His evidence is a variant reading of the first sentence of the work (*de genere Eogeni(s) Stagni Len regione Mumenensium*, instead of Selmer's *de genere Eogeni, stagnili regione Mumenensium*), which gives the *Navigatio* a topical significance in the politics of eighth-century Ireland by linking Brendan with the Eoganacht dynasty of Loch Léin. See Dumville, "Two Approaches to Dating the *Navigatio Sancti Brendani*," *Studi Medievali* 29 (1988): 87–102. A resolution to this issue seems unlikely without the emergence of more conclusive evidence. For the purpose of this study, it is reasonable to assume that the *Navigatio* was written on the continent by the middle of the tenth century.

[2] *Navigatio sancti Brendani abbatis* 12: "Statim ut agnouit sanctus pater illius loci decretum, fratres suos admonebat, dicens: Custodite ora uestra a locucionibus, ne polluantur isti fratres per uestram scurrilitatem." ed. Carl Selmer (South Bend, IN, 1959), p. 30.

[3] *Ibid.* p. 34.

came to this island eighty years ago," the old man said, breaking his silence to converse with Brendan, but speaking with the utmost reverence and humility. "We have heard no human voice except when we sing praises to God. Among the twenty-four of us, no voice is raised unless one of the older monks makes a sign with a finger or with the eyes." The unwavering discipline of these monks had an awesome efficacy. Silence guarded them from the weaknesses of the flesh and the sicknesses of the spirit that hovered around humankind.[4]

The island of the silent monks was one of many fantastic landscapes explored by Brendan and his followers, where the disciplinary ideals and spiritual rewards of cenobitic life were presented as examples and incentives for virtuous behavior.[5] But this episode also revealed a tension inherent in early monastic thought and practice. As Chapter 1 has shown, silence was an important principle of personal discipline for the monks of Cluny. In emulation of the heavenly host, the Cluniacs directed their voices to God with liturgical celebration and private prayer, but shunned any conversation that mired their thoughts in the concerns of this world. The strict avoidance of human speech raised challenging practical consequences in large religious communities like Cluny. In an ideal monastery, like the one depicted in *The Voyage of Saint Brendan*, the abbot could avoid speech altogether by reading the hearts of his monks. In reality, however, the necessities of communal life required that individuals communicate with one another, even when private discourse was forbidden. As a result, early medieval monks devised systems of nonverbal communication to express their needs without compromising their ideals of ascetic discipline.

This chapter investigates the forms and functions of silent communication in early medieval monasticism from the rudimentary signals employed in the earliest cenobitic communities to the use of monastic sign language at Cluny and related abbeys in the tenth and eleventh centuries. Late antique monks had many kinds of simple signs at their disposal, which they used to make numerical reckonings and to indicate their basic needs in specific contexts, when rules of silence forbade them from conversing. By the tenth century, however, these signals did not suffice to convey precise information in abbeys like Cluny, where the community followed

---

[4] *Ibid.*: "Nullam uocem humanam audiuimus excepto quando cantamus Deo laudes. Inter nos uiginti quattuor uox non excitatur nisi per signum digiti aut oculorum, tantum a maioribus natu. Nullus ex nobis sustinuit infirmitatem carnis aut spirituum qui uagantur circa humanum genus, postquam uenimus in istum locum." pp. 35–36.

[5] For an analysis of the "monastic archetype underlying the framework" of the Brendan story, see Dorothy Ann Bray, "Allegory in the *Navigatio Sancti Brendani*," *Viator* 26 (1995): 1–10 (quotation at p. 5).

unusually strict rules against speaking. To adapt to these conditions, Cluniac monks created a silent language of meaning-specific hand signs that allowed them to convey everything necessary without recourse to speech. The practice of using sign language was an ingenious solution to the challenges posed by the speech prohibitions in place at Cluny, but the brethren were well aware of the dangers attendant with this custom. A sign system that replicated the precision of spoken language was as perilous as an unbridled tongue because it could provide negligent monks with an outlet for the expression of idle thoughts. In fact, it will be shown that anxiety about the misuse of monastic signs played an important role in shaping the linguistic character of this silent language. After examining the history of nonverbal communication in early medieval abbeys, this chapter analyzes the structure and morphology of the monastic sign language employed at Cluny and considers the role of this custom in the training of Cluniac novices in the tenth and eleventh centuries.

FROM SIGNAL TO SIGN

The earliest evidence for the use of monastic sign language appeared in the tenth-century *Life of Odo*, a hagiographical account of the virtues and miracles of the second abbot of Cluny (925–942).[6] This text was written around 943 by the Italian monk John of Salerno, who had met Odo in Rome a few years earlier and had traveled with him to Pavia to take the monastic habit at the abbey of St. Peter.[7] John dedicated this composition to his brethren in Salerno, where in the 940s he was the abbot of a religious house affiliated with Cluny.[8] During their time together, Odo recounted for his disciple and biographer the customs he had found in place at the abbey of Baume-les-Moines, where he made his profession and spent fifteen years as a monk before becoming abbot of Cluny. According to John, the monks of Baume-les-Moines embraced an ideal of personal discipline that included strong precepts against personal conversation, a custom that Odo later upheld as Berno's successor at Cluny.[9] John's description of the details of this practice included a long digression, in which he set out to demonstrate for his Italian readers the lengths to

---

[6] John of Salerno, *Vita Odonis*, PL CXXXIII, cols. 43–86; trans. Gerald Sitwell, in *St. Odo of Cluny, Being the Life of St. Odo of Cluny by John of Salerno and the Life of St. Gerald of Aurillac by St. Odo* (London and New York, 1958), pp. 3–87. Further on this text and its author, see Chapter 1, p. 18, n. 16, above.

[7] *Ibid.* 4, col. 45cd.

[8] On the ambiguities surrounding John's monastic career in Salerno, see the comments of Sitwell in *St. Odo of Cluny*, p. 44, n. 3; and p. 59, n. 1.

[9] John of Salerno, *Vita Odonis* 1.32, PL CXXXIII, col. 57a.

which these Gallic monks would go to avoid the dangers of human discourse. When Odo first entered the abbey as a novice, he found that the brethren rarely spoke. Instead, they employed a system of hand signs that allowed them to convey precise information to one another without recourse to spoken words:

> Whenever it was necessary for them to ask for something, they made it known to each other through various signs, which I think grammarians would call *notas* of fingers and eyes. This practice had developed to such an extent among them that I believe, if they lost the use of their tongues, these signs would suffice to signify everything necessary.[10]

This code of manual communication captured the attention of Odo's biographer because it was unprecedented in the western monastic tradition. The novelty of this practice can only be understood in the context of habitual sign use in the abbeys of early medieval Europe. It was not uncommon for the earliest monks to employ a wide variety of hand signs in the course of their daily activities. By the tenth century, manual systems of numerical reckoning and the use of the hands as rudimentary signaling devices were age-old practices in many cloistered communities. The form and function of these modes of communication differed considerably, however, from the silent language developed by the brethren of Berno's abbeys.

Late antique monks were well acquainted with an elaborate system of finger numbers that was part of their cultural inheritance from Roman antiquity.[11] Although the use of finger numbers was widespread in the ancient Mediterranean world, written descriptions of these signs seldom appeared before the fourth century. Jerome provided medieval readers with their best-known example of this system, when he explained Christ's parable of the sower (Matt. 13.3–9) with reference to the shapes of the Roman hand signs for 30, 60 and 100.[12] According to the Gospel of Matthew, the sower's seeds that fell on good soil brought forth an abundance of grain, some thirty-fold, some sixty-fold and some a hundred-fold. Jerome equated the proportions of these yields with the three ranks of sexual relations acceptable to Christians: marriage, widowhood

---

[10] *Ibid.*: "Nam, quoties necessarias ad exposcendum res instabant, toties diversa in invicem fiebant ad perficiendum signa, quas puto grammatici digitorum et oculorum notas vocare voluerunt. Adeo nempe inter eos excreverat ordo iste, ut puto si sine officio linguae essent, ad omnia necessaria significanda sufficere possent signa ipsa." col. 57ab. On the meaning of the term *nota* in this context, see pp. 61–62, below.

[11] Burma P. Williams and Richard S. Williams, "Finger Numbers in the Greco-Roman World and the Early Middle Ages," *Isis* 86 (1995): 587–608, with a useful recapitulation of earlier literature and an appendix of relevant texts.

[12] Jerome, *Epistula* 48.2, *PL* XXII, col. 495ab. See also Jerome, *Epistola* 123.9, *PL* XXII, col. 1052c.

and virginity.[13] The number thirty referred to the state of marriage, because the ancient sign for thirty involved joining the tip of the left thumb and index finger "as if embracing and loving in a tender kiss" like a husband and wife.[14] The number sixty signified the state of widowhood, because the sign for this number, the pressing down of the left thumb with the index finger, symbolized the hardship and distress of widows, who had difficulty in abstaining from the sexual pleasures they had once known. The sign for 100 was especially significant because it was expressed on the right hand. Jerome understood the shift from the left hand to the right to indicate the transcendence of virginity over the state of marriage and widowhood. Moreover, the Roman sign for 100, made by placing the nail of the right index finger on the middle joint of the thumb, seemed to him to portray the crown of virginity. Depictions of these number signs appeared in manuscripts of Jerome's letters as well as later medieval texts on the praise of virginity that borrowed this analogy from them.[15]

Knowledge of this numerical system was well established by the late antique period, but full descriptions of it were not codified until the decades around 700. The anonymous *Romana computatio* (*c.* 688) presented a catalogue of number signs from one to 1 million.[16] This text provided the source for the first chapter of Bede's treatise *On the Reckoning of Time* (*c.* 725), the popularity of which led to the spread of information about this ancient practice throughout the abbeys of northern Europe.[17] According to Bede, numbers from one to ninety-nine were the province of the left hand, while numbers from 100 to 9,999 were expressed on the right. For even higher numbers, finger configurations combined with the placement of the left and right hands on the chest, stomach and thigh. The number 1 million, the highest reckoning allowed by the system, was made by clasping both hands together and interlacing the fingers. Drawings

---

[13] On Jerome's attitude toward human sexuality, see Peter Brown, *The Body and Society: Men, Women, and Sexual Renunciation in Early Christianity* (New York, 1988), pp. 366–386.

[14] Jerome, *Epistula* 48.2: "Triginta referuntur ad nuptias, quia et ipsa digitorum conjunctio, quasi molli osculo se complectens et foederans, maritum pingit et conjungem." *PL* XXII, col. 495ab; trans. Williams and Williams, "Finger Numbers in the Greco-Roman World," p. 600.

[15] See, for example, *Speculum virginum*, ed. Jutta Seyforth, *CCCM* V (Turnhout, 1990), fig. 15 (MS Cologne, Historisches Archiv, W 276a, fol. 66v). I am grateful to Michael Curschmann for drawing this image to my attention.

[16] *Romana computatio*, ed. Charles W. Jones, in *Bedae pseudepigrapha: Scientific Writings Falsely Attributed to Bede* (Ithaca, 1939), pp. 53–54 (discussion) and 106–108 (text).

[17] Bede, *De temporum ratione* 1, ed. Charles W. Jones, in *Bedae Opera de temporibus* (Cambridge, MA, 1943), pp. 179–181 (text) and 329–331 (commentary); and trans. Faith Wallis, *Bede: The Reckoning of Time* (Philadelphia, 2000), pp. 9–13.

depicting the shapes and positions of the hands accompanied the text of Bede's chapter in several medieval manuscripts.[18]

For ancient and early medieval people alike, Roman finger calculus was an important tool that assisted in mental computations. It enabled individuals to keep track of large sums on their hands while working through complex calculations in their minds. Its use was so widespread in the late antique world that knowledge of it could be taken for granted, even among the lowest classes of society. In a series of sermons on the significance of the number 153, the sum of all the numbers between 1 and 17, Augustine of Hippo could expect a large audience attending an Easter service to compute the total quickly using their hands: "Count to 17, from 1 all the way to 17, so that you add them all together, and you will arrive at 153. Do not wait for me. Add it up for yourselves."[19] Finger numbers were essential for calculating this figure quickly. "In this way," the bishop explained, "you reach 17, carrying 153 on your fingers."[20]

Bede recognized the utility of this practice for a more contentious calculation: the reckoning of the date of Easter. In the late seventh century, there was a clash of traditions on the Celtic fringe of northern Europe concerning the determination of the date of the most important feast day in the Christian liturgical calendar: the resurrection of Christ.[21] Roman tradition held that Easter fell on the first Sunday after the first full moon on or after the vernal equinox (20 March). Early Christians had always celebrated Easter on the Passover, which took place on the evening of the full moon on the fourteenth day of Nisan, the first month of the Jewish calendar. By the fourth century, a separation between the dates of Passover and Easter had occurred. The Council of Nicaea (325) decreed that the celebration of Easter should take place on

[18] See, for example, Anita Rieche, "*Computatio Romana*: Fingerzählen auf provinzialrömischen Reliefs," *Bonner Jahrbücher* 186 (1986): 165–192, at p. 169, fig. 3 (MS Biblioteca Vaticana, Urbinus Latinus 290, fol. 31r). For an eleventh-century illumination of a monk depicted in the act of counting using Roman finger calculus, see Thomas H. Ohlgren, "The Grumbling Monk in the Hereford Gospels," *Old English Newsletter* 24.3 (Spring, 1991), pp. 22–24 (MS Cambridge, Pembroke College 302, fol. 6r).
[19] Augustine, *Sermo* 250.3: "Decem et septem numera, ab uno usque ad decem et septem, ita ut omnes addas, et pervenies ad centum quinquaginta tres. Quid a me expectatis? Numerate vobis." *PL* XXXVIII, col. 1167b. See also Augustine, *Sermones* 248.5 and 249.3, *PL* XXXVIII, cols. 1161a and 1163c.
[20] *Ibid.* 270.7: "Sic pervenis usque ad decem et septem, portans in digitis centum quinquaginta tres." col. 1245a. This sermon was delivered on the feast of Pentecost.
[21] For what follows, see Bede, *Historia ecclesiastica* 3.25, ed. Bertram Colgrave and R. A. B. Mynors, in *Bede's Ecclesiastical History of the English People* (Oxford, 1969), pp. 294–309. See also the introduction by Charles W. Jones to *Bedae Opera de temporibus*, pp. 6–104; J. M. Wallace-Hadrill, *Bede's Ecclesiastical History of the English People: An Historical Commentary* (Oxford, 1988), pp. 124–129; and Stephen C. McCluskey, *Astronomies and Cultures in Early Medieval Europe* (Cambridge, 1998), pp. 77–96.

the first Sunday following Passover, that is, between 15 and 21 Nisan. If Easter happened to fall on the same day as Passover (14 Nisan), the observance of the feast day was deferred until the following Sunday (21 Nisan). Missionaries sent to England by Pope Gregory the Great introduced this custom to Anglo-Saxon converts to Christianity. The Celtic church employed a slightly different rationale for calculating this important date based on an older model than that adopted at the Council of Nicaea. Unlike the Roman tradition, Celtic Christians did not defer the celebration of Easter when it occurred on the same day as Passover. As a result, they calculated the date of Easter between 14 and 20 Nisan.

The consequences of this minor difference in liturgical reckoning were significant. Every few years, when Easter coincided with Passover, the Celtic church celebrated the most important Christian feast day a full week before its Roman counterpart. This occurred most dramatically in 664, when King Oswy of Northumbria, who was raised in the Celtic tradition, ended his Lenten fast on 14 April, a full week before his wife, who adhered to the Roman practice. Troubled by this inconsistency, the king convened a council of abbots and bishops at the monastery of Whitby to debate the merits of these divergent traditions. After hearing arguments from the representatives of both viewpoints, Oswy decided the case for the Roman tradition, which rested on the authority of St. Peter. The correct calculation of the date of Easter remained a contentious issue into the eighth century, in part due to the recalcitrance of Celtic monks who refused to recognize the Roman paschal calendar. Bede included a description of Roman finger calculus in his treatise *On the Reckoning of Time* because he recognized that the ability to make accurate computations was essential for forecasting the proper date of Easter. Without the aid of this system, ecclesiastical chronographers risked celebrating movable feast days at the wrong time. Such errors in liturgical time-keeping were greatly feared because they threatened to compromise the universality of the Roman church.

In Bede's imagination, the utility of these number signs transcended their function as an mnemonic aid to mental arithmetic. In the first chapter of his treatise, he suggested that this system could also be used as a medium for communication. By substituting the meaning of the number signs with their corresponding letters ("one" for "a," "two" for "b," etc.), an individual could use their left hand to spell out entire words and phrases and thereby share information with others in secret or at a distance. Bede provided the following example of this manual alphabet at work: "If you wish to warn a friend who is among enemies that he should be careful, show with your fingers the numbers three and one and twenty and nineteen and five and one and seven and five. In this order, the letters signify *caute age,* be careful."[22] Although a finger alphabet of this sort had considerable potential as a functional, if somewhat clumsy, substitute for speech in early medieval abbeys, Bede did not presume that monks would use these signs as a means to safeguard rules against speaking. In fact, he made it clear from the outset that this digression was simply an intellectual exercise.[23] Furthermore, despite the widespread diffusion of manuscript copies of his treatise, there is no evidence to suggest that any medieval monastic community ever adopted Roman finger numbers as a medium for silent conversation. The application of these signs as a manual alphabet was conceived too late to fulfill this function in any case, for by Bede's time the use of nonverbal cues for communication was already a long-established aspect of cenobitic life in western Europe.

In late antique abbeys, monks sometimes used auditory signals in the refectory, where the custom of silence *ad mensam* clashed with the practical necessities of food provision and distribution. In the fourth century, the deans of the Egyptian monastery of Tabennesi in the Thebaid communicated the needs of their brethren "with a sound rather than the voice."[24] Similarly, a precept in the near contemporary *Rule of Pachomius* indicated that the deans, or perhaps the monks themselves, could make "a sign with a sound" (*signum sonitu*) to attract the attention of their attendants when they required something at the table.[25] The sixth-century *Rule of Benedict* captured in words the idealized order of a refectory in which the monks ministered to their own needs without speaking: "Let the brothers tend to the things that are needful for eating and drinking, each for himself in turn, so that no one need ask for anything. If something is needed, however, let it be sought with the

---

[22] Bede, *De temporum ratione* 1: "Verbi gratia, si amicum inter insidiatores positum ut caute se agat admonere desideras, iii, et i, et xx, et xix, et v, et i, et vii, et v, digitis ostende; huius namque ordinis literae, 'caute age,' significant." ed. Jones, p. 181.

[23] *Ibid.*: "Potest autem et de ipso quem praenotavi computo quaedam manualis loquela, tam ingenii exercendi quam ludi agendi gratia figurari."

[24] John Cassian, *De coenobiorum institutis* 4.17: "Qui suae decaniae praeest, qui tamen si quid mensae superinferri uel auferri necessarium esse peruiderit, sonitu potius quam uoce significat." ed. Jean-Claude Guy, in *Jean Cassien: Institutions cénobitiques,* SC CIX (Paris, 1965), p. 144. In some early abbeys, deans (*decani* or *praepositi*) were instrumental in providing for the needs of the monks during meals. See, for example, Augustine, *Ordo monasterii* 7: "Sedentes ad mensam taceant, audientes lectionem. Si autem aliquid opus fuerit, praepositus eorum sit sollicitus." ed. George Lawless, in *Augustine of Hippo and His Monastic Rule* (Oxford, 1987), p. 76.

[25] Pachomius, *Praecepta* 33: "Si aliquid necessarium fuerit in mensa, nemo audebit loqui, sed ministrantibus signum sonitu dabit." *PL* XXIII, col. 71c. The use of these signals extended beyond the table as well. See *Praecepta* 116, *PL* XXIII, cols. 79d–80a. The compiler of an early sixth-century Gallic rule for monks copied the first precept almost verbatim into his work. See *Regula orientalis* 38, ed. Adalbert de Vogüé, in *Les règles des saints pères,* 2 vols., *SC* CCXCVII–CCXCVIII (Paris, 1982), vol. II, pp. 490–492.

sound of some sign rather than with the voice."[26] The authors of these prescriptive texts made no mention, however, of sound-making devices, like bells or wooden boards, so there is no way to know precisely what kind of sounds they intended in their precepts.

Some early cenobitic communities employed silent signals in those parts of the abbey where speech was forbidden. In the sixth century, Caesarius of Arles instructed the women of a local convent to indicate what they needed during meals "with a nod rather than with the voice."[27] The bishop may have wished them to make silent signals so as not to distract their neighbors from the words of the reader chosen each week to read aloud for the edification of the assembled community.[28] The fifth-century *Rule of the Master* permitted the use of similar forms of communication during periods of silence, but only when necessity demanded it. If there was sufficient light in the dormitory, a monk could convey information to another "with his hand or with a nod of his head or with a wink."[29] Likewise, *The Voyage of Saint Brendan* provided a model of monastic discipline for its readers that included the use of indeterminate nonverbal signals made with the fingers and eyes to cue the brethren to sing during the celebration of the divine office.[30] There were intrinsic limitations to the use of nods and winks as vehicles for information exchange in early medieval abbeys. Even when combined with helping mechanisms, like pointing or the mouthing of words, these actions did not have fixed meanings. Their message was entirely dependent on the context of their use.

In the early tenth century, the strict speech prohibitions of the Cluniacs required monks to express ever more complex concerns without talking and consequently shaped a more detailed and accurate system of manual communication. Unlike the nonverbal cues employed in other abbeys, the signs described in the *Life of Odo* were exacting instruments of language. John of Salerno referred to them specifically as *notae*, meaning

---

[26] *RB* 38.6–7, p. 574: "Quae uero necessaria sunt comedentibus et bibentibus sic sibi uicissim ministrent fratres ut nullus indigeat petere aliquid; si quid tamen opus fuerit, sonitu cuiuscumque signi potius petatur quam uoce."

[27] Caesarius, *Regula uirginum* 18.4–5: "Si uero aliquid opus fuerit, quae mensae praeest, sollicitudinem gerat, et quod est necessarium nutu magis quam uoce petat." ed. Joël Courreau and Adalbert de Vogüé, in *Césaire d'Arles: Oeuvres monastiques*, 2 vols., SC CCCXLV and CCCXCVIII (Paris, 1988–1994), vol. I, p. 192.

[28] On the importance of attending to the words of the reader during meals, see *ibid.* 18.2: "Sedentes ad mensam taceant, et animum lectioni intendant."

[29] *RM* 30.17–18, vol. II, pp. 164–166: "Sed ne forte, cum silentium custoditur, aliqua necessitas utilitatis ad loquendum fratrem perurgueat et frater fratri uult loqui, si lumen cicindeli aut lucernae fuerit, de manu uel nutu capitis uel nutu oculorum."

[30] See pp. 53–54, above.

"marks" or "characters." This term was a more precise qualification than the ambiguous *signum*, because it implied that each sign carried a specific value or meaning.[31] In contrast to arbitrary signals, the Cluniac sign language was a manual code of symbolic characters that allowed the brethren to articulate their needs with the same precision as the tongue.

Monastic sign language functioned as a medium for the exchange of necessary information between individuals when speaking was forbidden. Two episodes in the *Life of Odo* provide the earliest insight into the semantic specificity of Cluniac signs and their range of application in the abbey. John of Salerno described one instance when a child oblate approached Odo in the silence of the night and indicated with a sign that he sought permission to urinate.[32] In another case, a monk made a sign to communicate to a brother who was talking out of turn that he should refrain because the hour was unsuitable, that is, it was a time when conversation was prohibited.[33] These brief yet evocative anecdotes suggest that the monks of tenth-century Baume-les-Moines and Cluny used their silent language to convey specific information on topics ranging from the private needs of the body to the public concerns of the community. Unfortunately, the *Life of Odo* provided no further evidence concerning the operating principles of the Cluniac sign language or details of its vocabulary. John had learned about this custom secondhand from Odo during their travels together and not from direct experience in the abbey. As such, he was not prepared to write a practical guide for its use. Nor was this his goal in any case. For John, the custom of sign language was emblematic of the laudable standards of discipline embraced by the monks of Cluny. It provided his readers with an exemplary model of ascetic heroism that would inspire them to uphold the rules of silence specific to their own community.[34]

---

[31] See Charles du Cange, *Glossarium mediae et infimae latinitatis*, 10 vols. (Niort, 1883–1887), vol. V, pp. 609–610, s.v. nota.

[32] John of Salerno, *Vita Odonis* 1.33: "Adfuit nox, et ecce quidam de pueris signo secessum naturae petiit." *PL* CXXXIII, col. 57c. For an eleventh-century description of such a sign, see Walter Jarecki, *Signa Loquendi: Die cluniacensischen Signa-Listen eingeleitet und herausgegeben* (Baden-Baden, 1981), p. 275 (Fleury, no. 152).

[33] John of Salerno, *Vita Odonis* 2.23: "Ille nostro more signum ei fecit ut taceret, quia hora erat incompetens." *PL* CXXXIII, col. 73c.

[34] It is worth noting that later Cluniac redactors of John of Salerno's *Life of Odo* consistently omitted the chapter on sign language from their work, probably because it seemed redundant to readers who were already long familiar with this practice. See MS BN, Latin 5566, fols. 165r–175v (*BHL* 6298; an anonymous eleventh-century redaction dedicated to Abbot Hugh the Great); and the twelfth-century *vita* by Nalgod (*BHL* 6299; *PL* CXXXIII, cols. 85–104), who complained explicitly about John's redundancy (*PL* CXXXIII, col. 85b).

IMAGINATION AND RESEMBLANCE

Descriptions of the Cluniac sign vocabulary first appeared more than 100 years after the composition of the *Life of Odo* in the late eleventh-century customaries of Bernard and Ulrich.[35] These compilations of monastic customs preserved identical copies of a short manual of sign-forms, commonly known as the Cluniac sign lexicon.[36] This document, which may have circulated independently as a pamphlet before its incorporation into the customaries, prescribed a vocabulary of 118 hand signs that novices were required to commit to memory before their consecration as monks (Table 1). The anonymous author of the sign lexicon followed a precise formula of presentation. Each entry included the name of the signified item or object, a description of the sign and often an explanation of the sign-form. For example, the first entry in the lexicon reads: "For the sign of bread, make a circle using the thumbs and the index fingers, the reason being that bread is usually round."[37] The descriptions were organized into three thematic units comprising signs for food (*victus*), clothing (*vestitus*) and the divine office (*divinum obsequium*), followed by a miscellaneous section of signs for people, actions, qualities and abstract concepts (*mixtim de personis et rebus et causis*). The signs for food ranged from common foodstuffs like bread, beans and fish, to drinks and spices. They also included signs for items that monks associated with food, like serving trays and drinking vessels. In the same way, the lexicon mingled signs for clothing with those for bedding and personal tools, like the knife and the sewing kit that monks carried on their belts. The section on the liturgy comprised signs for chants, hymns and books used in the church, alongside signs for celestial and saintly persons. The lexicon concluded with a miscellany that comprised signs for categories of people, a short list of monastic officials, a string of verbs, as well as signs for concepts (like good and bad) and qualities (such as quickness and slowness).

Monastic sign language was the product of an imagination of resemblance that constructed meaning primarily from concrete visual associations. Cluniac sign-forms usually reflected some visual experience of the object in question and were in effect gestural renderings of a prominent observable attribute of their referent. The diversity of sign-forms in the

---

[35] Further on the customaries of Bernard and Ulrich, see the Introduction, pp. 9–10, above.

[36] Bernard 1.17, pp. 169–173 (*De notitia signorum*); and Ulrich 2.4 (*De signis loquendi*), cols. 703b–705a (this edition of Ulrich is truncated and incomplete). For a modern critical edition, see Jarecki, *Signa Loquendi*, pp. 121–142. Appendix A, below, provides an English translation of the Cluniac sign lexicon as it appeared in the customaries of Bernard and Ulrich. I have followed Jarecki's numbering system in the notes and appendix to facilitate reference to individual signs.

[37] Cluny, no. 1: "Pro signo panis fac unum circulum cum utroque pollice et his duobus digitis, qui secuntur, pro eo, quod et panis solet esse rotundus." ed. Jarecki, *Signa Loquendi*, p. 121.

Cluniac lexicon suggests, however, that there were no dominant principles in the process of sign creation. In some cases, signs made reference to easily recognizable physical attributes. Bread took its sign from the roundness of its shape, while the sign for a drink made with wormwood mimicked the distinctive arrangement of wormwood leaves.[38] Signs for general categories of people also drew their meanings from visual associations of this kind. The sign for monk called attention to the cowl; the sign for priest to the tonsure; and the sign for layman to the beard.[39] In other cases, signs imitated habitual actions associated with their referent, especially those related to the preparation of food and the tasks of monastic officials. Thus, a pressing motion represented cheese; a slicing motion, vegetables; and a stirring motion, porridge.[40] Likewise, monks imitated the ringing of a bell for the prior; the counting of coins for the chamberlain; and the turning of a key in a lock for the cellarer.[41]

Many monastic signs imitated a visual characteristic of their referent, but some relied on qualitative, cultural or even linguistic associations for their meaning. Several signs for food items drew on the distinctive qualities of their taste. The sign for honey required monks to lick their fingers because of its sweetness, while the sign for vinegar involved rubbing a finger on the throat due to the harshness of its aftertaste.[42] Some signs took their form from metaphorical representations of prevalent cultural attitudes toward the signified object or concept. The sign for a book written by a pagan author involved a gesture that mimicked a dog scratching its ear because, as the author of the sign lexicon explained, people without faith were comparable with dogs.[43] Other signs borrowed their meanings from an allusion to the word for the referent. The sign for a countryman or blood relative (*conpatriota vel consanguineus*) made direct reference to the word for blood (*sanguis*), requiring monks to hold a finger to the nose, because blood sometimes flowed from it.[44] In the case of the sign for trout, the relationship between the sign-form and its referent was

---

[38] Cluny, nos. 1 (*panis*) and 29 (*potio, que est melle et absintio temperata*), ed. Jarecki, *Signa Loquendi*, pp. 121 and 126.

[39] Cluny, nos. 80 (*monachus*), 81 (*clericus*) and 82 (*laicus*), ed. Jarecki, *Signa Loquendi*, p. 136.

[40] Cluny, nos. 17 (*caseus*), 7 (*pulmentum oleribus confectum*) and 15 (*milium*), ed. Jarecki, *Signa Loquendi*, pp. 122 and 124.

[41] Cluny, nos. 85 (*prior*), 88 (*camerarius*) and 89 (*cellararius*), ed. Jarecki, *Signa Loquendi*, p. 137.

[42] Cluny, nos. 21 (*mel*) and 31 (*acetum*), ed. Jarecki, *Signa Loquendi*, pp. 125 and 127.

[43] Cluny, no. 73: "Pro signo libri secularis, quem aliquis paganus conposuit, premisso generali signo libri adde, ut aurem cum digito tanga, sicut canis cum pede pruriens solet, quia nec inmerito infidelis tali animanti conparatur." ed. Jarecki, *Signa Loquendi*, p. 134.

[44] Cluny, no. 102: "Pro signo conpatriote vel consanguinei tene manum contra faciem et medium digitum naso inpone propter sanguinem, qui inde nonnumquam fluit." ed. Jarecki, *Signa Loquendi*, p. 140.

so obscure that it elicited an explanation from the author of the sign lexicon. To make this sign, monks combined the general sign for fish with a motion that represented the head-covering worn by women. This seemingly odd combination of signs was suitable for trout because the Latin word for the fish (*truta*) was a feminine noun.[45]

Signs involving arbitrary hand positions or abstract shapes were rare in the Cluniac sign lexicon, but a few appeared among the signs for books. This subset of signs comprised compounds of the general sign for book and a second sign that designated specifically what kind of book it was.[46] In most cases, the designating sign relied on a visual association for its meaning. The sign for psalter, for example, was a compound of the general sign for book and the sign for crown, the latter being an associative reference to King David, the author of the psalms.[47] When faced with competing visual analogues, however, monks relied on the arbitrary positioning of the designating sign to communicate its meaning. The signs for three related mass books – the missal, the Gospels and the Epistles – all combined the general sign for book and the sign for cross, but they differed in the positioning of the hand when it made the designating sign: in front of the body for the missal; on the forehead for the Gospels; and on the chest for the Epistles. Purely abstract signs were also exceedingly rare. Whenever possible, monks expressed theoretical or moral concepts with concrete visual analogies. For example, the sign for bad mimicked the claws of a bird grasping and tearing at the face. More often, however, monks constructed signs for concepts like assent and refusal with abstract hand motions, but provided no explanation of the relationship of these signs to their referent.[48]

In very few cases, Cluniac sign-forms carried two denotative meanings. The sign for angel was identical to the sign for Alleluia because, as the author of the sign lexicon explained, it was believed that angels sung these verses perpetually in heaven.[49] The monks of Cluny cultivated this semantic ambiguity to underscore their own identification with the heavenly host through their celebration of the divine office. Likewise, the sign for

---

[45] Cluny, no. 14: "Pro signo trute hoc adde, ut digitum de supercilio ad supercilium trahas propter ligaturas, que hoc in loco habentur a feminis, et qui truta femineo genere pronuntiatur." ed. Jarecki, *Signa Loquendi*, p. 124.

[46] See Cluny, nos. 64–72, ed. Jarecki, *Signa Loquendi*, pp. 133–134.

[47] Cluny, no. 72: "Pro signo psalterii adde, ut summitates digitorum cava manu ponas in caput propter similitudinem corone, quam rex portare solet, quia et auctor psalmorum David rex erat." ed. Jarecki, *Signa Loquendi*, p. 134.

[48] Cluny, no. 115 (*annuicio*) and 116 (*negacio*), ed. Jarecki, *Signa Loquendi*, p. 142.

[49] Cluny, no. 61: "Pro signo alleluia leva manum et summitates digitorum inflexas quasi ad volandum move propter angelos, quia, ut creditur, ab angelis cantatur in celo." and Cluny, no. 74: "Pro signo angeli fac idipsum, quod facis pro signo alleluia." ed. Jarecki, *Signa Loquendi*, pp. 132 and 135.

the *Rule of Benedict* shared its primary characteristics with the sign for abbot.[50] This visual parallel strengthened the association between the office of the living abbot and the fundamental precepts on the monastic life set down by the saint in his rule for monks. Lastly, the sign for sickness was indistinguishable from the sign for confession. Here physical sickness was expressly equated with the stain of sin. The need to make confession arose because the sinful monk suffered from a sickness of the soul.[51]

It would be presumptuous to conclude from the evidence of the Cluniac sign lexicon alone that the character of the early monastic imagination was purely concrete and associative rather than abstract and arbitrary. Nonetheless, the monk (or monks) who devised this silent language invested the sign-forms with meanings derived overwhelmingly from common visual experiences associated with the appearance, function or qualitative characteristics of their referents. Didactic concerns may have guided these choices. Abstract and arbitrary signs could have seemed less intuitive and therefore more difficult to memorize than signs that drew their meaning from observable attributes evident to all. There were exceptions to this, of course, but they accounted for a very small proportion of the monastic sign vocabulary.

SIGNS FOR THE SHADOW MONKS

Instruction in sign language was an important part of the preparation of novices for life in a Cluniac abbey.[52] Training in this custom may have been offered as early as the first decades of the tenth century, when Odo observed its use upon his entry to Baume-les-Moines. Monastic sign language was certainly taught at Cluny as a matter of course by the late eleventh century. According to the customaries of Bernard and Ulrich: "It is also necessary that he [the novice] learn with diligence the signs by

---

[50] Cluny, no. 70: "Pro signo regule adde [generali signo premisso libri] ut capillum super aurem pendentem cum duobus digitis aprehendas propter duo nomina, quibus abba appellatur: abba et domnus, quia et sanctus Benedictus auctor regule huius erat officii." and Cluny, no. 84: "Pro signo domni abbatis fac idipsum, quod pro signo regule est premissum." ed. Jarecki, *Signa Loquendi*, pp. 134 and 137.

[51] Cluny, no. 94: "Pro signo infirmarii, qui obsequitur infirmis, pone manum contra pectus, quod significat infirmitatem, quamvis non semper, quia et confessionem significat." ed. Jarecki, *Signa Loquendi*, p. 138.

[52] On the Cluniac novitiate, see Noreen Hunt, *Cluny Under Saint Hugh 1049–1109* (South Bend, IN, 1967), pp. 92–96; and Isabelle Cochelin, "Peut-on parler de noviciat à Cluny pour les Xe–XIe siècles?" *Revue Mabillon* n.s. 9 (1998): 17–52. Further on adult entry into the monastic life in the medieval period, see Hubertus Lutterbach, *Monachus factus est: Die Mönchwerdung im frühen Mittelalter, zugleich ein Beitrag zur Frömmigkeits- und Liturgiegeschichte* (Münster, 1995); and Charles de Miramon, "Embrasser l'état monastique à l'âge adulte (1050–1200): Etude sur la conversion tardive," *Annales: Economies, Sociétés, Civilisations* 54 (1999): 825–849.

which he may communicate in a certain manner while remaining silent, because after he has entered the monastery, he is rarely permitted to talk."[53] The training of the hand was twofold. Novices acquired proficiency in sign language by observing and imitating the master of novices, the official who was their instructor and model in all aspects of personal comportment. But there was a moral component to their instruction as well. The Cluniacs were well aware of the dangers that accompanied the use of sign language. A silent replacement for speech could easily become a medium for sinful utterances as potent and perilous as the spoken word. Like the mouth, which held the power of life and death (Prov. 18.21), the speaking hand required the guidance of a human will directed at all times by the principles of monastic virtue. Once the novices had mastered the vocabulary of the Cluniac sign language, they were also trained to control their desire to use the signs for idle purposes.

All manner of people sought entry into Cluny during the abbacy of Hugh the Great (1049–1109). Some were already professed monks from distant communities, who entered the monastery without delay or after spending an obligatory night in the guesthouse.[54] Others were children, consecrated to God's service by their parents through the ritual of oblation. Although common in the Carolingian period, this practice was on the wane by the year 1100. Nonetheless, throughout the eleventh century, children still accounted for an important source of recruitment for many large monastic communities, including Cluny. The vow made on behalf of these children was immediate and binding. Oblates became full participants in the community from the moment of their consecration.[55] Adult laymen and priests also petitioned to become monks, but they were first received as novices. Unlike professed monks and child oblates, however, great care was taken to instruct the novices in the demands of the *Rule* before their formal admission into the abbey.

The Cluniac customaries outlined at length the proper preparation of novices for entry into the community.[56] The attention given to describing this process may have been a response to an internal crisis caused by the remarkable increase in monastic vocations at Cluny under Hugh the

---

[53] Bernard 1.17, p. 169; and Ulrich 2.3, col. 703a: "Opus quoque habet ut signa diligenter addiscat, quibus tacens quodammodo loquatur, quia postquam adunatus fuerit ad conventum, licet ei rarissime loqui."

[54] Ulrich 2.1, cols. 700d–701a.

[55] Mayke de Jong, *In Samuel's Image: Child Oblation in the Early Medieval West* (Leiden, 1996).

[56] Giles Constable, "Entrance to Cluny in the Eleventh and Twelfth Centuries According to the Cluniac Customaries and Statutes," in *Mediaevalia Christiana, XIe–XIIIe siècles: Hommages à Raymonde Foreville*, ed. Coloman Etienne Viola (Paris, 1989), pp. 335–354; repr. in Giles Constable, *Cluny from the Tenth to the Twelfth Centuries: Further Studies* (Aldershot, 2000), no. III.

Great, when the number of monks tripled from 100 to 300.[57] It is probably not coincidental that the sign lexicon was written down at the very time that this increase occurred. After requesting the abbot's permission to join the society of the elect (*vestram societatem*), adult converts heard an explanation of the *Rule* and promised their obedience to it. They then submitted themselves for tonsure and exchanged their worldly garments for the monastic habit.[58] These visible transformations carried a powerful symbolic significance. The shearing of the hair represented the abandonment of the will.[59] The new clothing was a symbol of the vow of stability and obedience.[60] The novices were distinguished from the professed monks only by the absence of the cowl, which they were not permitted to wear until the ceremony of consecration that heralded their full membership in the community.[61]

The *Rule of Benedict* recommended a probationary period of a full year for converts to the cloistered life, but there is little evidence from Cluniac sources that this ancient precept was upheld in the eleventh century.[62] Bernard and Ulrich are silent on the matter, but in the twelfth century Peter the Venerable issued a statute enforcing a probation period of at least a month, which suggests that the novitiate had been severely curtailed by the time of his abbacy.[63] It is clear from the eleventh-century customaries, however, that initiates to Cluny undertook a program of moral formation and spiritual direction intended to temper their wills and prepare them for their new vocation. When their numbers were great, the novices were shadow monks, who formed a separate community on the fringes of the monastery.[64] They used their own dormitory, refectory and kitchen, where they imitated the activities and comportment of the professed monks in preparation for joining them.[65] They were sometimes permitted to attend the chapter meeting and played a limited role in liturgical celebrations, but they usually remained a group apart until their instruction was complete.[66]

---

[57] Cochelin, "Peut-on parler de noviciat à Cluny?" On the evidence for a dramatic rise in vocations in this period, see Hunt, *Cluny Under Saint Hugh*, pp. 82–83.

[58] Bernard 1.15, p. 165.

[59] Louis Trichet, *La tonsure: vie et mort d'une pratique ecclésiastique* (Paris, 1990), pp. 65–67.

[60] Giles Constable, "The Ceremonies and Symbolism of Entering Religious Life and Taking the Monastic Habit, from the Fourth to the Twelfth Centuries," in *Segni e riti nella chiesa altomedievale occidentales, Spoleto, 11–17 aprile 1985* (Spoleto, 1987), pp. 771–834, at pp. 808–816; repr. in Giles Constable, *Culture and Spirituality in Medieval Europe* (London, 1996), no. VII.

[61] Ulrich 2.1, col. 701c: "Vestis eorum nostrae debet omnino similis esse, praeterquam quod, quandiu erunt absque benedictione, sola cuculla carebunt."

[62] *RB* 58, pp. 626–632.   [63] *Statuta* 37, pp. 71–72.   [64] Ulrich 2.2, col. 701d.

[65] See, for example, Ulrich 2.2, col. 702b: "Nam et lectiones habent et scillam et aliis modis simulant eamdem disciplinam quam nos in refectorio habemus."

[66] On the liturgical role of the novices, see Chapter 3, pp. 86–87, below.

The demands of monastic discipline smothered the voices of the novices from the moment they entered the abbey. According to the *Liber tramitis*, an early eleventh-century Cluniac customary from Farfa, the novices were not allowed to speak unbidden with anyone except the master of novices, who supervised all of their activities.[67] When they did speak with another monk, their master sat between them to ensure the quality of the conversation.[68] Moreover, at Cluny and other places, silence was an essential component of the consecration ceremony that marked the formal admission of a novice into the community. This ritual represented a second baptism and cleansed the individual of the sins of his former life. In eleventh-century consecration formulas, the silence of the participant played a key role in his transformation from novice to monk. The novice covered his head with a cowl on the first day of the ceremony. He then spent three days veiled in utter silence, in imitation of the apostles, who went into hiding for three days after the death of Jesus. On the third day, the abbot summoned him and with the words "Peace be with you" removed the cowl from his head. The novice emerged from his silence as a monk.[69] Even after his profession, the new monk did not presume to speak in the chapter meeting for up to five years.[70] These lessons in conduct prepared the novice for the strict rules against speaking that characterized Cluniac monasticism in the tenth and eleventh centuries.

Little is known about the training of novices in the custom of sign language at Cluny, but it seems to have involved oral instruction supported by written texts. The large numbers of adult converts who entered the community under Hugh the Great challenged traditional methods of monastic education. Prior to this period, Cluniac monks learned and transmitted their customs orally. Observation and imitation were also important principles in monastic pedagogy, especially with regard to rules

---

[67] For the influence of Cluniac customs on Farfa in this period, see Susan Boynton, *Shaping a Monastic Identity: Liturgy and History at the Imperial Abbey of Farfa, 1000–1125* (Ithaca and London, 2006), pp. 106–143.

[68] *Liber tramitis aevi Odilonis abbatis* 18, ed. Peter Dinter, *CCM* X (Siegburg, 1980), p. 208.

[69] *Ex decreto beati Gregorii papae*: "Et ita usque in tercium diem uelatum habeat caput cum summo silentio et debita reuerentia, figuram gerens dominicae passionis ... Tribus diebus sunt in silentio iuxta apostolos, qui ob metum Iudeorum in conclaui residebant, usque dum tercio die dominus resurgens dixit illis: Pax uobis. Sic abbas pacem det monacho, et capitium de capite eius auferat." ed. Giles Constable, in "The Treatise 'Horatur nos' and Accompanying Canonical Texts on the Performance of Pastoral Work by Monks," in *Speculum Historiale: Geschichte im Spiegel von Geschichtsschreibung und Geschichtsdeutung (Festschrift Johannes Spörl)*, ed. Clemens Bauer, Laetitia Boehm and Max Müller (Freiburg and Munich, 1966), pp. 567–577, at pp. 575–576; repr. in Giles Constable, *Religious Life and Thought (11th–12th Centuries)* (London, 1979), no. IX.

[70] *Liber tramitis* 18, ed. Dinter, p. 208.

of personal comportment.[71] This implies that the novices learned sign language both by hearing the verbal encouragement of their master and by watching the muted movements of his hands.[72] By the late eleventh century, however, the unprecedented expansion of the community rendered oral methods of instruction inadequate, prompting the monks to write their customs down.[73] The earliest copies of the Cluniac sign lexicon appeared around 1080 as chapters in the customaries of Bernard and Ulrich. The sign lexicon was composed to support, rather than replace, an existing oral tradition at a time of rapid and unprecedented growth. While it is unlikely that the customaries were ever used by individuals as tools of instruction, copies of the Cluniac sign lexicon may have been made available to the novices for individual or collective study. If so, its existence is an indication of the growth of literacy in the eleventh century, or at the very least the level of literacy that could be expected of some novices. Although evidence is lacking for eleventh-century Cluny, the didactic use of sign lists for training in this custom was evident in other medieval abbeys and has endured in the monastic tradition down to the present day.[74]

Monastic signs were useful vehicles of information exchange so long as monks did not employ them with subversive intent. Studies in American Sign Language (ASL) have shown that modern sign systems for the deaf are comparable with spoken languages in terms of their complexity and expressiveness.[75] With a vocabulary of thousands of conventualized sign-forms supported by a complex system of syntactical markers, ASL and its equivalents in other countries are vivid and powerful narrative tools.[76]

---

[71] See, for example, Isabelle Cochelin, "Besides the Book: Using the Body to Mould the Mind – Cluny in the Tenth and Eleventh Centuries," in *Medieval Monastic Education*, ed. George Ferzoco and Carolyn Muessig (London and New York, 2000), pp. 21–34. This study concerns the training of child oblates, but its insights apply to adult novices as well.

[72] Bernard 1.15, pp. 165–166. See also Bernard 1.16, p. 169, and Ulrich 2.2, col. 702d: "De hoc autem praefatus scholaris Christi, non tam auditu quam visu instruitur."

[73] For a useful discussion of these problems in the context of the liturgical training at Cluny and elsewhere in this period, see Susan Boynton, "Orality, Literacy, and the Early Notation of the Office Hymns," *Journal of the American Musicology Society* 56 (2003): 99–168.

[74] See Chapter 4, pp. 107–108, below.

[75] The study of ASL as a system of gestural communication independent of spoken languages but analogous with them began in the 1960s with the pioneering work of William Stokoe. See, for example, William Stokoe, *Sign Language Structure* (Buffalo, 1960); and William Stokoe, Dorothy Casterline and Carl Croneberg, *A Dictionary of American Sign Language on Linguistic Principles* (Washington, DC, 1965). Stokoe was also the founding editor of *Sign Language Studies* (1972–present), the leading journal of deaf studies, history and education published by Gallaudet University in Washington, DC.

[76] See, for example, Edward S. Klima and Ursula Bellugi, *The Signs of Language* (Cambridge, MA, 1979); Scott K. Liddell, *American Sign Language Syntax* (New York, 1980); and John O. Isenhath, *The Linguistics of American Sign Language* (London, 1990).

A sign language with the expressive potential of ASL would have been as pregnant with peril as an undisciplined tongue in a medieval monastic context, especially for novices, whose commitment to the cloistered life was still dubious. In realization of this danger, the Cluniacs took specific precautions to prevent individuals from sinning through the garrulous use of their hands.

First, it is clear that the novices did not learn the full panoply of signs in use among the professed monks at Cluny. The customaries of Bernard and Ulrich implied that they were only instructed in the most pertinent and necessary signs chosen from the many employed in the abbey.[77] The contents of the Cluniac sign lexicon lend support to this inference. Several of its descriptions of compound signs – a string of two or more signs made in succession to indicate a single word or concept – have as one of their components a sign not otherwise attested among the entries in the lexicon. The incidental appearance of signs for pride, metal, long, cross, song, first, bishop, knowing, large, small, sickness, novice, seeing and refectory provides a sample of the wider range of sign vocabulary in use among professed monks, but not taught directly to the novices.[78] Moreover, Bernard did not provide a separate entry in the lexicon for the sign for confession, but chose instead to describe this important sign and its application in the chapter following the sign lexicon.[79]

Second, the brevity of the Cluniac sign lexicon meant that the novices could express little more than their basic needs with the few signs they knew. The initial vocabulary of the novices comprised 118 signs, primarily for specific nouns. Only fifteen of these signs represented verbs or abstract concepts.[80] Moreover, the sign lexicon contained no signs for pronouns, prepositions, conjunctions or possessive adjectives and made no mention of temporal and syntactical markers or other principles of grammar. Possessive adjectives were generally forbidden in monastic communities in any case, because their use implied private ownership. The monks of Cluny could only use the adjective "my" to refer to their parents or their sins.[81] As it was taught to the novices, the silent language of the Cluniacs was a limited repertoire of visual nouns with no means of connecting them to express full sentences or higher thoughts. In comparison to the rich expressive potential of ASL and other modern sign systems for the deaf, the Cluniac sign lexicon described a purposefully

---

[77] Bernard 1.17, p. 173; and Ulrich 2.4, cols. 704d–705a.
[78] See Cluny, nos. 12 (*superbia*), 51 (*metallum*), 63 (*longum*), 65 (*crux*), 71 (*presens tempus vel quod primum est*), 75 (*episcopus*), 83 (*sciendum*), 86 (*aliquid magnum*), 94 (*infirmitas*), 95 (*refectio*) and 98 (*novicius*), ed. Jarecki, *Signa Loquendi*, pp. 123, 130 and 132–139.
[79] Further on the sign for confession, see Chapter 3, pp. 89–90, below.
[80] Cluny, nos. 104–118, ed. Jarecki, *Signa Loquendi*, pp. 140–142.   [81] Bernard 1.19, p. 177.

disabled language that was useful only for the expression of single nominal concepts.

These limitations were aspects of monastic discipline. The novices learned a sufficient number of signs to express their basic needs and to understand instruction and reprimand when speaking was forbidden, but their prescribed vocabulary and the absence of syntactical principles hindered them from making sinful utterances with their hands. Even with these restrictions in place, the novices were warned repeatedly against the frequent use of the few signs they knew. The customary of Bernard instructed monks in no uncertain terms to use sign language sparingly and only when absolutely necessary.[82] Moreover, on a visit to Cluny in 1063 to settle a dispute between the abbey and the bishop of Mâcon, Peter Damian allegedly observed that the monks expressed themselves warily with signs and employed them only to communicate essential information, with the result that their silent exchanges did not bear the stain of empty or chiding remarks.[83] The fear of suspicious signing may also explain why the Cluniac sign lexicon comprised only hand signs and included no examples of the "signs made with the eyes" (*notae oculorum*) mentioned in the tenth-century *Life of Odo*.[84] The customary of Bernard instructed monks to avoid using signs in the dormitory as they prepared for sleep, but it also warned them specifically against directing a wink (*nutum oculorum*) toward the bed of another monk.[85] The novices apparently received no instruction in signs of this kind, perhaps because, as Bernard's warning implied, the eyes were thought to be a suspect and potentially provocative medium of silent communication.

The training of the hand involved more than the physical mastery of a manual code of discourse. Like the abnegation of the desire to speak, it was also a kind of mortification, a denial of the will to communicate freely with others, except by reason of necessity. Incapable of expressing more than single nominal concepts, the Cluniac sign system lingered on the

---

[82] Bernard 1.19, p. 178: "Signa, quae cum manu fiunt pro locutione, non amat frequenter facere, conventu maxime cernente, et quoties facit, facit reverenter, et pro necessitate, et numquam absque alicujus utilitatis ratione."

[83] *De Gallica Petri Damiani profectione et eius ultramontano itinere* 13: "Ita enim semper in ecclesiasticis atteruntur officiis, ut vix claustrensi et honesta locutione nisi signis possit alter alteri aliquid intimare. Quae quidem ita cauta et necessaria omnibus in locis facta deprehenduntur, ut nullius levitatis, nullius reprehensionis valeant macula denotari." *MGH SS* XXX, ed. Gerhard Schwartz and Adolf Hofmeister (Hanover, 1934), pp. 1034–1046, at p. 1042. On the significance of this journey for the relationship between Cluny and the papacy, see H. E. J. Cowdrey, *The Cluniacs and the Gregorian Reform* (Oxford, 1970), pp. 47–51.

[84] See n. 10, above.

[85] Bernard 1.19, p. 179: "Non modo ea signa, quae cum manu fiunt, devitat, sed etiam nutum oculorum nequaquam dirigit ad lectum alterius fratris."

threshold of language. Yet, it was the quasi-linguistic character of this system of communication that allowed it to function in a medieval monastic context. Signs with the expressive potential of ASL and its equivalents would have been unacceptable to monks because they presented the same opportunities for sinful utterances as the spoken word. With a strictly delimited vocabulary and a lack of organizing principles, Cluniac sign language provided a medium of communication already measured by the expectations of monastic discipline.

CONCLUSION

The silent language of the Cluniacs was a radical departure from the nonverbal signals traditionally employed in early medieval abbeys. Unlike the arbitrary signs attested in cenobitic communities from the fourth century onwards, this nuanced vocabulary of meaning-specific handshapes allowed the brethren to communicate silently with unprecedented precision. With knowledge of this custom, the monks of Cluny could overcome the practical difficulties of communal life attendant with austere rules against speaking. While Cluniac sign language safeguarded the souls of monks from the perils of human discourse, it also presented the possibility for individuals to express idle thoughts in secret and thereby undermine its purpose. The brethren of Cluny attempted to prevent the misuse of this custom by disabling the expressive potential of the signs as a medium of unregulated conversation. Although the potential always existed for mischievous or disobedient individuals to amplify the existing sign vocabulary for their own purposes or to misuse the few signs they knew, the Cluniac sign language was an original and largely effective system of regulated information exchange that satisfied the strict ascetic objectives of the brethren who used it.

Understanding the linguistic character of the Cluniac sign repertoire brings us no closer, however, to reconstructing the specific contexts in which the monks of Cluny applied this silent language in the course of their daily lives. The next chapter examines some of the possible applications of this custom at the great Burgundian abbey by comparing the sign vocabulary of the Cluniac lexicon and the numerous allusions to their referents in the customaries of Bernard and Ulrich. Taken together, these eleventh-century sources allow us to infer many of the discrete functions of monastic sign language for the brethren of Cluny. They also provide us with the opportunity to consider the role of this custom in shaping and supporting a sense of communal identity among the monks who used it.

Table 1: *The vocabulary of the Cluniac sign lexicon*

Signs for sustenance (*que ad victum pertinent*)

1. Bread (*panis*)
2. Bread cooked in water (*panis qui coquitur in aqua*)
3. Wheat bread (*panis sigalinus*)
4. Small loaf (*tortula*)
5. Beans (*fabae*)
6. Eggs (*ova*)
7. Dish of vegetables (*pulmentum oleribus confectum*)
8. Fish (*piscis*)
9. Squid (*sepiae*)
10. Eel (*anguilla*)
11. Lamprey (*lampreda*)
12. Salmon or sturgeon (*salmo vel sturio*)
13. Pike (*lucius*)
14. Trout (*truta*)
15. Millet (*milium*)
16. Crepes (*crispellae*)
17. Cheese (*caseus*)
18. Cheese tarts (*fladones*)
19. Bread of some kind (*rufeolae*)
20. Milk (*lac*)
21. Honey (*mel*)
22. Fruit (*poma*)
23. Cherries (*ceraseae*)
24. Raw lentils (*porrus crudus*)
25. Garlic or radish (*allium seu rafa*)
26. Water (*aqua*)
27. Wine (*vinum*)
28. Spiced drink (*potio pigmentata*)
29. Drink prepared with honey and wormwood (*potio melle et absintio temperata*)
30. Mustard seed (*sinapis*)
31. Vinegar (*acetum*)
32. Flat dish (*scutella*)
33. Cup (*cyphus*)
34. Shallow bowl (*patera*)
35. Glass drinking vessel (*phiala vitrea*)

Signs for apparel (*de his, que ad vestitum pertinent*)

36. Wool tunic (*staminia*)
37. Trousers (*femoralia*)
38. Frock (*froccus*)
39. Cowl (*cuculla*)

Table 1: (*cont.*)

40. Sleeves (*manicae*)
41. Hide garment (*pellicium*)
42. Shoes (*calcei*)
43. Night shoes (*nocturnales calcei*)
44. Ankle straps (*pedules*)
45. Blanket (*coopertorium*)
46. Coat (*cottus*)
47. Sheet (*strala*)
48. Pillow or cushion (*capitale vel cussinum*)
49. Strap for a tunic (*corrigia ad stamineam*)
50. Belt for trousers (*cingulum femoralium*)
51. Needle (*acus*)
52. Thread (*filum*)
53. Knife (*cultellus*)
54. Sheath (*vagina cultelli*)
55. Comb (*pecten*)
56. Writing boards (*tabulae*)
57. Writing instrument (*graphium*)

Signs for the divine office (*ad divinum maxime pertinent obsequium*)

58. Reading (*lectio*)
59. Response (*responsorium*)
60. Antiphon or verse of the response (*antiphona vel versus responsorii*)
61. Alleluia (*alleluia*)
62. Prose or sequence (*prosa vel sequentia*)
63. Tractus (*tractus*)
64. Book (*liber*)
65. Missal (*liber missalis*)
66. The Gospels (*textus evangelii*)
67. The Book of Epistles (*liber epistolaris*)
68. Book read at Nocturns (*liber in quo legendum est ad nocturnos*)
69. Antiphonary (*antiphonarium*)
70. *Rule of Benedict* (*regula*)
71. Hymnal (*ymnarium*)
72. Psalter (*psalterium*)
73. Secular book (*liber secularis*)
74. Angel (*angelus*)
75. Apostle (*apostolus*)
76. Martyr (*martyr*)
77. Confessor (*confessor*)
78. Holy virgin (*sacra virgo*)
79. Feast day (*festivitas*)

Table 1: (*cont.*)

Miscellany of signs for people and other things and events (*mixtim de personis et rebus aliis et causis*)

80. Monk (*monachus*)
81. Priest (*clericus*)
82. Layman (*laicus*)
83. Monk raised in the abbey (*monachus nutritus in monasterio*)
84. Abbot (*abbas*)
85. Prior (*prior*)
86. Major prior (*maior*)
87. Sacrist (*custos ecclesie*)
88. Chamberlain (*camerarius*)
89. Cellarer (*cellararius*)
90. Keeper of the granary (*granatarius*)
91. Gardener (*ortolanus*)
92. Keeper of the hospice (*custos hospicii*)
93. Almoner (*elemosinarius*)
94. Infirmarer (*infirmarius*)
95. Refectorer (*refectorarius*)
96. Librarian and precentor (*armarius et precentor*)
97. Master of the boys (*magister puerorum*)
98. Master of the novices (*magister noviciorum*)
99. Old man (*senex*)
100. Marshal (*marschalchus*)
101. Keeper of the donkeys (*asinarius*)
102. Countryman or blood relative (*conpatriota vel consanguineus*)
103. Man who speaks another language (*homo alterius lingue*)
104. To talk (*loqui*)
105. To hear (*audire*)
106. To not know (*nescire*)
107. To tell a lie (*mentiri*)
108. To kiss (*osculari*)
109. To dress (*vestire*)
110. To undress (*exuere*)
111. To wash feet (*lavare pedes*)
112. Something good (*bonum*)
113. Something bad (*malum*)
114. Something done (*res facta*)
115. Assent (*annuicio*)
116. Refusal (*negacio*)
117. Quickness (*celeritas*)
118. Slowness (*tarditas*)

Chapter 3

A SILENT COMMERCE OF SIGNS

On a winter night in the early twelfth century, the monks of Cluny awoke to the sound of screaming so persistent that it eventually roused the entire community. A novice named Armannus was raving in his sleep and no effort could wake him from his terrible dream. The alarmed monks rushed to the bedside of their abbot, but the lateness of the hour prohibited them from speaking, so they made it known to him with signs (*nutibus*) that something extraordinary was taking place. As it turned out, the novice had been terrified by a vision of the devil in the form of a ravenous bear. Peter the Venerable related this episode in his treatise *On Miracles*, but unlike John of Salerno, whose expository digression 200 years earlier in the tenth-century *Life of Odo* provided the earliest description of the character and function of the Cluniac sign language, the abbot felt no need to explain or otherwise qualify the actions of his brethren.[1] By the time of his abbacy (1122–1156), the custom of using signs in place of spoken words was woven so tightly into the fabric of monastic life at Cluny that knowledge of it was easily taken for granted by those who employed it. In fact, cloistered authors rarely mentioned the use of sign language at all.

Surprisingly little is known about the practical applications of monastic sign language at Cluny. Most studies have relied heavily on the Cluniac sign lexicon for information about this custom.[2] With its evocative

---

[1] Peter the Venerable, *De miraculis libri duos* 1.18, ed. D. Bouthillier, *CCCM* LXXXIII (Turnhout, 1988), pp. 55–56.

[2] Louis Gougaud, "Le langage des silencieux," *Revue Mabillon* 19 (1929): 93–100; Gérard van Rijnberk, *Le langage par signes chez les moines* (Amsterdam, 1953); Eric Buyssens, "Le langage par gestes chez les moines," *Revue de l'Institut de Sociologie* 29 (1954): 537–545; Paul Gerhard Schmidt, "*Ars loquendi et ars tacendi*: Zur monastischen Zeichensprache des Mittelalters," *Berichte zur Wissenschaftsgeschichte* 4 (1981): 13–19; and Lois Bragg, "Visual-Kinetic Communication in Europe Before 1600: A Survey of Sign Lexicons and Finger Alphabets Prior to the Rise of Deaf Education," *Journal of Deaf Studies and Deaf Education* 2 (1997): 1–25.

descriptions of the 118 hand signs taught to novices before their formal profession as monks, the lexicon is an unparalleled source for the linguistic character of this silent language. Unfortunately, it has generally been treated in isolation from other valuable evidence for cloistered life in the eleventh century, including the Cluniac customaries of Bernard and Ulrich. Such a narrow focus on a single source has led to some misleading inferences about the function of monastic sign language and its range of application in medieval abbeys. For example, Walter Jarecki, the modern editor of the Cluniac sign lexicon, has suggested that the boundaries of monastic discipline provided the organizing principle of the document because the first three thematic sections of signs (food, clothing and the divine office) seem to correspond to the three parts of the monastery (the refectory, the dormitory and the oratory) in which the *Rule of Benedict* forbade monks from speaking.[3] This conclusion is misleading, however, because the section headings in the Cluniac sign lexicon seem to indicate that thematic function was more important than spatial association in the organization of its contents. Moreover, as we will see, most of the signs were not confined in their use to a single part of the abbey.

It is the contention of this chapter that the Cluniac sign lexicon alone does not tell the full story of this practice. In the words of Canadian novelist Margaret Atwood, "The living bird is not its labeled bones."[4] The customaries of Bernard and Ulrich specified many of the rituals and other activities that Cluniac monks performed in silence and thus provide a rich descriptive context for the use of sign language in their community. Reading the sign lexicon in the context of the customaries yields two important insights about the application of this custom. First, whenever it was possible, monastic officials tried to minimize sign use among the brethren by finding ways for them to interact without recourse to words or signs. Sign language was employed primarily for otherwise unregulated situations, which raised anxiety that monks would abuse this custom through the garrulous use of their hands. Limited opportunities for sign use lessened the possibility of lapses in discipline. Second, the customaries suggest that monastic signs were particularly important as a medium of instruction and reprimand. The master of novices employed them most frequently to cue and prompt his charges during activities that would have been habitual or intuitive for more experienced monks. A comparative reading of the lexicon and the customaries allows us to reconstruct probable scenarios for the use of monastic signs and thereby infer their

---

[3] Walter Jarecki, *Signa Loquendi: Die cluniacensischen Signa-Listen eingeleitet und herausgegeben* (Baden-Baden, 1981), pp. 21–22.

[4] Margaret Atwood, *The Blind Assassin* (New York, 2000), p. 395.

practical applications for the brethren of Cluny. This analysis promises to change the way historians have imagined interpersonal communication between monks regarding the preparation of food, the maintenance of clothing and tools, and the orchestration of the divine office. In turn, it builds a detailed and unusually vivid tableau of daily life in one of the largest abbeys in western Christendom at the close of the eleventh century.

Attention to the discrete applications of Cluniac sign language by individual monks invites us to consider the inverse question of its function, that is, what the custom contributed to the formation of the identity of the monastic community as a whole. This chapter argues that sign language provided a kind of institutional lingua franca for monks with limited skills in Latin and no shared vernacular language. A universal proficiency in spoken Latin could not be presumed among adult converts to the monastic life after the linguistic reforms undertaken in the early ninth century to standardize its pronunciation.[5] Moreover, although a predominantly Gallic community, the abbey of Cluny attracted individuals from every part of Europe, many of whom crossed linguistic boundaries en route to Burgundy. Monastic sign language allowed brethren from different linguistic backgrounds to bridge the gap separating those who could not otherwise understand one another using spoken words. In the parlance of modern sociolinguists, Cluny was a speech community, a group of people whose shared understanding of a particular language, in this case a silent language of signs, set them apart from those around them.[6] As this chapter suggests, Cluniac sign language constructed and maintained a sense of solidarity among those who defined themselves through their emulation of the angels in opposition to the secular ideals that governed the world beyond their cloister walls. In short, the adoption of this custom was essential to the Cluniac monk's understanding of himself as the embodiment of angelic ideals embraced in anticipation of the life to come.

SIGNS FOR SUSTENANCE

Rules of silence forbade the monks of Cluny from speaking in the kitchens and the refectory, making sign language an important tool in the preparation and orchestration of meals. In the early Middle Ages, the monastic diet was a carbohydrate-rich combination of breads

[5] Further on this point, see pp. 90–92, esp. n. 78, below.
[6] On the application of this term to Cluny, see pp. 90–91, below.

and vegetables, supplemented with wine and high protein animal products.[7] The novices learned thirty-five signs for food and food-related items like bread, eggs and vegetables, fish, millet, cheese and baked goods, milk and honey, fruit, lentils and garlic, drinks, condiments and serving vessels.[8] It was important for the novices to learn these signs because they were expected to use them while performing kitchen duties and taking their meals in the refectory. The evidence of the customaries suggests that monastic sign language played a much more significant role in the preparation of meals than they did in the procurement of rations or the actual consumption of food and drink.

At Cluny and other early medieval abbeys, eating habits changed with the season and the liturgical significance of the day. Monks ate one meal per day in the winter and two meals in the summer when the days were longer. They ate once on fast days and twice on feast days, irrespective of the season.[9] Their standard meal comprised two dishes of cooked beans and vegetables and a dish of raw vegetables and fruit. Monks also received a pound of bread every day to eat with their meals. An extra portion was available to them in the evening as well, if their daily ration did not suffice.[10] The standard drink in the abbey was wine. Monks gathered together for a drink between their two meals in the summer or in the evening in place of the second meal during the winter and on fast days.[11] Attendance was mandatory, even if the monk chose not to drink.[12] In the early darkness of winter evenings, they drank their wine in the refectory by candlelight.[13] The name of this drink, the *caritas*, suggests that the custom was an outgrowth of the ration increase recommended in the *Rule of Benedict* and allowed at the kind discretion (*per caritatem*) of the abbot. It may have served originally as a supplement to the single meal provided in the winter season because of the harsher climates endured by monks who lived north of the Alps.[14]

---

[7] On the monastic diet in the late antique and early medieval periods, see Gerd Zimmermann, *Ordensleben und Lebensstandard: Die Cura corporis in den Ordensvorschriften des abendländischen Hochmittelalters* (Münster, 1973), pp. 37–87; Stéphane Boulc'H, "Le repas quotidien des moines occidentaux du haut moyen âge," *Revue Belge de Philologie et d'Histoire* 75 (1997): 287–328; Kathy L. Pearson, "Nutrition and the Early-Medieval Diet," *Speculum* 72 (1997): 1–32; and Mary Harlow and Wendy Smith, "Between Fasting and Feasting: The Literary and Archaeobiological Evidence for Monastic Diet in Late Antique Egypt," *Antiquity* 75 (2001): 758–768. For a discussion of the general economic trends that had an impact on food production in this period, see Jean-Pierre Devroey, "The Economy," in *The Early Middle Ages: Europe 400–1000*, ed. Rosamond McKitterick (Oxford, 2001), pp. 97–129.

[8] Cluny, nos. 1–35, ed. Jarecki, *Signa Loquendi*, pp. 121–127.

[9] Bernard 2.31, pp. 349–350 and 355.   [10] *RB* 39.3–5; and Bernard 2.11, p. 156.

[11] Ulrich 1.18, col. 668c.   [12] Ulrich 2.24, col. 712b.

[13] Bernard 1.74, no. 15, p. 269. On the evening drink in the winter, see also Bernard 2.32, p. 354.

[14] Zimmermann, *Ordensleben und Lebensstandard*, pp. 42–44.

It was forbidden for healthy monks to eat the flesh of quadrupeds, but they did consume a daily portion of high protein animal products, like cheese and eggs, as well as large quantities of fish as supplements to their standard meals. On Tuesdays, Thursdays and Saturdays, Cluniac monks ate the *pitantia*, a plate of four eggs or raw cheese shared between two people. On other days, they ate the *generale*, a more generous helping of five eggs and cooked cheese for each person, often accompanied by a serving of fish.[15] On fast days, the more frugal *pitantia* was served irrespective of the day of the week; on feast days, the *generale* or both portions at once.[16] Raw vegetables replaced the cheese and eggs of these dishes during Lent, but the consumption of fish was allowed throughout the fast.[17] In addition, important occasions earned the monks a celebratory repast. When the abbot returned from a journey, they enjoyed a *generale* of fish with spiced wine.[18] At his discretion, they could also receive wine flavored with wormwood and honey, especially when the weather was warm, though this practice changed in the twelfth century when Peter the Venerable forbade the use of honeyed or spiced wine except on Holy Thursday.[19] Similarly, on Sundays in the summer months the abbot allowed the children in the abbey a drink of milk in the evening, an indulgence warranted by the length of the day and the extent of their fast.[20]

The procurement of food for a large monastic community like Cluny required detailed conversations among high-ranking officials and multiple transactions with people outside of the abbey walls and thus did not involve the use of sign language. The purchase and harvest of fish is illustrative of this point. The cellarer was responsible for obtaining a fresh supply of fish, a standard component of the *generale* that was also in high demand on feast days and during Lent, when animal products like eggs and cheese were forbidden. He had an assistant who purchased the catch of local fishermen and oversaw the harvest of fish from rivers and ponds where the abbey had fishing rights.[21] The monks of Cluny primarily ate indigenous river fish, like salmon, pike and trout, as well as eel and lamprey.[22] They also consumed cuttlefish or squid. These marine creatures were probably salted at their point of harvest on the Mediterranean or Atlantic coast and preserved for shipment to the

---

[15] Ulrich 2.35 and 3.18, cols. 728ab and 761a.
[16] Bernard 1.6, pp. 147–148.   [17] Bernard 2.13, p. 302.
[18] Bernard 1.1, p. 138.   [19] Ulrich 1.30, col. 677a; and *Statuta* 11, p. 50.
[20] Bernard 1.27, p. 207.   [21] Bernard 1.6, pp. 147–150.
[22] Cluny, nos. 12 (*salmo vel sturio*), 13 (*lucius*), 14 (*truta*), 10 (*anguilla*) and 11 (*lampreda*), ed. Jarecki, *Signa Loquendi*, pp. 123–124.

interior of Burgundy.[23] The cellarer's assistant had permission to leave the abbey after Vespers to conduct his business with the fishermen.[24] It is unlikely that monastic signs played any role in these transactions. The responsibilities of the cellarer's assistant would have absolved him from the rule of silence when he conducted business on behalf of the community. Duties of this kind were assigned to experienced monks with a reputation for good judgment, who could be trusted not to abuse the freedom from discipline that accompanied their increased responsibility.[25] Moreover, it is unreasonable to assume that local fishmongers had any knowledge of the silent language of the Cluniacs.

Signs for sustenance played a much more evident role in the preparation of food than they did in its procurement. Monastic signs were a practical necessity in the abbey kitchens, where a team of monks prepared and orchestrated the communal meals in silence. Six of the brethren served in the kitchens every week on a rotating basis.[26] Some of them cooked vegetables and fish; others arranged food on trays; others carried the trays into the refectory.[27] These monks would have relied exclusively on signs for specific food items and utensils to perform their duties because spoken words were expressly forbidden at all times during the preparation of food. The kitchen crew worked under close supervision in a busy environment, so there was little fear that they would use sign language to express anything other than the concerns of their labors.

In contrast to the kitchens, the strict regulation of meal times and food portions minimized the need for sign use in the refectory, where the entire community gathered for meals. No one was allowed to eat outside of the established meal times or after Compline.[28] Each monk received the same portion of vegetables and fish and the same amount of bread and

---

[23] Cluny, no. 9 (*sepiae*), ed. Jarecki, *Signa Loquendi*, p. 122. Squid are seldom mentioned in early medieval sources, but the available evidence indicates that they were harvested in the Adriatic Sea and the Atlantic Ocean. On squid-fishers in the Adriatic, see Paulo Squatriti, *Water and Society in Early Medieval Italy, AD 400–1000* (Cambridge, 1998), p. 105, n. 16. In 1040, Geoffrey of Vendôme and his wife Agnes founded the abbey of La Trinité and endowed it with revenues including half of their share of the tax from squid harvested in the region of Saintonge on the Atlantic shore. See *Privilegium Gosfredi comitis et Agnetis comitissae* (31 May 1040), ed. Charles Métais, in *Cartulaire de l'abbaye cardinale de la Trinité de Vendôme*, 5 vols. (Paris, 1893–1904), vol. I, pp. 55–60 (no. 35), at p. 58. In her study of La Trinité, Penelope Johnson implied that the squid tax represented "a valuable source of income for the abbey" owing to the importance of squid in the production of ink, but she provided no evidence of this economy to support her statement. See Johnson, *Prayer, Patronage, and Power: The Abbey of La Trinité, Vendôme, 1032–1187* (New York and London, 1981), p. 20.

[24] Bernard 1.6, pp. 149–150.

[25] See, for example, *RB* 31.1–2 and *RB* 66.1–2 on the requisite character of the cellarer and the porter, respectively.

[26] Bernard 1.46, p. 236.   [27] Bernard 1.46, p. 238.

[28] Bernard 1.11, p. 156. Some allowance was made for the sick (Bernard 1.74, no. 62, p. 278).

wine. The prior kept a strict watch over the food portions and inspected the servings of fish to ensure that the cooks had divided them fairly among the brethren.[29] These mechanisms of control limited the need for sign use in the refectory. The strict regulation of food and drink meant that monks had no choice regarding the content or portions of their meals. This curbed opportunities for the misuse of sign language when the monks gathered to eat. Offences involving speech were undoubtedly rare when the entire community gathered for meals in the silence of the refectory, but there was some concern about the excessive use of sign language at the table. A monastic customary from the thirteenth century instructed officials explicitly to report monks observed making unnecessary signs while they ate.[30] Signs for condiments were an exception to this rule. The customary of Bernard allowed for servers to roam the refectory during meal times with trays of mustard seed and vinegar.[31] Monks may have used the signs for these food items to attract the attention of the servers and to indicate their choice of condiment.[32]

SIGNS FOR APPAREL

Sign language was also an important tool for maintaining personal discipline, particularly in the church and the dormitory, where rules of comportment applied both to the monks' bodies and to the clothing that covered them. The monastic official known as the chamberlain supplied the novices with their personal apparel. The customaries of Bernard and Ulrich provided inventories of the clothing, bedding and tools granted to each individual, along with an indication of their number and quality. According to these inventories, each monk received two frocks and two cowls made from inexpensive cloth, two woollen tunics, two pairs of trousers, two pairs of shoes, one pair of night shoes with felt to be worn in winter, one pair of night shoes without felt for summer nights, two pairs of boots, three garments (two made from hide and one from fur), one fur cap, five pairs of ankle straps, one wooden clasp (with which they fastened their pants), and one hide belt for their tunics, on which they carried a knife in a sheath, a wooden comb in a sheath and a sewing kit (needle and thread) in a small case. For their beds, they also received a

[29] Bernard 1.6, p. 148.
[30] *Consuetudines Affligenienses* 29: "Quamdiu autem comeditur, intente debent considerare circatores si qui dissoluti sint vel signa superflua faciant." ed. Robert J. Sullivan, *CCM* VI (Siegburg, 1975), p. 149.
[31] Bernard 1.11, p. 156.
[32] Cluny, nos. 30 (*sinapis*) and 31 (*acetum*), ed. Jarecki, *Signa Loquendi*, pp. 126–127.

pillow, an inexpensive blanket made from lamb, cat, polecat or rabbit, a heavy coat and a sheet.[33]

The novices learned signs for the majority of the items on the chamberlain's inventory when they entered the abbey.[34] This suggests that the signs for apparel in the Cluniac sign lexicon reflected the novices' initial allotment of clothing, bedding and tools. The sign for cowl was an exception.[35] Novices did not receive cowls until their formal consecration as monks.[36] Even so, it was an important sign for them to learn, because it was a common article of clothing and carried the added significance of visually distinguishing the professed monks from the novices. Among the signs for personal apparel, the novices also learned signs for writing tablet and stylus.[37] These items did not appear on the chamberlain's inventory because they were not supplied to monks on an individual basis. Their inclusion reflects the fact that writing and copying were important for all novices to learn.[38] Monks proficient in these skills applied them at the order of the cantor, the official who instructed the brethren in the production of manuscripts, charters, letters and other documents relevant to the needs of the monastic community.[39]

The chamberlain and his assistant supplied the monks with clothing and tools, but this interaction rarely involved the use of signs for apparel. The customary of Bernard instructed individuals to make requests for new items of clothing in the cloister at a time when speaking was permitted.[40] In addition, the chamberlain distributed new articles of clothing at certain times of the year, thus eliminating the need for direct communication. The brethren received a new frock and cowl every year at Christmas and a new hide garment every third year on the feast day of St. Michael. The chamberlain left the new

---

[33] Bernard 1.5, p. 146; and Ulrich 3.11, col. 752bd.

[34] Cluny, nos. 36–57, ed. Jarecki, *Signa Loquendi*, pp. 127–131. All but three items from the sign lexicon were present on the chamberlain's inventory. The absent items were sleeves, writing tablet and stylus (Cluny, nos. 40 and 56–57), all of which are discussed below.

[35] Cluny, no. 39 (*cuculla*), ed. Jarecki, *Signa Loquendi*, p. 128.

[36] On the consecration ceremony at Cluny, see Giles Constable, "Entrance to Cluny in the Eleventh and Twelfth Centuries According to the Cluniac Customaries and Statutes," in *Mediaevalia Christiana, XIe–XIIIe siècles: Hommages à Raymonde Foreville*, ed. Coloman Etienne Viola (Paris, 1989), pp. 335–354; repr. in Giles Constable, *Cluny from the Tenth to the Twelfth Centuries: Further Studies* (Aldershot, 2000), no. III.

[37] Cluny, nos. 56 (*tabulae*) and 57 (*graphium*), ed. Jarecki, *Signa Loquendi*, p. 131.

[38] On writing as a component of the training of novices, see Bernard 1.15, p. 166.

[39] On the office of the cantor (*armarius*) and his responsibility for book production, see Bernard 1.14, p. 161. Further on the duties of this official, see Margot Fassler, "The Office of the Cantor in Early Western Monastic Rules and Customaries: A Preliminary Investigation," *Early Music History* 5 (1985): 29–51.

[40] Bernard 1.5, p. 146; and Ulrich 3.11, cols. 752d–753a.

clothes on their beds during meal times.[41] Moreover, a system was in place for the monks to have their tunics and trousers repaired without recourse to words or signs. They left worn-out or damaged clothes at a designated place in the abbey, where the chamberlain's assistant collected them and delivered them to the resident tailors. The monks had their names sewn onto their clothes to prevent the inevitable confusion when their items returned from the tailors.[42] This measure was not always successful, however. In the twelfth century, Peter the Venerable assigned two custodians to the dormitory to avert quarrels resulting from the loss or confusion of clothing.[43]

The Cluniac signs for apparel were also an important medium of instruction and reprimand in the silence of the church. During the celebration of the divine office, expectations of discipline extended beyond the movements of the body to the clothing that covered it. The customary of Bernard drew attention to the proper manipulation of the frock and its wide sleeves several times in its discussion of personal comportment in the church.[44] The monastic habit was no doubt an unwieldy set of unfamiliar garments for most novices. During their indoctrination, the monks-in-training learned to draw the frock back to their elbows and knees to prevent it from hanging over their feet and touching the ground as they bowed in prayer. They were also instructed to gather up the folds of their sleeves with their hands during the regular hours and collect them onto their laps as they sat in the choir. The presence of a sign for sleeves in the Cluniac sign lexicon enforces the inference that the signs for apparel had a disciplinary function.[45] Sleeves were a part of the frock and not a separate article of clothing. The customary of Bernard mentioned them only in the context of comportment during the liturgy. Employing the sign for sleeves, the master of novices could teach and correct his charges as he guided them through ritual activities in the church, where speaking was forbidden.

Signs for clothing had a comparable function in the dormitory. With their new clothes, the novices donned a heightened sense of self-consciousness about their bodies. They slept in a communal dormitory, where lanterns burned throughout the night to dissuade suspicious activities.[46] There they learned to dress and undress in such a way that

---

[41] Bernard 1.5 and 2.31, pp. 146 and 351.   [42] Bernard 1.5, pp. 146–147; and Ulrich 3.11, col. 753a.
[43] *Statuta* 69, pp. 99–100.   [44] For what follows, see Bernard 1.18, p. 174.
[45] Cluny, no. 40 (*manicae*), ed. Jarecki, *Signa Loquendi*, p. 128.
[46] On the fear of sexual misconduct and strategies for its deterrence in Cluniac abbeys, see Scott G. Bruce, "Lurking with Spiritual Intent: A Note on the Origin and Functions of the Monastic Roundsman (*Circator*)," *Revue bénédictine* 109 (1999): 75–89, esp. p. 86; and Christopher A. Jones, "Monastic Identity and Sodomitic Danger in the *Occupatio* by Odo of Cluny," *Speculum* 82 (2007): 1–53.

their bodies remained hidden from their fellow monks. The customary of Bernard instructed all monks to don their cowls in bed before drawing back the blanket when they rose for the Night office.[47] Likewise, upon returning to bed, to keep their cowls on until they drew the blanket up past their elbows. Even in the summer heat, it was forbidden for them to expose more than their feet, arms and head as they slept.[48] Bernard also warned monks not to rely on the cowl alone to conceal their nakedness when they changed their clothes in the dormitory, advising that a frock or a tunic was also necessary to shield them sufficiently from the eyes of others.[49] These precautions applied to the novices as well. The scrutiny of their master followed their actions in the dormitory. With signs for apparel, he could instruct and admonish them to guard their modesty in the presence of their brethren.

SIGNS FOR THE DIVINE OFFICE

Sign language also facilitated the orchestration of the rituals central to the celebration of the divine office. In the eleventh century, the liturgy was the primary focus of monastic communities like Cluny.[50] The recitation of the psalter and the intonation of lessons from the Bible and the works of the church fathers directed the attention of the monks to God. The particulars of the services varied considerably from house to house and changed with the liturgical significance of the day and the season. Consequently, it has proven very difficult for historians to reconstruct a timetable that represents with accuracy the liturgical obligations of individual monks. Modern reconstructions of monastic timetables are potentially misleading in any case, because it is unreasonable to assume that every monk was obliged to take part in all of the services.[51] The Cluniacs were renowned for their intense commitment to the divine office, which they expressed in part by the staggering length of their services, especially during the penitential seasons. Throughout Lent, they sang over 150 psalms a day, invoking the *Rule of Benedict* to defend the severity of

---

[47] Bernard 1.18, p. 174.   [48] Bernard 1.18, p. 175.   [49] *Ibid.*

[50] For an invaluable overview of medieval liturgical practices, see David Hiley, *Western Plainchant: A Handbook* (Oxford, 1993). On the elaboration of liturgical customs in this period, see Kassius Hallinger, "Überlieferung und Steigerung im Mönchtum des 8. bis 12. Jahrhunderts," in *Eulogia: Miscellanea Liturgica in onore di P. Burckhard Neunheuser O.S.B.*, Studia Anselmiana 68 (Rome, 1979), pp. 125–187.

[51] On this point, see Jean Leclercq, "Prayer at Cluny," *Journal of the American Academy of Religion* 51 (1983): 651–665, at pp. 651–657.

this practice.[52] Ulrich of Zell remembered hearing the entire book of Isaiah read over six nights during Advent and the Epistle to the Romans read over two nights at another time.[53] The brethren took part according to their singing ability and their knowledge of the complex variations of liturgical chants.[54] The intricacies of these services were notoriously difficult to learn, unless one had grown up in the abbey.[55] Perhaps for this reason, monastic sign language distinguished between monks who had entered the abbey as adults and those who had been raised there from childhood.[56] Adult novices lacked the familiarity or expertise necessary to play more than a minor role in the divine office. They were forbidden from beginning antiphons, singing the response and intoning the lesson for the Night office.[57] Although the novices were not full participants in the services, it was important for them to learn the signs for every important aspect of the liturgy because, even as professed monks, they would have to rely on nonverbal cues from the precentor to guide them through the ceremonies.

The Cluniacs took the utmost care to orchestrate their long ceremonies without recourse to speech. Using hand signs, the precentor directed individual and communal participation in the divine office and the liturgy of the mass. Signs for liturgical books announced the need for particular texts. The most experienced monks could recite common services from memory, but they referred to books for the words of difficult or seldom used antiphons and hymns.[58] The novices learned to recognize hand signs for common choir books, like antiphonaries, hymnals and psalters as well as those for texts read during the mass, like missals, the Gospels and the Epistles.[59] The Cluniac sign lexicon also included a sign for angel, as well as signs for saintly persons like apostle, martyr, confessor and holy

[52] Ulrich 1.3, cols. 646b–647b, esp. 646c: "Invenitur autem in regula quod sanctus Benedictus praecipit ut in Quadragesimali quid addatur ad pensum solitae servitutis; quod nec dissimulatur a nobis." See *RB* 49.5–7: "Ergo his diebus augeamus nobis aliquid solito pensu seruitutis nostrae, orationes peculiares, ciborum et potus abstinentiam."

[53] Ulrich 1.1, cols. 644d and 645a.

[54] *RB* 47.3; and Bernard 1.14, p. 161. See generally Joseph Dyer, "Monastic Psalmody of the Middle Ages," *Revue bénédictine* 99 (1989): 41–73.

[55] Ulrich, col. 644a.

[56] Cluny, nos. 80 (*monachus*) and 83 (*monachus qui nutritus est in monasterio*), ed. Jarecki, *Signa Loquendi*, p. 136. For a discussion of the functional distinctions between child oblates and adult novices in early medieval abbeys, see Mayke de Jong, *In Samuel's Image: Child Oblation in the Early Medieval West* (Leiden, 1996), pp. 126–155. On the participation of children in the divine office at Cluny and elsewhere, see Susan Boynton, "The Liturgical Role of Children in Monastic Customaries from the Central Middle Ages," *Studia Liturgica* 28 (1998): 194–209.

[57] Bernard 1.15, p. 165.   [58] Bernard 1.19, p. 178.

[59] Cluny, nos. 65 (*liber missalis*), 66 (*textus evangelii*), 67 (*liber epistolaris*), 69 (*antiphonarium*), 71 (*ymnarium*) and 72 (*psalterium*), ed. Jarecki, *Signa Loquendi*, pp. 133–134.

virgin.[60] The close association of these signs with others for liturgical books and feast day suggests that they had some function related to the commemoration of the saints. The cantor may have employed them to cue the reader to begin the proper text for the Night office. An entry in a twelfth-century library catalogue from Cluny lends weight to this inference, for it described a compilation of lessons for the Night office that explicitly included sections on martyrs, confessors and virgins.[61]

The use of signs for books extended beyond the precincts of the church. The authority of the *Rule of Benedict* as a legislative document could account for its place in the Cluniac sign lexicon among signs for books used in the divine office, but it had no liturgical function.[62] The abbot or the prior may have employed this sign in the daily chapter meeting to signal the monk who read a chapter of the *Rule* to the assembled community. The presence of a sign for a secular text suggests that signs for books also came into play in the abbey library. The rhetoric of disdain for ancient authors was common in monastic sources from this period and implicit in the Cluniac sign for a book composed by a pagan author:

For the sign of a secular book that some pagan composed, add to the aforesaid general sign for book that you touch your ear with your finger, just as a dog usually does when scratching with his foot, because a person without faith deserves to be compared with such an animal.[63]

Cluniac monks were among the most vociferous of those who expressed their disdain for classical authors. Odo of Cluny allegedly dreamed that Virgil handed him a vase full of serpents that represented the dangers of his poetry.[64] Likewise, Ralph Glaber reported that demons appeared to a young man in the guises of Virgil, Horace and Juvenal and compelled him to preach heretical doctrines.[65] Despite this sentiment, the library at Cluny preserved dozens of volumes of Roman history and poetry, including

[60] Cluny, nos. 74 (*angelus*), 75 (*apostolus*), 76 (*martyr*), 77 (*confessor*) and 78 (*sacra virgo*), ed. Jarecki, *Signa Loquendi*, p. 135.
[61] Léopold Delisle, *Inventaire des manuscrits de la Bibliothèque nationale: Fonds de Cluni* (Paris, 1884), p. 338 (no. 12). This redaction of the library catalogue was probably compiled during the abbacy of Hugh III (1158–1161). On its organization and contents, see Veronika von Büren, "Le grand catalogue de la Bibliothèque de Cluny," in *Le gouvernement d'Hugues de Semur à Cluny: Actes du Colloque scientifique international (Cluny, septembre 1988)* (Mâcon, 1990), pp. 245–263, who argues that it was originally composed under Abbot Hugh the Great (1049–1109).
[62] Cluny, no. 70 (*regula*), ed. Jarecki, *Signa Loquendi*, p. 134.
[63] Cluny, no. 73: "Pro signo libri secularis, quem aliquis paganus conposuit, premisso generali signo libri adde, ut aurem cum digito tangas, sicut canis cum pede pruriens solet, quia nec inmerito infidelis tali animanti conparatur." ed. Jarecki, *Signa Loquendi*, p. 134.
[64] John of Salerno, *Vita Odonis* 1.12, PL CXXXIII, col. 49a.
[65] Rodulphus Glaber, *Historiarum libri quinque* 2.23, ed. John France, in *Rodulphus Glaber: The Five Books of Histories and the Life of St. William* (Oxford, 1989), p. 92.

works of Virgil, Horace, Terence, Pliny, Sallust and Cicero.[66] Some of these works were among the books distributed to the monks during the Lenten season for personal reading, a custom that did not involve the use of sign language. In 1040, for example, a monk of Cluny named Peter borrowed a copy of Livy's *Roman History* in this manner.[67] The customaries of Bernard and Ulrich made no reference to sign use in the library, but a late eleventh-century customary from Hirsau warned its readers against speaking in the chamber where they stored their books unless there was an urgent concern that they could not express with signs.[68] This warning clearly implied that sign language was the accepted means of communication in the Hirsau library. Hirsau's dependency on Cluniac customs suggests that this may have been the case at Cluny as well.[69]

The customaries of Bernard and Ulrich passed over the mundane applications of monastic signs for food, clothing and the divine office with little comment, but they described in considerable detail the role of this custom in the act of confession. A new concern with sin and its absolution through confession confronted novices as soon as they entered the monastic community. In the tenth and eleventh centuries, an increasing number of Cluniac monks became ordained priests.[70] As Dominique Iogna-Prat has noted, their "gradual access to the priesthood was linked in large part to the pastoral funerary role entrusted to them and to the fact that the service of the dead was in the first instance eucharistic."[71] The provision of pastoral care for the secular world and its inhabitants reflected an outward-facing aspect of Cluniac ecclesiology that achieved its fullest expression in the twelfth century under Abbot Peter the Venerable.[72] This development stood in marked contrast, though not in direct contradiction, to the tight regulations on oral communication observed within the walls of the abbey itself.

---

[66] See Delisle, *Inventaire des manuscrits de la Bibliothèque nationale*, Appendix 1, pp. 337–373, *passim*; and von Büren, "Le grand catalogue de la Bibliothèque de Cluny," pp. 245–263. For a discussion of these contradictory tendencies in medieval monastic thought, see Jean Leclercq, *The Love of Learning and the Desire for God: A Study of Monastic Culture*, trans. Catharine Misrahi (New York, 1961), pp. 112–143.

[67] *Liber tramitis aevi Odilonis abbatis* 2.190, ed. Peter Dinter, *CCM* X (Siegburg, 1980), p. 264. Further on this custom, see Karl Christ, "In Caput Quadragesimae," *Zentralblatt für Bibliothekswesen* 60 (1943): 33–59.

[68] William 2.25, col. 1077cd.

[69] On the relationship between Hirsau and Cluny, see Chapter 4, pp. 118–120, below.

[70] The essential works on this topic remain Otto Nussbaum, *Kloster, Priestermönch und Privatmesse: Ihr Verhältnis im Westen von den Anfängen bis zum hohen Mittelalter* (Bonn, 1961); and Angelus Häussling, *Mönchskonvent und Eucharistiefeier: Eine Studie über die Messe in der abendländischen Klosterliturgie des frühen Mittelalters und zur Geschichte der Messhäufigkeit* (Münster, 1973).

[71] Dominique Iogna-Prat, *Order and Exclusion: Cluny and Christendom Face Heresy, Judaism, and Islam (1000–1150)*, trans. Graham Robert Edwards (Ithaca and London, 2002), pp. 68–75 (quotation at p. 70).

[72] *Ibid.* pp. 84–95.

Frequent confession was essential for monk-priests because absolution from sin was a prerequisite for the celebration of private masses, which took place on a daily basis in most abbeys in this period.[73] Since laymen rarely received communion and were not required to confess their sins with nearly the same frequency as monks, it was vitally important for novices to learn how to initiate the ritual of confession in the silence of the church.[74] At Cluny, the brethren used sign language to signal their need for confession and absolution. According to the customary of Bernard:

> If he [the novice] needs to go to confession for some transgression, he approaches the priest who is most preferable to him. Standing before him, he draws his right hand from his sleeve and places it upon his chest, because this is the sign for confession.[75]

Once he had signaled his intention, the novice followed the priest into the chapter room where he prostrated himself on the floor and asked for forgiveness for his sins.[76] The sign for confession warranted such a detailed treatment in the customary of Bernard because, unlike other signs in the Cluniac lexicon, it was directly relevant to the spiritual well-being of the novice and played a pivotal role in his transition from layman to monk.

SIGN LANGUAGE AND COMMUNITY

Monastic sign language was a useful tool for discrete acts of unsupervised communication at eleventh-century Cluny, but it also played an important role in the formation and expression of the identity of the cloistered

---

[73] On the history of the private mass in the early Middle Ages, see Arnold Angenendt, "Missa specialis: Zugleich ein Beitrag zur Entstehung der Privatmessen," *Frühmittelalterliche Studien* 17 (1983): 153–221.

[74] The decrees of the Fourth Lateran Council (1215) required all Christians to confess their sins and take communion at least once a year (usually at Easter), but lay participation in these activities in the early medieval period was probably much less frequent. On the practice of confession in this period, see Joseph Avril, "Remarques sur un aspect de la vie religieuse paroissiale: La pratique de la confession et de la communion du Xe au XIVe siècle," in *L'encadrement religieux des fidèles au moyen âge et jusqu'au Concile de Trente: Actes du 109e Congrès national des société savantes (Dijon, 1984)* (Paris, 1985), pp. 345–363; Jean Chélini, *L'aube du moyen âge: Naissance de la chrétienté occidentale* (Paris, 1991), pp. 410–424; Alexander Murray, "Confession Before 1215," *Transactions of the Royal Historical Society*, 6th series, 3 (1993): 51–81; and Rob Meens, "The Frequency and Nature of Early Medieval Penance," in *Handling Sin: Confession in the Middle Ages*, ed. Peter Biller and A. J. Minnis, York Studies in Medieval Theology II (Woodbridge, 1998), pp. 35–63.

[75] Bernard 1.18, p. 175: "Si opus habet ad confessionem pro aliquo excessu venire, accedit ad sacerdotem ad quem potissimum voluerit, et stans ante eum dextram de manica abstractam ponit super pectus, quod est signum confessionis." Cf. Cluny, no. 94: "Pro signo infirmarii, qui obsequitur infirmis, pone manum contra pectus, quod significat infirmitatem, quamvis non semper, quia et confessionem significat." ed. Jarecki, *Signa Loquendi*, p. 138.

[76] Bernard 1.18, p. 175.

community as a whole. Sharing a prescribed repertoire of hand signs as their principal method of information exchange, the brethren of Cluny comprised a "speech community," defined by modern sociolinguists as a group of people "all of whose members share at least a single speech variety and the norms for its appropriate use."[77] Although they had already distinguished themselves from lay society by emulating the character of chaste and reverential angels, the Cluniacs set themselves apart even further by adopting an unspoken code of manual signs. The distinctiveness and exclusiveness of this silent language lent their collective enterprise a more cohesive sense of purpose. There were internal benefits to the use of this custom as well. Like many large abbeys in this period, Cluny was a heterogeneous community that attracted monks from across Europe. While many of these individuals adapted to life in the abbey without difficulty, there is a strong likelihood that some of them would have felt a pronounced sense of linguistic dislocation, either because their pronunciation of Latin differed from that of the resident monks or because they spoke vernacular dialects alien to the Romance-speaking inhabitants of Burgundy. Cluniac legislators recognized the benefit of imposing a silent language of signs as a common idiom for speakers who may have found it increasingly difficult to communicate in their native tongues. The use of monastic sign language to the exclusion of oral means of communication was an effective way of assuring proper decorum during rituals and fostering a sense of communal identity among individuals from different and perhaps mutually incomprehensible linguistic backgrounds.

At eleventh-century Cluny and elsewhere, the Latin language was the dominant medium of oral expression in every aspect of monastic life from the solemn choruses of liturgical celebration to the discrete confessions of individuals burdened with sin. It would be misleading to assert, however, that spoken Latin enjoyed the universal comprehension among monks that historians have long presumed for the early medieval period.[78] Carolingian reformers of the ninth century embarked on the project to

---

[77] Joshua Fishman, *Sociolinguistics: A Brief Introduction* (Rowley, MA, 1970), p. 28. In thinking about the problem of group cohesion and language diversity at Cluny, I have received valuable orientation from Peter Burke, *Languages and Communities in Early Modern Europe* (Cambridge, 2004).

[78] For what follows, see Roger Wright, *Late Latin and Early Romance in Spain and Carolingian France* (Liverpool, 1982); Rosamond McKitterick, *The Carolingians and the Written Word* (Cambridge, 1989), pp. 1–22; and *Latin and the Romance Languages in the Early Middle Ages*, ed. Roger Wright (University Park, PA, 1991), particularly the historical essays by Van Uytfanghe, "The Consciousness of a Linguistic Dichotomy," McKitterick, "Latin and Romance: A Historian's Perspective," Heene, "*Audire, legere, vulgo*: An Attempt to Define Public Use and Comprehensibility of Carolingian Hagiography" and Banniard, "Rhabanus Maurus and the Vernacular Languages" (pp. 114–174).

standardize the morphology and pronunciation of the Latin language on the model of the writings of the church fathers. By doing so, they effectively disenfranchised most of their contemporaries whose regional dialects of Latin sounded quite different from the ideal sought by the schoolmen fostering the reform. As a result, in the post-Carolingian period the Latin taught and used in monastic schools was generally an affected and anachronistic idiom that had little relation to the lived Latin and proto-Romance vernaculars spoken in the towns and villages of the European countryside. The practical value of a silent language of signs becomes clear in this context. In an institution like Cluny that measured human behavior against an ideal of angelic conduct, especially during the divine office and other ceremonial activities, a mutual reliance on monastic sign language as a means of communication prevented the momentary confusion and resultant loss of decorum that could have easily resulted from misunderstanding instructions in Latin spoken by individuals with widely differing pronunciations. Unimpaired by the centuries of linguistic development that made spoken Latin an unreliable medium of communication in a monastic setting that mingled experts and novices, the silent language of the Cluniacs provided them with a shared and homogeneous conduit of information that was resistant to the troubling ambiguities of the spoken word.

Although sources for the perception of language and its role in the formation of personal identity are scarce from the decades around 1100, there can be little doubt that some monks understood themselves in terms of the vernacular speech community to which they belonged. Take the example of Orderic Vitalis, a monastic chronicler who flourished in the early twelfth century.[79] Born in 1075 to an English mother and a Norman father near Atcham, a village in the newly conquered Marcher region around Shrewsbury, young Orderic grew up speaking the English dialect of his mother's family. He may have also learned some Latin from a local priest named Siward, who looked after the boy's early education. At the age of ten, however, Orderic's father sent him as an oblate to the Norman abbey of St. Evroult. Over half a century later, the chronicler vividly recounted crossing the physical and linguistic boundary separating England and Normandy in biblical terms: "And so, a boy of ten, I crossed the English Channel and came into Normandy as an exile, unknown to all, knowing no one. Like Joseph in Egypt, I heard a language which I did not

---

[79] Orderic Vitalis, *Historia ecclesiastica*, ed. Marjorie Chibnall, in *The Ecclesiastical History of Orderic Vitalis*, 6 vols. (Oxford, 1969–1980); and Marjorie Chibnall, *The World of Orderic Vitalis* (Oxford, 1984).

understand."[80] Language was an important cultural marker in the monastic community at St. Evroult, so much so that the Norman monks who adopted Orderic insisted on changing his name to Vitalis, the saint whose feast was being celebrated on the day of his arrival at the abbey. As the chronicler later explained, his English name, Ordric, which he Latinized as Ordricus, sounded too harsh to Norman ears.[81] The renaming of the boy did little, however, to diminish his sense of himself as an Englishman. Even though he had lived for decades at St. Evroult in Normandy, the monk presented himself in his chronicle as Orderic of England (*Ordricus angligena*).[82] This identity, forged in childhood and intimately bound to the language of his English mother, endured both his move to northern France and his life-long immersion in a foreign tongue.

While Orderic's chronicle is unparalleled for the insight that it offers into the role of language in shaping the identity of an individual monk, his personal story of relocation and reorientation was not unique in this period. Several individuals whose first language was a German vernacular underwent a similar process of linguistic enculturation at eleventh-century Cluny, where Latin and Gallo-Romance dialects were the most common spoken languages. The Rhineland is generally considered to have been the boundary separating indigenous Romance-speakers and German-speakers in the early Middle Ages.[83] From the eighth century onwards, Old High German (in its various dialectical guises) emerged as an important medium of oral exchange and written knowledge throughout the East Frankish realms.[84] Manuscripts of Latin texts with Old High German glosses number well into the hundreds in the late Carolingian period, a striking testimony to the effort made by German monks to maintain their grasp of Latin.[85] The gulf separating the oral cultures of German and Romance vernaculars is illustrated by the so-called *Paris*

---

[80] Orderic Vitalis, *Historia ecclesiastica* 13.45: "Decennis itaque Britannicum mare transfretaui, exul in Normanniam ueni, cunctis ignotus neminem cognoui. Linguam ut Ioseph in Ægipto quam non noueram audiui." ed. and trans. Chibnall, vol. VI, pp. 554–555.

[81] *Ibid.*: "Nomen quoque Vitalis pro anglico uocamine quod Normannis absonum censebatur michi impositum est, quod ab uno sodalium sancti Mauricii martiris cuius tunc martirium celebrabatur mutuatum est." ed. Chibnall, vol. VI, p. 554.

[82] *Ibid.* 5.1, ed. Chibnall, vol. III, p. 6; and Chibnall, *The World of Orderic Vitalis*, p. 3.

[83] A. Joris, "On the Edge of Two Worlds in the Heart of the New Empire: The Romance Regions of Northern Gaul during the Merovingian Period," *Studies in Mediaeval and Renaissance History* 3 (1966): 1–52; and McKitterick, *The Carolingians and the Written Word*, p. 7 and map 1 (p. 6).

[84] Dennis Green, *Medieval Listening and Reading: The Primary Reception of German Literature 800–1300* (Cambridge, 1994); and Cyril Edwards, "German Vernacular Literature: A Survey," in *Carolingian Culture: Emulation and Innovation*, ed. Rosamond McKitterick (Cambridge, 1994), pp. 141–170.

[85] On Old High German glosses and glossaries from the early Middle Ages, see J. Knight Bostock, *A Handbook on Old High German Literature*, 2nd edn (Oxford, 1976), pp. 90–107, who described their quantity as "immense" (p. 90).

Conversations, a late ninth-century phrase-book written to help a Romance-speaking warrior learn simple sentences in Old High German.[86] The work provided German words and phrases for various situations (spelled out as they would be pronounced by a Romance-speaker) with corresponding Latin translations:

> Gueliche land cumen ger? De qua patria? [Which land do you come from?]
> Gimer min ros. Da mihi meum equum. [Give me my horse.]
> Guaz queten ger, erra? Quid dicitis vos? [What are you saying?][87]

The distinction between Old High German and Latin is clear from these model sentences. For German-speaking monks who had recently arrived in Burgundy, the Cluniac community would have resounded with a cacophony of unfamiliar accents and outlandish idioms.

During the late eleventh century, many Germans from Lotharingia, Bavaria and the Black Forest region crossed the Rhine into Burgundy to make Cluny their home.[88] Some came by order of their superiors to learn the customs of the community firsthand; others came by choice in their old age to await death and find burial at the abbey.[89] Those among them who entered the monastic life as adults probably had little knowledge of Latin as a spoken idiom. Due to the long and arduous course of study required to learn Latin, the proficiency of late entrants to the monastic life was often poor. Child oblates like Ulrich, the German author of one of the two great Cluniac customaries compiled in this period, and literate elites who took monastic vows as adults were usually the only ones who achieved mastery of the language.[90] This is apparent from an anecdote about three German monks from aristocratic backgrounds told in the mid-eleventh century by Ekkehard IV of St. Gall.[91] With the permission

---

[86] *Gespräche aus Paris*, ed. W. Braune, in *Althochdeutsches Lesebuch*, 17th edn (Tübingen, 1994), pp. 9–11 (V.2). Further on this text, see J. A. Huisman, "Die Pariser Gespräche," *Rheinischer Vierteljahrsblätter* 33 (1969): 272–296; Bostock, *Handbook on Old High German Literature*, pp. 101–103; Edwards, "German Vernacular Literature," p. 143; and Paul Kershaw, "Laughter After Babel's Fall: Misunderstanding and Miscommunication in the Ninth-Century West," in *Humour, History and Politics in Late Antiquity and the Early Middle Ages*, ed. Guy Halsall (Cambridge, 2002), pp. 179–202, at pp. 200–201.

[87] *Gespräche aus Paris* nos. 20, 51 and 64; ed. Braune, pp. 9–10.

[88] For a list of known individuals, see Joachim Wollasch, "Cluny und Deutschland," *Studien und Mitteilungen zur Geschichte des Benediktinerordens und seine Zweige* 103 (1992): 7–32, at pp. 22–23.

[89] Further on the traffic in personnel between Hirsau, Regensburg and Cluny in this period, see Chapter 4, pp. 118–119, below.

[90] On the duties assigned to child oblates, including the memorization of Latin chants and readings and the preparation of the *brevis* (the liturgical assignments for individual monks), see Boynton, "The Liturgical Role of Children."

[91] Ekkehard, *Casus sancti Galli* 35–36, ed. Hans F. Haefele, in *St. Galler Klostergeschichten* (Darmstadt, 1980), pp. 80–84. For further discussion of this episode, see de Jong, *In Samuel's Image*, pp. 126–132.

of their superior, these learned monks gathered at night in the scriptorium to talk about the Bible. Their language of conversation was an Old German vernacular. When they noticed, however, that a nosy German-speaking monk named Sindolf was eavesdropping on their conversation at a window, they immediately switched to speaking Latin "which Sindolf did not understand at all" (*qui nihil intellegeret*). Their intentions thus veiled by their fellow monk's ignorance, the three friends success-fully conspired to seize the meddler and gave him a sound beating for his presumptuous behavior.

Sindolf was not alone in his difficulties with Latin. Although the number of monolingual German-speakers at Cluny was probably never very large, especially as the community swelled into the hundreds toward the end of the century, the presence of this foreign element was prominent enough to warrant the inclusion of two German synonyms for Latin words in the Cluniac sign lexicon. The first synonym appeared among the signs for the divine office, calling attention to a difference in liturgical terminology. The kind of long melodies that the brethren of Cluny referred to as the prose (*prosa*), Germans called the sequence (*sequentia*).[92] The inclusion of this synonym solved a disparity between local customs, a situation that was not unknown at eleventh-century Cluny. When Spanish monks visited the abbey in the early 1030s, they successfully petitioned Abbot Odilo for permission to celebrate the feast of the Annunciation on 18 December according to their local tradition, rather than on 25 March like the rest of the community.[93] The second synonym turned up in the description of the sign for a kind of bread (*rufeolae*) "which the Germans call *craphoium*."[94] The word *craphoium* was a phonetic Latin rendering of the Old German *Grapfen*, which designated a confection baked from flour and butter.[95] Unlike the first example, however, this was an issue of language rather than custom. By including this synonym in the sign lexicon, Cluniac legislators were accommodating the needs of German-speaking novices who may have had difficulties learning sign language through the medium of Latin. Their choice to use these synonyms

---

[92] Cluny, no. 62: "Pro signo prose vel quod a theutonicis sequentia vocatur, leva manum inclinatam et a pectore amovendo eam inverte ita, ut, quod prius erat sursum, sit deorsum." ed. Jarecki, *Signa Loquendi*, p. 132.

[93] Rodulphus Glaber, *Historiarum libri quinque* 3.12, ed. France, p. 114. For a discussion of this episode in its liturgical context, see Susan Boynton, *Shaping a Monastic Identity: Liturgy and History at the Imperial Abbey of Farfa, 1000–1125* (Ithaca and London, 2006), pp. 27–28.

[94] Cluny, no. 19: "Pro signo rufeolarum vel, ut theutonici loquuntur, craphoium premisso generali signo panis simula cum duobus digitis illas minutas involutiones, que in eis sunt facte, ex ea parte, qua sunt conplicate et quasi rotunde." ed. Jarecki, *Signa Loquendi*, p. 125.

[95] Charles du Cange, *Glossarium mediae et infimae latinitatis*, 10 vols. (Niort, 1883–1887), vol. III, p. 607, s.v. cratones.

strongly affirms the presence of German monks as a distinct and significant linguistic subgroup in the great Burgundian abbey.

Considered in this multilingual context, the imposition of monastic sign language fostered solidarity in a community that viewed linguistic diversity as a challenge to the demands of monastic decorum and personal discipline. Sources for the cloistered life at Cluny in this period do not permit us to speak with precision about contemporary perceptions of this threat, but they do suggest that sign language played an important part in building a sense of communal identity among the individuals who used it. In his treatise *On Miracles*, with which we began the chapter, Peter the Venerable described how a monk of Cluny named Bernard Savinellus left his brethren singing in the church one evening and set out for the dormitory to sleep. On a dark stairway, another monk approached him and broke the silence of the night with ominous words. "Where are you going?" he asked Bernard aloud. "Stop and hear what I have to say." According to Peter, Bernard was stunned (*miratus*) by the sound of the voice and angered (*indignans*) that someone had presumed to disobey the precept against speaking at night. When he attempted to respond with signs (*nutibus*) the sinister monk ignored him and proceeded with his message.[96] This disobedient individual was, in fact, a ghost, who had come to petition the brethren of Cluny for prayers to hasten the release of his soul from purgatory. This anecdote shows that the custom of sign language had a strong unifying effect on the monastic community. The use of signs played such a significant role in the imaginative transformation of the abbey into a celestial space that their unexpected replacement with spoken words roused shock and indignation among the brethren. The sound of the ghost's voice signaled that it did not belong to the world of the living. At Cluny, human discourse had become an attribute of otherworldliness in an institution where a silent language of signs was the expected medium of communication.

CONCLUSION

A comparative reading of the Cluniac sign lexicon and the customaries of Bernard and Ulrich has illuminated many of the discrete applications of sign language at eleventh-century Cluny. In doing so, it has also brought to light important features concerning the purpose of this custom. Monastic signs were not intended to serve in every instance as a functional replacement for speech. The Cluniacs were naturally guarded in their use

---

[96] Peter the Venerable, *De miraculis libri duos* 1.10, ed. Bouthillier, p. 38.

of this silent language. In many cases, the anxiety attendant with the fear of its abuse led monastic officials to devise ways for monks to conduct their activities without the need for speaking or signing. Moreover, it is clear that novices learned the sign vocabulary first and foremost to understand signs of instruction and reprimand from the master of novices. The active use of this custom was primarily the province of more experienced monks. Nonetheless, the shared knowledge of this exclusive language forged a strong sense of solidarity among the brethren. In a large and linguistically heterogeneous community like Cluny, where rustic forms of Latin were spoken side by side with foreign vernaculars, the silent language of the Cluniacs provided a shared medium of discourse that prevented misunderstandings that could arise from linguistic differences and thereby preserved the angelic decorum so valued in the community. Like the practice of celibacy and the cultivation of an unearthly silence, the use of sign language set the monks of Cluny apart from their contemporaries, lending strength to their communal purpose as they abandoned the world to embrace a celestial life realized on earth.

The utility of Cluniac sign language captured the attention of monks in other abbeys as well. Although no other religious community in this period followed rules against speaking as strict as those embraced by the Cluniacs, esteem for the virtue of silence was still a fundamental component of personal discipline in most monasteries. Before the close of the eleventh century, several houses with ties to Cluny appropriated the custom of sign language for their own use. Through a network of textual borrowings and human agents, knowledge of Cluniac signs spread from Burgundy to the Loire Valley, the Black Forest and as far away as southern England. The following chapter traces the channels of transmission through which three abbeys in northern Europe acquired expertise in this silent language. In turn, it examines how each of these houses adapted the Cluniac sign vocabulary to meet the needs and expectations of their respective communities.

Chapter 4

TRANSMISSION AND ADAPTATION

Despite the dangers of long-distance travel in an uncertain age, monks of ability and promise were continually on the move between the monasteries of northern Europe in the tenth and eleventh centuries.[1] The *Rule of Benedict* generally frowned on itinerant monks, but its precepts made allowance for individuals to leave the abbey precincts for legitimate reasons with the abbot's permission.[2] Some took to the roads in an official capacity as royal escorts, like the Anglo-Saxon monk-bishop Coenwald, who in 929 escorted two sisters of King Æthelstan to the court of Henry the Fowler in Germany. Coenwald took the opportunity on this journey to visit local abbeys, including St. Gall, where he entered the names of his kinfolk and king into the confraternity book.[3] Others traveled more discreetly between monastic centers as teachers and students. In 985, Abbo of Fleury went to Ramsey abbey in England, where he stayed for two years to instruct monks in the customs of his community.[4] Likewise, throughout the tenth century, promising Anglo-Saxon youths were sent to the abbey of Fleury in the Loire Valley to learn the monastic life. Among them were Oda, who became archbishop of Canterbury (941–958), and his nephew Oswald, later archbishop of York

---

[1] For a comprehensive treatment of modes of travel and perils to travelers around the year 1000, see Heinrich Fichtenau, "Reisen und Reisende," in *Beiträge zur Mediävistik*, 3 vols. (Stuttgart, 1975–1986), vol. III, pp. 1–79.

[2] *RB* 1.10–11 (on wandering monks) and 67 (on the conduct expected of monks who left the abbey to travel), pp. 438–440 and 662. A moral ambiguity shadowed wayward monks in early medieval thought. See Maribel Dietz, *Wandering Monks, Virgins, and Pilgrims: Ascetic Travel in the Mediterranean World, 300–800* (University Park, PA, 2005).

[3] For the text of Coenwald's entry, see *Councils and Synods with Other Documents Relating to the English Church I, A.D. 871–1204, part 1: 871–1066*, ed. D. Whitelock, M. Brett and C. N. L. Brooke (Oxford, 1981), pp. 40–43 (no. 10).

[4] Marco Mostert, "Le séjour d'Abbon de Fleury à Ramsey," *Bibliothèque de l'Ecole des Chartes* 144 (1986): 199–208.

(972–992).[5] Whatever their purpose or destination, these brethren bore with them an intimate knowledge of the customs of their own houses as well as a curiosity about the traditions of the foreign monks they encountered or among whom they lived for a short time.

A consequence of these travels was the development of a broad network of cultural exchange between northern European abbeys in the decades around 1000. Studies of this phenomenon have generally concentrated on the relationship between England and influential monasteries or regions on the continent.[6] Itinerant scribes and shared manuscripts provide some of the most important evidence for interaction between religious communities in this period.[7] Among those tenth-century individuals whose movements modern scholars have been able to reconstruct through the study of manuscript texts is Fredegaud of Brioude.[8] This Frankish poet wrote commemorative verses for Sts. Wilfrid and Ouen at Canterbury under the patronage of Archbishop Oda. After Oda's death in 958, Fredegaud returned to France and took up residence at a religious house in Brioude. There he found a new patron, Duke William IV of Aquitaine (963–995), for whom he composed a series of drinking-verses for the celebration of liturgical feast days. Like the poems of Fredegaud, the literary products of his tenth-century contemporaries allow us to chart the movements of itinerant monks back and forth across the English Channel.[9]

---

[5] On the lure of Fleury as a center of learning in this period, see John Nightingale, "Oswald, Fleury and Continental Reform," in *St. Oswald of Worcester: Life and Influence*, ed. Nicholas Brooks and Catherine Cubitt (London and New York, 1996), pp. 23–45.

[6] See, for example, Louis Gougaud, "Les relations de l'abbaye de Fleury-sur-Loire avec la Bretagne armoricaine et les Iles britanniques (Xe et XIe siècles)," *Mémoires de la Société d'Histoire de Bretagne* 4 (1923): 3–30; and Karl Leyser, "The Ottonians and Wessex," in *Communications and Power in Medieval Europe: The Carolingian and Ottonian Centuries*, ed. Timothy Reuter (London and Rio Grande, 1994), pp. 73–104. For a convenient, though not altogether reliable, summary of evidence for cultural interaction between England and mainland Europe in this period, see Veronica Ortenberg, *The English Church and the Continent in the Tenth and Eleventh Centuries: Cultural, Spiritual, and Artistic Exchanges* (Oxford, 1992).

[7] D. Gremont and Lin Donnat, "Fleury, le Mont Saint-Michel et l'Angleterre à la fin du Xe et au début du XIe siècle à propos du manuscrit d'Orléans, no. 127 (105)," in *Millénaire monastique du Mont Saint-Michel*, ed. J. Laporte *et al.*, 5 vols. (Paris, 1966–1967), vol. I, pp. 751–793; Lin Donnat, "Recherches sur l'influence de Fleury au Xe siècle," in *Etudes ligériennes d'histoire et d'archéologie médiévales*, ed. R. Louis (Auxerre, 1975), pp. 165–174; and J. Vezin, "Leofnoth: un scribe anglais à Saint-Benoît-sur-Loire," *Codices manuscripti* 4 (1977): 109–120.

[8] For what follows, see Michael Lapidge, "A Frankish Scholar in Tenth-Century England: Frithegod of Canterbury/Fredegaud of Brioude," *Anglo-Saxon England* 17 (1988): 45–65; repr. in Michael Lapidge, *Anglo-Latin Literature, 900–1066* (London and Rio Grande, 1993), pp. 157–181.

[9] See, for example, Michael Lapidge, "B. and the Vita S. Dunstani," in *St. Dunstan: His Life, Times and Cult*, ed. Nigel Ramsay, Margaret Sparks and Tim Tatton-Brown (Woodbridge, 1992), pp. 247–259, repr. in Lapidge, *Anglo-Latin Literature, 900–1066*, pp. 279–291; and Michael Hare, "Abbot Leofsige of Mettlach: An English Monk in Flanders and Upper Lotharingia in the Late Tenth Century," *Anglo-Saxon England* 33 (2004): 109–144.

Silence and sign language in medieval monasticism

Knowledge of Cluniac customs, including its sign language, was a commodity in this environment of religious and cultural exchange. As Cluny's reputation for sanctity grew, reform-minded abbots looked to the monastery as a model for the improvement of their own communities. Early proponents of the great Burgundian abbey praised the austere lives of its monks, claiming that their prayers could redeem souls from infernal punishment. In the early eleventh century, partisan authors circulated a legend concerning a hermit who had a vision that the vigils and alms-giving of Cluniac monks released the souls of the damned from the clutches of demons. News of this vision allegedly inspired Abbot Odilo (994–1049) to establish the feast of All Souls.[10] At the same time, the papacy extended its own interests north of the Alps by confirming and protecting Cluny's exemption from the spiritual jurisdiction of the bishop of Mâcon.[11] Pope Benedict VIII (1012–1024) trumpeted the preeminence of Cluny in a letter to Gallic prelates that urged them to protect the abbey's lands from the depredations of rapacious lords. He feared that any harm that came to Cluny, where the pious activities of the monks provided respite for the living and the dead in Christ, would injure the whole of the Church as well.[12] For their part, the abbots of Cluny were eager to encourage any endorsement of their way of life. Hugh the Great (1049–1109) provided prospective emulators with texts describing the traditions of his abbey and even tolerated the potentially disruptive presence of monks from other communities, who had been sent by their superiors to observe these customs firsthand.

Before the year 1100, knowledge of monastic sign language had spread from Cluny to abbeys in the Loire Valley, the south of England and the Black Forest. Unfortunately, the tissue of evidence for the transmission of this custom is very thin. Sign lexicons composed in the eleventh century for monastic communities at Fleury, Canterbury and Hirsau allow us to follow the transmission of Cluniac signs and examine

---

[10] On Cluniac sources related to this tradition, see Umberto Longo, "Riti e agiografia: L'istituzione della *commemoratio omnium fidelium defunctorum* nelle *Vitae* di Odilone di Cluny," *Bullettino dell'Istituto storico italiano per il Medio Evo e Archivio Muratoriano* 103 (2002): 163–200; and Chapter 1, p. 23, n. 43, above.

[11] For what follows, see H. E. J. Cowdrey, *The Cluniacs and the Gregorian Reform* (Oxford, 1970), pp. 3–43.

[12] Pope Benedict VIII (1 April 1021–1023): "Igitur quia in eodem loco iuges orationes et missarum caelebrationes et elemosine fiunt pro statu sanctae Dei aecclesiae et omnium fidelium vivorum et defunctorum salute et requie, ipsius dispendium commune omnium nostrum est detrimentum." ed. H. Zimmermann, in *Papsturkunden, 896–1046*, 3 vols. (Vienna, 1984–1985), vol. II, pp. 1007–1010 (no. 530), at p. 1009. More generally on the "sacred ban" that protected Cluny in this period, see Barbara Rosenwein, *Negotiating Space: Power, Restraint, and Privileges of Immunity in Early Medieval Europe* (Ithaca and London, 1999), pp. 156–183.

their adaptation in new contexts. These three religious houses were the only ones besides Cluny to produce textual evidence for their use of sign language before the twelfth century. This may be an accident of manuscript survival. It is certainly possible that many more abbeys adopted Cluniac sign language in this period, but if they did, no record of it survives. In a series of case studies, this chapter establishes the most plausible points of contact between these abbeys and Cluny and considers the role of textual sources and human actors in the appropriation of this custom (see Table 2 for a summary of the evidence). The appeal of monastic sign language clearly owed something to its adaptability. As this chapter shows, the monks who adopted it abandoned or retailored Cluniac signs that they deemed irrelevant or inadequate for their purposes. Moreover, they also fashioned new signs to make up for the deficiencies that they perceived in their model. With these interventions, each abbey created regionally specific variations of the Cluniac sign system to express cultural expectations and monastic ideals distinct from the experiences of the brethren of Cluny. Even so, fundamental principles of monastic sign language remained unchanged, even when translated to new environments. The chapter concludes with a consideration of these principles and explains their importance for the success of this custom.

FLEURY (THE ABBEY OF SAINT-BENOÎT-SUR-LOIRE)

The abbey of Saint-Benoît-sur-Loire, also known as Fleury, was the first monastic community outside of Burgundy to adopt the silent language of the Cluniacs. Founded in 651, Fleury was located in the Loire Valley near the city of Orléans. In the early eighth century, the community acquired the relics of St. Benedict and thereafter benefited from the prestige afforded by his holy presence.[13] According to the late ninth-century hagiographer Adrevald of Fleury, Benedict had been a restless shade. Tired of neglect, he appeared in a vision to the monks and urged them to retrieve his bones from the blackened ruins of Montecassino. In return, the saintly abbot assured his adopted community that he would protect

---

[13] Problems surround the date of Benedict's translation: Paul Meyvaert, "Peter the Deacon and the Tomb of Saint Benedict: The Cassinese Tradition," *Revue bénédictine* 65 (1955): 3–70, repr. in Paul Meyvaert, *Benedict, Gregory, Bede and Others* (London, 1977), no. I; Walter Goffart, "Le Mans, St. Scholastica, and the Literary Tradition of the Translation of St. Benedict," *Revue bénédictine* 77 (1967): 107–141; and the relevant articles of Jacques Hourlier in *Studia Monastica* 21 (1979), a collection of studies devoted to the theme "Le culte et les reliques de saint Benoît et de sainte Scholastique."

Table 2: *Narrative and legislative sources for Cluniac sign language to 1100*

Cluny	Fleury	Canterbury	Hirsau
(943) First mention of monastic sign language at Baume-les-Moines during the novitiate of Odo, later abbot of Cluny (925–942), in John of Salerno's *Life of Odo*.	(938) Odo of Cluny may have introduced the custom of sign language at Fleury during his reform of the community.	(970) Monks from Fleury participating in the Council of Winchester may have introduced the custom of sign language to England.	(before 1091) The Hirsau sign lexicon (359 signs) appears in the customary composed by Abbot William of Hirsau on the model of Ulrich's customary.
	(c. 1015) First mention of the use of monastic sign language at Fleury in the customary of Thierry, which claimed to relate the customs in place under Abbot Abbo (998–1004).	(c. 1000) First mention of the use of monastic sign language in England in Wulfstan of Winchester's *Life of Saint Æthelwold*.	
(1078/84) Bernard of Cluny and Ulrich of Zell copy the Cluniac sign lexicon (118 signs) into their respective customaries.	(7 December 1087) The Fleury sign lexicon (154 signs) is composed or copied at Saint-Benoît-sur-Loire.	(mid-11th cent.) The Canterbury sign lexicon (127 signs written in Old English) is copied into a miscellany of texts relevant to the reform of English monastic life preserved at Christ Church.	

them from harm as long as they lived according to his monastic rule.[14] In the early tenth century, however, the harmony of this relationship threatened to change. After dispersing in the wake of the Northmen invasions, the monks of Fleury returned home to resume their way of life, but there was such discord among them that the shade of Benedict departed to find a man after his own heart (*secundum cor meum*) to restore the abbey to its former glory. That man was Odo, the second abbot of Cluny (925–942).[15]

Abbot Odo's reform provided the earliest context for the introduction of monastic sign language at Fleury. Despite initial resistance to the intrusion of an abbot from another community, the brethren eventually accepted Odo as their spiritual leader.[16] His primary task as abbot was the reestablishment of regular observance on the model of his interpretation of the *Rule of Benedict*. Contemporaries considered his standards to be strict and severe. In fact, a papal privilege from 938 conceded that monks of Saint-Benoît-sur-Loire who were unable to shoulder the burden of the new abbot's demands should be allowed to leave the monastery so as not to distract the more serious brethren from their holy purpose.[17] According to John of Salerno's account of the reform, Odo forbade the consumption of meat and the possession of private property.[18] He may have also introduced the custom of sign language from Cluny at this time.[19] In response to local opposition, Odo enlisted St. Benedict's support for his reforming measures. In a sermon delivered at Fleury on the feast day of the saint, he called attention to the continued veneration

[14] Adevaldus, *Miracula Benedicti* 1.20, ed. Eugène de Certain, in *Les miracles de saint Benoît écrits par Adevald, Aimoin, André, Raoul Tortaire et Hugues de Sainte Marie, moines de Fleury* (Paris, 1858), p. 49. On the cult of Benedict at Fleury in the Carolingian period, see Thomas Head, *Hagiography and the Cult of Saints: The Diocese of Orléans, 800–1200* (Cambridge, 1990), pp. 20–57.

[15] John of Salerno, *Vita Odonis* 3.8, PL CXXXIII, cols. 80c–81d.

[16] On Odo of Cluny's reforming efforts at Fleury and elsewhere, see Ernst Sackur, *Die Cluniacenser in ihrer kirchlichen und allgemeingeschichtlichen Wirksamkeit bis zur Mitte des elften Jahrhunderts*, 2 vols. (Halle an der Saale, 1892), vol. I, pp. 88–93; and Joachim Wollasch, "Königtum, Adel und Klöster im Berry während des 10. Jahrhunderts," in *Neue Forschungen über Cluny und die Cluniacenser*, ed. Gerd Tellenbach (Freiburg, 1959), pp. 17–165, at pp. 88–142.

[17] Pope Leo VII (9 January 938): "Econtra permittimus, ut si alicui de [ipsis fratribus] onerosa conversatio fuerit, ut suo potius detrimento [ipse] discedat, ut non alios inquietet." ed. Zimmermann, in *Papsturkunden, 896–1046*, vol. I, pp. 140–142 (no. 83).

[18] John of Salerno, *Vita Odonis* 3.9, PL CXXXIII, col. 81d.

[19] Kassius Hallinger has refuted the notion that Odo instituted Cluniac customs at Saint-Benoît-sur-Loire in the tenth century. Citing numerous minute differences in liturgical practices evident in customaries composed for these communities in the decades around the year 1000, Hallinger has argued that Fleury maintained its autonomy from Cluny until the middle of the eleventh century. See CCM VII.1, pp. 345–350 ("Der Einfluss Klunys auf Fleury im 10. Jahrhundert"). This thesis may hold true for the liturgy, but, as we will see below, it does not seem to apply to the custom of sign language.

of Benedict's tomb and the miracles performed there, but he also reminded his monastic audience to respect the letter of the *Rule* and to esteem the holy abbot as a second Moses, that is, as a law-giver as well as a miracle-worker.[20] His stratagem was successful. Around the year 1015, Thierry of Fleury promoted the disciplinary standards of his brethren in a book that purported to reflect the customs practiced under Abbot Abbo (998–1004), many of which were introduced from Cluny at the time of Odo's reform.[21] Thierry claimed that their way of life was so virtuous that it protected the monks from the intrigues of the devil and warded off the wrath of the Last Judgment for all humankind.[22]

The first explicit reference to the use of sign language at Saint-Benoît-sur-Loire appeared in this early eleventh-century customary. The text did not include a sign lexicon like those preserved in the later Cluniac customaries of Bernard and Ulrich. Nonetheless, in a chapter on the duties of the roundsmen (*circatores*), Thierry described a sign employed by these officials to identify monks who had fallen asleep and yet remained obstinately disobedient even after the discovery of their negligence. The condemning gesture was made by placing an open palm under the chin.[23] The care taken to describe this sign suggests that it was a purposeful act and not an arbitrary motion. While it had no exact equivalent in the Cluniac sign repertoire, the Fleury sign for disobedience bore a close resemblance to the monastic sign for pride, which involved putting a fist with an upturned thumb beneath the chin.[24] The touching of the chin was a potent symbol of sexual indiscretion in eleventh-century

---

[20] Odo of Cluny, *Sermo de sancto Benedicto abbate, PL* CXXXIII, cols. 721–729, esp. col. 724c: "Et hunc quidem beatissimum patrem legislatio specialiter Moysi comparat."

[21] *Consuetudines Floriacenses Antiquiores,* ed. Anselme Davril and Lin Donnat, *CCM* VII.3 (Siegburg, 1984), pp. 7–60. This edition has been reprinted with a French translation in *L'abbaye de Fleury en l'an mil* (Paris, 2004), pp. 147–251. All references are to the original *CCM* edition. On the date and audience of this customary, see Davril's introduction to the critical edition in *CCM* VII.1, pp. 333–338. Although its author is not named, most historians believe it to be the work of Thierry of Fleury. On his monastic career and works, see A. Poncelet, "La vie et les oeuvres de Thierry de Fleury," *Analecta Bollandiana* 27 (1908): 5–27; and Anselme Davril, "Un moine de Fleury aux environs de l'an mil: Thierry, dit d'Amorbach," in *Etudes ligériennes,* ed. Louis, pp. 97–104.

[22] *Consuetudines Floriacenses Antiquiores,* prol., ed. Davril and Donnat, pp. 7–9.

[23] *Ibid.* 10, ed. Davril and Donnat, p. 19: "Si autem aliquis, ut persepe provenit, taurina cervice rigidus et sibimetipsi stultior resupinus – cui pro signo palmus extentus subtus mentum ponitur – qui crassitudine contumacie surgere dedignatur postquam deprehensus fuerit obdormisse et secundum prefatum modum neglexerit satisfactionem agere, in conventu fratrum grassante censura iustitie ultione corporali noverit se permulctandum." On the duties of the roundsmen, see Chapter 1, pp. 48–50, above.

[24] Cluny, no. 12: "Pro signo salmonis vel sturgionis premisso generali signo piscium hoc adde, ut pugnum erecto pollice subponas mento, quo superbia significatur, quia superbi maxime et divites tales pisces solent habere." ed. Walter Jarecki, *Signa Loquendi: Die cluniacensischen Signa-Listen eingeleitet und herausgegeben* (Baden-Baden, 1981), p. 123.

iconography, as the scene depicting Ælfgyva in the Bayeux Tapestry illustrates.[25] The symmetry of hand placement shared by these signs underscores their complementary meanings: disobedience and pride were grave sins for monks. This leaves little doubt that they belonged to the same semantic system, namely, the silent language of the Cluniacs.

By the late eleventh century, the brethren of Saint-Benoît-sur-Loire had composed a sign lexicon of their own. A miscellany of texts compiled at the abbey in the fourteenth century preserved a descriptive catalogue of 154 hand signs (Table 3).[26] The scribe of this manuscript reproduced the original colophon of his exemplar, thereby revealing that the Fleury sign lexicon was originally composed or copied on 7 December 1087. This document shared many formal and verbal parallels with the contemporary sign catalogue from Cluny, which undoubtedly served as its textual model. In most respects, the Fleury sign lexicon conformed to the general structure of its source. The two documents had more than 100 signs in common and employed similar principles of organization. Like its Cluniac model, the Fleury sign lexicon framed its list of sign descriptions with a short preface and epilogue explaining the rationale for their use. It also organized its contents into thematic groupings, employing both headings and marginal notations to denote the beginning of each new subsection of sign entries.[27]

The brethren of Fleury were more than slavish imitators in this endeavor, for they clearly augmented and revised the Cluniac sign lexicon in significant ways to adapt this custom to their own needs.[28] In particular, they invented signs unique to Saint-Benoît-sur-Loire, reflecting local and regional differences between the two communities in several aspects of monastic life. A new sign for herring indicates that the location of Fleury, in the Loire Valley, gave the community access to an Atlantic maritime economy that was unknown at Cluny.[29] Similarly, a new sign for a bitter drink made from white wine and spices may have been a response to the

---

[25] J. Bard McNulty, "The Lady Aelfgyva in the Bayeux Tapestry," *Speculum* 55 (1980): 659–668, at p. 665.

[26] The contents of this manuscript (MS Orléans, Bibliothèque municipale 2293) included a martyrology of St. Usuard, a copy of the *Rule of Benedict*, lessons for the chapter office and the sign lexicon (the latter on fols. 105r–110r). See Charles Cuissard, *Inventaire des manuscrits de la Bibliothèque d'Orléans, fonds de Fleury* (Paris, 1885), pp. 201–203. Jarecki's edition of the Fleury sign lexicon (*Signa Loquendi*, pp. 250–275) is technically superior to that of Anselme Davril, "La langage par signes chez les moines: Un catalogue de signes de l'abbaye de Fleury," in *Sous la règle de saint Benoît: Structures monastiques et sociétés en France du moyen âge à l'époque moderne* (Geneva, 1982), pp. 51–74, at pp. 55–70.

[27] Jarecki, *Signa Loquendi*, pp. 54–55.   [28] For a summary of these changes, see *ibid.* pp. 56–62.

[29] Fleury, no. 13 (*alec*), ed. Jarecki, *Signa Loquendi*, p. 252.

popularity of a local recipe favored in the cloister, an inference suggested by the inclusion of the Gallic name for its main ingredient (*aloigne*) in the sign description.[30] The most striking revisions appeared among the signs for personnel, where the brethren of Fleury added fourteen new entries for specialized officials and their helpers, both lay and monastic. These included signs for the master of the work (perhaps an overseer of building projects), the treasurer and four grades of prior, as well as signs for lay assistants both to the refectorer and to the monk responsible for ringing the bells.[31] There were also new signs for specialists, like doctors, barbers and cooks, who either frequented the abbey with regularity or inhabited the place with the monks.[32] The multiplication of signs for officials underscores the fact that active participation in the operation and maintenance of the community was an important characteristic of the monastic ideal fostered at Saint-Benoît-sur-Loire. After describing the duties of nineteen officials, the customary composed by Thierry claimed with a measure of pride that almost all of the brethren were responsible for some specialized task (*obedientia particularis*) in the abbey. Selfless participation of this kind was considered to be the greatest glory of the monks.[33] These statements may have been enthusiastic exaggerations, but they suggest that the specialization of function expressed in the Fleury sign lexicon reflected an ideal of service that differentiated the brethren of Saint-Benoît-sur-Loire from their contemporaries at Cluny.

A concern for textual clarity led the monks of Fleury to revise ambiguous and potentially confusing sign descriptions borrowed from the Cluniac sign lexicon. In several cases, they provided general Cluniac signs with greater specificity by replacing them with more precise signs or by building more complex, and therefore more exacting, compounds. For example, they added a gesture denoting speech to the Cluniac sign for

---

[30] Fleury, no. 44: "Pro signo pocionis, que sit ex vino albo et quadam herba, que galice vocatur aloigne, signo vini premisso hoc adde, ut manum ante os ponas, sicut ille qui sentit amarum." ed. Jarecki, *Signa Loquendi*, p. 257.

[31] Fleury, nos. 122 (*magister operis*), 123 (*thauserarius*), 104 (*grandis prior*), 105 (*subprior*), 106 (*tercius prior*), 107 (*quartus prior*), 128 (*famulus refectorii*) and 124 (*famulus pulsatoris*), ed. Jarecki, *Signa Loquendi*, pp. 270, 267–268 and 271, respectively.

[32] Fleury, nos. 125 (*medicus*), 126 (*barbitor*) and 127 (*coquus*), ed. Jarecki, *Signa Loquendi*, p. 271. Scholars have only recently begun to exploit the evidence of monastic customaries for insight into the care of the sick in this period. See Riccardo Cristiani, "*Infirmus sum et non possum sequi conventum*: L'esperienza della malattia nelle consuetudini cluniacensi dell'XI secolo," *Studi Medievali* 41 (2000): 777–807; and Riccardo Cristiani, "Integration and Marginalization: Dealing with the Sick in Eleventh-Century Cluny," in *From Dead of Night to End of Day: The Medieval Customs of Cluny / Du coeur de la nuit à la fin du jour: Les coutumes clunisiennes au moyen âge*, ed. Susan Boynton and Isabelle Cochelin (Leiden, 2005), pp. 287–295.

[33] *Consuetudines Floriacenses Antiquiores* 22, ed. Davril and Donnat, p. 33: "maxima monachorum gloriatio."

confession to eliminate its visual ambiguity with the sign for sickness.[34] Likewise, they favored individual signs for apple and pear over the generic Cluniac sign for fruit.[35] While they appropriated the Cluniac sign for foreigner, the brethren of Fleury used qualifying signs to indicate whether the foreigner in question was a layman or a monk.[36] This concern for precision applied to the smallest details of sign construction. The Cluniac sign lexicon noted the action and placement of individual fingers in many of its sign descriptions, particularly those for verbs, but never specified which fingers the brethren were supposed to use to express these concepts: "For the sign of hearing, hold your finger against your ear. For the sign of not knowing, wipe your lips with a raised finger. For the sign of telling a lie, place a finger inside of your lips and then draw it out again."[37] All of these entries were rewritten with greater precision in the Fleury sign lexicon, each stating precisely which finger was used to make the sign in order to prevent any confusion that may have resulted from their misinterpretation: "For the sign of hearing, hold your index finger against your ear. For the sign of not knowing, touch your lips with your index and middle fingers. For the sign of telling a lie, place your index and middle fingers inside of your lips and then draw them out again."[38]

These revisions for relevance and clarity raise questions about the function of the sign lexicon at Saint-Benoît-sur-Loire, particularly its role as a teaching tool. Like the eleventh-century Cluniacs, the monks of Fleury probably used texts to support, rather than supplant, the oral transmission of customs in their community. As we have seen, the Cluniac sign lexicon survived as a chapter in the customaries of Bernard and Ulrich, where it functioned as an instrument of reference, providing a sanctioned catalogue of signs that novices should learn before their

---

[34] Cluny, no. 94: "Pro signo infirmarii, qui obsequitur infirmis, pone manum contra pectus, quod significat infirmitatem, quamvis non semper, quia et confessionem significat." and Fleury, no. 116: "Pro signo infirmarii, qui obsequitur infirmis, pone manum contra pectus, quod significat infirmitatem, quamvis non semper, quia et confessionem significat adiungendo indicem ori." ed. Jarecki, *Signa Loquendi*, pp. 138 and 269.

[35] Cluny, no. 22 (*pomi, maxime piri vel mali*); and Fleury, no. 29 (*pomum*) and 30 (*pirus*), ed. Jarecki, *Signa Loquendi*, pp. 125 and 255.

[36] Cluny, no. 103: "Pro signo hominis, qui est alterius lingue, cum digito labia tange propter loquelam." and Fleury, no. 130: "Pro signo hominis, qui est alterius lingue, cum digito labia tange propter loquelam; si sit laycus, facias primo signum layci, et si sit monachus, eciam primo facias signum monachi." ed. Jarecki, *Signa Loquendi*, pp. 140 and 271.

[37] Cluny, nos. 105–107: "Pro signo audiendi tene digitum contra aurem. Pro signo nesciendi cum digito erecto labia terge. Pro signo mentiendi digitum intra labia positum trahe." ed. Jarecki, *Signa Loquendi*, pp. 140–141.

[38] Fleury, nos. 132–134: "Pro signo audiendi indicem tene contra aurem. Pro signo nesciendi cum indice et medio labia tange. Pro signo mentiendi indicem et medium inter labia positos trahe." ed. Jarecki, *Signa Loquendi*, p. 272.

consecration as monks and serving as an authoritative witness to tradition in the event of disagreement over the interpretation of received customs.[39] In contrast, the Fleury sign lexicon seems to have circulated independently as a supplement to, rather than an integral part of, a monastic customary. In this form, it may have played a more direct role in the instruction of this custom than the Cluniac sign catalogue. The revisions undertaken to make its sign descriptions more precise and intelligible imply the expectations of a readership for whom textual clarity was of the utmost importance. These interventions suggest that the monks of Fleury supplemented oral instruction in this custom by reading and studying a sign catalogue that had been revised and clarified for that very purpose.[40]

The brethren of Saint-Benoît-sur-Loire adopted the custom of sign language from Cluny as early as the tenth century. Although this practice was likely introduced during the reform of the community by Odo of Cluny, concrete evidence for its use first appeared in a customary that claimed to describe the monastic ideal fostered under Abbot Abbo (998–1004). By the late eleventh century, the monks of Fleury composed a sign lexicon of their own. Although it drew heavily on a Cluniac model for its form and content, the addition of new signs and the revision of adopted signs show that the brethren made efforts to adapt this custom to the specific needs of their community. This process of imitation and adaptation was not unique to the abbey of Saint-Benoît-sur-Loire. Like their counterparts at Fleury, with whom they had close contact in the tenth century, monks in southern England adopted the silent language of the Cluniacs as well. As the following case study shows, they made significant modifications to their adopted sign vocabulary that reflected expectations and ideals unique to the reformed monasticism of the late Anglo-Saxon church.

CANTERBURY (CHRIST CHURCH CATHEDRAL)

In the late tenth century, a steady traffic in monastic personnel between the Loire Valley and southern England provided the context for the spread of Cluniac signs from the abbey of Fleury to Christ Church, Canterbury. Established in 597 as a staging ground for the Roman mission

---

[39] See Chapter 2, pp. 69–73, above.

[40] In kind response to an inquiry from me about learning a modern form of monastic sign language in his youth, Father Anselme Davril of the abbey of Saint-Benoît-sur-Loire underscored the pedagogical importance of reading a sign catalogue for gaining proficiency in this custom: "Eh bien c'est très simple, nous disposions d'un petit catalogue de signes, en français, et l'assistant du maître des novices nous enseignait comment réaliser pratiquement ces signes." (Personal communication, 13 April 2002).

to the lost province of Britain, the see of Canterbury had a long history as a foothold for continental influence in early medieval England.[41] The unprecedented reform of religious life sponsored by King Edgar the Peaceful (959–975) and his successors transformed the Christ Church community from a house of canons to a chapter of monks.[42] Drawing on an earlier tradition, the twelfth-century chronicler William of Malmesbury portrayed Edgar as a ruler who was mindful of his promises. As a young man, the future king had happened upon a dilapidated abbey while hunting. The depredations of the Northmen and the inability of the landed classes to part with their wealth had both played a role in the widespread decline in English monasticism in the ninth century.[43] Edgar was so moved by the sight of the ruin that he vowed to rebuild the abbey and others like it when he ascended to the throne.[44] True to his word, once he became king, Edgar summoned an episcopal council to lay out a plan for the restoration of religious life in his kingdom. This council took place at Easter sometime between 964 and 969.[45] With the cooperation of monk-bishops like Æthelwold, Dunstan and Oswald, the king expelled canons from important urban cathedrals and replaced them with monks.[46] He defended this action in his royal privilege for the monks of New Minster in Winchester, stating that the vices of the canons had nullified the beneficial effects of their intercessory prayers.[47] On the occasion of the same council, Edgar ordered the construction of more than forty houses for monks.[48] He fostered houses for religious women as well, but entrusted the care of them to his queen, Ælfthryth, to avoid any rumor of

---

[41] Nicholas Brooks, *The Early History of the Church of Canterbury: Christ Church from 597–1066* (Leicester, 1984); and more generally the classic study of Wilhelm Levison, *England and the Continent in the Eighth Century* (Oxford, 1946).

[42] Brooks, *Early History of the Church of Canterbury*, pp. 255–310.

[43] For an expression of both views, see Asser, *De rebus gestis Ælfredi* 93, ed. William H. Stevenson (Oxford, 1904), pp. 80–81. On the waning of female religious communities in the ninth century, see Sarah Foot, *Veiled Women I: The Disappearance of Nuns from Anglo-Saxon England* (Aldershot, 2000).

[44] William of Malmesbury, *Vita Dunstani* 2.2, ed. William Stubbs, in *Memorials of Saint Dunstan*, Rolls Series LXIII (London, 1874), p. 290. This anecdote was an embellishment of a well-attested tenth-century tradition that Edgar had promised to advance the cause of English monasticism in his youth after receiving guidance from "a certain abbot," commonly thought to be Æthelwold, bishop of Winchester. See *Regularis Concordia*, prol., ed. and trans. Thomas Symons, in *Regularis Concordia: The Monastic Agreement of the Monks and Nuns of the English Nation* (London, 1953), p. 1.

[45] See *Councils and Synods*, ed. Whitelock, Brett and Brooke, pp. 113–118 (no. 30).

[46] On the three churchmen who acted as Edgar's principal advisors in the reform, see *Bishop Æthelwold: His Career and Influence*, ed. Barbara Yorke (Woodbridge, 1988); *St. Dunstan: His Life, Times and Cult*, ed. Ramsey, Sparks and Tatton-Brown; and *St. Oswald of Worcester: Life and Influence*, ed. Brooks and Cubitt.

[47] *Councils and Synods*, ed. Whitelock, Brett and Brooke, p. 125 (no. 31).

[48] Byrhtferth, *Vita Oswaldi* 3, ed. Whitelock, Brett and Brooke, in *ibid.* p. 118 (no. 30).

scandal.[49] The king's reputation as a champion of religious renewal grew to such an extent that the abbots of St. Ouen in Rouen and St. Geneviève in Paris requested his help in restoring their communities.[50]

The *Rule of Benedict* provided the reformed abbeys of late tenth-century England with a model of monastic discipline, but there were disagreements among the brethren over the correct interpretation of its precepts. The resulting discord threatened to undermine the progress of the reform. Around 970, Edgar convened a council of abbots, abbesses and bishops at Winchester to deal with the problem. He encouraged them to compose a written agreement on the proper observance of the *Rule*, known as the *Regularis Concordia*, and to swear an oath to adhere to its contents and enforce them in the abbeys of the realm.[51] The participants in the Council of Winchester turned to the monastic traditions of their own country to find precedents to guide them in this national under-taking. Recalling that Pope Gregory the Great (590–604) had advised Augustine of Canterbury to gather customs from Gaul and Rome for the nascent English church, the reformers summoned monks from Fleury and Ghent to participate in their endeavor.[52]

There was a strong sense of pollination at the Council of Winchester. Monks came from different parts of England and from across the sea to share the traditions of their communities and to forge them into a national observance suitable to the ideals of the English reform. Anglo-Saxon monks likened themselves to bees in this enterprise. They gathered the most worthy customs of their foreign brethren like nectar from wild flowers and collected them in a little book, as though it was their hive.[53] The monks of Fleury and Ghent shared their traditions at the council, but they also introduced into England customs imposed on their respective communities during the tenth-century reforms of Odo of

---

[49] *Regularis Concordia*, prol., ed. Symons, p. 2. Further on relations between queens and female monastic communities in this period, see Pauline Stafford, "Queens, Nunneries and Reforming Churchmen: Gender, Religious Status and Reform in Tenth- and Eleventh-Century England," *Past and Present* 163 (1999): 3–35.

[50] *Memorials of Saint Dunstan*, ed. Stubbs, pp. 363–364 and 366–368 (nos. 6 and 8).

[51] *Regularis Concordia*, prol., ed. Symons, pp. 1–3.

[52] *Ibid*. p. 3. The participants in the council knew the letter of Pope Gregory to Augustine either from Bede or from an independent manuscript of Gregory's responses. See Paul Meyvaert, "Bede's Text of the *Libellus Responsionum* of Gregory the Great to Augustine of Canterbury," in *England Before the Conquest: Studies in Primary Sources Presented to Dorothy Whitelock*, ed. Peter Clemoes and Kathleen Hughes (Cambridge, 1971), pp. 15–33; repr. in Meyvaert, *Benedict, Gregory, Bede and Others*, no. X. On the writings of Bede as a model for the tenth-century reformers, see Antonia Gransden, "Traditionalism and Continuity during the Last Century of Anglo-Saxon Monasticism," *Journal of Ecclesiastical History* 40 (1989): 159–207, at pp. 164–170.

[53] *Regularis Concordia*, prol., ed. Symons, p. 3. For medieval comparisons of monks and bees, see Chapter 1, p. 13, n. 1, above.

Cluny and Gerard of Brogne.[54] As a result, the *Regularis Concordia* bore the indelible imprint of contemporary practices from monastic centers in Burgundy and the Rhine Valley.[55]

The participants in the Council of Winchester agreed unanimously that the cultivation of silence was a virtuous pursuit for the monks of Anglo-Saxon England. Following the example of the *Rule of Benedict*, they forbade speech during most hours of the day and throughout the night, making allowance for the study of Latin and any other words deemed necessary, so long as the monks spoke them softly.[56] The teaching of Latin in pre-conquest English abbeys involved the memorization and recitation of Latin conversational texts known as colloquies, the most famous of which were composed by the monk Ælfric of Eynsham (*c.* 950–*c.* 1010) and his pupil Ælfric Bata (fl. early eleventh century).[57] The reformers also drew from continental traditions that elaborated on the general precepts of the *Rule*. The *Regularis Concordia* called for complete silence in the cloister on feast days in the same manner as the brethren of tenth-century Baume-les-Moines and Cluny.[58] It also advised monks to refrain from idle speech when they warmed themselves around the fire permitted in the months of winter.[59] In general,

---

[54] For a discussion of tenth-century reformers like Gerard and Odo and their possible influence on Æthelwold, see Patrick Wormald, "Æthelwold and his Continental Counterparts: Contact, Comparison, Contrast," in *Bishop Æthelwold*, ed. Yorke, pp. 13–42, esp. pp. 19–22 and 25–26; repr. in Patrick Wormald, *The Times of Bede, 625–865: Studies in Early English Christian Society and its Historian* (Oxford, 2006), pp. 169–206.

[55] For an overview of continental monastic rules available in England during this period, see Mary Bateson, "Rules for Monks and Secular Canons After the Revival under King Edgar," *English Historical Review* 9 (1894): 690–708; and David Knowles, *The Monastic Order in England: A History of its Development from the Times of Dunstan to the Fourth Lateran Council, 940–1216* (Cambridge, 1963), pp. 31–56. The studies of Thomas Symons on the sources of the *Regularis Concordia* remain indispensable: "The Sources of the *Regularis Concordia*," *Downside Review* 59 (1941): 14–36, 143–170 and 264–289; the introduction to his critical edition of the text (London, 1953), pp. xlv–lii; and "*Regularis Concordia*: History and Derivation," in *Tenth-Century Studies: Essays in Commemoration of the Millennium of the Council of Winchester and Regularis Concordia*, ed. David Parsons (London, 1975), pp. 37–59. Scholars are divided on the extent of the influence of Fleury's customs on the legislation of the English reform. For a sample of contrasting opinions, see Eric John, "The Sources of the English Monastic Reformation: A Comment," *Revue bénédictine* 70 (1960): 197–203; Donnat, "Recherches sur l'influence de Fleury au Xe siècle," pp. 165–174; and the comments of Kassius Hallinger in *CCM* VII.1 (Siegburg, 1984), pp. 351–359 ("Fleurys Einfluβ auf die Synode von Winchester"), esp. p. 354: "Fleury's Einfluβ auf die *Regularis Concordia* ist überbewertet worden."

[56] *Regularis Concordia* 56, ed. Symons, pp. 54–55.

[57] Further on this genre and its pedagogical function, see David W. Porter, "The Latin Syllabus in Anglo-Saxon Monastic Schools," *Neophilologus* 78 (1994): 463–482; and Scott Gwara and David W. Porter, *Anglo-Saxon Conversations: The Colloquies of Aelfric Bata* (Woodbridge, 1997).

[58] *Regularis Concordia* 24, ed. Symons, p. 20. On this practice in tenth-century Burgundy, see Chapter 1, p. 25, above.

[59] *Regularis Concordia* 29, ed. Symons, p. 25. This custom may have derived from continental practice as well. See Chapter 1, p. 40, above.

the new legislation recommended that monks guard their tongues at all times, because silence was the most favorable condition for the well-being of their souls.[60]

Monastic sign language appealed to the Anglo-Saxon reformers as a means to ensure the discipline of silence in their abbeys. Knowledge of this custom arrived in England in the late tenth century, a time of significant religious and cultural exchange with monasteries on the continent. The agents of this event are unknown, but modern scholars have consistently cast the abbey of Fleury as the point of contact between Cluny and England in this period.[61] As we have seen, the custom of sign language was very likely instituted at Saint-Benoît-sur-Loire as early as the 930s, when Odo of Cluny reformed the community. The monks of Fleury who attended the Council of Winchester around 970 were the heirs of this tradition and plausibly introduced it to England. Anglo-Saxon monks may also have acquired proficiency in sign language during their frequent visits to Saint-Benoît-sur-Loire, an attractive destination for aspiring youths eager to learn the rhythms of cenobitic life in the abbey that housed the bones of St. Benedict.[62]

The earliest evidence for the use of monastic sign language in England appeared around the year 1000 in Wulfstan of Winchester's *Life of Saint Æthelwold*.[63] Like other references to sign use in narrative sources from this period, Wulfstan's description of this custom was brief and opaque. He used it as a literary prop to set the scene for a miraculous episode, in this case a demonstration of saintly power that occurred in the middle of the night.[64] The incident began when a monk named Theodric approached Æthelwold while he was reading by candlelight during the

---

[60] *Regularis Concordia* 56, ed. Symons, p. 55: "Alias autem de Deo et animae suae salute cum silentio meditandum, uti ipse (beatus Benedictus) censuit, hortamur."

[61] On the role of Fleury as a conduit of information between England and the continent in this period, see the works cited in nn. 5–7, above.

[62] See, for example, Wulfstan, *Vita sancti Æthelwoldi* 14: "Ætheluuoldus autem misit Osgarum monachum trans mare ad monasterium sancti patris Benedicti Floriacense, ut regularis obseruantiae mores illic disceret ac domi fratribus docendo ostenderet." ed. Michael Lapidge and Michael Winterbottom, in *Wulfstan of Winchester: Life of St Æthelwold* (Oxford, 1991), p. 26; and Eadmer, *Vita Oswaldi* 5: "Regulam, inquit, Beati Benedicti servare sub obedientia volo; et idcirco in Gallia apud Floriacum, ubi ipsius patris reliquiae dicuntur haberi, monachus fieri, mente revolvo. Nam juxta quod mihi mea aestimatio dicit, nusquam rectius servanda sunt, nec forte servantur quae idem pater instituit, quam in loco quem ipsemet sua corporali praesentia in perpetuum honorare non desistit." ed. James Raine, in *The Historians of the Church of York and its Archbishops*, 3 vols. (London, 1879–1894), vol. II, pp. 7–8.

[63] Wulfstan composed the *vita* in late 996 or shortly thereafter. See *Wulfstan of Winchester: Life of St Æthelwold*, eds. Lapidge and Winterbottom, pp. xv–xvi.

[64] The translation of the opening clause of this episode ("Tempore quodam hiemali") as "One winter's day" in the most recent edition of this work is misleading (*ibid.* p. 53). The setting and purpose of the narrative make it abundantly clear that the episode in question took place after dark.

interval between the Night office and the coming of dawn. The monk had important news to discuss with his bishop, but since it was forbidden to converse after dark, Theodric intended to inform him of the matter using sign language (*uolens indiciis . . . ei indicare*).[65] He was distracted from his original purpose, however, by the old man's uncanny ability to read so well by candlelight. This prompted him to test his healthy eyes against the aged vision of the saint. On the following evening, Theodric incurred a divine punishment for his presumption. Although the use of sign language played a minor role in the episode, Wulfstan's work gives a clear indication that the monks of the Old Minster had adopted this custom by the last decades of the tenth century.

A mid-eleventh-century manuscript associated with Christ Church, Canterbury, preserved the first descriptions of these signs. Between 988 and 1020, under the guidance of five successive archbishops from mon-astic backgrounds, the cathedral chapter underwent a slow evolution from a community of secular canons to a house of professed monks.[66] At the same time, the scriptorium of Christ Church emerged as a major center of book production and illumination. Sixty-two manuscripts composed by Canterbury scribes have survived from the late Anglo-Saxon period.[67] These ranged in quality from sumptuous decorated altar-books to anthologies of moral verse for private contemplation. Among them was an illuminated collection of texts relevant to the tenth-century reform of English monastic life (MS British Library, Cotton Tiberius A.iii).[68] Preserved alongside the *Rule of Benedict* and one of two known copies of the *Regularis Concordia*, both with vernacular glosses, was a catalogue of 127 hand signs composed in Old English (Table 4).[69]

The internal organization of the Canterbury sign lexicon differed considerably from that of its Latin counterparts, which it predated by

---

[65] Wulfstan, *Vita sancti Æthelwoldi* 35: "Quidem monachus, nomine Theodricus, ad Dei hominem perrexit, uolens indiciis de quadam necessitate ei indicare." ed. Lapidge and Winterbottom, p. 52.

[66] See n. 42, above.

[67] There is a complete list and discussion of these manuscripts and their contents in Brooks, *Early History of the Church of Canterbury*, pp. 266–278.

[68] For a description of the manuscript, see N. R. Ker, *Catalogue of Manuscripts Containing Anglo-Saxon* (Oxford, 1957), pp. 240–248 (no. 186), esp. p. 248 on its association with Christ Church, Canterbury.

[69] MS British Library, Cotton Tiberius A.iii, fols. 97v–101v. The Old English sign lexicon has been edited and translated most recently in Debby Banham, *Monasteriales Indicia: The Anglo-Saxon Monastic Sign Language* (Pinner, 1991). For a thorough analysis of the text, with reference to earlier literature, see Juan C. Conde-Silvestre, "The Code and Context of *Monasteriales Indicia*: A Semiotic Analysis of Late Anglo-Saxon Monastic Sign Language," *Studia Anglica Posnaniensia* 36 (2001): 145–169. I am very grateful to Professor Conde-Silvestre for making an offprint of his article available to me.

several decades. Unlike continental sign lists, which commenced with signs for food, the Canterbury document began with the sign for abbot, followed directly by signs for other monastic officials (nos. 1–6).[70] This ordering may have been an attempt on the part of its author to assert the supreme authority of the abbot in a climate of monastic reform. One modern commentator has inferred that the presence of a sign for abbot indicated that the Canterbury sign lexicon had not been adapted to specific conditions at Christ Church, because the archbishop filled the role of this official for the cathedral chapter.[71] It is not unreasonable to assume, however, that the monks referred to their archbishop as "abbot," since he fulfilled the role of spiritual father for their community. Following the signs for officials came signs for books and items used in the church (nos. 7–37), actions related to comportment and personal discipline (nos. 38–43), books and items pertaining to the chapter meeting (nos. 44–48), utensils and foodstuffs (nos. 49–86), items related to the dormitory (nos. 87–94), items and actions concerned with washing and hygiene (nos. 95–98), tools and clothing (nos. 99–110), the bakehouse (no. 111), writing instruments and supplies (nos. 112–117), and lastly signs for persons, both lay and ordained (nos. 118–127). In several cases, these subsections commenced with the sign for the building most readily associated with their use: church (no. 7), chapter house (no. 44), refectory (no. 49), dormitory (no. 87) and bathhouse (no. 95).[72] These building signs very likely served as thematic headings for their respective sections, indicating to the readers of the lexicon the kinds of signs to follow in the manuscript.

The Canterbury sign lexicon, like that of Fleury, borrowed much of its vocabulary from the silent language of the Cluniacs. It also described signs that were Cluniac in origin, but unattested in the identical sign lexicons preserved in the customaries of Bernard and Ulrich. This requires some explanation. As Chapter 2 has argued, the Cluniac sign lexicon was a carefully prescribed list of 118 hand signs compiled for the instruction of novices and not an exhaustive inventory of every sign in use at Cluny. When the monks of the Black Forest abbey of Hirsau adopted Cluniac sign language in the 1080s, they composed a sign lexicon with a vastly expanded vocabulary of 359 signs.[73] The close interaction between monks of Cluny and Hirsau suggests that these hundreds of new signs represented contemporary Cluniac usage rather than innovations in this

---

[70] I have followed Banham's numbering of the Canterbury signs throughout this section (*Monasteriales Indicia*, pp. 22–49).

[71] *Ibid.* p. 9.

[72] Canterbury, nos. 7 (*cyrcean*), 44 (*capitel huse*), 49 (*beoddern*), 87 (*slæpern*) and 95 (*bæðern*), ed. Banham, *Monasteriales Indicia*, pp. 22, 30, 38 and 40.

[73] On the transmission of monastic sign language from Cluny to Hirsau, see pp. 118–123, below.

custom undertaken at Hirsau. Nine of the new signs in the Hirsau sign lexicon also appeared in the Old English sign list copied earlier in the eleventh century at Canterbury. Most of these signs represented items related to the celebration of the liturgy: provost, humeral, alb, chasuble, chalice, mass-bread, censer, Bible and lamp.[74] There is no question that these signs would have been as relevant at Cluny as they were at Canterbury and Hirsau. The limited role played by novices in liturgical services explains their absence from the Cluniac sign lexicon.[75] Although the Canterbury sign list was composed several decades before the earliest Latin sign inventories, all of which date from the last quarter of the eleventh century, its contents were nonetheless influenced by contemporary usage of this custom at Cluny.

Anglo-Saxon monks did not hesitate to adapt Cluniac sign language to the needs of their communities. The most striking adaptation was their decision to compose their sign lexicon in Old English. This document was the product of a reform movement that privileged access to monastic customs written in the vernacular. The translation and glossing of Latin texts relevant to religious reform became an industry in late Anglo-Saxon England. Before his death in 975, King Edgar promised the manor of Sudbourne to Bishop Æthelwold on the condition that he produce a vernacular translation of the *Rule of Benedict* to improve the king's understanding of its precepts.[76] Monastic scribes performed similar tasks without the need for royal sponsorship.[77] Vernacular translations and glosses of important didactic and legislative texts were essential for the spread and adoption of reform policies in Anglo-Saxon abbeys, because Latin was a foreign language to most English monks.[78] By couching the Canterbury

---

[74] Compare Canterbury, nos. 3 (*profost*), 13 (*superumerale*), 14 (*halba*), 17 (*mæssan hacele*), 20 (*calic*), 21 (*oflæt*), 24 (*storfæt*), 29 (*bibliodece*) and 34 (*leoht fæt*), ed. Banham, *Monasteriales Indicia*, pp. 22, 24, 26 and 28; and Hirsau, nos. 254 (*prepositus*), 181 (*humerale*), 182 (*alba*), 180 (*casula*), 156 (*calix*), 158 (*oblata*), 162 (*turibulum*), 215 (*biblioteca*) and 315 (*laterna*), ed. Jarecki, *Signa Loquendi*, pp. 213, 197, 193–195, 205 and 223, respectively.

[75] See Chapter 3, p. 87, above.

[76] *Liber Eliensis* 2.37, ed. E. O. Blake, Camden Third Series XCII (London, 1962), p. 111. Further on this work, see Mechthild Gretsch, "Aethelwold's Translation of the *Regula Sancti Benedicti* and its Latin Exemplar," *Anglo-Saxon England* 3 (1974): 125–151.

[77] See, for example, Ker, *Catalogue of Manuscripts*, pp. 74–75 (no. 46: a bilingual *Rule of Chrodegang*) and 196–197 (no. 155: an Old English *Regularis Concordia*).

[78] For grim assessments of Latin proficiency in ninth-century England and its slow recovery toward the turn of the millennium, see C. E. Hohler, "Some Service-Books of the Later Saxon Church," in *Tenth-Century Studies*, ed. Parsons, pp. 60–83, at pp. 72–74; Michael Lapidge, "The Study of Latin Texts in Late Anglo-Saxon England," in *Latin and the Vernacular Languages in Early Medieval Britain*, ed. N. P. Brooks (Leicester, 1984), pp. 99–140, repr. in Michael Lapidge, *Anglo-Latin Literature, 600–899* (London and Rio Grande, 1996), pp. 455–498; and Michael Lapidge, "Latin Learning in Ninth-Century England," in Lapidge, *Anglo-Latin Literature, 600–899*,

sign lexicon in the vernacular, its anonymous author ensured that its contents would reach and benefit the widest possible audience of monastic readers. In fact, this was true of MS British Library, Cotton Tiberius A.iii as a whole. According to Debby Banham, "[a] consistent concern in Tiberius A.iii is to make the reform, or at least its texts, comprehensible to English speakers."[79]

The Canterbury sign lexicon also boasted new signs tailored to meet the cultural expectations of its Anglo-Saxon readers. The brethren of Christ Church consumed fish and eel like monks in Europe, but their regular diet apparently included shellfish as well, a marine commodity unknown at Cluny and Fleury.[80] Likewise, a cluster of new signs related to washing and the bathhouse underscored a concern for personal hygiene unattested in other monastic sign lexicons.[81] These signs throw light on the cultural sensibility that informed the construction of the elaborate waterworks built at Christ Church around 1160. A contemporary scribe of Canterbury illuminated this impressive system of water distribution and drainage on the last folios of the Eadwine Psalter.[82] New signs for king and queen reflected the fact that royal patronage was a defining aspect of monastic reform in tenth-century England.[83] The Canterbury sign for king seems to have derived from the Cluniac sign for psalter.[84] Both signs involved the placement of the hand and outstretched fingers over the head in imitation of a crown. In the Cluniac sign, the crown represented King David, the author of the psalms. The *Regularis Concordia* recognized the royal couple as the supreme lords and protectors of the abbeys of the realm.[85] Male and female houses alike sought their advice and consent in the election of abbots and abbesses.[86] After

---

pp. 409–454. Further on the vernacular glossing of the *Regularis Concordia*, see Lucia Kornexl, "The *Regularis Concordia* and its Old English Gloss," *Anglo-Saxon England* 24 (1995): 95–130.

[79] See Debby Banham, "Part of the Kit: The *Monasteriales Indicia* and the Monastic Reform," *Old English Newsletter* 30.3 (1997): A-69 (the summary of a paper presented at the Eighth Biennial Meeting of the International Society of Anglo-Saxonists in July 1997).

[80] Canterbury, no. 72 (*ostre*), ed. Banham, *Monasteriales Indicia*, p. 36.

[81] Canterbury, nos. 95 (*bæðern*), 96 (*heafod þwean*), 97 (*wæter*) and 98 (*sape*), ed. Banham, *Monasteriales Indicia*, pp. 40–42.

[82] MS Cambridge, Trinity College R.17.1, fols. 284–286 (c. 1147), described in C. M. Kauffmann, *Romanesque Manuscripts 1066–1190*, A Survey of Manuscripts Illuminated in the British Isles III (London, 1975), pp. 96–97 (no. 68) and fig. 181.

[83] Canterbury, nos. 118 (*cyning*) and 119 (*cyninges wif*), ed. Banham, *Monasteriales Indicia*, p. 46. The classic study of this topic remains Robert Deshman, "*Benedictus Monarcha et Monachus*: Early Medieval Ruler Theology and the Anglo-Saxon Reform," *Frühmittelalterliche Studien* 22 (1988): 204–240.

[84] Cluny, no. 72 (*psalterium*), ed. Jarecki, *Signa Loquendi*, p. 134.

[85] *Regularis Concordia* 10, ed. Symons, p. 7.   [86] *Regularis Concordia* 9, ed. Symons, p. 6.

Nocturns, Anglo-Saxon monks intoned two psalms for the royal house, one specifically for the king and the other for the king, the queen and their entire households.[87] The addition of these new signs gave the silent language of the brethren an Anglo-Saxon inflection that expressed the concerns of reformed English monasticism.

Principles of exclusion were applied to this custom as well. As Debby Banham has observed, the modification of monastic sign language in England involved the choice to exclude Cluniac signs that were not fitting or relevant in Anglo-Saxon abbeys.[88] Generally speaking, the Canterbury sign lexicon eschewed signs for specialty items in favor of their generic equivalents. The monks of Christ Church employed all-purpose signs for bread, fish and the need to drink, but omitted the more specific signs for varieties of bread, species of fish and spiced wine known at Cluny. Absent as well were many of the Cluniac signs for verbs. While these changes suggested to Banham that Anglo-Saxon monks lived more austere and simple lives than the brethren of Cluny, it is equally plausible that their reserved vocabulary was an aspect of monastic discipline. Generic signs streamlined the system of communication, making it easier to learn and more difficult to abuse. To be sure, the semantic ambiguity of these signs made them more dependent on context for their meaning, but they clearly sufficed to meet the needs and expectations of Anglo-Saxon monks at Christ Church and elsewhere.

In the decades before the year 1000, knowledge of monastic sign language arrived in England from Cluny, most probably by way of Saint-Benoît-sur-Loire. Throughout the tenth century, the relics of St. Benedict drew Anglo-Saxon monks to the abbey of Fleury and endorsed the quality of the customs introduced there in the 930s during Odo of Cluny's reform. A monk traveling from Fleury carried knowledge of Cluniac signs to England, where it was codified in Old English to facilitate its use among Anglo-Saxon monks in an age of reform that privileged texts composed in the vernacular. The author of the Canterbury sign lexicon modified the Cluniac sign vocabulary, adding new signs for items and people familiar to Anglo-Saxon monks and omitting traditional vocabulary that had no relevance to their experience. In doing so, he created a new idiom of monastic sign language tailored to the cultural and religious environment of reformed English monasticism.

---

[87] *Regularis Concordia* 18, ed. Symons, p. 13: "Peractis Nocturnis dicant duos psalmos, *Domine ne in furore tuo* [Ps. 6] et *Exaudiat te Dominus* [Ps. 19], unum uidelicet pro rege specialiter, alterum uero pro rege et regina ac familaribus."

[88] Banham, *Monasteriales Indicia*, pp. 12–13.

HIRSAU (THE MONASTERY OF ST. PETER AND PAUL)

Traffic in the knowledge of Cluniac sign language did not flow east across the Rhine River until the end of the eleventh century. It was difficult for Cluniac influence to infiltrate the imperial monastic system before the height of the Gregorian reform, in part due to Ottonian policies that were hostile to the exemption of abbeys from the spiritual jurisdiction of bishops.[89] A Bavarian monk named Ulrich of Zell was instrumental in the transmission of Cluniac customs, including monastic signs, to the Black Forest abbey of Hirsau.[90] Reliable and industrious, Ulrich entered Cluny around 1060 and was soon entrusted with duties that took him far beyond the walls of the abbey for months at a time. After a short tenure as the claustral prior of the Cluniac convent of Marcigny-sur-Loire, he founded priories in the Alpine forests to the east of Burgundy at Rüggisberg, Peterlingen, Grüningen and Zell, as well as a convent for women at Bollschweil.[91] Ulrich's activity as an agent of Cluny reunited him with his old friend William of Hirsau. In their youth, the two had served together at the monastery of St. Emmeram in Regensburg.[92] In 1069, a decade after Ulrich's departure for Cluny, William left Bavaria to lead the newly refounded abbey of St. Peter and Paul at Hirsau.[93] He proved to be a conscientious administrator. In the late 1070s, with the counsel of Bishop Bernard of Marseille, William decided to reform his community on the model of Cluny.[94] Abbot Hugh the Great was so

---

[89] On the right of exemption as a defining aspect of the relationship between Cluny and the papacy, see n. 12, above. On the Ottonian monastic system and the obligations involved for German abbeys, see John W. Bernhardt, *Itinerant Kingship and Royal Monasteries in Early Medieval Germany, c. 936–1075* (Cambridge, 1993).

[90] *Vita sancti Udalrici prioris Cellae (vita posterior)*, ed. Roger Wilmans, *MGH SS* XII (Hanover, 1856), pp. 253–267. The most thorough study of Ulrich's career remains Ernst Hauviller, *Ulrich von Cluny: Ein biographischer Beitrag zur Geschichte der Cluniacenser im 11. Jahrhundert* (Münster, 1896). For the influence of Cluny on German monasticism in this period, see Cowdrey, *The Cluniacs and the Gregorian Reform*, pp. 191–213, esp. p. 196, n. 3 for a convenient summary of older works on Hirsau; and Joachim Wollasch, "Cluny und Deutschland," *Studien und Mitteilungen zur Geschichte des Benediktinerordens und seiner Zweige* 103 (1992): 7–32, esp. pp. 23–27 on the role of Ulrich of Zell.

[91] *Vita sancti Udalrici prioris Cellae* 21, 25, 27, 29 and 32, ed. Wilmans, pp. 258–263. It was customary for Cluniac monks to serve as officials at the convent. See Else Maria Wischermann, *Marcigny-sur-Loire: Gründungs- und Frühgeschichte des ersten Cluniacenserinnenpriorates (1055–1150)* (Munich, 1986), pp. 93–110. Further on Ulrich's activities in this period, see Hauviller, *Ulrich von Cluny*, pp. 41–64.

[92] Ulrich, prol., col. 643a; and Hauviller, *Ulrich von Cluny*, p. 26.

[93] Haimo, *Vita Willihelmi abbatis Hirsaugiensis* 2, *MGH SS* XII, ed. W. Wattenbach (Hanover, 1856), p. 212. Count Adalbert II of Calw began the restoration of Hirsau in 1049 at the request of his cousin, Pope Leo IX. The abbey had been founded in the Carolingian period, but subsequently fell into ruin. On the early history of Hirsau, see Stephan Molitor, "*Ut fertur, sub Pippino rege*: Zur karolingerzeitlichen Gründung Hirsaus," in *Hirsau St. Peter und Paul 1091–1991*, 2 vols. (Stuttgart, 1991), vol. II, pp. 45–54, which argues for an original foundation date between 765 and 768.

[94] William, prol., cols. 928–929.

impressed with his reputation that he sent a representative to Hirsau to indoctrinate the monks of Hirsau in the Cluniac way of life. Ulrich was the obvious choice for the assignment. His friendship and cultural affinity with Abbot William aside, he was experienced as a founder of monastic dependencies and boasted an intimate knowledge of Cluniac traditions. His visit to the Black Forest was a success. Upon his return to Cluny, Ulrich composed a book of customs to serve as a template for the reform underway at Hirsau.[95]

The customary of Ulrich provided a rich storehouse of information culled from the archives of Cluny and from its author's long experience as an overseer of priories and convents. It comprised three books on the order of the liturgy, the instruction of novices and the duties of monastic officials.[96] Like the customary of Bernard, Ulrich's chapters on novice training outlined the rules against speaking at Cluny and included a copy of the Cluniac sign lexicon.[97] Writing in dialogue form, Ulrich responded at length to Abbot William's inquiries concerning the character of Cluniac customs and their relationship to the precepts of the *Rule of Benedict*. Despite its length and specificity, the customary of Ulrich left its readers with many unanticipated questions, prompting William to take action. On three separate occasions during the 1080s, he sent a pair of monks to Cluny where they lived for an unspecified period of time to learn the traditions of the abbey firsthand.[98] These brethren returned to the Black Forest with empirical knowledge of Cluniac monasticism that complemented and in many ways superseded Ulrich's written account. They also carried back an important message from Abbot Hugh the Great. Concerned that William would adopt Cluniac practices without full consideration of their appropriateness to conditions in Germany, Hugh urged him to make whatever changes he considered necessary to adapt these traditions to the local customs of his community and to the location and climate of Hirsau.[99]

---

[95] Ulrich, prol., col. 643a; and William, prol., col. 929b.

[96] On the structure and content of Ulrich's customary, see Burkhardt Tutsch, *Studien zur Rezeptionsgeschichte der Consuetudines Ulrichs von Cluny* (Münster, 1998), pp. 39–54.

[97] See Chapter 1, pp. 26–27; and Chapter 2, p. 63, above.

[98] William, prol., col. 929c. The brethren of eleventh-century Montecassino also endorsed the practice of visitation as a means of learning alien customs. See *Die ältere Wormser Briefsammlung*, ed. Walther Bulst, *MGH Briefe* III (Weimar, 1949), pp. 13–18 (no. 1).

[99] William, prol., col. 929cd: "Illis tandem redeuntibus, et tam fructuosi operis manipulos cum gaudio reportantibus, accepimus per eos mandatum a Domino Hugone venerabili Cluniacensium abbate, ut sua freti auctoritate, coadunato seniorum nostrorum consilio, prout ipsa declarat ratio, secundum morem patriae, loci situm, et aeris temeriem, de eisdem consuetudinibus, si quid esset superfluum demeremus; si quid mutandum, mutaremus; si quid addendum, adderemus."

Abbot William took the advice to heart. Before his death in 1091, he composed a body of legislation modeled on the customary of Ulrich, but tailored specifically to life at Hirsau.[100] The customary of William echoed Ulrich's concern with the preservation of monastic silence, but also extended the boundaries of its application in the abbey.[101] Following Ulrich's example, William forbade conversation in the church, the refectory, the dormitory and the kitchens, and instructed his monks to remain silent before the close of the litany on twelve-lesson feast days in the summer and before the third hour during winter months. In a break from received tradition, however, the customary of William imposed on novices much stricter rules against speaking than those observed at Cluny. A total ban on conversation extended at all times throughout their cells. No one was ever allowed to converse there, except for the abbot, the prior and the master of novices, and then only when the novices made their confession.

Abbot William adopted the silent language of the Cluniacs to foster this rigorous ideal of silence, but he made considerable changes to this custom to prepare it for use in his community.[102] The Hirsau customary included a descriptive catalogue of hand signs modeled on the sign lexicon included in Ulrich's work, but William expanded its repertoire dramatically from 118 to 359 signs (Table 5).[103] This unprecedented elaboration of the monastic sign vocabulary made the Hirsau sign lexicon the longest catalogue of sign-forms to survive from the Middle Ages. William may have undertaken this expansion to accommodate the unusually strict prohibitions against speaking observed by the Hirsau novices. Their imposed silence would have increased their reliance on a much broader range of sign vocabulary than that taught to prospective monks during the Cluniac novitiate. This is not to suggest that the new signs in the Hirsau customary were the invention of William and his community. In fact, the majority of these signs were probably already in use at Cluny, but did not find their way into the Cluniac sign lexicon because they did not have a direct bearing on the instruction of novices. The monks of Hirsau who visited the great

---

[100] For a description of the Hirsau customary and its contents, see Norbert Reimann, "Die Konstitutionen des Abtes Wilhelm von Hirsau: Bermerkungen zur Überlieferungs- und Wirkungsgeschichte," in *Hirsau St. Peter und Paul*, vol. II, pp. 101–108. Burkhardt Tutsch has prepared a comparative chapter breakdown of the customaries that demonstrates William of Hirsau's dependence on his Cluniac model. See Tutsch, *Studien zur Rezeptionsgeschichte*, pp. 358–371 (Appendix 1).

[101] For what follows, see William 1.5, cols. 940b–d.

[102] Tutsch, *Studien zur Rezeptionsgeschichte*, pp. 91–97.

[103] William 1.6–25, cols. 940d–957c (*De signis loquendi*). For a critical edition of the Hirsau sign lexicon, see Jarecki, *Signa Loquendi*, pp. 163–230.

Burgundian abbey to learn its traditions firsthand were in an opportune position to observe the application of the full panoply of Cluniac signs by professed monks with considerable experience in this custom. Their newfound expertise undoubtedly informed the composition of the Hirsau sign lexicon, thereby allowing William to triple the number of signs recorded in Ulrich's customary, which was his only other source of information for this practice. It was particularly important for William to expand on the vocabulary provided by the novice-oriented lexicon available at Cluny because, unlike the Cluniacs, the monks of Hirsau had no reservoir of oral knowledge and practice to draw on for information about the use of this custom.

There were, in fact, so many new signs that Abbot William had to reorganize the structure of his textual model to present them in a meaningful way. He accomplished this by dividing the four sections of the Cluniac sign lexicon into more discrete and coherent units, each with its own heading. The signs for food and vessels (Cluny, nos. 1–35) became ten sections of signs for bread (Hirsau, nos. 1–7), vegetables (nos. 8–10), fish (nos. 11–26), staples (nos. 27–44), common fruit (nos. 45–54), exotic fruit (nos. 55–57), herbs (nos. 58–82), spices (nos. 83–85), liquids (nos. 86–96) and serving vessels (nos. 97–113). The signs for apparel remained an autonomous section, but the number of entries increased from twenty-two (Cluny, nos. 36–57) to twenty-nine (Hirsau, nos. 114–142). The signs for the divine office (Cluny, nos. 58–79) expanded to six sections of signs pertaining to the church (Hirsau, nos. 143–166), masses and hours (nos. 167–178), liturgical vestments (nos. 179–191), the celebration of the office (nos. 192–202), books (nos. 203–228) and objects made of wood (nos. 229–231). Lastly, the miscellany of signs for people, actions and concepts that concluded the Cluniac sign lexicon (Cluny, nos. 80–118) was subdivided into ten sections of signs for people and special officials (Hirsau, nos. 232–265), diverse actions and concepts (nos. 266–294), buildings (nos. 295–309), a procession (no. 310), wax and candles (nos. 311–316), signs pertaining to the act of writing and the scriptorium (nos. 317–322), metals (nos. 323–345), laughter and sickness (nos. 346–348), domesticated animals (nos. 349–357) and wild animals (nos. 358–359).

The rationale for most of these thematic groupings is self-evident, but the deliberate association of signs for laughing, nosebleed and vomiting (nos. 346–348) challenges modern expectations and invites closer inquiry.[104] As we have seen, the earliest Christian ascetics condemned

---

[104] Hirsau, nos. 346 (*ridere*), 347 (*sanguis de naso fluens*) and 348 (*vomere*), ed. Jarecki, *Signa Loquendi*, p. 228.

laughter as antithetical to the penitential spirit of the desert. Tempering this tradition, early medieval monks were curiously ambivalent about the expression of mirth.[105] Their prohibitions against laughter tended to focus on amusement that was raucous and unbridled. Consequently, physical comportment emerged as an important factor in the moral economy of monastic humor. The *Rule of Benedict* specifically forbade "movements of laughter" (*risum mouentia*), an ambiguous phrase that presumably referred to the uncontrollable and indecorous shaking of the body that attends strong feelings of levity.[106] Carolingian authors inflated the authority of this ruling by repeating it verbatim in the legislation that governed their religious communities.[107] This attitude toward unrestrained mirth provides the clearest insight into the association of the sign for laughing with those for nosebleed and vomiting at Hirsau. Like these conditions, which involved the spontaneous expulsion of blood and bile from the body, laughter in its worst sense was an uncontrollable eruption of sound and movement that interrupted the monk's control of his personal comportment and disturbed the cultivated tranquility of those around him.

The breadth of the Hirsau sign vocabulary makes it difficult to perceive whether Abbot William exercised any principles of exclusion when he adopted this custom from Cluny. Modifications to the signs for fish suggest that he did. The catalogue of fish signs in the Cluniac sign lexicon yields a comprehensive profile of the local aquatic ecosystem.[108] The specificity of these signs made them particularly sensitive to change. The monks of Hirsau appropriated Cluniac signs for freshwater fish that were indigenous to the Black Forest region, but they also created signs that reflected differences in local ecology, regional trade routes and dietary customs. The Hirsau sign lexicon included new signs for barbel, bream and burbot, but these fish were also native to waters in the vicinity of Cluny, so their absence from the Cluniac sign lexicon may indicate that they were eaten less frequently than the other species represented there.[109] Less surprising are new signs for grayling, carp and

---

[105] See Chapter 1, pp. 32–33, above.   [106] *RB* 6.8, p. 472.

[107] See, for example, Benedict of Aniane, *Concordia regularum* 9.1, *PL* CIII, col. 825a; and Smaragdus, *Expositio in regulam sancti Benedicti* 6, ed. Alfred Spannagel and Pius Engelbert, *CCM* VIII, p. 161, where the phrase "risum mouentia" was qualified as: "risum supra modum."

[108] Cluny, nos. 8–14, ed. Jarecki, *Signa Loquendi*, pp. 122–124. See Richard C. Hoffmann, "Economic Development and Aquatic Ecosystems in Medieval Europe," *American Historical Review* 101 (1996): 631–669, esp. pp. 634–635.

[109] Hirsau, nos. 20 (*piscis qui barbo vocatur*), 23 (*brahsima*) and 24 (*ruppa*), ed. Jarecki, *Signa Loquendi*, p. 167. See Frédérique Audoin-Rouzeau, *Ossements animaux du moyen âge au monastère de La Charité-sur-Loire* (Paris, 1986), pp. 146–147.

herring.[110] Grayling are native to cold running waters across northern continental Europe and would have been more at home in Black Forest streams around Hirsau than in water systems near Cluny. The Hirsau sign for carp is the earliest reference to this fish so far west and in the Rhine watershed, whence it had spread from its natural range in the lower and middle Danube. It was unknown at Cluny and would not appear in more western rivers for another 150 years.[111] Herrings are marine fish harvested in northern seas and then salted or smoked for inland distribution. For this reason, the sign for herring at Hirsau was a compound of the generic sign for fish and the sign for salt.[112] The brethren of Hirsau probably obtained this catch from traders on the Rhine. Cluny was too far from herring habitats and production zones to take part in this trade network. This reasoning may also explain why the abbot of Hirsau did not adopt the Cluniac sign for squid. This sign would have had no relevance to German monks, because the routes of trade that brought salted squid from the Mediterranean Sea to Burgundy did not extend to the Black Forest region.[113]

Like the monks of Fleury and Canterbury, Abbot William also made changes to Cluniac sign-forms to meet the cultural expectations of his brethren. The sign for milk is one such example. At Cluny and other eleventh-century abbeys, the sign for milk was made by placing the little finger to the lips in imitation of a suckling infant.[114] In contrast, the monks of Hirsau expressed the need for milk with a sign that mimicked the milking of a cow.[115] Abbot William may have altered this sign-form because the Cluniac sign for milk called to mind a woman's nipple and was therefore an inappropriate action for monks to contemplate. It is also possible that he made this change because the image of milking a cow carried a stronger cultural resonance for his charges than that of a suckling infant and thus would have been easier to remember. Whatever his reason, Abbot William's intervention shows that he did not hesitate to recast Cluniac sign-forms to facilitate their use in his community.

---

[110] Hirsau, nos. 21 (*piscis qui asco appellatur*), 17 (*piscis qui vulgari nomine carpho dicitur*) and 22 (*allec*), ed. Jarecki, *Signa Loquendi*, pp. 166–167.

[111] On the westward spread of carp in the eleventh and twelfth centuries, see Hoffmann, "Economic Development and Aquatic Ecosystems," pp. 662–665.

[112] Hirsau, no. 22: "Pro signo allecis premisso generali signum salis adde." ed. Jarecki, *Signa Loquendi*, p. 167.

[113] On the harvest of squid in the early medieval period, see Chapter 3, pp. 81–82, above.

[114] Cluny, no. 20: "Pro signo lactis minimum digitum labiis inpinge pro eo, quod ita sugit infans." The same sign was in use at Fleury (no. 26). See Jarecki, *Signa Loquendi*, pp. 125 and 254.

[115] Hirsau, no. 31: "Pro signo lactis omnes digitos dextere manus minimo alterius manus digito circumponas et sic inante trahas ipsum lac emulgentem simulans." ed. Jarecki, *Signa Loquendi*, p. 169.

CONCLUSION

As the holy reputation of Cluniac monks increased in the decades around 1000, abbots throughout northern Europe encouraged the emulation of their way of life. From the tenth century onwards, their silent language of signs was adopted in monastic communities from the Black Forest to the Loire Valley and as far afield from Burgundy as southern England. As the three case studies in this chapter have shown, the custom of sign language was not a static commodity in tenth- and eleventh-century monastic culture. It is clear that monks displayed both discernment and pragmatism when they appropriated signs from Cluny and other communities in its orbit of influence. While signs for people and items common in early medieval cloisters passed unchanged between abbeys, those expressive of indigenous ideals and local conditions varied considerably from place to place. The modification of the Cluniac sign vocabulary evinced at Fleury, Canterbury and Hirsau provides compelling insight into the local character of monastic experience in this period, but close attention to these details threatens to obscure a feature of this custom that persisted throughout this process of transmission and adaptation. While monks across northern Europe tailored the Cluniac sign vocabulary as they saw fit, they did not think to alter the quasi-linguistic properties of this custom. In other words, every community considered in this chapter held to the Cluniac ideal that the replication of human discourse was not the purpose of monastic sign language. At no point did the brethren of Fleury, Canterbury or Hirsau attempt to introduce principles of language that would have altered the semiotic structure of the sign system and thereby undermined its function in the abbey. This consistency in practice over such a broad geographical range emphasizes the fact that the intrinsic limitations of the Cluniac sign language as a form of expression were an appealing and enduring attribute of this custom in early medieval monasticism.

The transmission and adaptation of monastic sign language continued unabated into the twelfth century, even as the new religious orders that proliferated at that time challenged received traditions about the dangers of human speech. The final chapter of this study examines how monks, canons and hermits reconciled the discipline of silence with the varieties of active piety that were so important to the evangelical spirit of their reform. Praise for the virtue of silence was universal in twelfth-century religious discourse, but the parameters of its practice were open to interpretation and negotiation. The centrality of silence as a monastic virtue assured, however, that the silent language of the Cluniacs would appeal to the new religious orders. In fact, as the next chapter shows, this custom became so widespread by the end of the twelfth century that it was widely recognized and often maligned as a stereotypical attribute of cloistered life throughout western Europe.

Table 3: *The vocabulary of the Fleury sign lexicon*

Signs for sustenance (*que ad victum pertinent*)

1. Bread (*panis*)
2. Bread cooked in water (*panis qui coquitur in aqua*)
3. Wheat bread (*panis sigalinus*)
4. Small loaf (*tortula*)
5. Malt bread (*panis bracellorum*)
6. Beans (*fabae*)
7. Eggs (*ova*)
8. Eggs cooked in oil or lard (*ova in oleo vel in pinguedine cocta*)
9. Peas (*pisa*)
10. Millet (*milietum*)
11. *Navetum* (*navetum*)
12. Fish (*piscis*)
13. Herring (*alec*)
14. Squid (*sepiae*)
15. Eel (*anguilla*)
16. Lamprey (*murena vel lampreda*)
17. Salmon (*salmo*)
18. Pike (*lucius*)
19. Trout (*truta*)
20. Mullet (*muletum*)
21. Crepes (*crispellae*)
22. Barbel (*barbelum*)
23. Cheese (*caseus*)
24. Cheese tarts (*tocapae*)
25. Bread of some kind (*rufeolae*)
26. Milk (*lac*)
27. Bread pudding (*morteus*)
28. Honey (*mel*)
29. Apple (*pomum*)
30. Pear (*pirus*)
31. Nut (*nux*)
32. Cherries (*ceraseae*)
33. Cabbage (*poreta vel caulis*)
34. Raw lentils (*porrus crudus*)
35. Garlic (*alium*)
36. Water (*aqua*)
37. Wine (*vinum*)
38. Drink prepared with honey and wormwood (*pocio melle et absinthio temperata*)
39. Spiced drink (*pigmentum seu nectar*)
40. Mustard seed (*sinapis*)
41. Vinegar (*acetum*)
42. Flat dish (*scutella*)
43. Cup (*tacea*)

Table 3: (*cont.*)

44. Drink made from white wine and a certain plant called *aloigne* in the Gallic tongue (*pocio, que sit ex vino albo et quadam herba, que galice vocatur aloigne*)
45. *Mensura*, from which the daily wine is dispensed (*mensura ex qua cotidie vinum distribuitur*)
46. *Verves* (*verves*)
47. Glass drinking vessel (*fiola vitrea*)

Signs for apparel (*de his, que ad vestitum pertinent*)

48. Woollen tunic (*staminea*)
49. Trousers (*femoralia*)
50. Frock (*froteus*)
51. Cowl (*cuculla*)
52. Sleeves (*manicae*)
53. Hide garment (*pelliceum*)
54. Hood (*capuceum*)
55. Shoes (*calcei*)
56. Night shoes (*nocturnales calcei*)
57. Ankle straps (*pedules*)
58. Blanket (*coopertorium*)
59. Linen garment in which we sleep (*linteamen in quo cubamus*)
60. Coat (*cottus*)
61. Similar item (*simile*)
62. Pillow or cushion (*capitale* vel *cussinum*)
63. Strap (*corrigia*)
64. Belt (*cingulum*)
65. Needle (*acus*)
66. Thread (*filum*)
67. Knife (*cultellus*)
68. Sheath (*vagina cultelli*)
69. Comb (*pecten*)
70. Writing boards (*tabulae*)
71. Writing instrument (*stillus sive graphium*)

Signs for the divine office (*ad divinum maxime pertinent obsequium*)

72. Reading (*lectio*)
73. Response (*responsorium*)
74. Alleluia (*alleluya*)
75. Prose or what the Germans call sequence (*prosa vel quod a teutonicis sequencia nominatur*)
76. Tractus (*tractus*)
77. Book (*liber*)
78. Missal (*liber missalis*)
79. The Book of Epistles (*liber epistolaris*)
80. The Gospels (*liber in quo dicitur evangelium*)

Table 3: (*cont.*)

81. Book read at Nocturns (*liber in quo legendum est ad nocturnas*)
82. Antiphonary (*antiphonarum*)
83. Psalter (*psalterium*)
84. Book containing the collects (*collectarium*)
85. Hymnbook (*gradualis*)
86. To sing (*cantare*)
87. To sing quietly (*pacifice cantare*)
88. *Rule of Benedict* (*regula*)
89. Hymnal (*hympnarium*)
90. Customary (*liber consuetudinum*)
91. Angel (*angelus*)
92. Apostle (*apostolus*)
93. Martyr (*martir*)
94. Confessor (*confessor*)
95. Abbot (*abbas*)
96. Holy virgin (*sacra virgo*)
97. All Saints (*omnes sancti predicti*)
98. Feast day (*festivitas*)
99. Monk (*monachus*)
100. Priest (*clericus*)
101. Layman (*laicus*)
102. Monk raised in the abbey (*monachus nutritus in monasterio*)
103. Abbot (*abbas*)
104. Major prior (*grandis prior*)
105. Subprior (*subprior*)
106. Third prior (*tercius prior*)
107. Fourth prior (*quartus prior*)
108. Custodian of the church (*custos ecclesie*)
109. Chamberlain (*camerarius*)
110. Cellarer (*cellararius*)
111. Keeper of the granary (*granatarius*)
112. Gardener (*ortolarius*)
113. Keeper of the hospice (*custos hospicii*)
114. Almoner, who receives the poor (*elemosinarius, qui pauperes recipit*)
115. Almoner, who offers alms in the absence of bread (*elemosinarius, qui peccunias debet in defectu panis*)
116. Infirmarer (*infirmarius*)
117. Refectorer (*refectorarius*)
118. Cantor (*cantor*)
119. Master of the boys (*magister puerorum*)
120. Master of the novices (*magister noviciorum*)
121. Sacrist (*secretinus*)
122. Master of the work (*magister operis*)
123. Treasurer (*thauserarius*)
124. Servant of the monk who sounds the bells (*famulus pulsatoris*)

Table 3: (*cont.*)

125. Doctor (*medicus*)
126. Barber (*barbitor*)
127. Cook (*coquus*)
128. Refector's servant (*famulus refectorii*)
129. Keeper of the donkeys (*asinarius*)
130. Man who speaks another language (*homo alterius lingue*)
131. To talk (*loqui*)
132. To hear (*audire*)
133. To not know (*nescire*)
134. To tell a lie (*mentiri*)
135. To kiss (*osculari*)
136. To dress (*vestire*)
137. To undress (*exuere*)
138. To wash feet (*lavare pedes*)
139. Something good (*bonum*)
140. Something bad (*malum*)
141. Something done (*res facta*)
142. Command (*preceptum*)
143. Refusal (*negacio*)
144. Quickness (*celeritas*)
145. Slowness (*tarditas*)
146. Wax (*cereum*)
147. Wax candle (*candela cerea*)
148. Oil (*oleum*)
149. Incense (*thus*)
150. Censer (*turribulum*)
151. Permission to go somewhere (*licencia eundi alicubi*)
152. Permission to go and urinate (*licencia eunci mictum aquam*)
153. Defecation (*purgacio ventris*)
154. To say: you will be in the chapter meeting (*dicere: tu eris in capitulo*)

Table 4: *The vocabulary of the Canterbury sign lexicon*

1. Abbot (*abbud*)
2. Dean (*diacan*)
3. Provost (*profost*)
4. Cellarer (*hordere*)
5. Master (*magister*)
6. Sacrist (*cyricweard*)
7. The church (*cyrcean*)

Signs for books used in the liturgy (*þara boca tacn þe mon on cyrican to god cundun þeowdome notigan sceal*)

---

8. Gradual (*antiponaria*)
9. Sacramentary (*maesse boc*)
10. Epistolary (*pistol boc*)
11. Troper (*troper*)
12. Any rectangular book (*hwilce langwyrpe boc*)
13. Superhumeral (*superumerale*)
14. Alb (*halba*)
15. Girdle (*gyrder*)
16. Stole (*stola*)
17. Mass vestment (*mæssan hacele*)
18. Maniple (*handlin*)
19. Offering-cloth (*offrung*)
20. Chalice and paten (*calic and disc*)
21. Mass-bread (*oflæt*)
22. Wine (*win*)
23. Wine-flask (*winhorn*)
24. Censer (*storfæt*)
25. Tapers (*tapers*)
26. Candlestick (*candel sticca*)
27. Thin candle (*smael candel*)
28. Candle board (*candel bord*)

Signs for books used at Matins (*þara boca tacna þe mon æt uhtsange notian sceal*)

---

29. Bible (*biblioðece*)
30. Legendary (*martirlogium*)
31. Any other book containing the Gospels (*hwylce oþre boc þe god spelles traht on sy*)
32. Psalter (*salter*)
33. Hymnal (*hymner*)
34. Lamp (*leoht fæt*)
35. Large cross (*micel rod*)
36. Small cross (*litel rod*)
37. Small candlestick (*gewæd candel sticca*)
38. To sit in church because of some infirmity (*inne cyricean sittan for wylcere untrumnysse*)
39. To request someone sitting down to stand up (*willan þæt hwa sittendra manna up arise*)

Table 4: (*cont.*)

40. To request someone standing up to sit down (*willan þæt he sytte þonne*)
41. To reject more of something, of which one has enough (*gyf man hwylcum breþer byt hwæt on ufan þæt he genoh hæbbe*)
42. To accept an offering (*gyf he þæt ge bodene habban wille*)
43. To reject an offering (*gyf he hyt nelle*)
44. The chapter house (*capitel huse*)
45. Small martyrology (*gewæd martirlogium*)
46. *Rule of Benedict* (*regol*)
47. Rod (*gyrd*)
48. Scourge (*swypa*)
49. The refectory (*beoddern*)
50. Seat covering (*setrægel*)
51. Folding stool for the mealtime reader (*meterædere flydstol*)
52. Cloth or napkin (*sceat oððe wapan*)
53. Dish (*disc*)
54. Bread (*laf*)
55. Knife (*syx*)
56. Skewer (*sticca*)
57. Boiled vegetables (*gesodenra wyrta*)
58. Raw vegetables (*grene wyrta*)
59. Leeks (*læces*)
60. Porridge (*briw*)
61. Pepper (*pipor*)
62. Beans (*beana*)
63. Peas (*peosenan*)
64. Cheese (*cyse*)
65. Butter (*butere oððe smeoru*)
66. Milk (*meolc*)
67. Eggs (*ægrera*)
68. Salt (*scealt*)
69. Honey (*hunig*)
70. Fish (*fisc*)
71. Eel (*æl*)
72. Oyster (*ostre*)
73. Apple (*æpple*)
74. Pear (*peru*)
75. Plum (*plyme*)
76. Cherry (*cyrsen*)
77. Sloe (*slan*)
78. Salt meat (*sealtflæsc*)
79. Cup or measure (*cuppe oððe iustitia*)
80. Lid (*hlid*)
81. Large bowl (*micel bledu*)
82. Little drinking vessel (*lytel drencefæt*)
83. To drink (*drincan*)

Table 4: (*cont.*)

84. Dripped wine (*gedrypt win*)
85. Beer (*beor*)
86. Herbal drink (*wyrtdrenc*)
87. The dormitory (*slæpern*)
88. Lamp (*blacern*)
89. Bedcover (*bedreaf*)
90. Pillow (*pyle*)
91. Slippers (*swyftlera*)
92. Socks (*socca*)
93. Shoes (*sceona*)
94. Lavatory (*tun*)
95. The bathhouse (*bæðern*)
96. To wash your head (*þine heafod þwean*)
97. Water (*wæter*)
98. Soap (*sape*)
99. Nail-knife (*nægel seax*)
100. Comb (*camb*)
101. Shirt (*hemeþe*)
102. Pants (*brecce*)
103. Leg bands (*wynynga*)
104. Stockings (*hosa*)
105. Pelisse (*pylece*)
106. Cowl (*cugle*)
107. Scapular (*scapular*)
108. Glove (*glofa*)
109. Scissors (*sceara*)
110. Needle (*nædle*)
111. Bakehouse (*bæcern*)
112. Stylus (*græf*)
113. Small wax tablets (*gehwæde wæxbreda*)
114. Large wax tablet (*micel weax bred*)
115. Ruler (*reogol sticca*)
116. Ink-well (*blec horn*)
117. Quill (*fiþer*)
118. King (*cyning*)
119. Queen (*cyninges wif*)
120. Bishop (*bisceop*)
121. Any monk (*munec*)
122. Nun (*mynecenu*)
123. Priest (*mæsse preost*)
124. Deacon (*diacon*)
125. Celibate priest (*mædenneshad preost*)
126. Layman (*lædeman*)
127. Laywoman (*ungehadod wif*)

Table 5: *The vocabulary of the Hirsau sign lexicon*

Signs for sustenance (*que ad victum pertinent*)

1. Bread (*panis*)
2. Bread cooked in water (*panis qui coquitur in aqua*)
3. Twice-cooked bread (*panis biscoctus*)
4. Small loaf (*tortula*)
5. Major offering (*oblata maioris*)
6. Unleavened bread (*panis azimus*)
7. Wheat bread (*panis siligineus*)

Concerning vegetables (*De leguminis*)

8. Beans (*fabae*)
9. Peas (*pisae*)
10. Lentil (*lens*)

Concerning the signs for fish (*De signis piscium*)

11. Fish (*piscis*)
12. Sturgeon (*sturio*)
13. Salmon (*salmo*)
14. Lachs (*lahso*)
15. Lamprey (*murena sive lampreda*)
16. Pike (*lucius*)
17. Carp (*carpho*)
18. Trout (*trutta*)
19. Eel (*anguilla*)
20. Barbel (*barbo*)
21. Grayling (*asco*)
22. Herring (*allec*)
23. Bream (*brahsima*)
24. Burbot (*ruppa*)
25. Dried fish (*piscis assus*)
26. Crayfish (*cancer*)

Concerning the signs for staples (*De signis ciborum*)

27. Cheese (*caseus*)
28. Cigara (*cigara*)
29. Eggs (*ova*)
30. Eggs cooked in lard (*ova que in sagimine coquuntur*)
31. Milk (*lac*)
32. Cheese tarts (*fladones*)
33. Crepes (*crispellae*)
34. Bread of some kind (*crafonnes vel rufeolae*)

Table 5: (*cont.*)

35. Bread cooked in a frying pan (*panis qui in sartagine coquitur*)
36. Dish of vegetables (*pulmentum oleribus confectum*)
37. Little snack of raw greens and herbs (*sorbiciuncula, id est cibum ex herbis et holeribus confectum*)
38. Millet (*milium*)
39. To eat (*comedere*)
40. Meat (*caro*)
41. Lard (*sagimen*)
42. Oil (*oleum*)
43. Natural oil (*oleum naturale*)
44. Honey (*mel*)

Concerning the signs for fruit (*De signis pomorum*)

45. Fruit (*poma*)
46. Pear (*pirum*)
47. Small fig (*cottanus*)
48. Peach (*persicum*)
49. Medlar (*nespela*)
50. Greater nut (*nux maior*)
51. Grape (*botrum*)
52. Greater plum (*pruna maior*)
53. Cherries (*ceraseae*)
54. Mulberries (*fraga*)

Concerning the signs for exotic fruit. For the signs of fruit, which are unusual or rare in our lands (*De signis pomorum peregrinorum. Ad signa pomorum, que terris nostris rara et inusitata sunt*)

55. Cedar berry (*pomum cedrinum*)
56. Fig (*ficus*)
57. Chestnut (*castenea*)

Concerning the signs for herbs (*De signis holerum*)

58. Herb (*holus*)
59. Onion (*cepa*)
60. Gourd (*cucurbita*)
61. Pumpkin (*pepo*)
62. Bitter herb (*ruta*)
63. Fennel (*feniculum*)
64. Panacea or all-heal (*panaceta vel reinevano*)
65. Dill (*anetum*)
66. Parsley (*apium*)
67. Sage (*salvia*)

Table 5: (*cont.*)

68. Burciolum (*burciolum*)
69. Lettuce (*lactuca*)
70. Wax-leaf (*cerefolium*)
71. Cabbage (*caulis*)
72. Rock-parsley (*petrosilinum*)
73. Cardamina or nasturcium, which is commonly called cress (*cardamum vel nasturcium, quod vulgariter cresso dicitur*)
74. Poppy (*papaver*)
75. Lily (*lilium*)
76. Rose (*rosa*)
77. Hyssopum (*ysopum*)
78. Southern-wood (*abrotanum*)
79. Wormwood (*absinthium*)
80. Garlic (*allium*)
81. Radish (*rafa*)
82. Turnip (*rapa*)

Concerning the signs for smells (*De signis aromatum*)

83. Ginger (*gingiber*)
84. Pepper (*piper*)
85. Frankincense (*tus*)

Concerning the signs for various liquids (*De signis diversi liquoris*)

86. Water (*aqua*)
87. Holy water (*aqua benedicta*)
88. Beer (*cervisia*)
89. Mead (*medo*)
90. Wine (*vinum*)
91. Spiced drink (*potio pigmentata*)
92. Drink prepared with honey and wormwood (*potio melle et absintio temperata*)
93. Mustard oil (*sinapis*)
94. Vinegar (*acetum*)
95. Red wine (*vinum rubeum*)
96. Clear wine (*vinum clarum*)

Concerning the signs for vessels (*De signis vasorum*)

97. Flat dish (*scutella*)
98. Bowl (*cavata*)
99. Spoon (*coclear*)
100. Cup (*sciphus*)
101. Shallow bowl (*patera*)

Table 5: (*cont.*)

102. Beaker (*becharius*)
103. Glass drinking vessel (*phiala vitrea*)
104. Salt container (*vasculum in quo sal habetur*)
105. Little basket (*sportula*)
106. Wood (*lignum*)
107. Vessel commonly called a jug (*vas quod vulgo cannata dicitur*)
108. Vessel in which vinegar is carried (*vas in quo acetum portari solet*)
109. Wine vessel (*vas vinarium*)
110. Cask (*fustis*)
111. Flat dish, in which crumbs are collected (*scutella in qua mice recolligi solent*)
112. Fan (*flabellum*)
113. Wine cup (*cuppa vinaria*)

Concerning the signs for clothing (*De signis vestimentorum*)

114. Wool tunic (*stamineum*)
115. Trousers (*femoralia*)
116. Frock (*froccus*)
117. Hide garment (*pellicium*)
118. Fur cloak (*gunella*)
119. Shoes (*calcei*)
120. Night shoes (*nocturnales calcei*)
121. Boots (*pedules, id est socci*)
122. Shoes made of hide (*pedules villosi*)
123. Felt slippers (*filtrones*)
124. Leg straps (*fasciolae*)
125. Blanket (*coopertorium*)
126. Coat (*cottus*)
127. Hairshirt (*cilicium*)
128. Sheet (*strala*)
129. Pillow or cushion (*capitale vel cussinum*)
130. Quilt (*culcitra*)
131. Belt or strap for a tunic (*zona sive corrigia ad stamineam*)
132. Belt for trousers (*cingulum femorialium*)
133. Needle (*acus*)
134. Knife (*cultellus*)
135. Sheath (*vagina cultelli*)
136. Comb (*pecten*)
137. Writing boards (*tabulae*)
138. Board, on which things are written down (*tabula in qua notari solet*)
139. Writing instrument (*graphium*)
140. Spurs (*calcares*)
141. Gloves (*cirothecae*)
142. Stone (*lapis*)

Table 5: (*cont.*)

Concerning the signs for things related to the church (*De signis ecclesiasticorum*)

---

143. Altar (*altare*)
144. High altar (*altare principale*)
145. Altar of any virgin (*altare cuiuslibet virginis*)
146. Altar of Saint Michael (*altare sancti Michahelis*)
147. Altar of Saint John the Baptist (*altare sancti Johannis Baptiste*)
148. Altar of Saint Peter or all of the apostles (*altare sancti Petri sive omnium apostolorum*)
149. Altar of bishops (*altare episcoporum*)
150. Altar of confessors (*altare confessorum*)
151. Altar of Saint Paul the Apostle (*altare sancti Petri apostoli*)
152. Altar of Saint Lawrence (*altare sancti Laurentii*)
153. Altar of Saint Benedict or others who were abbots (*altare sancti Benedicti sive aliorum, que abbates fuerunt*)
154. Cross (*crux*)
155. Reliquary (*capsa*)
156. Goblet (*calix*)
157. Shallow dish (*patena*)
158. Offering (*oblata*)
159. Vessel from which we are accustomed to take the blood of the Lord (*fistula sive harundo ex qua sanguinem domini percipere solemus*)
160. Liturgical cloth (*corporale*)
161. Cloth prepared for the offering (*pannum ad offerendum aptatum*)
162. Censer (*turibulum*)
163. Candlestick (*candelaber*)
164. Incense casket (*acerra*)
165. Bellows (*follis*)
166. Basins (*bacina*)

Concerning the signs for masses and hours (*De signis missarum vel horarum*)

---

167. The mass (*missa*)
168. High mass (*missa maior*)
169. Mass for the dead (*missa defunctorum*)
170. Matins (*matutini nocturnales*)
171. Lauds (*matutinae laudes*)
172. Prime (*prima*)
173. Terce (*tercia*)
174. Sext (*sexta*)
175. None (*nona*)
176. Vespers (*vespera*)
177. Meeting (*collatio*)
178. Compline (*completorium*)

Table 5: (*cont.*)

Concerning the signs for liturgical vestments (*De signis indumentorum sacerdotalium*)

179. Cope (*cappa*)
180. Cape (*casula*)
181. Veil (*humerale*)
182. Alb (*alba*)
183. Maniple (*fano*)
184. Dalmatic (*dalmatica*)
185. Subdeacon's liturgical garment (*subtile*)
186. Pallium (*pallium*)
187. Curtain (*cortina*)
188. Dossal (*dorsale*)
189. Tapestry (*tapes*)
190. Feast day (*festivitas*)
191. Mat (*matta*)

Concerning those signs pertaining to the divine office (*De his que ad divinum pertinent obsequium*)

192. Reading (*lectio*)
193. Response (*responsorium*)
194. Verse (*versus*)
195. Antiphon (*antiphona*)
196. Introit (*introitus*)
197. Response to the Gradual (*responsorium graduale*)
198. Alleluia (*alleluia*)
199. Prose or sequence (*prosa vel sequentia*)
200. Tractus (*tractus*)
201. Offertory anthem of the mass (*offertorium*)
202. Communion (*communio*)

Concerning the signs for the books (*De signis librorum*)

203. Book (*liber*)
204. Missal (*liber missalis*)
205. Book of the Offices (*liber officialis*)
206. The Gospels (*textus evangelii*)
207. The Book of Epistles (*liber epistolaris*)
208. Book read at Nocturns (*liber in quo legendum est ad nocturnos*)
209. Antiphonary (*antiphonarium*)
210. Gradual (*liber gradualis*)
211. *Rule of Benedict* (*regula*)
212. Hymnal (*ymnarium*)
213. Psalter (*psalterium*)

Table 5: (*cont.*)

214. Book of the Prophets (*liber prophetarum*)
215. Library (*biblioteca*)
216. Letters of Saint Paul (*epistolae sancti Pauli*)
217. Book of Job (*liber Iob*)
218. Glossarium (*glosarium*)
219. Book of homilies (*liber omeliarum*)
220. Book of conferences (*liber collationum*)
221. Book of litanies (*liber letaniaris*)
222. Breviary (*breviarium*)
223. Customary (*liber consuetudinum*)
224. Parchment (*pergamenum*)
225. Scroll (*rotula*)
226. Schedule (*breve*)
227. Martyrology (*martyrologium*)
228. Secular book (*liber secularis*)

Concerning the signs for pulpit, choir-stall and wooden lantern (*De signis analogii, formule et ligni, in quo lumen habetur*)

229. Pulpit (*analogium*)
230. Wooden lantern (*lignum ad lumen tenendum compositum*)
231. Choir-stall (*formula*)

Concerning the signs for persons (*De signis personarum*)

232. Abbot (*abbas*)
233. Monk (*monachus*)
234. Recluse (*inclusus*)
235. Monk raised in the abbey (*monachus nutritus in monasterio*)
236. Prior (*prior*)
237. Major prior (*maior*)
238. Claustral prior (*prior claustralis*)
239. Assistant to the claustral prior (*adiutor illius*)
240. Librarian and precentor (*armarius et precentor*)
241. Choir official (*cantor ebdomarius*)
242. Roundsman (*circator*)
243. Sacrist (*custos ecclesie*)
244. Chamberlain (*camerarius*)
245. Cellarer (*cellararius*)
246. Keeper of the granary (*granatarius*)
247. Gardener (*hortulanus*)
248. Keeper of the hospice (*custos hospicii*)
249. Almoner (*elemosinarius*)
250. Infirmarer (*infirmarius*)

Table 5: (*cont.*)

251. Refectorer (*refectorarius*)
252. Master of the boys (*custos iuvenum*)
253. Someone well educated (*aliquis bene literatus*)
254. Provost (*prepositus*)
255. Building master (*magister cementariorum*)
256. Old man (*senex*)
257. Countryman or blood relative (*conpatriota vel consanguineus*)
258. Father (*pater*)
259. Brother (*frater*)
260. Mother (*mater*)
261. Sister (*soror*)
262. Priest (*clericus*)
263. Layman (*laicus*)
264. Man who speaks another language (*homo alterius lingue*)
265. Shoemaker (*sutor*)

Concerning signs for diverse things (*De signis diversarum rerum*)

266. Everyone (*omnes*)
267. To talk (*loqui*)
268. To hear (*audire*)
269. To not know (*nescire*)
270. To forget (*oblivisci*)
271. To tell a lie (*mentiri*)
272. To kiss (*osculari*)
273. Abandoned custom (*consuetudo derelicta*)
274. To dress (*vestire*)
275. To undress (*exuere*)
276. To take off shoes (*discalciare*)
277. To wash feet (*lavare pedes*)
278. Something good (*bonum*)
279. Something bad (*malum*)
280. To agree (*innuere*)
281. Refusal (*negatio*)
282. Quickness (*celeritas*)
283. Slowness (*tarditas*)
284. To become angry (*irasci*)
285. To be negligent (*delinquere*)
286. Something done (*res facta*)
287. To do something freely (*facere libenter*)
288. Similitude (*similitudo*)
289. To divide (*dividere*)
290. To anoint the sick (*unguere infirmum*)
291. To cry (*lacrimare*)

Table 5: (*cont.*)

292. To ask: what are you called (*querare: quis vocaris*)
293. To put out a light (*extinguere lumen*)
294. Cemetery (*cymiterium*)

Concerning the signs for buildings (*De signis edificiorum*)

295. Building (*edificium*)
296. Church (*ecclesia*)
297. Chapter hall (*capitolium*)
298. Auditorium (*auditorium*)
299. Dormitory (*dormitorium*)
300. Lavatories (*necessariae*)
301. Warming room (*calefactorium*)
302. Treasury (*camera*)
303. Infirmary (*infirmaria*)
304. Kitchen (*coquina*)
305. Library (*armarium*)
306. Cloister (*claustrum*)
307. Refectory (*refectorium*)
308. Cell of the novices (*cella noviciorum*)
309. Sacristy (*sacristia*)

And so that I may draw this to a close, if you want to signify any of these things,
you must always join the following signs to their aforesaid general sign
(*Et ut conclusionem de talibus faciam, quiquid huiusmodi signare volueris, generali
semper premisso consequentia adiungas*)

310. Procession (*processio*)

Concerning the signs for wax, candle, any lantern and a portable lamp (*De signis cere,
candele, cuislibet laterne et absconse*)

311. Wax (*cera*)
312. Candle (*candela*)
313. Greater candle (*candela maior*)
314. Candle bent in a circle (*candela in modum circuli contorta*)
315. Lantern (*laterna*)
316. Portable lantern (*absconsa*)

Concerning those signs pertaining to writing (*De his que ad
scribendum pertinent*)

317. Sciptorium (*scriptorium*)
318. Ink (*incaustum*)
319. Red lead (*minium*)
320. Pumice stone (*pumex*)

321. Feather quill (*penna*)
322. Compass (*circinus*)

Concerning the signs for metals (*De signis ferramentorum*)

323. Metal used for making offerings (*ferramentum ad oblatas faciendas compositum*)
324. Pair of scissors (*forpex*)
325. Razor or sharp knife (*rasorium sive novacula*)
326. Whetstone (*cotis*)
327. Axe, pick-axe, plane, borer or adze (*securis, dolabrum, runcina, terebrum*)
328. Awl (*subula*)
329. Gold (*aurum*)
330. Silver (*argentum*)
331. Copper (*es*)
332. Lead (*plumbum*)
333. Bit (*frenum*)
334. Saddle (*sella*)
335. Staff (*baculum*)
336. Seal (*sigillum*)
337. Warming pot (*caldarius*)
338. Metal, by which the warming pot is suspended (*ferramentum quo caldarius suspenditur*)
339. Frying pan (*sartago*)
340. Oil, which comes from metal (*olla que est de metallo*)
341. Small fork (*fuscinula*)
342. Pair of tongs (*forcipis*)
343. Snuffers (*emunctorium*)
344. Cymbal (*cimbalum*)
345. Board, which is struck to signal permission for speaking (*tabula que ad loquendum percutitur*)

Concerning the signs for laughing and nosebleed and vomiting (*De signo ridendi et sanguinis de naso fluentis et vomendi*)

346. To laugh (*ridere*)
347. Nosebleed (*sanguis de naso fluens*)
348. To vomit (*vomere*)

Concerning different kinds of animals (*De diversis animalibus*)

349. Packhorse (*caballus*)
350. Donkey (*asinus*)
351. Mule (*mulus*)
352. Sheep (*ovis*)

Table 5: (*cont.*)

353. Ram (*aries*)
354. Lamb (*agnus*)
355. Goat (*caper*)
356. Pig (*porcus*)
357. Cat (*catta*)

Concerning wild animals (*De agrestibus animalibus*)

358. Deer (*cervus*)
359. Hare (*lepor*)

Chapter 5

CONTINUITY AND CRITICISM

Around the year 1100, men and women in all stations and ages of life experienced the awakening of new religious sentiments. Across western Europe, individuals set out to attain ideals of personal perfection on their own terms. Some fled to remote places to live as hermits and solitaries. Others founded or entered houses of new religious orders, where they attempted to recover and embrace the more austere and authentic forms of ascetic life observed in the distant past by the apostles and exemplary monastic saints like Anthony and Benedict.[1] The emergence of new religious orders in this period was not symptomatic of a "crisis" or decline in cenobitic monasticism, but represented instead the attempts of a generation of reformers to encourage the practice of religious values beyond abbey walls. These reformers sought to provide for the spiritual needs of laymen and women, who desired to fulfill their ideals of Christian perfection without having to enter the highly structured life of the cloister.[2] The service of others through itinerant preaching and other forms of active piety was a prominent aspect of this revival, but the personal obligations implicit in the new wave of reform often involved some form of verbal

---

[1] Further on the ideology of religious reform movements in the Middle Ages and the metaphors associated with them, see Gerhart B. Ladner, *The Idea of Reform: Its Impact on Christian Thought and Action in the Age of the Fathers* (Cambridge, MA, 1959), who defined the idea of Christian reform as "free, intentional and ever perfectible, multiple, prolonged and ever repeated efforts by man to reassert and augment values pre-existent in the spiritual-material compound of the world" (p. 35); and Giles Constable, "Renewal and Reform in Religious Life: Concepts and Realities," in *Renaissance and Renewal in the Twelfth Century*, ed. Robert L. Benson and Giles Constable, with Carol D. Lanham (Cambridge, MA, 1982), pp. 37–67. On the new articulations of religious life available to men and women at the beginning of the twelfth century, see Richard Southern, *Western Society and the Church in the Middle Ages* (London, 1970), pp. 214–272; and Giles Constable, *The Reformation of the Twelfth Century* (Cambridge, 1996), pp. 44–87.

[2] For a review of the historiography of the "crisis" of cenobitic monasticism and a strong corrective to this trend, see John Van Engen, "The 'Crisis of Cenobitism' Reconsidered: Benedictine Monasticism in the Years 1050–1150," *Speculum* 61 (1986): 269–304; repr. in John Van Engen, *Religion in the History of the Medieval West* (Aldershot, 2004), no. III.

143

expression and therefore clashed with the cultivation of silence, a virtuous practice that retained its strong currency among the new religious orders.[3]

The collision of righteous speech and pious silence put pressure on reformed monastic communities to find ways to meet their evangelical ideals without compromising time-honored standards of personal discipline. This chapter examines how monks, canons and hermits of the twelfth century negotiated the boundaries of silence in their communities. In contrast to the conventional portrait in modern scholarship of religious controversy in this period, the sources betray a striking continuity between traditional and reformed observances. In fact, by the turn of the thirteenth century, most of the new orders had adopted the silent language of the Cluniacs as a means of fostering the cultivation of silence in their communities. The risks inherent in this custom were transparent to contemporaries. Allegations about the misuse of monastic sign language became a feature of satirical portraits of wayward monks. As this chapter argues, the inclusion of this practice in popular forms of invective was not an indication of its widespread abuse, but rather a barometer of its success, a reliable indication that it had become a common attribute of cloistered life by the close of the twelfth century.

BENEDICT'S HEIRS

By the late eleventh century, many aspects of the cloistered life practiced at Cluny and elsewhere were no longer consonant with the literal precepts of the *Rule of Benedict*. These developments troubled Abbot Robert of Molesme. In the 1090s, he urged his brethren to abandon customs foreign to the *Rule*, like the collection of tithes and oblations, and to follow its precepts literally regarding diet, clothing and especially manual labor, which monks had long eschewed in favor of a protracted liturgy. There was significant resistance to his proposal. The brethren of Molesme argued that Benedict and his followers did not insist on strict adherence to the *Rule*, but encouraged abbots to adapt its precepts to meet local contingencies and to accommodate individuals with delicate constitutions. In the face of overwhelming opposition, Robert and twelve of his followers abandoned Molesme to found the abbey of Cîteaux in the wilderness of northern Burgundy. After several precarious years, the community acquired a reputation for ascetic rigor and sanctity that attracted many adherents. Within a few decades, the monks of Cîteaux

---

[3] The classic work on this topic remains M.-D. Chenu, "Monks, Canons, and Laymen in Search of the Apostolic Life," in *Nature, Man, and Society in the Twelfth Century: Essays on New Theological Perspectives in the Latin West*, ed. and trans. Jerome Taylor and Lester K. Little (Chicago, 1968), pp. 202–238.

and her daughter houses developed into a powerful religious order that threatened to eclipse the prominence of the Cluniacs.[4]

In the early twelfth century, the rivalry between Cluny and Cîteaux was played out in an exchange of letters between Peter the Venerable and Bernard of Clairvaux. Modern treatments of this controversy have tended to isolate and polarize relatively minor differences in custom at the expense of broader and more deep-rooted similarities shared by both orders that received no representation in contemporary propaganda.[5] It has generally escaped the attention of historians that the custom of silence was not an issue of contention between the Cluniacs and the Cistercians. A letter of Peter the Venerable from 1127 addressing a list of criticisms of Cluniac customs made by unnamed Cistercian monks underscores this point.[6] Some of the charges were indeed substantial, but most involved relatively minor details in observance, such as objections to the wearing of trousers while traveling. Cistercian critics also made no complaints regarding customs fundamental to the spirit of the common life, like the cultivation of silence. As Giles Constable has noted, "[These critics of Cluny] concentrated on many points of detail precisely because there was no serious disagreement on many of the substantial issues."[7] It is very telling that in an early twelfth-century account of the issues at stake between Robert of Molesme and his more traditional brethren, the Norman monastic chronicler Orderic Vitalis presented the virtue of silence as a principal component of the ascetic profile of both parties.[8]

---

[4] On the founding of Cîteaux, see *DHGE*, vol. XII, cols. 852–874, s.v. Cîteaux, and cols. 1050–1061, esp. cols. 1050–1051, s.v. Clairvaux; *Dictionnaire de spiritualité*, vol. II, cols. 736–814, esp. cols. 736–778, s.v. Robert of Molesme; the historical introduction of Jean Baptiste Van Damme, in *Les plus anciens textes de Cîteaux*, ed. Jean de la Croix Bouton and Jean Baptiste Van Damme (Achel, 1974), pp. 9–23; and Louis Lekai, *The Cistercians: Ideals and Realities* (Kent, OH, 1977), pp. 11–32. For a controversial reinterpretation of the sources relevant to the early history of the Cistercian Order, see Constance Berman, *The Cistercian Evolution: The Invention of a Religious Order in Twelfth-Century Europe* (Philadelphia, 2000). This work has inspired a substantial volume of critical response. See, in particular, Chrysogonus Waddell, "The Myth of Cistercian Origins: C. H. Berman and the Manuscript Sources," *Cîteaux: Commentarii Cistercienses* 51 (2000): 299–386.

[5] See, for example, David Knowles, *Cistercians and Cluniacs: The Controversy Between St. Bernard and Peter the Venerable* (London, New York and Toronto, 1955); and A. H. Bredero, "Cluny et Cîteaux au XIIe siècle: Les origines de la controverse," *Studi Medievali* 12 (1971): 135–175.

[6] Peter the Venerable, *Epistola* 28, ed. Giles Constable, in *The Letters of Peter the Venerable*, 2 vols. (Cambridge, MA, 1967), vol. I, pp. 52–101, and vol. II, pp. 270–274.

[7] Constable, *Reformation of the Twelfth Century*, p. 186.

[8] Orderic Vitalis, *Historia ecclesiastica* 8.26, ed. Marjorie Chibnall, in *The Ecclesiastical History of Orderic Vitalis*, 6 vols. (Oxford, 1969–1980), vol. IV, pp. 310–327, esp. p. 318, where the monks of Molesme are distinguished by their silence from the laymen for whom they prayed: "Inde semper meditantes taciturnitati delectabiliter insistant, a prauis et ociosis sermonibus os suum coherceant." and p. 324, where the chronicler characterized the discipline of Robert and his followers in this way: "Omni tempore silentio student." Further on the context of Orderic's work, see Marjorie Chibnall, *The World of Orderic Vitalis* (Oxford, 1984).

Surprisingly little is known about rules against speaking in early twelfth-century Cistercian communities, but there is reason to believe that their parameters were similar to those enforced in other contemporary monasteries. The foundation history of Clairvaux (*Exordium parvum*) and the earliest constitution of the Cistercian Order (*Carta caritatis*) stressed adherence to the letter of the *Rule of Benedict* in all matters of personal discipline, implying that early Cistercians refrained from speaking in certain parts of their abbeys and held their tongues throughout the night.[9] A decree of the Cistercian General Chapter from 1152 evoked the authority of the *Rule* directly in support of its mandates against speaking.[10] Like the Cluniacs, however, the white monks felt it necessary to augment these precepts with specific directives of their own devising. The earliest collection of Cistercian customs (*Instituta ecclesiastica*) dating from the 1130s states that they discouraged unnecessary speech in the chapter house and in those places where the monks labored.[11] In addition, the Cistercians extended the boundaries of silence in the refectory to the abbot's table, a detail assumed, but not stated explicitly, in the *Rule of Benedict*.[12] A twelfth-century English chronicler also noted that the abbots of Cistercian houses strove to remain as silent as possible when fulfilling the duties of their office.[13]

Religious women who followed Cistercian customs seem to have emulated the standards of discipline embraced by their male counterparts.[14] An early thirteenth-century Old French translation of Cistercian legislation written for an unidentified female community near Dijon

---

[9] *Exordium parvum* 15.2–3; and *Carta caritatis prior* 2.2, ed. Chrysogonus Waddell, in *Narrative and Legislative Texts from Early Cîteaux* (Brecht, 1999), pp. 253 and 444, respectively.

[10] *Statuta anni 1152* 3 (*De poena loquentium ad mensam*): "Omni tempore secundum Regulae praeceptum decet monachum silentio studere, sed maxime nocturnis horis et ad mensam." ed. Joseph-Maria Canivez, in *Statuta Capitulorum Generalium ab anno 1116 ad annum 1786*, 8 vols. (Louvain, 1933–1941), vol. I, p. 46. Compare *RB* 42.1, p. 584: "Omni tempore silentium debent studere monachi, maxime tamen nocturnis horis."

[11] *Ecclesiastica officia* 70.62 and 75.16, ed. Danièle Choisselet and Placide Vernet, in *Les Ecclesiastica Officia cisterciens du XIIe siècle* (Reiningue, 1989), pp. 206 and 220, respectively.

[12] *Ecclesiastica officia* 110.14: "Silentium ad mensam teneat [abbas], in quantum rationabiliter poteri." ed. Choisselet and Vernet, p. 312.

[13] William of Malmesbury, *Gesta regum anglorum* 336, ed. and trans. R. A. B. Mynors, and completed by R. M. Thomson and M. Winterbottom, in *William of Malmesbury: The History of the English Kings*, 2 vols. (Oxford, 1998–1999), vol. I, p. 582.

[14] On the affiliation of women with the Cistercian Order, see Brigitte Degler-Spengler, "The Incorporation of Cistercian Nuns into the Order in the Twelfth and Thirteenth Century," in *Hidden Springs: Cistercian Monastic Women*, ed. John A. Nichols and Lillian Thomas Shank, 2 vols. (Kalamazoo, 1995), vol. I, pp. 85–134; and Constance Berman, "Were There Twelfth-Century Cistercian Nuns?" *Church History* 68 (1999): 824–864, reproduced in slightly abbreviated form in *Medieval Religion: New Approaches*, ed. Constance Berman (New York and London, 2005), pp. 217–248.

shows that the *Rule of Benedict* provided a model of personal comportment for women as well.[15] This collection made explicit reference to the *Rule* in its precepts on the need for silence at night and during meals.[16] Likewise, it instructed its readers to hold their tongues whenever they traveled to their convent's rural holdings, and also while they worked in the scriptorium and the cloister.[17] In 1242, reports of suspicious activities around female Cistercian communities drew the attention of the General Chapter. A decree of that year ordered that no woman of the order was allowed to speak with anyone outside of her convent, except through a heavily barred window. Only abbesses and prioresses were exempt from this restriction, because their duties demanded frequent dealings with the outside world.[18] Exceptions were also made for visitors with outstanding reputations who would interpret the precept as an affront to their character. The General Chapter recommended excommunication as punishment for women who persisted in committing offenses involving wayward speech.[19]

Like cloistered men and women, Cistercian lay brothers (*conversi*) also adhered to strict rules of silence. These were typically illiterate members of the religious community who did not take monastic vows, but performed manual labor on behalf of the monks as an act of devotion to God.[20] Whether they served as cooks, shoemakers, tanners, fishermen or

---

[15] "Ancienne traduction française des Ecclesiastica officia, Instituta generalis Capituli, Usus conversorum et Regula sancti Benedicti, publié d'après le manuscrit 352 de la bibliothèque publique de Dijon," ed. Philip Guignard, in *Les monuments primitifs de la règle cistercienne* (Dijon, 1878), pp. lxxiv–lxxxviii and 407–642 (Appendix 1).

[16] *Les establissemens del general capitle* 87; *Les usages des conviers* 6 (*U il doivent tenir silence*); and *Le riule saint Benoit* (*De silence tenir*), ed. Guignard, in *Les monuments primitifs*, pp. 572, 578 and 596.

[17] *Les establissemens del general capitle* 72 and *Les usages des conviers* 6–8 (rules governing speech on Cistercian granges); and *Les establissemens del general capitle* 75 (silence in the scriptorium and the cloister), in "Ancienne traduction," ed. Guignard, in *Les monuments primitifs*, pp. 569, 578–579 and 572, respectively.

[18] *Statuta anni 1242* 17, ed. Canivez, in *Statuta Capitulorum Generalium*, vol. II, p. 248.

[19] *Ibid.* pp. 248–249. The General Chapter tempered these rules slightly in the following year, perhaps in response to protest in Cistercian nunneries. See *Statuta anni 1243* 6–8 and 61–68, ed. Canivez, pp. 260 and 270–273. Further on this episode specifically and the topic of female Cistercian disobedience in general, see Southern, *Western Society and the Church*, p. 317; and Anne E. Lester, "Cleaning House in 1399: Disobedience and the Demise of Cistercian Convents in Northern France at the End of the Middle Ages," in *Oboedientia: Zu Formen und Grenzen von Macht und Unterordnung im mittelalterlichen Religiosentum*, ed. Sébastien Barret and Gert Melville (Münster, 2005), pp. 423–444.

[20] On the Cistercian *conversi*, see R. P. Othon, "De l'institution et des us des convers dans l'ordre de Cîteaux (XIIe et XIIIe siècles)," in *Saint Bernard et son temps*, 2 vols. (Dijon, 1928–1929), vol. II, pp. 139–201; and James S. Donnelly, *The Decline of the Cistercian Laybrotherhood* (New York, 1949). On the sources relevant to their early history, see Chrysogonus Waddell, *Cistercian Lay Brothers: Twelfth-Century Usages with Related Texts* (Brecht, 2001). Further on the religious meaning of the term *conversus*, the use of which changed in this period, see Constable, *Reformation of the Twelfth Century*, pp. 77–80.

shepherds, they were instructed to refrain from conversation at all times. Only the mandate of the abbot or reason of necessity permitted them to speak.[21] These rules were modified, however, for lay brothers who worked on rural granges. Shepherds and herdsmen were allowed to converse freely with each other and their helpers, but limited their discussion to topics relevant to their tasks. They were also encouraged to return a word of greeting to any travelers who hailed them and to provide directions when asked the way.[22]

The monks of twelfth-century Cluny shared the concerns of the Cistercians regarding the preservation of silence in their community. Some scholars have portrayed Cluny as the last bastion of monastic conservatism in this age of reform, interpreting the activities of Abbot Peter the Venerable as a late response to Cistercian criticisms about the erosion of traditional standards of discipline at the great Burgundian abbey and its dependencies. Among other abuses, they have posited a relentless decay in the custom of silence to explain the abbot's new decrees on this practice.[23] Support for such statements has been found in highly polemical works by Bernard of Clairvaux and Idung of Prüfening, which derided the talkativeness of Cluniac monks.[24] In fact, it is unlikely that the integrity of this observance was ever in doubt at twelfth-century Cluny. Peter the Venerable was the product of the spiritual climate of his age. His reforming efforts were not the rash response of a leader stung by the criticism of external adversaries, but an attempt to foster and preserve, in his own terms, the perfect tenor of monastic life in his community, especially in the wake of the tumultuous abbacy of his predecessor, Pontius of Melgueil (1109–1122). Silence was his ally in this endeavor. Abbatial decrees and other sources for his activities show that he was always seeking to extend its protective boundaries to safeguard the spiritual well-being of his monks.[25]

---

[21] *Usus conversorum* 6, ed. Waddell, in *Cistercian Lay Brothers*, p. 65.   [22] *Ibid.*

[23] See, for example, David Knowles, "The Reforming Decrees of Peter the Venerable," in *Petrus Venerabilis 1156–1956*, ed. Giles Constable and James Kritzeck, Studia Anselmiana 40 (Rome, 1956), pp. 1–20, esp. pp. 10–11 on "the decay of silence" at Cluny (quote from p. 10).

[24] Bernard of Clairvaux, *Apologia ad Guillelmum abbatatem* 9.19, ed. Jean Leclercq, Charles H. Talbot and Henri-Marie Rochais, in *Sancti Bernardi Opera*, 8 vols. (Rome, 1957–1977), vol. III, p. 97; and Idung of Prüfening, *Dialogus duorum monachorum* 3.1–2, ed. R. B. C. Huygens, "Le moine Idung et ses deux ouvrages: *Argumentum super quatuor questionibus* et *Dialogus duorum monachorum*," *Studi Medievali* 13 (1972): 291–470, at pp. 438–439.

[25] Further on the view that Peter the Venerable's reforming decrees were sympathetic expressions of the new religious sentiment rather than reactions against criticisms from the new orders, see Giles Constable, "The Monastic Policy of Peter the Venerable," in *Pierre Abélard – Pierre le Vénérable: Les courants philosophiques, littéraires et artistiques en occident au milieu du XII siècle (Abbaye de Cluny, 2 au 9 juillet 1972)* (Paris, 1975), pp. 119–142, repr. in Giles Constable, *Cluniac Studies* (London, 1980), no. III.

When Peter the Venerable assumed the abbacy of Cluny in 1122, the house was bitterly divided. The tenure of Abbot Pontius had ended in scandal.[26] Standards of discipline had suffered during a long season of discord and dissent. Peter immediately set out to restore order to the community. Despite encountering resistance from his own brethren, within two years he felt that he had succeeded in correcting many abuses and eliminating excesses in food and drink as well as general lapses in discipline.[27] The abbot was not content, however, to rest on his achievements at home. In 1133, he summoned the priors of 200 Cluniac dependencies to Burgundy to hear new decrees on the proper observance of monastic life. Orderic Vitalis attended the assembly and described the outline of Peter's program of reform: "He imposed new fasts on his subject monks and took away times for conversation and various supports of bodily infirmity, which the moderate mercy of reverend fathers had previously allowed them."[28] The new rules met with resistance from the priors, who were unsettled by their severity and novelty. Their reaction was predictable. The introduction of new precepts almost always aroused suspicion among monks, especially when they diverged from the tenor of long-standing customs. When the abbots of the province of Reims agreed at a council in 1131 to adopt perpetual silence in their cloisters, Matthew of Albano, a cardinal-legate of the pope, condemned their resolutions in the harshest terms, in part because they did not accord with the precepts of the *Rule of Benedict*.[29] The priors assembled at Cluny reacted in a similar fashion. As a result, the abbot decided to withdraw his most severe precepts out of consideration for the less stalwart members of his extended community.

Despite this setback, Peter the Venerable remained a powerful advocate for the saving virtue of silence. Throughout his abbacy, he issued statutes

---

[26] On the career of Pontius, possible reasons for his downfall, and the events surrounding his resignation, see Hayden White, "Pontius of Cluny, the Curia Romana, and the End of Gregorianism in Rome," *Church History* 27 (1958): 195–219; Gerd Tellenbach, "Die Sturz des Abtes Pontius von Cluny," *Quellen und Forschungen aus italienischen Archiven und Bibliotheken* 42–43 (1963): 13–55; H. E. J. Cowdrey, "Two Studies in Cluniac History 1049–1126," *Studi Gregoriani* 11 (1978): 5–298, at pp. 177–268 ("Part II: Abbot Pontius of Cluny"); and Joachim Wollasch, "Das Schisma des Abtes Pontius von Cluny," *Francia* 23 (1996): 31–52.

[27] Peter the Venerable, *De miraculis libri duos* 2.11, ed. D. Bouthillier, *CCCM* LXXXIII (Turnhout, 1988), p. 116.

[28] Orderic Vitalis, *Historia ecclesiastica* 13.13: "Ille uero suiectis auxit ieiunia, abstulit colloquia, et infirmi corporis quaedam subsidia quae illis moderata patrum hactenus permiserat reuerendorum clementia." ed. and trans. Chibnall, vol. VI, pp. 426–427.

[29] See Matthew of Albano, *Epistola*, ed. Stanislaus Ceglar, in "William of Saint Thierry and His Leading Role at the First Chapters of the Benedictine Abbots (Reims 1131, Soissons 1132)," in *William, Abbot of St. Thierry: A Colloquium at the Abbey of St. Thierry*, trans. Jerry Carfantan (Kalamazoo, 1987), pp. 65–86 (here at pp. 78–79).

to modify received traditions that he believed to be obsolete or harmful.[30] In 1146/1147, he compiled these decrees into a single volume, appending to each an explanation of his reason for emending established customs. The senior monks of Cluny endorsed these amendments, which were intended with few exceptions to take effect in all Cluniac dependencies, although Peter admitted his doubt that every priory would enforce them.[31] Five of these decrees dealt specifically with the custom of silence. Through them, the reader can chart the abbot's persistent efforts to impose this practice on any situation that fostered an opportunity for harmful speech in the abbey. The first of these decrees was the most general. It extended the traditional boundaries of silence to the infirmary, the cells of the novices, the cemetery, and other small chambers and halls overlooked in earlier legislation. The reason for this, Peter explained, was the fundamental utility of silence to all monks, and especially to the Cluniacs, whose traffic with the secular world required them to embrace a more austere mode of discipline within the confines of their abbey.[32] Other decrees limited conversation in specific settings. One restricted talking in the cloister on weekdays during Lent. Conversation had traditionally been allowed at this time, but the abbot felt that silence was a more fitting expression of reverence during the holy season.[33] Another decree eliminated one of the two times for speaking in the cloister previously permitted to monks. Peter stated his rationale for this amendment in no uncertain terms: the extra period was a waste of time because the brethren often busied themselves with useless chatter.[34] Another directive extended the rule of silence observed in the refectory to all meals, no matter where the monks took them. Peter marshaled biblical and patristic precedents to support this decree, adding that it was unfitting for Cluniac monks to appear lax in such a fundamental aspect of personal conduct, when they had earned a reputation for rekindling religious life throughout Europe.[35] The abbot also issued new rules to regulate conduct in even the smallest dependencies. In communities with fewer than twelve monks, he ordered that everyone should refrain from speech at all times in the refectory and the dormitory, and guard their tongues in the cloister as well. That way, he stated with more than a hint of frustration, they would at least avoid wasting their days in foolish conversations

---

[30] *Statuta*, p. 39. Further on the date and character of this work, see the introduction to the *Statuta* by Constable, in *CCM* VI, pp. 21–25, repr. in Constable, *Cluniac Studies*, no. IV.
[31] *Statuta* 61, p. 93.   [32] *Statuta* 19, p. 58.   [33] *Statuta* 20, p. 59.
[34] *Statuta* 21, p. 59.   [35] *Statuta* 22, p. 60.

in the manner of laymen and thereby preserve "some shadow, some vestige, some small particle" of their hallowed way of life.[36]

The currents of reform that shaped Peter the Venerable's initiatives to preserve the integrity of monastic silence at Cluny and its dependencies also exerted influence on early twelfth-century authors who addressed the religious life of women. In a letter written to Abbess Heloise on the organization of convents and the spiritual directives that govern them, Peter Abelard recommended a program of silence that reflected the ascetic sensibilities fostered among the Cluniacs. Using biblical precedents and metaphors of claustration, his treatise emphasized the vulnerability of women to sins of the tongue and prescribed strict rules against conversation to overcome this weakness.[37] Abelard cast silence as a tether that keeps the soul tied inside the manger of the Lord where it chews on sacred words. Without it, he explained, the soul was free to abandon God and roam the world with its thoughts. Women were especially vulnerable to the danger of errant words. According to Abelard, their tongues were a plague, for which silence was the only remedy. The apostle James had advised Timothy on this matter when he wrote that married women were not permitted to speak in church and should learn in submissive silence (1 Tim. 2.11–12; see also 1 Cor. 14.34–35). To this end, Abelard advised the abbess to enforce a perpetual silence (*continua taciturnitas*) throughout her convent, entombing the spoken word at all times in the church, the cloister, the dormitory, the refectory and the kitchens, and forbidding all human discourse throughout the night.

This move toward the complete mortification of the will to speak through the adoption of totalizing rules of silence was not endorsed by all twelfth-century monastic thinkers. In a commentary on the *Rule of Benedict* written around 1160 for a community of reformed canons, Hildegard of Bingen stressed that discretion and moderation were the guiding principles of the monastic way of life.[38] In her opinion, the practice of perpetual silence was cruel, uncharitable and completely alien to the spirit of the *Rule*:

Since it is inhuman for someone to be silent always and never to speak, the same father [Benedict] left it in the power and discretion of the abbot, as he did with

---

[36] *Statuta* 42, p. 75: "Causa instituti huius fuit, ut si fratres in talibus locis plenum ordinem tenere aut non possent, aut nollent, saltem aliquam umbram, vel vestigium, vel particulam ordinis retinerent, ne integra die nugacibus verbis, aut rebus vacantes, in nullo a secularibus differre viderentur."

[37] For what follows, see Peter Abelard, *Institutio seu regula sanctimonialium*, ed. T. P. McLaughlin, in "Abelard's Rule for Religious Women," *Mediaeval Studies* 18 (1956): 241–292, at pp. 245–246.

[38] Hildegard of Bingen, *Regula sancti Benedicti explicata*, PL CXCVII, cols. 1053b–1066a; with Giles Constable, "Hildegard's Explanation of the Rule of St. Benedict," in *Hildegard von Bingen in ihrem historischen Umfeld: Internationaler wissenschaftlicher Kongreß zum 900jährigen Jubiläum, 13.–19. September 1998, Bingen am Rhein*, ed. Alfred Haverkamp (Mainz, 2000), pp. 163–187.

many other things, to provide a suitable time for the monks to speak with each other about honest and necessary matters, so that they should not be afflicted by the unmitigated boredom of silence, since after being permitted in this way to speak together they could more fittingly and severely be incited and coerced to the taciturnity of silence.[39]

In response to reforming mentalities that encouraged the complete cessation of spoken words in religious communities, Hildegard recommended a program of discipline in which times set aside for holy conversation relieved the tediousness of silence. Abbots who showed such charitable discretion would thereby encourage monks to embrace the virtue of this custom all the more rigorously during those times when speaking was forbidden.

In the twelfth century, Cluniacs and Cistercians alike recognized the cultivation of silence as a saving virtue and took measures to prevent idle speech in their communities. Although modern historiography has tended to portray the relationship between them as competitive and antagonistic, this interpretation has overshadowed the fact that these religious orders had many fundamental values in common. While they were certainly influenced by the currents of reform that molded twelfth-century monastic thought, their shared esteem for the custom of silence derived primarily from their mutual reliance on the same textual tradition. From the beginning, Cluniacs and Cistercians camped back-to-back on common ground mapped out in the *Rule of Benedict*. Their dependence on this sixth-century authority distinguished them from newly founded communities of reformed canons and the private asceticism of hermits, who turned to other ancient precedents in the monastic tradition to direct them in their search for the apostolic life.

THE CRUELTY OF SILENCE

The cultivation of silence was not always interpreted as a benefit in twelfth-century religious thought. In contrast to the Cluniacs and the Cistercians, reformed canons sought to redefine the purpose and parameters of this custom against long-established monastic ideals. In the early Middle Ages, canons were usually priests who performed liturgical and

---

[39] Hildegard, *Regula sancti Benedicti explicata:* "Attamen quia inhumanum est hominem in taciturnitate semper esse, et non loqui, idem Pater in potestate et discretione abbatis dimittit, uemadmodum alia plurima ei concedit, ut discipulis suis horam competentem praevideat, qua ipsi haec, quae honesta et necessaria sunt, adinvicem loquantur, et ne in indiscreto silentio taedio afficiantur, quoniam post huiusmodi ad invicem loquendi permissionem, convenientius et severius ad taciturnitatem silentii admoneri et coerceri poterunt." *PL* CXCVII, col. 1056a; trans. Constable, "Hildegard's Explanation of the Rule," p. 184 (slightly modified).

ceremonial functions in urban cathedrals and collegiate churches. The Aachen synod of 816 established Archbishop Chrodegang of Metz's *Rule for Canons* as the normative text for canonical life in the Carolingian period.[40] Unlike monks, canons were allowed to eat meat, take wives, own property and maintain private residences. It was also common for them to receive a share of their church's resources, usually the income of a landed estate. By the tenth century, many canons passed their office and its endowment (or prebend) down to their sons as an inheritance and generally lived in the same manner as laymen (hence the term "secular" canon). During the eleventh century, Peter Damian and other prelates urged secular canons to abandon their worldly trappings and embrace a life in common under the guidance of a rule. Those who did so became "regular" canons. The most earnest adherents to this new religious sentiment adopted as their code of conduct a small corpus of documents allegedly composed by the renowned fifth-century bishop, Augustine of Hippo. The so-called *Rule of Augustine* comprised a short code of monastic discipline (*ordo monasterii*) and a longer directive on the principles of the common life (*praeceptum*), both possibly written by the bishop himself, as well as an adaptation of a letter of reprimand that he sent to a community of female religious (*Epistola* 211). An anonymous Gallic or Italian author compiled these works in the later fifth century.[41] This collective work provided a seasonal timetable for psalmody, while exhorting its readers to renounce private property and observe the principles of the apostolic life, namely, obedience, humility, abstinence and silence. Although it was more akin to a letter of spiritual advice than normative legislation, the association of the *Rule* with a celebrated saint gave it great authority, lending the enterprise of the canons a sense of authenticity rooted firmly in the Christian past and thereby ensuring its appeal to an entire generation of reformers.[42]

---

[40] Chrodegang of Metz, *Regula canonicorum, PL* LXXXIX, cols. 1057–1120. On Chrodegang and the ascetic program underlying his *Rule for Canons*, see M. A. Claussen, *The Reform of the Frankish Church: Chrodegang of Metz and the Regula canonicorum in the Eighth Century* (Cambridge, 2004).

[41] For modern editions and commentaries on the *Rule of Augustine*, see *La règle de saint Augustin*, ed. Luc Verheijen, 2 vols. (Paris, 1967); and George Lawless, *Augustine of Hippo and His Monastic Rule* (Oxford, 1987). On the authorship and dates of its component parts, see C. Lambot, "Un *ordo officii* du 5e siècle," *Revue bénédictine* 42 (1930): 77–80; and Lawless, *Augustine of Hippo and His Monastic Rule*, pp. 121–154.

[42] On the early history of the regular canons and their adoption of the *Rule of Augustine*, see *DHGE*, vol. XII, cols. 353–405, s.v. Chanoines; *Dictionnaire de spiritualité*, vol. II, cols. 463–477, s.v. Chanoines réguliers; C. Dereine, "Vie commune, règle de Saint Augustin et chanoines réguliers au XIe siècle," *Revue d'Histoire Ecclésiastique* 41 (1946): 365–406; J. C. Dickinson, *The Origins of the Austin Canons and Their Introduction into England* (London, 1950), pp. 7–90; and Lester Little, *Religious Poverty and the Profit Economy in Medieval Europe* (Ithaca, 1978), pp. 99–112.

Twelfth-century canons articulated theories about their distinctiveness from monks in commentaries on the *Rule of Augustine* and works of spiritual instruction written for their brethren. Living both as priests and monks, they preached and performed pastoral duties, but slept and prayed in cloistered seclusion. It was difficult for canons to reconcile the utility of verbal exhortation and the cultivation of silence. Many of them argued that the denial of the will to speak was not an end unto itself, as monks believed, but only useful insofar as it prepared the individual to utter wise and helpful words.[43] The responsibility to correct faults verbally found its roots in the *Rule of Augustine* in the context of individuals who cast sinful glances toward women. Companions of the sinner were urged to admonish him immediately and thereby curb the progress of his transgression:

Do not consider yourselves unkind when you point out such faults. Quite the contrary, you are not without fault yourself when you permit your brothers to perish because of your silence. Were you to point out their misdeeds, correction would at least be possible. If your brother had a bodily wound which he wished to conceal for fear of surgery, would not your silence be cruel and your disclosure merciful? Your obligation to reveal the matter is, therefore, all the greater in order to stem the more harmful infection of the heart.[44]

This statement was a fundamental departure from the precept on silence expressed in the *Rule of Benedict* and repeated by generations of monastic commentators:

Let us do what the prophet says: I said, I will guard my ways so that I do not commit a fault with my tongue. I have set a watchman to my mouth. I was mute and was humbled and I remained silent from good things (Ps. 38.2–3).[45]

For monks, the pursuit of silence was a purposeful humbling of the will to speak, made in the realization that all words, even those expressed with good intention, could tangle the speaker in sin. Despite the perils

---

[43] The subsequent discussion of canonical views of silence has benefited from the work of Caroline Walker Bynum on the distinctive aspects of the spirituality of reformed canons in this period. See Bynum, *Docere Verbo et Exemplo: An Aspect of Twelfth-Century Spirituality* (Cambridge, MA, 1979); and "The Spirituality of the Regular Canons in the Twelfth Century," in *Jesus as Mother: Studies in the Spirituality of the High Middle Ages* (Missoula, 1982), pp. 22–58.

[44] *Praeceptum* 4.8: "Nec uos iudicetis esse maliuolos, quando hoc indicatis. Magis quippe innocentes non estis, si fratres uestros, quos indicando corrigere potestis, tacendo perire permittitis. Si enim frater tuus uulnus haberet in corpore, quod uellet occultare, cum timet secari, nonne crudeliter abs te sileretur et misericorditer indicaretur? Quanto ergo potius eum debes manifestare, ne perniciosius putrescat in corde?" ed. and trans. Lawless, *Augustine of Hippo and His Monastic Rule*, pp. 90–91.

[45] *RB* 6.1: "Faciamus quod ait propeta: dixi: custodiam vias meas, ut non delinguam in lingua mea. Posui ori meo custodiam. Obmutui et humiliatus sum et silui a bonis."

commonly associated with speech, reformed canons weighed the value of useful and edifying words against the virtue of silence. An early twelfth-century commentary on the *Rule of Augustine* usually associated with the abbey of St. Victor in Paris expressly condemned excessive silence as a cruel and damning practice because it prevented canons from preaching and thereby uttering the admonitions that could rescue souls from sin.[46]

Speaking in the service of others made reformed canons more vulnerable than monks to allegations of sins of the tongue. Before his death in 1148, Odo of St. Victor underscored this distinction in a letter to his fellow canons. It was natural for people to assume that canons were susceptible to temptations involving speech, he explained. While monks guarded themselves from the dangers of human discourse with a schedule of silence and prayer, canons seemed to have no protection from the lure of sinful utterances.[47] Odo argued that this was not in fact the case. Like monks, reformed canons followed a spiritual program that included periods of mandatory silence. Their greatest protection, however, was their power of discernment. The license to speak was not intended to concede the power of sinning. With this in mind, the old canon warned his readers to avoid entering quarrels or indulging themselves in unwholesome conversations.[48]

Twelfth-century treatises on the precepts of canonical life flesh out the spiritual program outlined by Odo of St. Victor. The *Rule of Augustine* instructed its readers to remain silent when seated together for their common meal, so that they could attend to the words of the reader who read aloud for their edification.[49] It also advised them to busy their hands with labor rather than working their tongues with idle conversation, warning them specifically to avoid topics unrelated to the benefit of their souls or the task at hand.[50] In the 1120s, the Victorines added more specific directives against wayward speech in their community. At the beginning of the Lenten season and on important feast days, they observed a solemn silence throughout the entire day, a mute expression of their reverence.[51] On most days, however, they were permitted to gather for an hour between services to converse, but one of their number

---

[46] *Expositio in regulam sancti Augustini* 7, *PL* CLXXVI, col. 902cd. The author and precise date of this commentary are unknown, but it is commonly attributed to Hugh of St. Victor and dated to the twelfth century. On the early history of the community of canons at St. Victor, see F. Bonnard, *Histoire de l'abbaye royale et des chanoines réguliers de l'ordre de St.-Victor de Paris*, 2 vols. (Paris, 1904–1907), vol. I, pp. 1–14.

[47] Odo of St. Victor, *Epistola* 4, *PL* CXCVI, col. 1408a. [48] *Ibid.* col. 1408ab.

[49] Augustine, *Ordo monasterii* 7, ed. Lawless, *Augustine of Hippo and His Monastic Rule*, p. 76.

[50] *Ibid.* 9, ed. Lawless, *Augustine of Hippo and His Monastic Rule*, p. 76.

[51] *Liber ordinis sancti Victoris Parisiensis* 31, ed. Luc Jocqué and Ludo Milis, *CCCM* LXI (Turnhout, 1984), p. 145.

was always required to sit apart, watching over them to ensure that they avoided contentious words and gossip.[52]

Using the power of discernment, reformed canons were permitted to temper their silence with words of spiritual instruction, warning and reprimand. Around 1125, Hugh of St. Victor composed a treatise on the training of novices that displayed an acute concern for this aspect of their education. Unlike new recruits in monastic communities, who were rarely permitted to speak, the novices at the abbey of St. Victor learned to discern the places most suitable for speech and to choose the most fitting content for their utterances.[53] Certain chambers of the abbey rarely heard a human voice, while others echoed continuously with the celebration of the divine office and the measured tones of teachers.[54] It was the responsibility of the novices to avoid words that were contrary to the spirit of these activities.[55] For their benefit, Hugh constructed a taxonomy of harmful speech as a tool for the recognition and evasion of idle words of every kind. These, he wrote, were words that were hurtful, shameful or useless in their application. Hurtful words lured the spirit of the listener toward depravity and error. Shameful words did not befit the dignity of the speaker, the listener or the subject matter. Useless words were in no way beneficial to their author or his audience.[56]

The canons of St. Victor and other reformed communities viewed the monastic ideal of an all-embracing silence as a hindrance to their vocation. Strict adherence to rules against speaking would have prevented them from preaching the word of God and correcting the faults of the listeners with verbal admonitions, thereby plunging them both into sin. Instead of abandoning human discourse like monks, they exercised the power of discernment, seasoning their speech with the salt of wisdom by condemning evil words and giving voice to good and useful utterances.[57] The benefits of silence were not entirely lost on the reformed canons, however. Like the desert fathers of late antiquity, they articulated an understanding of silence as a necessary preparation for wise and helpful words.[58] According to Hugh of St. Victor, a time of silence should always precede speech, because the silent mind informs the pattern and content

---

[52] *Liber ordinis* 34, ed. Jocqué and Milis, pp. 163–164.

[53] Hugh of St. Victor, *De institutione novitiorum* 13, *PL* CLXXVI, col. 943d. See also the chapter on silence in the anonymous late twelfth-century *De novitiis instruendis*, ed. Mirko Breitenstein, in *De novitiis instruendis: Text und Kontext eines anonymen Traktates vom Ende des 12. Jahrhunderts* (Dresden, 2003), pp. 135–136.

[54] Hugh of St. Victor, *De institutione novitiorum* 15, *PL* CLXXVI, col. 946ab.

[55] *Ibid.* 6 and 15, cols. 932b and 946b.   [56] *Ibid.* 13, cols. 943d–944a.

[57] *Expositio in regulam sancti Augustini* 6, *PL* CLXXVI, col. 898d.

[58] See Chapter 1, p. 35, above.

of the spoken word before its actual utterance.[59] For Hugh and his brethren, silence was more than a safeguard against sins of the tongue. In a departure from contemporary monastic thought that recalled the enlightened discernment of the hermit saints, they dared to imagine this virtue as a cradle for words of wisdom and warning.

THE WHISPERERS WITH GOD

Early medieval Christians considered physical withdrawal from the distractions of human society to be a powerful expression of their devotion to Christ. In the decades around 1100, an increasing number of individuals practiced the art of living alone throughout western Europe from the arid highlands of Italy to the forested valleys of England and France. The term "hermit" is misleading unless it is understood in its broadest possible sense as one who lives in the wilderness because few reformers sought total isolation from the world and many lived in small groups.[60] Hermits of this sort did not live according to the *Rule of Benedict* or any other code of monastic conduct – at least, not at first – but nonetheless practiced on their own terms many of the same virtuous activities as monks, including the cultivation of silence. In fact, many hermits and their disciples underwent a process of cenobitization in the early twelfth century, that is, they adopted an authoritative rule and swore obedience to an abbot. Some, like the followers of Norbert of Xanten (later called the Premonstratensians) became canons and followed the *Rule of Augustine.*[61]

Among the new religious orders that emerged in this period, the Carthusians astounded their contemporaries with their heroic disdain for human discourse. The currents of piety that directed these hermits in their pursuit of silence flowed in the opposite direction to those that inspired the tempered speech of the reformed canons. The collective will of the Carthusians to deny the need for conversation earned them the respect of the Cluniacs, whose strict rules of silence paled before the mortifications endured by these ascetics in their isolated hermitage. Founded in 1084 by Bruno of Cologne (*c.* 1032–1101), a former schoolmaster from Reims, La Chartreuse was perched high above the city of

[59] Hugh of St. Victor, *De institutione novitiorum* 16, *PL* CLXXVI, col. 946d.
[60] Further on the character and prevalence of the eremetical life in this period, see Chapter 1, pp. 46–48, above.
[61] For a discussion of this process, see Ludo Milis, "Ermites et chanoines réguliers au XIIe siècle," *Cahiers de Civilisation Médiévale* 22 (1979): 39–80.

Grenoble in the western Alps.[62] Surrounded by precipitous slopes and lashed by frigid winds, the hermitage had a terrifying and hostile remoteness that evoked the otherworldly terrain of the desert, the battleground of the saints and the demons of their will.[63] The Alpine weather was a constant source of danger for the hermits, many of whom died in great snowstorms and avalanches in the winter months.[64] Although the Carthusians did not openly dissuade people from visiting them, they refused to accommodate horses because they had none of their own and lacked the resources to feed and shelter them. Visitors were thus forced to make the last part of their journey on foot, an inconvenience that dissuaded all but the most serious and devout from disturbing the solitude of the hermits.[65] Despite these conditions, Peter the Venerable so esteemed the Carthusians that he visited their Alpine hermitage once a year.[66]

Guibert of Nogent was also a pilgrim to La Chartreuse, whose record of his visit in 1112 provides the earliest description of the austere lives of its inhabitants.[67] Guibert found thirteen recluses living around a cloister in individual cells, in which they devoted themselves to private prayer, silent contemplation and some form of manual labor, usually the production of manuscripts.[68] In comparison to the Cluniacs, the Carthusians did not place a great emphasis on liturgical prayer. They gathered as a community only on Sundays and feast days to celebrate the mass in a small, unadorned church. Their personal asceticism was severe by contemporary standards. Despite the cold, they survived on a meager diet of bread, vegetables and diluted wine. Hairshirts mortified their flesh and tamed their will. Hidden from human society in their mountain fastness,

---

[62] On the early history of the Carthusian Order, see *DHGE*, vol. XXI, cols. 1088–1107, s.v. Grande Chartreuse (La); *Dictionnaire de spiritualité*, vol. II, cols. 705–776, s.v. Chartreux; the first section of articles collected in *La naissance des Chartreuses: Actes du VIe colloque international d'histoire et de spiritualité cartusiennes (Grenoble, 12–15 septembre 1984)*, ed. Bernard Bligny and Gérald Chaix (Grenoble, 1984), pp. 6–191 ("Les temps des origines"); and, most recently, Adelindo Giuliani, *La formazione dell'identità certosina (1084–1155)* (Salzburg, 2002).

[63] *Vita altera Brunonis* 31, *PL* CLII, cols. 505c–506a.

[64] Peter the Venerable, *Epistola* 48, ed. Constable, vol. I, pp. 146–148, and vol. II, p. 130.

[65] *Consuetudines Cartusiae* 19.1, ed. An anonymous monk of La Chartreuse, in Guigues 1er, *Coutumes de Chartreuse*, SC CCCXIII (Paris, 1984), p. 201.

[66] Radulf, *Vita Petri Venerabili* 17: "Unde ad sanctos Carthusiae quos nimio affectu diligebat, semel in anno pergebat." *PL* CLXXXIX, col. 28b.

[67] For what follows, see Guibert of Nogent, *De vita sua sive monodiarum libri tres* 1.11, ed. Edmond-René Labande, in *Guibert de Nogent: Autobiographie* (Paris, 1981), pp. 62–74. Further on the life and thought of Guibert, see Jay Rubenstein, *Guibert of Nogent: Portrait of a Medieval Mind* (New York and London, 2002).

[68] Bernard Bligny, "L'érémitisme et les Chartreux," in *L'eremitismo in occidente nei secoli XI e XII: Atti della seconda Settimana internazationale di studio (Mendola, 30 agosto–6 settembre 1962)* (Milan, 1965), pp. 248–268.

they denied themselves the comfort and consolation of any social discourse.[69] Silence was the ever-present companion of their solitude.[70]

The avoidance of spoken words had an eschatological significance in Carthusian spirituality. In the quiet of their cells, the hermits meditated on the account that each individual would render on the Day of Judgment for every careless word they ever spoke.[71] It was this constant state of awareness of the eternal consequences of idle conversation that motivated their flight from human contact and differentiated them from other religious orders of this period. Only the most dire circumstances, like the sudden outbreak of fire or the threat of contagious illness, warranted interrupting this meditation with speech.[72] Their solitude afforded them considerable protection from the dangers of sinful words, but a collection of Carthusian customs compiled before the death of Prior Guigo in 1136 expressed concern for the regulation of their personal interaction with the lay servants who looked after the practical needs of their community. The hermits and their attendants were instructed to remain silent in the church, resisting the temptation to converse when they gathered on certain feast days to shave one another.[73] This code of conduct even extended to the servants who tended the livestock. Unlike the Cistercian *conversi*, who were allowed to talk about their tasks and respond to passing travelers, these shepherds preserved the strict silence fostered by the hermits. Wherever they grazed the flocks, even in the most remote pastures, they were forbidden from speaking at all.[74]

Although their seclusion deterred almost all human contact, the Carthusians did not relinquish the sense of responsibility for the spiritual well-being of others that characterized religious thought in the early twelfth century. They considered the production and dissemination of sacred manuscripts as an evangelical act that did not threaten their silence. The Carthusians busied themselves with transcribing the books of the Bible and works of the church fathers. Their cells contained all of the

---

[69] Guibert of Nogent, *De vita sua* 1.11: "Nusquam pene loquuntur." ed. Labande, p. 68.
[70] See, for example, *Consuetudines Cartusiae* 14.5, p. 196: "Raro quippe hic missa canitur, quoniam precipue studium et propositum nostrum est, silentio et solitudini celle vacar, iuxta illud iheremiae: Sedebit solitarius, et tacebit. (Lam. 3.28)."
[71] Guigo II, *Liber de exercitio cellae* 17, *PL* CLIII, cols. 829b–830c. This treatise was actually the work of Adam Scot, a monk of the Carthusian abbey of Witham in Kent, who composed it around 1186. Further on this work and its author, see M. M. Davy, "La vie solitaire cartusienne d'après le *de quadripartito exercitio cellae* d'Adam le Chartreux," *Revue d'Ascétique et de Mystique* 14 (1933): 124–145.
[72] *Consuetudines Cartusiae* 56.1, p. 266: "Si alicubi vel morbi subitanei, vel ignis, vel alicuius talis periculi necessitas ingruerit, soluto silentio qui prius potent succurrit."
[73] *Consuetudines Cartusiae* 9.1, 42.2–4 and 72.2, pp. 184, 249 and 278.
[74] *Consuetudines Cartusiae* 61.3, p. 270: "In mulgendo ubicumque sint, semper silentium tenent." On the comportment of Cistercian *conversi*, see pp. 147–148, above.

implements necessary for preparing parchment and transcribing texts.[75] A letter of Peter the Venerable listed some of the manuscripts that the hermits had borrowed from Cluny during his abbacy, including works of Hilary of Poitiers, Ambrose of Milan and Prosper of Aquitaine, as well as saints' lives, biblical commentaries and devotional poetry.[76] In the same letter, the abbot asked to borrow a specific volume of Augustine's letters from La Chartreuse, because a bear had recently eaten its exemplar at a Cluniac dependency.[77] A late twelfth-century treatise on topics of meditation for Carthusian hermits exhorted individuals to direct their will toward all aspects of book production, from the preparation of materials to the binding, correction and decoration of manuscript folios.[78] The benefits of these labors were legion. Attentive to their work, the hermits warded off the sins of pride and laziness, long recognized by monastic thinkers as enemies of the soul. They modeled themselves on the first Christian community at Thessalonica, who were encouraged by the apostle Paul to live quietly while toiling day and night with the labor of their hands (1 Thes. 4.11–12 and 2 Thes. 3.12). Every manuscript that they produced was a messenger of truth, allowing them to preach with their hands the word of God that could not escape their lips.[79]

Hidden away at the top of the world, the Carthusians earned the respect and admiration of their most renowned contemporaries, who believed that they embraced the highest ideals of the monastic life. As a young man, the future Pope Urban II had been a student of Bruno at Reims. In 1090, he implored his trusted teacher to come down from the mountain to serve as his advisor in a turbulent time for the papacy.[80] Bruno heeded the call to Rome and never returned to La Chartreuse, but his absence did not diminish the devotion and vitality of the community.

[75] *Consuetudines Cartusiae* 28.1–5, pp. 222–225.

[76] Peter the Venerable, *Epistola* 24, ed. Constable, vol. I, pp. 44–47. Further on the exchange of manuscripts between these two communities, see also *ibid.* 132, 169 and 170, pp. 333–334 and 402–404.

[77] *Ibid.* 24: "Mittite et uos nobis si placet maius uolumen epistolarum sancti patris Augustini, quod in ipso pene initio continet epistolas eiusdem ad sanctum Ihronimum et sancti Ieronimi ad ipsum. Nam magnam partem nostrarum in quadam obaedientia casu comedit ursus." ed. Constable, vol. I, p. 47.

[78] For what follows, see Guigo II, *Liber de exercitio cellae* 36, *PL* CLIII, cols. 880b–884d. On the authorship of this treatise, see n. 71, above.

[79] *Consuetudines Cartusiae* 28.3, p. 224: "Libros quippe tanquam sempiternum animarum nostrarum cibum cautissime custodiri et studiosissime volumus fieri, ut qui ore non possumus, dei verbum manibus predicemus."

[80] H. E. J. Cowdrey, "The Gregorian Papacy and Eremitical Monasticism," in *San Bruno et la Certosa di Calabria: Atti del Convegno Internazionale di Studi per il IX Centenario della Certosa di Serra S. Bruno (Squillace, Serra S. Bruno 15–18 settembre 1991)*, ed. Pietro de Leo (Messina, 1991), pp. 31–54, esp. pp. 44–54 on Bruno and Pope Urban II; repr. in H. E. J. Cowdrey, *Popes and Church Reform in the Eleventh Century* (Aldershot, 2000), no. V.

A few decades later, Peter the Venerable compared the Carthusians to the desert fathers in their pursuit of many virtues, including the denial of the will to converse.[81] Abbot Peter of Celle (d. 1183) marveled at the superhuman exertions of the hermits, summing up their ascetic virtuosity with the words: "They have mouths and speak not."[82] Likewise, Bernard of Clairvaux confessed in a letter to Prior Guigo that he was loath to disturb for even a moment their holy silence from the world and their whispering with God.[83]

THE SIGNS OF THE CENOBITES

The discipline of silence triumphed over the discordant chorus of right-eous claims and polemical rhetoric that accompanied the clash of twelfth-century reform ideologies. Monks, canons and hermits alike fostered this virtuous practice as a means of safeguarding their souls from sinful speech and as a preparation for the utterance of words of instruction, admonish-ment and correction. Universal esteem for the custom of silence con-sequently elevated the currency of monastic sign language as a useful and valuable custom in twelfth-century religious communities. Without exception, the new religious orders adopted the use of hand signs to preserve silence in their cells and cloisters. In fact, these orders borrowed many features of their administration and customs from successful, long-established abbeys like Cluny. Their appropriation of monastic sign language was but one aspect of the currents of reform that molded and reshaped the character of religious foundations in this period.[84] The widespread adoption of this custom by the year 1200 made it vulnerable to criticism, especially in the polemical climate of the twelfth century. For the first time, authors of satire openly derided monks for the excessive use of sign language and branded them hypocrites for using their hands to express the sinful thoughts that the discipline of silence prevented their mouths from uttering. The inclusion of this custom in popular forms of invective was not symptomatic of a general decline in the standards of monastic conduct. Rather, it was a poignant and powerful indication that

[81] Peter the Venerable, *De miraculis libri duos* 2.27, ed. Bouthillier, pp. 149–152, esp. p. 151.
[82] Peter of Celle, *Epistola* 28, ed. and trans. Julian Haseldine, in *The Letters of Peter of Celle* (Oxford, 2001), p. 98: "Os habent et non loquuntur."
[83] Bernard of Clairvaux, *Epistola* 11, ed. Leclercq *et al.*, vol. VII, pp. 52–60, esp. pp. 52–53: "Verebar nimirum sanctam, quam in Domino habetis, importunis scriptitationibus infestare quietem, iuge illud vestrum sacrumque silentium a saeculo, susurrium cum Deo, vel ad modicum interrumpere, nostraque ingerere auribus secretis penitus occupatis supernis eulogiis."
[84] On this point, see Constable, *Reformation of the Twelfth Century*, pp. 88–124, esp. pp. 109–111.

sign language had become a commonly acknowledged characteristic of cloistered communities by the late 1100s.

The earliest sources for the internal life of Cistercian monks indicate that the use of sign language was already a feature of their disciplinary regime in the twelfth century.[85] According to the *Instituta ecclesiastica*, signs replaced the voices of the white monks in the cloister, the refectory and the infirmary.[86] In 1152, the Cistercian General Chapter laid out punishment for anyone who chose words over signs during meals, but made allowances for visiting monks who were not familiar with local sign-forms.[87] The master of novices employed signs as a tool for instruction whenever the rule of silence prevented him from teaching with spoken words.[88] Women associated with the Cistercian Order adopted this custom as well. In the thirteenth century, the residents of one convent communicated with signs during periods of manual labor and when they took meals together in the refectory.[89] Sign language was also a feature of monastic discipline on Cistercian granges. The monks who managed these rural holdings were instructed specifically not to use signs to converse with the lay brothers or resident servants.[90] This admonition implied that *conversi* shared some knowledge of sign language with the monks. Caesarius of Heisterbach affirms this inference with the story of a garrulous lay brother who was felled by a sudden illness. After experiencing a vision of the punishments that awaited him in the afterlife, he warned his fellow *conversi* in desperate tones not to underestimate the seriousness of sins involving unbridled speech and the undisciplined use of sign language.[91]

Evidence for the character of Cistercian sign language does not survive from the twelfth century, but late medieval manuscripts of Cistercian provenance preserved copies of descriptive sign lexicons, the contents of which may reflect the features of a twelfth-century predecessor.

[85] On the history of monastic sign language in the Cistercian tradition, see Jens Rüffer, *Orbis Cisterciensis: Zur Geschichte der monastischen ästhetischen Kultur im 12. Jahrhundert*, Studien zur Geschichte, Kunst und Kultur der Zisterzienser VI (Berlin, 1999), pp. 202–218; and Scott G. Bruce, "The Origins of Cistercian Sign Language," *Cîteaux: Commentarii cistercienses* 52 (2001): 193–209.

[86] *Ecclesiastica officia* 71.5–9, 108.20 and 116.11, ed. Choisselet and Vernet, pp. 212, 306 and 328, respectively.

[87] *Statuta anni 1152* 3 (*De poena loquentium ad mensam*), ed. Canivez, in *Statuta Capitulorum Generalium*, vol. I, p. 46.

[88] *Ecclesiastica officia* 113.1, ed. Choisselet and Vernet, p. 318. It was expressly forbidden, however, for novices to use signs to initiate communication with other monks. See *ibid.* 102.14, p. 294.

[89] *Les offices ecclésiastiques* 79 and *Le riule saint Benoit* (*De le semaniere ki list au mangier*), in "Ancienne traduction," ed. Guignard, in *Les monuments primitifs*, pp. 488–489 and 618.

[90] *Ecclesiastica officia* 84.26–27: "Caveant etiam ne cum conversis vel cum familia significent. Inter se etiam locis et horis incompetentibus signa non faciant." ed. Choisselet and Vernet, p. 242.

[91] Caesarius of Heisterbach, *Libri miraculorum* 2.32, ed. Alfons Hilka, in *Die Wundergeschichten des Caesarius von Heisterbach*, 3 vols. (Bonn, 1933–1937), vol. III, p. 115.

Cistercian sign lexicons appeared in many different forms. Some were prose compositions similar in structure and content to the Cluniac lexicon.[92] Many more were written in verse. These metrical works varied in length and seem to have undergone considerable adaptation over time. The most detailed of them described 216 sign-forms in 275 lines of hexameter.[93] The choice of verse would not have been unusual for Cistercian authors of the twelfth century, who were known to have composed poems on historical and religious topics. Two of them, Hélinant de Froidmont and Bertran of Born, succeeded in rousing the enmity of the king of France and the suspicions of the Cistercian General Chapter with poems critical of secular life.[94] The recasting of prose sign lexicons into hexameter served a didactic function as well. The acquisition of proficiency in sign language was undoubtedly a slow and laborious process for Cistercian novices. The measured rhythms of verse may have served as a mnemonic device for the reader or listener, thereby facilitating the memorization of specific signs and contributing to the eventual mastery of this custom.[95]

Cluniac sign-forms provided the Cistercians with the raw material from which they fashioned their own silent language. Although recast from prose into verse, many Cistercian sign descriptions retained the imprint of their Cluniac exemplars. Take, for instance, the sign for bread. The eleventh-century sign lexicon from Cluny described the sign in this way: "For the sign of bread, make a circle using the thumbs and the index fingers, the reason being that bread is usually round." Two centuries later the Cistercians versified this description in their own sign catalogue: "With two thumbs and two index fingers like a circle joined, thus is bread signified."[96] Many

---

[92] See, for example, Gérard van Rijnberk, "De Gebarentaal in een Cisterciënserklooster der Nederlanden in de XVe eeuw," *Cîteaux in de Nederlanden* 2 (1951): 55–68.

[93] See Walter Jarecki, "Die 'Ars signorum Cisterciensium' im Rahmen der metrischen Signa-Listen," *Revue bénédictine* 99 (1989): 329–399. Other editions of Cistercian verse sign lexicons include Axel Nelson, "Teckenspråket I Vadstena Kloster," *Nordisk Tidskrift för Bok- och Biblioteksväsen* 22 (1935): 25–43 (127 sign-words in 156 lines of verse); and Bruno Griesser, "Ungedruckte Texte zur Zeichensprache in den Klöstern," *Analecta Sacri Ordinis Cisterciensis* 3 (1947): 111–137 (two separate lists of 165 sign-words in 190 lines of verse and 141 sign-words in 141 lines of verse).

[94] William D. Paden, Jr., "*De monachis rithmos facientibus*: Hélinant de Froidmont, Bertran of Born, and the Cistercian General Chapter of 1199," *Speculum* 55 (1980): 669–685, esp. pp. 669–671 on the activities of Cistercian poets in the twelfth century.

[95] On this point, see Pierre Riché, "Le rôle de la mémoire dans l'enseignement médiéval," in *Jeux de mémoire: Aspects de la mnémotechnie médiévale*, ed. Bruno Roy and Paul Zumthor (Montréal and Paris, 1985), pp. 133–148. Further on didactic verse in the Middle Ages, see Thomas Haye, *Das lateinische Lehrgedicht im Mittelalter: Analyse einer Gattung* (Leiden, 1997).

[96] "Pro signo panis fac unum circulum cum utroque pollice et his duobus digitis, qui secuntur, pro eo, quod et panis solet esse rotundus." ed. Walter Jarecki, *Signa Loquendi: Die cluniacensischen Signa-Listen eingeleitet und herausgegeben* (Baden-Baden, 1981), p. 121 (Cluny, no. 1); and "Cum duplex pollex quasi spera sic sociatur / Et duplex index, sic panis significatur." ed. Jarecki, "Die 'Ars signorum Cisterciensium,'" p. 360 (lines 59–60).

Cluniac signs represented people and items that were common to medieval abbeys and thus readily applicable in Cistercian houses as well. The white monks adopted Cluniac signs for different kinds of people (like priest and monk) and specific monastic officials (like abbot, prior and chamberlain) as well as signs related to sustenance (common foodstuffs and serving vessels), apparel (articles of clothing and personal tools) and the divine office (liturgical items and candles).[97] The Cistercians also conceived of new signs to express words and concepts outside of the scope of the Cluniac sign vocabulary. A new sign for lay brother was specific to their monastic experience.[98] Moreover, signs for enemies of the faith (heretics and pagans) and sick people (lepers and the blind) reflected the active involvement of white monks in late medieval society as preachers against heresy and as caregivers to the disenfranchised and destitute in hospitals and leper-houses, which they often founded themselves.[99] In the thirteenth century, women associated with the Cistercians were particularly inclined to minister to the needs of lepers as an expression of their piety.[100] Lastly, new signs for the reception of payment and for specific monetary currencies suggest that the Cistercians had cause to use this custom to signal their participation in some aspects of the emergent money-based economy of the twelfth and thirteenth centuries. The reckoning and tallying of rents, tithes and other incomes may explain the need for these terms in the Cistercian sign vocabulary, but the specific context of their use remains elusive.[101]

---

[97] Signs for people and monastic officials: Griesser, "Ungedruckte Texte zur Zeichensprache," pp. 116 (*abbas*), 119 (*clericus*), 118 (*prior*), 120 (*monachus*) and 121 (*camerarius*). For the numerous signs related to sustenance, apparel and the divine office, see Jarecki, "Die 'Ars signorum Cisterciensium,'" *passim*. For the Cluniac prototypes of these signs, see Jarecki, *Signa Loquendi*, pp. 136 (*monachus* and *clericus*), 137 (*abbas, prior* and *camerarius*) and *passim*.

[98] Griesser, "Ungedruckte Texte zur Zeichensprache," p. 120 (*conversus*). Further on the Cistercian *conversi*, see pp. 147–148, above.

[99] Jarecki, "Die 'Ars signorum Cisterciensium,'" pp. 371 (*paganus* and *Bohemus vel hereticus*) and 369 (*cecus, luscus, scabidus* and *leprosus*), respectively. On the activities of white monks who opposed heretics in southern France, see Beverly Mayne Kienzle, *Cistercians, Heresy and Crusade in Occitania, 1145–1229: Preaching in the Lord's Vineyard* (York, 2001). For an important study of Cistercian contributions to the care of the sick, with references to earlier literature, see David N. Bell, "The English Cistercians and the Practice of Medicine," *Cîteaux: Commentarii Cistercienses* 40 (1989): 139–173.

[100] Anne E. Lester, "Cares Beyond the Walls: Cistercian Nuns and the Care of Lepers in Twelfth- and Thirteenth-Century Northern France," in *Religious and Laity in Northern Europe, 1000–1400: Interaction, Negotiation and Power*, ed. E. Jamroziak and J. Burton (Turnhout, 2006), pp. 197–224.

[101] Jarecki, "Die 'Ars signorum Cisterciensium,'" p. 372 (*munus accipere, nummus, marca* and *librum / talentum*). For a useful introduction to the problem of monastic participation in the profit economy, see Little, *Religious Poverty and the Profit Economy*, esp. pp. 90–96 on the Cistercians. Further on Cistercian attitudes toward tithes, see Giles Constable, *Monastic Tithes from their Origins to the Twelfth Century* (Cambridge, 1964), esp. pp. 138–139 and 251–255; and Constance Berman, "Cistercian Women and Tithes," *Cîteaux: Commentarii Cistercienses* 49 (1998): 95–127.

Continuity and criticism

In imitation of the Cluniacs, the white monks confined their use of signs to a small vocabulary of nouns, with no means of connecting them to express full sentences or higher thoughts. These limitations protected the monks from sinning through the garrulous use of their hands. Around 1200, Conrad of Eberbach included the love of excessive signing in a list of actions and qualities contrary to the ideals of Cistercian monks.[102] Legislation from the twelfth century onwards bristled with prescriptions against the inappropriate use of sign language. White monks were warned specifically to refrain from making unnecessary signs in the cloister and the dormitory, during their labors and in the evening after Vespers.[103] Sick monks were forbidden from using sign language in the infirmary.[104] Tales of divine punishment for breaches in discipline were used to dissuade Cistercian monks from making improper signs. In a thirteenth-century account of a vision of purgatory, a Cistercian novice was allowed to witness the torments suffered by the souls of dead monks as a reminder to the living that seemingly inconsequential excesses may result in terrible otherworldly ordeals.[105] This story was part of a compilation that provided edifying examples and spiritual guidance culled from patristic authors and saints' lives for the cultivation of virtues and the avoidance of vices. The episode in question, "Concerning the vision of a certain monk" (*De visione cuiusdam monachi*), was part of a thematic section entitled "On the punishments of souls after death" (*De penis animarum post mortem*).[106] Among the sufferers were those who had dared to use signs to utter lewd and silly words. Their punishment included flaying and beatings.[107]

Like the Cistercians, communities of reformed canons also adopted the custom of sign language from the Cluniacs in the twelfth century. The earliest customary of the order of St. Victor in Paris recommended the use

[102] Conrad of Eberbach, *Exordium magnum cisterciense* 5.19, ed. Bruno Griesser, *CCCM* CXXXVIII (Turnhout, 1994), p. 379.
[103] See, for example, *Ecclesiastica officia* 71.19 (sign restrictions in the cloister), 72.25 (limits to sign use in the dormitory), 75.16 (sign restrictions for laboring monks) and 79.1 (limits to sign use after Vespers), ed. Choisselet and Vernet, pp. 212, 214, 220 and 232, respectively.
[104] *Ecclesiastica officia* 92.16, ed. Choisselet and Vernet, p. 264.
[105] MS BN, Latin 15912, fol. 64r: "Gravissime in purgatorio inferuntur pene pro his excessibus quos levissimos estimamus."
[106] *Ibid.* fols. 64v–65r. For a description of the manuscript and its contents, see Léopold Delisle, *Inventaire des manuscrits de la Sorbonne* (Paris, 1870), p. 28 (no. 15912); and Brian Patrick McGuire, "The Cistercians and the Rise of the Exemplum in Early Thirteenth-Century France: A Reevaluation of Paris B.N. MS lat. 15912," *Classica et Medievalia* 34 (1983): 211–267, repr. in Brian Patrick McGuire, *Friendship and Faith: Cistercian Men, Women, and their Stories, 1100–1250* (Aldershot, 2002), no. V.
[107] MS BN, Latin 15912, fol. 64r: "Pro signorum numerositate superflua quibus ludicra quaeque et iocosa intulissent ad invicem digiti negligentium vel excoriabantur et tunsionibus quassabantur."

of hand signs to facilitate communication when conversation was forbidden.[108] Canons learned a list of 110 hand signs for books, food, clothing and other common items in their community.[109] With the exception of a new sign for reformed canon, their sign vocabulary was drawn directly from the Cluniac sign lexicon.[110] Recognizing that proficiency in sign language was a difficult and time-consuming process, the canons of St. Victor made allowances for individuals who had trouble learning the sign-forms. In extreme circumstances, individuals were permitted to speak a single word during times of silence, if they could not remember the corresponding sign. Fearful that some would interpret this exception to the rule as an invitation to speak, the author of their customary followed it with a warning that judgment awaited any canon who used more signs than necessary or uttered a single extra word and thereby broke the silence.[111]

The hermits of La Chartreuse also employed a language of signs to protect the silence of their cells. Unique among their contemporaries, however, they explicitly rejected Cluniac sign-forms in favor of a system of their own devising. In principle, the Carthusians agreed with monks and canons that the custom of sign language was a useful tool for the exchange of necessary information when speech was forbidden. Their earliest customary stated plainly that the hermits should use signs to convey their need for important items or to call attention to potential danger.[112] In practice, however, the hermits claimed to have little or no knowledge of the "signs of the cenobites" (*signa cenobiorum*).[113] They employed instead what they called simple signs (*signa rustica*) that in their words were free from the subtleties of wit and innuendo and therefore more fitting to their austere way of life.[114] No descriptions of these signs have survived, but this comment was without doubt intended as a critique of the Cluniac sign language. It is unclear, however, if it was aimed at the forms of the signs, the manner of their execution or the linguistic

---

[108] *Liber ordinis* 31, ed. Jocqué and Milis, p. 147: "Debent quippe singuli signa necessaria diligenter addiscere, ut in hora silentii quod lingua non licet, sibi inuicem, quando necesse fuerit, signis ualeant insinuare."

[109] Jarecki, *Signa Loquendi*, pp. 231–249; and *Liber ordinis* 25, ed. Jocqué and Milis, pp. 116–134. This sign list later circulated independently of the customary. See Jarecki, *Signa Loquendi*, pp. 110–111.

[110] Jarecki, *Signa Loquendi*, p. 244, no. 76 (*canonicus regularis*).

[111] *Liber ordinis* 31, ed. Jocqué and Milis, p. 147: "Quod si aliquando necesse habent aliquid dicere, et signum non habent, quo id ualeant significare, conceditur eis pro necessitate unum tantummodo uerbum proferre. Si autem aliquis in hora silentii signa multiplicauerit, aut etiam unum uerbum superflue dixerit, si percipi potest, ita iudicetur, ac si fregisset silentium."

[112] *Consuetudines Cartusiae* 45.1, p. 254.

[113] *Consuetudines Cartusiae* 31.3, p. 232: "Signa cenobiorum aut nulla aut pauca novimus."

[114] *Consuetudines Cartusiae* 45.1, p. 254: "Habent enim signa pleraque rusticana, et ab omni facetia vel lascivia aliena."

system as a whole. The hermits of La Chartreuse seem to have set out to create a muted version of the silent language of the Cluniacs, a new idiom of sign language that had a more silent quality than that of the monks. In fact, the Carthusians were not the only hermits to develop a new sign system in the early twelfth century. Independent of the prevalent tradition, an English recluse named Godric of Finchale (d. 1170) also invented signs to facilitate communication with his servants when he wished to remain silent.[115] Unfortunately, no record of these signs has survived.

The criticism voiced by the Carthusians calls attention to the fact that suspicion followed monastic sign language into the twelfth century. As we have seen, the Cluniacs were self-conscious of the fact that a silent language of signs with the expressive potential of spoken words invited the risk of abuse among negligent individuals, especially those who were new to the monastic vocation. Following the lead of the black monks, the new religious orders likewise treated this custom with caution so that signs would not become a medium of sinful discourse in their communities. Nonetheless, the widespread adoption of Cluniac sign-forms after the year 1100 drew the attention of authors of satire, who often included some reference to its misuse whenever they ridiculed monks. Toward the end of the century, Gerald of Wales (d. c. 1223) lampooned the comportment of the brethren of Canterbury. His disdain for these monks arose from his opposition to the policy of their archbishop of electing English bishops to Welsh sees. Their power of excommunication over Welsh congregations was a strong deterrent to regional uprisings.[116] With firsthand authority, Gerald claimed that the monks of Canterbury avoided speech in their refectory by employing an inexhaustible repertoire of signs made with the fingers, hands and arms. Their actions were so unrestrained that Gerald felt as though he dined on a stage among actors and jesters.[117] This comparison carried strong moral overtones in ecclesiastical circles. Like prostitutes, entertainers of this kind put their bodies to shameful use, inciting lust in their audience by means of rude stories and suggestive gestures.[118] It would have been more appropriate for the monks of Canterbury to speak human words with modesty, Gerald sneered, than to allow their talkative hands to usurp the duties of their silent tongues.

---

[115] Reginaldus of Durham, *Libellus de vita et miraculis sancti Godrici* 58.127, 86.182 and 118.228, ed. J. Stevenson (London, 1845), pp. 136–137, 190 and 241.

[116] Robert Bartlett, *Gerald of Wales 1146–1223* (Oxford, 1982), pp. 48–57.

[117] Gerald of Wales, *De rebus a se gestis* 1.5, ed. J. S. Brewer, in *Giraldi Cambrensis Opera*, Rolls Series XXI, 2 vols. (London, 1861), vol. I, p. 51.

[118] John W. Baldwin, "The Image of the Jongleur in Northern France around 1200," *Speculum* 72 (1977): 635–663, esp. p. 639.

Similarly, an early thirteenth-century sermon attributed to Jacques de Vitry (d. 1240) drew the parallel between talkative women and cloistered monks. It told how a husband and his wife could not agree whether a certain field had been mown with a scythe or cut with shears. Enraged by his wife's relentless opposition, the man cut out her tongue. To his surprise, however, she persisted with her argument, expressing with her fingers what she could no longer say with her mouth. Although unable to speak, her busy hands allowed her to carry on their quarrel unabated. The preacher ended the anecdote with a humorous analogy. Just as the wife bickered endlessly with her hands, he explained, so too do certain monks speak incessantly with their fingers, even when they are instructed to remain silent.[119] By harnessing the practice of sign language among monks to the image of a scolding wife unhindered by the loss of her tongue, Jacques de Vitry compounded the ironic humor of his anecdote at the expense of brethren who employed this custom.[120]

Another sermon from the same collection suggested the lengths to which some disobedient monks would go to gossip and tell stories when both speech *and* sign language were prohibited to them:

> I have heard of some monks that, when they had been enjoined to keep silent and even manual signs had been forbidden to them (seeing that they used such signs to tell vain and curious things to their fellows) no longer daring to employ any other means, they would converse together with their toes, thus communicating to their brothers the battles of kings and the deeds of warriors and almost all the news and tidings of this world.[121]

Fanciful satires of this kind achieved their ironic intention by playing on the paradox inherent in monastic sign language. As a system of nonverbal communication that served as a functional replacement for speech, this custom invited ridicule from critics of the monastic endeavor because it appeared to allow the brethren to partake in all of the luxuries of idle conversation that they professed so strenuously to avoid. Satirical portraits of monks with garrulous hands belie the fact that in most cases the

---

[119] Jacques de Vitry, *Exempla ex sermonibus vulgaribus* 222: "Sic faciunt quidam monachi quando eis silentium imperatur." ed. Thomas Frederick Crane, in *The Exempla or Illustrative Stories from the Sermones Vulgares of Jacques de Vitry* (New York, 1890), p. 92.

[120] On the popularity of the image of the scold in late medieval thought, see Sandy Bardsley, *Venomous Tongues: Speech and Gender in Late Medieval England* (Philadelphia, 2006).

[121] Jacques de Vitry, *Exempla ex sermonibus vulgaribus* 48: "Audivi de quibusdam monachis, cum interdiceretur eis quod silentium tenerent nec etiam manibus signa facerent, eo quod vana et curiosa per signa sociis cum manibus nunciabant, cum alio modo non auderant, pedibus invicem loquebantur, regum prelia et gesta pugnatorum et fere omnia nova et rumores de toto mundo sociis intimantes." ed. Crane, p. 19; trans. G. G. Coulton, *Five Centuries of Religion*, 4 vols. (Cambridge, 1923–1950), vol. I, p. 87 (slightly modified).

responsibility of using signs in place of spoken words was not habitually abused in cloistered communities. In fact, the appearance of this custom in the early thirteenth century among the vices attributed to negligent monks speaks to the widespread acceptance of signs as a useful medium of silent discourse among religious orders that otherwise fostered divergent ideals about the ends and means of ascetic renunciation and participation in the world beyond their walls.

CONCLUSION

In the twelfth century, the positive valuation of silence was a unifying element in a religious world of increasing diversity. This sentiment was expressed clearly in the writings of Abbot Peter of Celle. In a treatise on the discipline of the cloister that addressed followers of St. Benedict and St. Augustine alike, Peter asserted that, despite their seeming differences, monks, canons and hermits belonged to the same family and were obliged to cultivate the virtue of silence among the highest principles of their shared vocation.[122] With words resonant of the Revelation of John, he invited his readers to imagine claustral silence as a book closed with seven seals. These seals represented both the seven kinds of evil words that closed lips would never utter and the seven benefits that the denial of the will to speak gave to the mortal soul.[123] In Peter of Celle's "inclusive vision of the monastic order," the discipline of silence transcended the boundaries of ascetic vocations, providing a common focus for the aspiration of all individuals who strove to abandon the prison of their will and voice their desire for God.[124]

Esteem for the virtue of silence among the new religious orders of the twelfth century led to the adoption of Cluniac sign language in cloisters and hermitages throughout northern Europe. The utility and adaptability of this silent language accounted for its pervasiveness and vitality in the medieval monastic tradition. Monks showed considerable pragmatism and creativity in their appropriation of this custom by retiring old signs that had no relevance to their experience and fashioning new ones that better reflected their practical needs and cultural expectations. Translations of Latin sign lexicons into vernacular languages in the later medieval and early modern periods ensured the accessibility of this custom to new generations of Christian ascetics, including religious

---

[122] Peter of Celle, *De disciplina claustrali* 18, ed. G. de Martel, in *Pierre de Celle: L'école du cloître, SC* CCXL (Paris, 1977), pp. 224–232.
[123] *Ibid.* 18.2–3, ed. Martel, pp. 226–230.
[124] The quotation is from the introduction of *The Letters of Peter of Celle*, ed. Haseldine, p. xiv.

169

women.[125] Although a cause of concern for some authors, the benefits of using signs in religious communities always outweighed the fear of their misuse. As a result, by the end of the twelfth century, the custom of sign language was firmly rooted in the medieval imagination as an inalienable feature of monastic discipline. Bridging the ideological divide that separated the new religious orders of the twelfth century from one another, this silent language remained a fundamental aspect of the cloistered experience throughout the later Middle Ages and beyond.

---

[125] The translation of sign lexicons into vernacular languages began in the eleventh century with the Old English *Monasteriales Indicia* (see Chapter 4, pp. 108–117, above), but became much more common in the early modern period, when Portuguese and French translations appeared in Cistercian circles. See Mario Martins, "Livros de Sinais dos Cistercienses Portugueses," *Boletin de Filologia* 17 (1958): 293–357; and Louis du Bois, *Histoire civile, religieuse et littéraire de l'abbaye de la Trappe* (Paris, 1824), pp. 248–258. The first sign lexicon addressed specifically to women was a Middle English product of the fifteenth century composed for the nuns of Sion, a convent of the order of St. Brigit in Middlesex. See "A Table of Signs Used During the Hours of Silence by the Sisters in the Monastery of Sion," ed. Samuel Bentley, in *Excerpta Historica or Illustrations of English History* (London, 1833), pp. 414–419; repr. in *Monastic Sign Languages*, ed. Jean Umiker-Sebeok and Thomas A. Sebeok (Berlin, New York and Amsterdam, 1987), pp. 489–494.

CONCLUSION

As this study has shown, the monks of tenth-century Cluny developed an elaborate system of meaning-specific hand signs as a means to achieve an ideal of angelic conduct that included the cultivation of an all-embracing silence. The inhabitants of early medieval abbeys generally esteemed the abnegation of the will to speak as a virtuous practice that protected monks from the sins of slander and murmuring. Unlike their contemporaries, however, the Cluniacs also freighted this custom with positive moral and eschatological associations. With their thoughts fixed firmly on the life to come, they strove to live in consonance with their angelic counterparts in heaven. By embracing strict regulations against idle conversation, the monks of Cluny set themselves apart in the Christian tradition in their unrivaled effort to actualize within the walls of their monastery the eternal silence enjoyed by the elect at the end of time.

The development of monastic sign language was a corollary to the rigorous prohibitions against speaking embraced at Cluny. The cultivation of silence raised practical difficulties in large religious houses, where the responsibilities of communal life required that individuals communicate with one another on a regular basis. The use of signs in place of speech was not unknown in late antique and early medieval monasticism, but the silent language of the Cluniacs was unprecedented in its range of vocabulary and precision of expression, causing some contemporaries to complain that this custom was incongruent with received tradition. For their part, the brethren of Cluny were well aware that their sign system posed considerable risks to monastic discipline, especially if employed with cunning or negligence. An eleventh-century lexicon of Cluniac sign-forms intended for the instruction of novices provides remarkable insight into the linguistic character of monastic sign language and the measures taken to curb its abuse in the abbey. The Cluniacs did not consider their silent language to be a functional replacement for speech. In fact, they only devised signs for single nominal concepts (primarily nouns), the result being that these signs could not be used to express higher thoughts. Similarly, they took care to teach new monks only those few signs that they would need to understand rudimentary instruction and reprimand during their novitiate. Only after many years in the abbey would individual monks learn the full panoply of signs that comprised this silent language.

While the Cluniac sign lexicon sheds light on the form and character of monastic sign language, it actually tells us very little about the contexts of its use until it is read alongside the eleventh-century customaries of Bernard and Ulrich, which together provide a rich descriptive context for the practical applications of this custom at Cluny. A comparative reading of these sources suggests that the Cluniacs encouraged their brethren to interact in matters of mundane practicality without recourse to words or signs, thereby limiting the venues in which sign language was permissible. Since the use of signs was always considered to be an opportunity to make sinful utterances, it was in the interest of the Cluniacs to restrict the application of this custom as much as possible. Moreover, it is apparent that novices learned this silent language primarily to recognize signs of instruction and reprimand employed by their master during their novitiate. The active expression of this custom was not nearly as import-ant a skill for new monks to cultivate as their passive understanding of the sign-forms used most frequently by their superiors. Even so, the shared language of the Cluniacs reinforced their sense that their monastic com-munity was a place distinct and separate from the secular world. Moreover, this custom also provided a mutually intelligible medium of communi-cation for monks who came from increasingly divergent linguistic backgrounds.

As Cluny's reputation for sanctity grew in the tenth and eleventh centuries, abbeys in its orbit of influence began to emulate the customs fostered by its monks, including the use of sign language. Before the turn of the twelfth century, knowledge of Cluniac sign-forms had migrated from Burgundy to monastic communities in neighboring regions of northern Europe. The adaptability of monastic sign language was the key to its successful adoption in other religious houses. Sign lexicons produced by these abbeys show that the brethren who adopted this custom readily adapted it to local contingencies by abandoning irrelevant signs from the Cluniac vocabulary and creating new ones better suited to their needs. The creative adaptation of the Cluniac sign system continued unabated in the twelfth century, as new orders of monks and canons appropriated this custom as a means to foster silence in their communities. Although the reformed orders differed considerably in their views of the religious meaning of silence and its proper measure in the cloister, most of them agreed that the silent language of the Cluniacs was both useful and necessary as a safeguard against sins of the tongue. The Carthusians were alone in their outspoken disdain for what they called the signs of the cenobites, favoring instead a sign system of their own devising (now lost) that was somehow a more fitting idiom for the tenor of their austere lives. By the year 1200 Cluniac signs had obtained an immense significance throughout western Europe. So ubiquitous was the practice of this custom that the use (and abuse) of sign language became synonymous with monastic discipline and its failings in the cultural vocabulary of the medieval west.

There is an ironic epilogue to this study of silence and sign language in medieval monasticism. In the sixteenth century, a Spanish monk named Pedro Ponce de León achieved celebrity and notoriety throughout Europe when he succeeded in teaching deaf children to speak aloud.[1] His feat was seen as nothing short of miraculous. Throughout the medieval and early modern periods, it was generally believed that deaf individuals had no recourse to the benefits of civil society because of their inability to speak. Despite the fact that most premodern deaf people were not natural mutes, they did not cultivate any form of oral discourse and thus were considered incapable of speech in the eyes of the law. This in turn led to considerable legal disenfranchisement. In sixteenth-century Spain, deaf people were typically excluded from rights of succession and inheritance and denied a general education. Moreover, social dishonor followed them and their families. The disabled children of aristocrats often found themselves sequestered away in monasteries, because their physical flaws were an embarrassing reflection on the moral failings of their parents.[2] This practice dated back to the Middle Ages. In the late eleventh century, the Cluniac monk Ulrich of Zell remarked on it explicitly in the prologue of the customary he sent to Abbot William of Hirsau:

Sometimes the pleasing and happy memory comes to me of your promise to avoid the genius of certain worldly men, who evidently caring for nothing other than this temporal life alone, and once they have, so to speak, a house full of sons and daughters, if one of them is missing a leg or an arm, or is deaf or blind, hunchbacked or leprous, or anything of this kind that makes him in some way less acceptable to the world, they offered this one to God with the exceedingly urgent will that he become a monk, although clearly not for God, but only to

[1] For what follows, see Susan Plann, "Pedro Ponce de León: Myth and Reality," in *Deaf History Unveiled: Interpretations from the New Scholarship*, ed. J. V. Van Cleve (Washington, DC, 1993), pp. 1–12; and Susan Plann, *A Silent Minority: Deaf Education in Spain, 1550–1835* (Berkeley, Los Angeles and London, 1997), pp. 13–35.
[2] John Boswell, *The Kindness of Strangers: The Abandonment of Children in Western Europe from Late Antiquity to the Renaissance* (New York, 1988), pp. 228–321, esp. pp. 298–299 and pl. 12.

save themselves the trouble of educating and feeding those children, or in order to favor their other children – not to mention those who are not lacking in bodily health or integrity of limbs, but who are half-men or half-alive, as we know by experience that this happens very often.[3]

Hidden away in cloistered seclusion, the deaf children of aristocrats were effectively erased from the legal and political histories of their families.

Contrary to received opinion, however, the grim social fate of pre-modern deaf children was not mirrored by the teaching of the Church on the issue of their salvation. Over the past hundred years, historians of deaf education have drawn repeatedly, but selectively, from the letters of the apostle Paul and the writings of Augustine of Hippo to construct and perpetuate the argument that ancient and medieval Christian thinkers adhered literally to the notion that faith comes by hearing (Rom. 10.17) and therefore denied the hope of salvation for deaf people.[4] This presumption has been shown to be completely false. In a brilliant piece of revisionist history, Leslie A. King has argued that uncritical reverence for nineteenth-century scholars of deaf education has allowed their erroneous presumptions about medieval attitudes toward the deaf to circulate unquestioned and unexamined down to the present day.[5] Her careful analysis of the Latin terminology for deafness employed by Augustine and other patristic authors and their respective opinions about the deaf and their hope of salvation has led her to conclude that "[t]he tradition that Augustine condemned the deaf to hell on account of Romans 10:17 is utterly unfounded and is completely at odds with the ideas and attitudes he displays at length and in detail in *De Quantitate Animae* and *De Magistro*."[6] In short, the condemnation of premodern deaf people as beyond the pale with respect to Christian salvation has more to do with the

---

[3] Ulrich, prol.: "Accedit aliquociens admodum grata et iocunda memoria pollicitationis tue de cauendo ingenio quorumdam hominum saecularium. Qui nimirum, non magnopere curantes de alio quam de hac sola temporali uita, postquam domum habuerint, ut ita dixerim, plenam filiorum et filiarum, aut si quis eorumdem claudus erit aut mancus, surdaster aut cecus, gibbosus aut leprosus, uel aliud quid huiusmodi quod eum aliquo modo saeculo facit minus acceptum, hunc quidem impensissimo uoto ut monachus fiat offerunt Deo, quamquam plane non propter Deum, sed propter hoc tantum ut seipsos expediant ab eis educandis et pascendis, uel allis suis liberis possit magis esse consultum. Erog ut taceam de his qui non carent sanitate corporali et membrorum integritate, ab his ipsis qui sunt ita semihomines uel ita semiuiui, qualia sepius experti sumus perpetrari." ed. and trans. Susan Boynton and Isabelle Cochelin, in *From Dead of Night to End of Day: The Medieval Customs of Cluny / Du cœur de la nuit à la fin du jour: Les coutumes clunisiennes au moyen âge*, ed. Boynton and Cochelin (Leiden, 2005), pp. 329–347, at pp. 330–331.

[4] For recent examples, see Plann, *Silent Minority*, pp. 17–18; and Marilyn Daniels, *Benedictine Roots in the Development of Deaf Education: Listening with the Heart* (Westport, CT and London, 1997), pp. 3–4.

[5] Leslie A. King, "*Surditas*: The Understandings of the Deaf and Deafness in the Writings of Augustine, Jerome, and Bede" (Ph.D. dissertation, Boston University, 1996). I am very grateful to Beverley Kienzle for bringing this work to my attention.

[6] *Ibid.* p. 214.

unfounded presumptions of modern scholars than it does with any medieval prejudices toward those with an inability to hear and speak aloud.

Sources from the Middle Ages seem to indicate that the positive and inclusive attitude toward the deaf expressed by patristic authors was prevalent in the medieval period as well. A compelling episode that supports this inference appears in Herman of Tournai's early twelfth-century account of the history of the abbey of St. Martin.[7] According to Herman, a cathedral canon named Galbert consulted a disfigured deaf-mute famous for his skill at divination. Despite that fact that church authorities generally frowned on the consultation of diviners, Galbert asked the oracle which schoolmaster it was better to follow, Odo of Tournai or his rival Rainbert of Lille. The deaf-mute expressed his inspired opinion using hand signs: "Drawing his right hand over his left palm as if cleaving the earth with a plow, he indicated that Odo's doctrine was most correct. Extending his finger toward the city of Lille, by contrast, he applied his hand to his mouth and, by blowing, indicated that the lectures of Master Rainbert were nothing but windy chatter."[8] While his prophetic utterances required some interpretation on the part of his petitioners, the deaf-mute diviner described by Herman of Tournai was clearly a respected person who held a position of considerable authority in his community and was by no means socially or spiritually disadvantaged by the fact that he could not speak.

By the sixteenth century, the legal disadvantages facing the deaf children of noble parents had become so harsh that it was desirable to find a way for them to learn how to speak aloud. Monastic sign language seems to have played a pivotal role in Pedro Ponce's enterprise to educate his deaf charges.[9] The boys in question were Pedro Fernández and Francisco de Velasco, the sons of Juan Fernández de Velasco y Tovar, the marquis of Berlanga and Astudillo and the patron of the abbey of San Salvador at Oña, where Pedro Ponce served as a monk. Hereditary deafness was a relatively common characteristic of aristocratic children in sixteenth-century Spain due to generations of intermarriage between noble families. Indeed, four of the nine Velasco children were born deaf. Two

---

[7] Herman of Tournai, *Liber de restauratione monasterii Sancti Martini Tornacensis*, ed. Georg Waitz, *MGH SS* XIV (Hanover, 1883), pp. 274–317; trans. Lynn H. Nelson, in *Herman of Tournai: The Restoration of the Monastery of Saint Martin of Tournai* (Washington, DC, 1996).

[8] *Ibid.* 2: "Dexteramque manum per sinistre palmam instar aratri terram scindentis pertrahens digitumque versus magistri Odonis scolam protendens, significabat, doctrinam eius esse rectissimam; rursus vero digitum contra insulense oppidum protendens manuque ori admota exsufflans, innuebat, magistri Raimberti lectionem nonnisi ventosam esse loquacitatem." ed. Waitz, p. 275; trans. Nelson, p. 15.

[9] The information in this paragraph is drawn from Plann, *Silent Minority*, pp. 13–35.

sisters, Juliana and Bernardina, were likewise removed to religious communities. Drawing the analogy between the Velasco boys and deaf children in modern households, Susan Plann has inferred that Pedro Fernández and Francisco, who were about eleven and seven years of age respectively when they came to the abbey of San Salvador, would have arrived with knowledge of some kind of gestural system that they had invented and employed among themselves at home, so-called "home sign." For their part, the brethren of San Salvador also employed a silent language of signs, although the derivation of their sign system and its precise relationship to Cluniac sign language is unknown. After reconciling their divergent sign vocabularies, Pedro Ponce was able to use signs to bridge the gulf of silence that separated the children from civil society and eventually succeeded in teaching them to enunciate words until they mastered the ability to speak aloud. His success prompted other monks in Spain and France to follow his example.

There is a wonderful irony to Pedro Ponce's achievement. In the tenth century, monks of Cluny first invented a vocabulary of meaning-specific hand signs to promote the glorification of silence that was central to their imitation of the angelic life. Through the use of these signs, they avoided uttering the human sounds that mired their thoughts in the world and thereby made their abbey a semblance of the dwelling place of the angels in heaven. Centuries later, Pedro Ponce employed a distant descendant of the Cluniac sign language as a way to communicate with deaf children. Unlike his medieval predecessors, however, the Spanish monk employed this custom with a new pragmatism. Rather than serving as tools for the preservation of silence in the pursuit of an ascetic ideal, in the hands of Pedro Ponce monastic signs became a medium of inquiry into the silent world of the hearing impaired, an instrument of first contact in an unprecedented pedagogical program, the goal of which was teaching deaf children to speak aloud. The monasteries which fostered a signing culture since the Middle Ages laid the foundations for the first experiments in deaf education.

Appendix A

THE CLUNIAC SIGN LEXICON

This translation of the Cluniac sign lexicon is based on the edition of Walter Jarecki, *Signa Loquendi* (Baden-Baden, 1981), pp. 121–142. Numerical markers did not accompany the sign descriptions in the customaries of Bernard (1.17) and Ulrich (2.4), but they have been added here to facilitate reference to individual signs.

LET ME SET DOWN SOME THINGS CONCERNING THESE
SIGNS, BY GRACE OF THE WORD, AND FIRST,
THOSE PERTAINING TO FOOD

[1] For the sign of bread, make a complete circle using each thumb and the next two fingers, the reason being that bread is usually round. [2] For the sign of bread cooked in water and considered better than ordinary bread, add to the aforesaid general sign for bread that you place the palm of one hand over the outside of the other hand and move the uppermost hand around as though smearing or moistening (something). [3] For the sign of wheat bread that is commonly called twisted loaf, add to the aforesaid general sign for bread that you make a cross through the center of your palm, the reason being that this kind of bread is usually divided into squares. [4] For the sign of a small loaf given beyond the usual measure on the five principal feast days, slightly divide the two fingers that follow the thumb and place them obliquely over the same two fingers on the other hand divided in the same way. [5] For the sign of beans, place the tip of the forefinger on the first joint of the thumb and then make the thumb stick out. [6] For the sign of eggs, with one finger on another, simulate someone peeling the top of an egg. [7] For the sign of a dish of vegetables, drag one finger over another finger, like someone cutting vegetables that he is about to cook. [8] For the general sign of fish, simulate with your hand the tail of a fish moving in the water. [9] For the sign of squid, divide all of the fingers from each other and then move them together, because squid are made up of many parts. [10] For the sign of an eel, close each hand, like someone holding and squeezing an eel in this way. [11] For the sign of lamprey, indicate with a finger on your jaw three or four marks because of those marks that a lamprey has under its eyes. [12] For the sign of salmon or sturgeon, to the aforesaid general sign for fish add that you place a fist with an erect thumb on the chin, which signifies pride, since the very proud and rich are accustomed to have fish of this kind. [13] For the sign of pike, again to the aforesaid general sign for fish add that you make with your hand the sign for speed, because the pike swims faster than other fish. [14]

For the sign of trout, add (to the aforesaid general sign for fish) that you draw a finger from eyebrow to eyebrow because of the bands that women wear in this place and because trout are spoken of with the feminine case. [15] For the sign of millet, make a circular motion with your finger, the reason being that millet is stirred in this manner in a pot with a spoon. [16] For the sign of crepes or, as others say, beignets, take hold of some of your hair with a closed hand as though you want to curl it. [17] For the sign of cheese, join each hand at an angle, like someone pressing cheese. [18] For the sign of cheese tarts, to the aforesaid general sign both for bread and for cheese (add that) you curl all of the fingers on one hand and then place the cupped hand on the surface of the other hand. [19] For the sign of a certain kind of bread or, as the Germans say, *craphoia*, to the aforesaid general sign of bread (add that) you simulate with two fingers those small folds that are made in them, which are rolled up and somewhat round. [20] For the sign of milk, bring a little finger to your lips, the reason being that an infant sucks in this way. [21] For the sign of honey, stick out your tongue for a moment and touch your fingers (with it), as though you want to lick them. [22] For the sign of fruit, especially a pear or an apple, enclose the thumb with the other fingers. [23] For the sign of cherries, (to the aforesaid sign for fruit) add that you place a finger under the eye. [24] For the sign of raw lentils, join together your thumb and the finger next to it and hold them out. [25] For the sign of garlic or radish, open your mouth a little and point a finger towards it, because of the kind of smell that one smells from them. [26] For the sign of water, join all of your fingers and move them at an angle. [27] For the sign of wine, bend your finger and then touch it to your lips. [28] For the sign of a spiced drink, close your hand and then simulate someone grinding (herbs). [29] For the sign of a drink prepared with honey and wormwood, separate your index and middle fingers from the rest and then separate them from each other and move them in turn, because wormwood leaves are divided in this way. [30] For the sign of mustard seed, place your thumb beneath the first joint of your little finger. [31] For the sign of vinegar, rub your throat with a finger, because the sharpness of its taste is felt in the throat. [32] For the sign of a flat dish, extend your outspread hand. [33] For the sign of the cup that holds the daily allowance of wine, turn your hand downwards and then hold it cupped with the fingers slightly bent. [34] For the sign of the shallow bowl, from which one drinks (the wine), bend three of your fingers slightly and hold them upwards. [35] For the sign of a glass drinking vessel, to the aforesaid sign preceding this one add that you place two of your fingers around your eye, so that the brightness of the glass is signified by the brightness of the eye.

CONCERNING THOSE SIGNS PERTAINING TO CLOTHING

[36] For the sign of a wool tunic, hold its sleeve with three of your fingers, that is, with the little finger and the two following it. [37] For the sign of trousers, add (to the aforesaid sign for wool tunic) that you draw your hand upwards along your leg, like someone putting on trousers. [38] For the sign of a frock, hold its sleeve in the same way that you hold the sleeve of a wool tunic. [39] For the sign of a cowl, add (to the aforesaid sign for frock) that you touch the back of your hood with two fingers. [40] For the sign of sleeves, hold the sleeve of the frock and add the sign for trousers. [41] For the sign of a hide garment, spread out all of your fingers on one hand and place them on your chest and then draw them together like someone gathering wool.

[42] For the sign of shoes, move one finger in a circular motion around another, like someone tying shoes with laces. [43] For the sign of night shoes, add (to the aforesaid sign for shoes) that you place your hand on your jaw like a sleeper is accustomed to do. [44] For the sign of ankle straps, make the same sign that you make for shoes and add this that you take hold of the sleeve of the frock with your fingers. [45] For the sign of a blanket, make the same sign that you make for a hide garment and add this that you draw your hand along your arm from the lower part upwards, like someone who wants to pull a blanket over himself. [46] For the sign of a coat, draw your hand along your arm in the same manner that it is drawn for the sign of a blanket, and add that you hold the sleeve of the frock with your fingers because each one, both the frock and the coat, is made from wool. [47] For the sign of a bed sheet that is spread out beneath you and called "light" by St. Benedict, place the fingers of both hands overtop of each other and draw them back once and then a second time and moving one hand from the chest, spread it out, like someone spreading out something rolled up. [48] For the sign of a pillow or what is commonly called a cushion, lift your hand, bend your fingertips, and then move them as though for the purpose of flying; after this, place your hand on your jaw, like a sleeper is accustomed to do. [49] For the sign of a strap for a tunic, make a circular motion with one finger around another and from each side bring the fingers of each hand together, like someone girding himself with a strap. [50] For the sign of a belt for trousers, make the same sign (for tunic strap) and add that you draw your hand upwards along your leg because of the trousers and boots, into which this belt is inserted. [51] For the sign of a needle, strike your fists together, because this signifies metal, and after that pretend that you are holding a piece of thread in one hand and a needle in the other and that you want to send the thread through the eye of the needle. [52] For the sign of thread, make a circular motion with one finger around another and add (that you pretend) that you want to send thread through the eye of a needle. [53] For the sign of a knife, draw your hand through the middle of your other palm, like someone cutting something with a knife. [54] For the sign of a sheath for a knife, draw the tip of one of your hands across the end of the other, like someone putting a knife into a sheath. [55] For the sign of a comb, draw three of your fingers through your hair, like someone combing their hair. [56] For the sign of writing boards, fold up both hands and once they have been folded, unfold them at the same time. [57] For the sign of a writing instrument, strike your fists together, then hold out your finger against your thumb and use them to simulate someone writing.

CONCERNING THOSE SIGNS PERTAINING ESPECIALLY TO THE DIVINE OFFICE

[58] First, for the sign of reading, press your finger to your hand or chest, then draw it back slightly and make it move back again, like someone turning the page of a book. [59] For the sign of the Response, place your thumb under the joint of your finger and then flick it downwards. [60] For the sign of the Antiphon or the verse of the Response, place your thumb under the joint of your little finger and add the aforesaid flicking action. [61] For the sign of Alleluia, raise your hand, bend the tips of your fingers, and move them as though for the purpose of flying on account of the angels, because, as it is believed, the Alleluia is sung by the angels in heaven. [62] For the sign of the Prose, or what Germans call the Sequence, incline your hand and raise it, and

then turn it by moving it away from your chest, with the result that, what previously was held upwards, is now facing downwards. [63] For the sign of the Tractus, draw your hand across your stomach from below, which always signifies something long, and then place your hand against your mouth, which signifies song. [64] For the general sign of a book, hold out your hand and move it like the page of a book is usually moved. [65] For the sign of the Missal, to the aforesaid general sign (for book) add that you make the sign for cross. [66] For the sign of the Gospels, add (to the aforesaid general sign for book) that you make the sign for cross on your forehead. [67] For the sign of the Book of Epistles, add (to the aforesaid general sign for book) that you make the sign for cross on your chest. [68] For the sign of the book read at Nocturns, to the aforesaid general sign for book and reading add that you place your hand on your jaw. [69] For the sign of the Antiphonary, to the aforesaid general sign (for book) add that you bend your thumb because of the musical notes that are bent in this way. [70] For the sign of the Rule (to the aforesaid sign of book), add that you take hold of the hair hanging above your ear with two fingers because of the two names by which the abbot is called: abbot and lord; because St. Benedict, the author of the Rule, also held this office. [71] For the sign of the Hymnal, add (to the aforesaid general sign for book) that you join the tips of your thumb and the finger next to it and bring them forward, by which the present time or what is first is signified; and this sign is relevant to the hymnal because of the particular word that begins the hymnal: *primo dierum*. [72] For the sign of the Psalter (to the aforesaid general sign for book), add that you cup your hand and place your fingertips on your head because of the similarity to a crown that a king is accustomed to wear, because David, the author of the psalms, was a king. [73] For the sign of a secular book that some pagan composed, add to the aforesaid general sign for book that you touch your ear with your finger, just as a dog usually does when scratching with his foot, because a person without faith deserves to be compared with such an animal. [74] For the sign of an angel, make the same sign that you make for the sign for Alleluia. [75] For the sign of an apostle, draw your right hand downwards from the right side to the left and again from the left to the right because of the similarity to the pallium, which archbishops use. And also there is no other sign for bishop. [76] For the sign of a martyr, place your right hand against your neck, like someone cutting something with a knife. [77] For the sign of a confessor, make the same sign that you make for an apostle, if he is a bishop; if he is an abbot, make the sign that you make for the Rule of St. Benedict by grabbing the hair. [78] For the sign of a holy virgin, draw your finger along the forehead from eyebrow to eyebrow, because that is the sign for a woman. [79] For the sign of a feast day, first make the sign of reading, and (then) hold out all of the fingers of each of your hands.

NOW A VARIETY OF SIGNS CONCERNING PEOPLE AND OTHER THINGS AND EVENTS

[80] For the sign of a monk, hold the cap of the cowl with your hand. [81] For the sign of a priest, make a circular motion with your finger around your ear because of the similarity to the tonsure that a priest has on his head. [82] For the sign of a layman, hold your chin with your right hand because of the beard that this sort of man did not shave long ago. [83] For the sign of a monk raised in the abbey, to the aforesaid general sign (for monk) add that you move your little finger to your lips, the reason

being that an infant sucks in this way; if he is well educated, place a finger against your chest, because this is the sign for knowing. [84] For the sign of the lord abbot, make the same sign as the aforesaid sign for the Rule. [85] For the sign of the prior, pretend that you are holding a small bell with two fingers and then pretend to make it ring. [86] For the sign of the major prior, add (to the aforesaid sign for prior) that you hold out your hand, because that is always the sign for something big, just as, on the contrary, something small is signified with the little finger. [87] For the sign of the sacrist, pretend to sound a bell with your hand. [88] For the sign of the chamberlain, pretend to count coins. [89] For the sign of the cellarer, pretend to hold a key in your hand and turn it as though it was set in a lock. [90] For the sign of the keeper of the granary, who receives and preserves the ration of grain, join both of your hands together and pretend to pour out the ration of some container as though for the purpose of measuring it. [91] For the sign of the gardener, bend your finger and draw it towards you, like someone dragging a rake along the ground. [92] For the sign of the keeper of the hospice, where wealthier guests are received, pretend to draw a sword from its sheath. [93] For the sign of the almoner, who receives the poor, draw your hand from the right shoulder down to the left side, just like the strap of a bag that the poor usually carry. [94] For the sign of the infirmarer, who looks after the sick, place your hand against your chest, which signifies sickness, although not always, because it also signifies confession. [95] For the sign of the refectorer, make the same sign that is used for the refectory, that is, join the tips of your thumb and index finger and move them toward your mouth. [96] For the sign of the librarian and precentor, lift the interior surface of the hand and move it, like someone directing the choir, so that it is sung together by all. [97] For the sign of the master of the boys, move your little finger to your mouth and then place your finger next to your thumb under your eye, because this is the sign for seeing. [98] For the sign of the master of the novices, draw your hand obliquely through the hair against your forehead, which is the sign for a novice, and add the aforesaid sign for seeing. [99] For the sign of an old man, draw a rigid hand through the hair against your ear. [100] For the sign of the marshal, with two fingers take hold of the outermost hairs (on your head) because of the mane that packhorses have. [101] For the sign of the keeper of the donkeys, raise your hand near to your ear and move it like a donkey moves its ear. [102] For the sign of a countryman or a blood relative, hold your hand against your face and place the middle finger to your nose because of the blood that sometimes flows from there. [103] For the sign of a man who speaks another language, touch your lips with your finger because of speech. [104] For the sign of talking, hold your hand against your mouth and then move it. [105] For the sign of hearing, hold your finger against your ear. [106] For the sign of not knowing, wipe your lips with a raised finger. [107] For the sign of telling a lie, place a finger inside of your lips and then draw it out again. [108] For the sign of kissing, place two of your fingers, that is, the middle and the index fingers, to your lips. [109] For the sign of dressing, especially with an alb, draw your hand downwards across your chest. [110] For the sign of undressing, with your thumb and the adjacent finger draw the alb away from your chest. [111] For the sign of the washing of feet, turn the insides of both hands toward one another and then move the tips of the upper hand slightly. [112] For the sign of something good, whatever it is that you say is good, place your thumb on (one side of) your jaw and your other fingers on the other side and then draw them down gently to the end of the chin. [113] For the sign of something bad, place your fingers spread out on your face and pretend that it is the claw of a bird grasping and tearing at something. [114] For the sign of something that has already been done, hold your hand perpendicular to the chest and then turning the interior part of your hand upwards raise it up away from the heart. [115] For the sign of assent, lift your hand in a measured way and do not turn it over, but move it so that the outer surface is turned up. [116] For the sign of refusal, place the tip of your middle finger under your thumb and then cause it to move back again. [117] For the sign of quickness, place one hand above the other hand in the manner of a saw and then move it quickly like someone using a saw. [118] For the sign of slowness, draw your hand upwards from the bellybutton slightly across the stomach.

BIBLIOGRAPHY

PRIMARY SOURCES

Adevaldus, *Miracula Benedicti*, ed. Eugène de Certain, in *Les miracles de saint Benoît écrits par Adevald, Aimoin, André, Raoul Tortaire et Hugues de Sainte Marie, moines de Fleury* (Paris, 1858).

Alcuin, *Epistolae, MGH Epistolae* IV, ed. Ernest Dümmler (Munich, 1978).

Die ältere Wormser Briefsammlung, ed. Walther Bulst, *MGH Briefe* III (Weimar, 1949).

Ambrose, *Enarrationes in XII Psalmos Davidicos, PL* XIV.

"Ancienne traduction française des Ecclesiastica officia, Instituta generalis Capituli, Usus conversorum et Regula sancti Benedicti, publié d'après le manuscrit 352 de la bibliothèque publique de Dijon," ed. Philip Guignard, in *Les monuments primitifs de la règle cistercienne* (Dijon, 1878).

Apophthegmata Patrum, in *Patrologia cursus completus: Series graeca*, ed. J. P. Migne, 161 vols. (Paris, 1857–1903), vol. LXV.

Ardo, *Vita Benedicti abbatis Anianensis et Indensis*, ed. G. Waitz, *MGH SS* XV.1 (Hanover, 1887).

Asser, *De rebus gestis Ælfredi*, ed. William H. Stevenson (Oxford, 1904).

Augustine, *In Johannis evangelium tractatus cxxiv*, ed. D. R. Willems, *CCSL* XXXVI (Turnhout, 1954).

    Ordo monasterii, ed. and trans. Lawless, in *Augustine of Hippo and His Monastic Rule*, pp. 74–79.

    Praeceptum, ed. and trans. Lawless, in *Augustine of Hippo and His Monastic Rule*, pp. 80–103.

    Sermones, PL XXXVIII–XXXIX.

Aurelianus, *Regula ad monachos, PL* LXVIII, cols. 385–398.

Basil of Caesarea, *Regula*, ed. K. Zelzer, *CSEL* LXXXVI (Vienna, 1986).

Bede, *De temporum ratione*, ed. Charles W. Jones, in *Bedae Opera de temporibus* (Cambridge, MA, 1943); trans. Faith Wallis, *Bede: The Reckoning of Time* (Philadelphia, 2000).

    Historia ecclesiastica, ed. Bertram Colgrave and R. A. B. Mynors, in *Bede's Ecclesiastical History of the English People* (Oxford, 1969).

Benedict of Aniane, *Concordia regularum, PL* CIII.

Bernard of Clairvaux, *Apologia ad Guillelmum abbatem*, ed. Jean Leclercq, Charles H. Talbot and Henri-Marie Rochais, in *Sancti Bernardi Opera*, 8 vols. (Rome, 1957–1977), vol. III, pp. 61–108.

    Epistolae, ed. Leclercq *et al.*, vols. VI–VIII.

183

Bibliography

Bernard of Cluny, *Ordo Cluniacensis sive Consuetudines*, ed. M. Herrgott, in *Vetus Disciplina Monastica* (Paris, 1726; repr. Siegburg, 1999), pp. 136–364. See also *The Cluniac Customary of Bernard / Le coutumier clunisien de Bernard*, ed. and trans. Susan Boynton and Isabelle Cochelin, forthcoming.

Berno, *Testamentum, PL* CXXXIII, cols. 853–858.

Caesarius, *Regula virginum*, ed. Joël Courreau and Adalbert de Vogüé, in *Césaire d'Arles: Oeuvres monastiques*, 2 vols., SC CCCXLV and CCCXCVIII (Paris, 1988–1994), vol. I, pp. 170–273.

Caesarius of Heisterbach, *Libri miraculorum*, ed. Alfons Hilka, in *Die Wundergeschichten des Caesarius von Heisterbach*, 3 vols. (Bonn, 1933–1937).

Carta caritatis prior, ed. Chrysogonus Waddell, in *Narrative and Legislative Texts from Early Cîteaux* (Brecht, 1999), pp. 442–452.

Cartulaire de l'abbaye cardinale de la Trinité de Vendôme, ed. Charles Métais, 5 vols. (Paris, 1893–1904).

Chrodegang of Metz, *Regula canonicorum, PL* LXXXIX, cols. 1057–1120.

Columbanus, *Regula coenobialis fratrum*, ed. and trans. G. S. M. Walker, in *Sancti Columbani Opera* (Dublin, 1957), pp. 142–168.

Regula monachorum, ed. G. S. M. Walker, in *Sancti Columbani Opera* (Dublin, 1957), pp. 120–142.

Conrad of Eberbach, *Exordium magnum cisterciense*, ed. Bruno Griesser, CCCM CXXXVIII (Turnhout, 1994).

Consuetudines Affligenienses, ed. Robert J. Sullivan, CCM VI (Siegburg, 1975).

Consuetudines Cartusiae, ed. An anonymous monk of La Chartreuse, in Guigues 1er, *Coutumes de Chartreuse*, SC CCCXIII (Paris, 1984).

Consuetudines Cluniacensium antiquiores cum redactionibus derivatis, ed. Kassius Hallinger, CCM VII.2 (Siegburg, 1983).

Consuetudines Corbeienses, ed. J. Semmler, CCM I (Siegburg, 1963), pp. 355–422.

Consuetudines Floriacenses Antiquiores, ed. Anselme Davril and Lin Donnat, CCM VII.3 (Siegburg, 1984), pp. 7–60; repr. with a French translation in *L'abbaye de Fleury en l'an mil* (Paris, 2004), pp. 147–251.

Councils and Synods with Other Documents Relating to the English Church I, A.D. 871–1204, part 1: 871–1066, ed. D. Whitelock, M. Brett and C. N. L. Brooke (Oxford, 1981).

De Gallica Petri Damiani profectione et eius ultramontano itinere, MGH SS XXX, ed. Gerhard Schwartz and Adolf Hofmeister (Hanover, 1934), pp. 1034–1046.

De novitiis instruendis, ed. Mirko Breitenstein, in *De novitiis instruendis: Text und Kontext eines anonymen Traktates vom Ende des 12. Jahrhunderts* (Dresden, 2003).

Decreta Lanfranci: The Monastic Constitutions, ed. and trans. David Knowles (London, 1951).

Defensor of Ligugé, *Liber scintillarum*, ed. H. M. Rochais, 2 vols., SC LXXVII and LXXXVI (Paris, 1961–1962).

Donatus, *Regula ad virgines*, ed. Adalbert de Vogüé, in "La règle de Donat pour l'abbesse Gauthstrude," *Benedictina* 25 (1978): 219–313

Eadmer, *Vita Oswaldi*, ed. James Raine, in *The Historians of the Church of York and its Archbishops*, 3 vols. (London, 1879–1894), vol. II, pp. 1–59.

Vita sancti Anselmi, ed. Richard W. Southern (Oxford, 1972).

Ecclesiastica officia, ed. Danièle Choisselet and Placide Vernet, in *Les Ecclesiastica Officia cisterciens du XIIe siècle* (Reiningue, 1989).

Bibliography

Ekkehard, *Casus sancti Galli*, ed. Hans F. Haefele, in *St. Galler Klostergeschichten* (Darmstadt, 1980).

Epistola cum duodecim capitulis quorundam fratrum ad Auvam directa, ed. H. Frank, *CCM* I (Siegburg, 1963), pp. 330–336.

Eusebius "Gallicanus": Collectio Homiliarum, ed. John Leroy and Fr. Glorie, 3 vols., *CCCM* CI (Turnhout, 1970–1971).

Exordium parvum, ed. Chrysogonus Waddell, in *Narrative and Legislative Texts from Early Cîteaux* (Brecht, 1999), pp. 233–259.

Expositio in regulam sancti Augustini, *PL* CLXXVI, cols. 881–924.

Gerald of Wales, *De rebus a se gestis*, ed. J. S. Brewer, in *Giraldi Cambrensis Opera*, Rolls Series XXI, 2 vols. (London, 1861), vol. I, pp. 3–122.

Gespräche aus Paris, ed. W. Braune, in *Althochdeutsches Lesebuch*, 17th edn (Tübingen, 1994), pp. 9–11 (V.2).

Gilo, *Vita Hugonis*, ed. H. E. J. Cowdrey, in "Two Studies in Cluniac History 1049–1126," *Studi Gregoriani* 11 (1978): 5–298, at pp. 45–109.

Gregory the Great, *Libri dialogorum*, ed. Adalbert de Vogüé, in *Grégoire le Grand: Dialogues*, 3 vols., *SC* CCLI, CCLX and CCLXV (Paris, 1978–1980).

Moralium Libri, *PL* LXXV, cols. 509–1162; and *PL* LXXVI, cols. 9–782.

Guibert of Nogent, *De vita sua sive monodiarum libri tres*, ed. Edmond-René Labande, in *Guibert de Nogent: Autobiographie* (Paris, 1981).

Guigo II, *Liber de exercitio cellae*, *PL* CLIII, cols. 787–884.

Haimo, *Vita Willihelmi abbatis Hirsaugiensis*, *MGH SS* XII, ed. W. Wattenbach (Hanover, 1856), pp. 209–225.

Herman of Tournai, *Liber de restauratione monasterii Sancti Martini Tornacensis*, ed. Georg Waitz, *MGH SS* XIV (Hanover, 1883), pp. 274–317; trans. Lynn H. Nelson, in *Herman of Tournai: The Restoration of the Monastery of Saint Martin of Tournai* (Washington, DC, 1996).

Hildegard of Bingen, *Regula sancti Benedicti explicata*, *PL* CXCVII, cols. 1053–1066.

Hildemar, *Expositio regulae sancti Benedicti*, ed. Rupert Mittermüller, in *Vita et Regula SS. P. Benedicti una cum Expositio Regulae a Hildemaro tradita* (Regensburg, New York and Cincinnati, 1880).

Hugh, *Vita Hugonis*, ed. H. E. J. Cowdrey, in "Two Studies in Cluniac History 1049–1126," *Studi Gregoriani* 11 (1978): 5–298, at pp. 113–139.

Hugh of St. Victor, *De institutione novitiorum*, *PL* CLXXVI, cols. 926–952.

Idung of Prüfening, *Dialogus duorum monachorum*, ed. R. B. C. Huygens, "Le moine Idung et ses deux ouvrages: *Argumentum super quatuor questionibus* et *Dialogus duorum monachorum*," *Studi Medievali* 13 (1972): 291–470.

Jacques de Vitry, *Exempla ex sermonibus vulgaribus*, ed. Thomas Frederick Crane, in *The Exempla or Illustrative Stories from the Sermones Vulgares of Jacques de Vitry* (New York, 1890).

Jerome, *Epistulae*, *PL* XXII.

John Cassian, *De coenobiorum institutis*, ed. Jean-Claude Guy, in *Jean Cassien: Institutions cénobitiques*, *SC* CIX (Paris, 1965).

John of Salerno, *Vita Odonis*, *PL* CXXXIII, cols. 43–86; trans. Gerald Sitwell, in *St. Odo of Cluny, Being the Life of St. Odo of Cluny by John of Salerno and the Life of St. Gerald of Aurillac by St. Odo* (London and New York, 1958), pp. 3–87.

Bibliography

Jotsaldus, *Vita Odilonis*, ed. Johannes Staub, in *Iotsald von Saint-Claude, Vita des Abtes Odilo von Cluny, MGH SRG* LXVIII (Hanover, 1999).

Liber Eliensis, ed. E. O. Blake, Camden Third Series XCII (London, 1962).

Liber ordinis sancti Victoris Parisiensis, ed. Luc Jocqué and Ludo Milis, *CCCM* LXI (Turnhout, 1984).

Liber tramitis aevi Odilonis abbatis, ed. Peter Dinter, *CCM* X (Siegburg, 1980).

Matthew of Albano, *Epistola*, ed. Stanislaus Ceglar, in "William of Saint Thierry and His Leading Role at the First Chapters of the Benedictine Abbots (Reims 1131, Soissons 1132)," in *William, Abbot of St. Thierry: A Colloquium at the Abbey of St. Thierry*, trans. Jerry Carfantan (Kalamazoo, 1987), pp. 65–86.

Memoriale qualiter II, ed. C. Morgand, *CCM* I (Siegburg, 1963), pp. 263–282.

Memorials of Saint Dunstan, ed. William Stubbs, Rolls Series LXIII (London, 1874).

Nalgod, *Vita Odonis*, *PL* CXXXIII, cols. 85–104.

Navigatio sancti Brendani abbatis, ed. Carl Selmer (South Bend, IN, 1959).

Notitia de servitio monasteriorum, ed. P. Becker, *CCM* I (Siegburg, 1963), pp. 493–499.

Odo of Cluny, *Epitome moralium sancti Gregorii in Job*, *PL* CXXXIII, cols. 105–512.

    Occupatio, ed. Anton Swoboda (Leipzig, 1900).

    Sermo de sancto Benedicto abbate, *PL* CXXXIII, cols. 721–729.

    Vita Geraldi, *PL* CXXXIII, cols. 639–710; trans. Gerard Sitwell, in *Soldiers of Christ: Saints and Saints' Lives from Late Antiquity and the Early Middle Ages*, ed. Thomas F. X. Noble and Thomas Head (University Park, PA, 1995), pp. 293–362.

Odo of St. Victor, *Epistolae*, *PL* CXCVI, cols. 1397–1418.

Orderic Vitalis, *Historia ecclesiastica*, ed. Marjorie Chibnall, in *The Ecclesiastical History of Orderic Vitalis*, 6 vols. (Oxford, 1969–1980).

Ordo Casinensis I, ed. T. Leccisotti, *CCM* I (Siegburg, 1963), pp. 94–104.

Pachomius, *Praecepta*, *PL* XXIII, cols. 67–82.

Papsturkunden, 896–1046, ed. H. Zimmermann, 3 vols. (Vienna, 1984–1985).

Peter Abelard, *Institutio seu regula sanctimonialium*, ed. T. P. McLaughlin, in "Abelard's Rule for Religious Women," *Mediaeval Studies* 18 (1956): 241– 292.

Peter of Celle, *De disciplina claustrali*, ed. G. de Martel, in *Pierre de Celle: L'école du cloître, SC* CCXL (Paris, 1977).

    Epistolae, ed. and trans. Julian Haseldine, in *The Letters of Peter of Celle* (Oxford, 2001).

Peter Damian, *De ordine eremitarum (Opusculum* 14), *PL* CXLV, cols. 327–336.

    Epistolae, *PL* CXLIV, cols. 205–498.

Peter the Venerable, *De miraculis libri duos*, ed. D. Bouthillier, *CCCM* LXXXIII (Turnhout, 1988).

    Epistolae, ed. Giles Constable, in *The Letters of Peter the Venerable*, 2 vols. (Cambridge, MA, 1967).

    Statuta, ed. Giles Constable, *CCM* VI (Siegburg, 1975), pp. 19–106.

Les plus anciens documents originaux de l'abbaye de Cluny, ed. Hartmut Atsma, Sébastien Barret and Jean Vezin, 2 vols. (Turnhout, 1997–2000).

Radulf, *Vita Petri Venerabili*, *PL* CLXXXIX, cols. 15–28.

Raynald, *Vita Hugonis*, *PL* CLIX, cols. 893–906.

Recueil des chartes de l'abbaye de Cluny, ed. Auguste Bernard and Alexandre Bruel, 6 vols. (Paris, 1876–1903).

Bibliography

Reginaldus of Durham, *Libellus de vita et miraculis sancti Godrici*, ed. J. Stevenson (London, 1845).

Les règles des saints pères, ed. Adalbert de Vogüé, 2 vols., *SC* CCXCVII–CCXCVIII (Paris, 1982).

Regula Benedicti, ed. Adalbert de Vogüé, in *La règle de saint Benoît*, 7 vols., *SC* CLXXXI–CLXXXVII (Paris, 1971–1972).

Regula magistri, ed. Adalbert de Vogüé, in *La règle de Maître*, 3 vols., *SC* CV–CVII (Paris, 1964–1965).

Regula orientalis, ed. Adalbert de Vogüé, in *Les règles des saints pères*, vol. II, pp. 462–495.

Regula Pauli et Stephani, ed. J. M. Villanova, in *Regula Pauli et Stephani: Edició crítica i comentari* (Montserrat, 1959).

Regula sanctorum patrum, ed. Adalbert de Vogüé, in *Les règles des saints pères*, vol. I, pp. 180–205.

Regularis Concordia, ed. and trans. Thomas Symons, in *Regularis Concordia: The Monastic Agreement of the Monks and Nuns of the English Nation* (London, 1953).

Rilke, Rainer Maria. *Sämtliche Werke*, ed. Rilke Archiv with Ruth Sieber-Rilke, 7 vols. (1955–1997).

Rimbert, *Vita Anskarii*, ed. G. Waitz, *MGH SRG* LV (Hanover, 1884), pp. 3–79; repr. in *Quellen des 9. und 11. Jahrhunderts zur Geschichte der hamburgischen Kirche und des Reiches* (Darmstadt, 1961).

Rodulphus Glaber, *Historiarum libri quinque*, ed. and trans. John France, in *Rodulphus Glaber: The Five Books of Histories and the Life of St. William* (Oxford, 1989).

Romana computatio, ed. Charles W. Jones, in *Bedae pseudepigrapha: Scientific Writings Falsely Attributed to Bede* (Ithaca, 1939), pp. 106–108.

Smaragdus, *Expositio in regulam sancti Benedicti*, ed. Alfred Spannagel and Pius Engelbert, *CCM* VIII (Siegburg, 1974).

Speculum virginum, ed. Jutta Seyforth, *CCCM* V (Turnhout, 1990).

Statuta Capitulorum Generalium ab anno 1116 ad annum 1786, ed. Joseph-Maria Canivez, 8 vols. (Louvain, 1933–1941).

Statuta Patrum, ed. Adalbert de Vogüé, in *Les règles des saints pères*, vol. I, pp. 274–283.

Sulpicius Severus, *Vita sancti Martini*, ed. Jacques Fontaine, in *Sulpice Sévère: Vie de saint Martin*, 3 vols., *SC* CXXXIII–CXXXV (Paris, 1967–1969).

Synodi primae decreta authentica 21, ed. J. Semmler, *CCM* I (Siegburg, 1963), pp. 452–468.

"A Table of Signs Used During the Hours of Silence by the Sisters in the Monastery of Sion," ed. Samuel Bentley, in *Excerpta Historica or Illustrations of English History* (London, 1833), pp. 414–419; repr. in *Monastic Sign Languages*, ed. Jean Umiker-Sebeok and Thomas A. Sebeok (Berlin, New York and Amsterdam, 1987), pp. 489–494.

Thegan, *Gesta Hludovici imperatoris*, ed. E. Tremp, in *Thegan: Täten Kaiser Ludwigs*, *MGH SRG* LXIV (Hanover, 1995).

Theodomar, *Epistula ad Theodoricum gloriosum*, ed. J. Winandy and K. Hallinger, *CCM* I (Siegburg, 1963), pp. 126–136.

Ulrich of Zell, *Consuetudines Cluniacensis*, *PL* CXLIX, cols. 643–779.

Usus conversorum, ed. Waddell, in *Cistercian Lay Brothers*, pp. 55–78.

Valerian of Cimiez, *Homiliae*, *PL* LII, cols. 691–755; trans. Georges E. Ganss, in *Saint Peter Chrysologus, Selected Sermons and Saint Valerian, Homilies*, The Fathers of the Church XVII (New York, 1953).

Bibliography

Vita altera Brunonis, PL CLII, cols. 491–526.

Vita Anastasii, PL CXLIX, cols. 423–434.

Vitae patrum, PL LXXIII; trans. Benedicta Ward, *The Desert Fathers: Sayings of the Early Christian Monks* (New York, 2003).

Vita sancti Udalrici prioris Cellae (vita posterior), ed. Roger Wilmans, *MGH SS* XII (Hanover, 1856), pp. 253–267.

Waddell, Chrysogonus, ed. *Cistercian Lay Brothers: Twelfth-Century Usages with Related Texts* (Brecht, 2001).

Waldebertus, *Regula ad virgines* 14, PL LXXXVIII, cols. 1051–1070.

William of Hirsau, *Constitutiones Hirsaugienses*, PL CL, cols. 923–1146.

William of Malmesbury, *Gesta regum anglorum*, ed. and trans. R. A. B. Mynors, and completed by R. M. Thomson and M. Winterbottom, in *William of Malmesbury: The History of the English Kings*, 2 vols. (Oxford, 1998–1999).

Vita Dunstani, ed. William Stubbs, in *Memorials of Saint Dunstan*, Rolls Series LXIII (London, 1874), pp. 250–324.

Wulfstan, *Vita sancti Æthelwoldi*, ed. Michael Lapidge and Michael Winterbottom, in *Wulfstan of Winchester: Life of St Æthelwold* (Oxford, 1991).

SECONDARY SOURCES

Alexander, Pedro Max. "La prohibición de la risa en la Regula Benedicti: Intento de explicación e interpretación," *Regulae Benedicti Studia* 5 (1976): 225–284.

Ambrose, Kirk. "A Visual Pun at Vézelay: Gesture and Meaning on a Capital Representing the Fall of Man," *Traditio* 55 (2000): 105–123.

The Nave Sculpture of Vézelay: The Art of Monastic Viewing (Toronto, 2006).

Angenendt, Arnold. "Missa specialis: Zugleich ein Beitrag zur Entstehung der Privatmessen," *Frühmittelalterliche Studien* 17 (1983): 153–221.

Aniel, Jean-Pierre. "Le scriptorium de Cluny au Xe et XIe siècles," in *Le gouvernement d'Hugues de Semur*, pp. 265–281

Anton, Hans Hubert. *Fürstenspiegel und Herrscherethos in der Karolingerzeit* (Bonn, 1968).

Arnaldi, Girolamo. "Il biografo 'romano' di Oddone di Cluny," *Bulletino dell'Istituto Storico Italiano per il Medioevo e Archivio Muratoriano* 71 (1959): 19–37.

Arnoux, M. "Un Vénitien au Mont-Saint-Michel: Anastase, moine, ermite et confesseur († vers 1085)," *Médiévales* 28 (1995): 55–78.

Asad, Talal. *Genealogies of Religion: Discipline and Reasons of Power in Christianity and Islam* (Baltimore and London, 1993).

Atwood, Margaret. *The Blind Assassin* (New York, 2000).

Audoin-Rouzeau, Frédérique. *Ossements animaux du moyen âge au monastère de La Charité-sur-Loire* (Paris, 1986).

Avril, Joseph. "Remarques sur un aspect de la vie religieuse paroissiale: La pratique de la confession et de la communion du Xe au XIVe siècle," in *L'encadrement religieux des fidèles au moyen âge et jusqu'au Concile de Trente: Actes du 109e Congrès national des société savantes (Dijon, 1984)* (Paris, 1985), pp. 345–363.

Bailey, Lisa K. "Preaching and Pastoral Care in Late Antique Gaul: The Eusebius Gallicanus Sermon Collection" (Ph.D. dissertation, Princeton University, 2004).

Baldwin, John W. "The Image of the Jongleur in Northern France around 1200," *Speculum* 72 (1977): 635–663.

Bibliography

Banham, Debby. *Monasteriales Indicia: The Anglo-Saxon Monastic Sign Language* (Pinner, 1991).

"Part of the Kit: The *Monasteriales Indicia* and the Monastic Reform," *Old English Newsletter* 30.3 (1997): A-69 (the summary of a paper presented at the Eighth Biennial Meeting of the International Society of Anglo-Saxonists in July 1997).

Barakat, Robert A. *Cistercian Sign Language* (Kalamazoo, 1975).

Bardsley, Sandy. *Venomous Tongues: Speech and Gender in Late Medieval England* (Philadelphia, 2006).

Barret, Sébastien. "Cluny et son scriptorium (Xe–XIIe siècles)," in *Cluny ou la puissance des moines: Histoire de l'abbaye et de son ordre, 910–1790* (Dijon, 2001), pp. 48–53.

Bartlett, Robert. *Gerald of Wales 1146–1223* (Oxford, 1982).

Bateson, Mary. "Rules for Monks and Secular Canons After the Revival under King Edgar," *English Historical Review* 9 (1894): 690–708.

Bell, David N. "The English Cistercians and the Practice of Medicine," *Cîteaux: Commentarii Cistercienses* 40 (1989): 139–173.

Berlière, U. "Le nombre des moines dans les anciens monastères," *Revue bénédictine* 41 (1929): 231–261.

Berman, Constance. "Cistercian Women and Tithes," *Cîteaux: Commentarii Cistercienses* 49 (1998): 95–127.

"Were There Twelfth-Century Cistercian Nuns?" *Church History* 68 (1999): 824–864.

The Cistercian Evolution: The Invention of a Religious Order in Twelfth-Century Europe (Philadelphia, 2000).

Berman, Constance, ed. *Medieval Religion: New Approaches* (New York and London, 2005).

Bernhardt, John W. *Itinerant Kingship and Royal Monasteries in Early Medieval Germany, c. 936–1075* (Cambridge, 1993).

Bligny, Bernard. "L'érémitisme et les Chartreux," in *L'eremitismo in occidente nei secoli XI e XII: Atti della seconda Settimana internazationale di studio (Mendola, 30 agosto–6 settembre 1962)* (Milan, 1965), pp. 248–268.

Bligny, Bernard and Chaix, Gérald, eds. *La naissance des Chartreuses: Actes du VIe colloque international d'histoire et de spiritualité cartusiennes (Grenoble, 12–15 septembre 1984)* (Grenoble, 1984).

du Bois, Louis. *Histoire civile, religieuse et littéraire de l'abbaye de la Trappe* (Paris, 1824).

Bonnard, F. *Histoire de l'abbaye royale et des chanoines réguliers de l'ordre de St.-Victor de Paris*, 2 vols. (Paris, 1904–1907).

Bostock, J. Knight. *A Handbook on Old High German Literature*, 2nd edn (Oxford, 1976).

Boswell, John. *The Kindness of Strangers: The Abandonment of Children in Western Europe from Late Antiquity to the Renaissance* (New York, 1988).

Bouchard, Constance B. "Merovingian, Carolingian and Cluniac Monasticism: Reform and Renewal in Burgundy," *Journal of Ecclesiastical History* 41 (1990): 365–388.

Boulc'H, Stéphane. "Le repas quotidien des moines occidentaux du haut moyen âge," *Revue Belge de Philologie et d'Histoire* 75 (1997): 287–328.

Bouton, Jean de la Croix and Van Damme, Jean Baptiste, eds. *Les plus anciens textes de Cîteaux* (Achel, 1974).

Bibliography

Boynton, Susan. "The Liturgical Role of Children in Monastic Customaries from the Central Middle Ages," *Studia Liturgica* 28 (1998): 194–209.

"Orality, Literacy, and the Early Notation of the Office Hymns," *Journal of the American Musicology Society* 56 (2003): 99–168.

Shaping a Monastic Identity: Liturgy and History at the Imperial Abbey of Farfa, 1000–1125 (Ithaca and London, 2006).

Boynton, Susan and Cochelin, Isabelle, eds. *From Dead of Night to End of Day: The Medieval Customs of Cluny / Du coeur de la nuit à la fin du jour: Les coutumes clunisiennes au moyen âge* (Leiden, 2005).

Braga, Gabriella. "Problemi di autenticà per Oddone di Cluny: l'Epitome dei 'Moralia' di Gregorio Magno," *Studi Medievali* 18 (1977): 45–145.

Bragg, Lois. "Visual-Kinetic Communication in Europe Before 1600: A Survey of Sign Lexicons and Finger Alphabets Prior to the Rise of Deaf Education," *Journal of Deaf Studies and Deaf Education* 2 (1997): 1–25.

Bray, Dorothy Ann. "Allegory in the *Navigatio Sancti Brendani*," *Viator* 26 (1995): 1–10.

Bredero, A. H. "Cluny et Cîteaux au XIIe siècle: Les origines de la controverse," *Studi Medievali* 12 (1971): 135–175.

Brooks, Nicholas. *The Early History of the Church of Canterbury: Christ Church from 597–1066* (Leicester, 1984).

Brooks, Nicholas and Cubitt, Catherine, eds. *St. Oswald of Worcester: Life and Influence* (London and New York, 1996).

Brown, Peter. *The Body and Society: Men, Women and Sexual Renunciation in Early Christianity* (New York, 1988).

Bruce, Scott G. "Lurking with Spiritual Intent: A Note on the Origin and Functions of the Monastic Roundsman (*Circator*)," *Revue bénédictine* 109 (1999): 75–89.

"The Origins of Cistercian Sign Language," *Cîteaux: Commentarii Cistercienses* 52 (2001): 193–209.

Brunhölzl, Franz. *Geschichte der lateinischen Literatur des Mittelalters*, 2 vols. to date (Munich, 1975–).

von Büren, Veronika. "Le grand catalogue de la Bibliothèque de Cluny," in *Le gouvernement d'Hugues de Semur à Cluny*, pp. 245–263.

Burke, Peter. *Languages and Communities in Early Modern Europe* (Cambridge, 2004).

Burrow, J. A. *Gestures and Looks in Medieval Narrative* (Cambridge, 2002).

Burton-Christie, Douglas. *The Word in the Desert: Scripture and the Quest for Holiness in Early Christian Monasticism* (New York and Oxford, 1993).

Buyssens, Eric. "Le langage par gestes chez les moines," *Revue de l'Institut de Sociologie* 29 (1954): 537–545.

Bynum, Caroline Walker. *Docere Verbo et Exemplo: An Aspect of Twelfth-Century Spirituality* (Cambridge, MA, 1979).

"The Spirituality of the Regular Canons in the Twelfth Century," in *Jesus as Mother: Studies in the Spirituality of the High Middle Ages* (Missoula, 1982), pp. 22–58.

du Cange, Charles. *Glossarium mediae et infimae latinitatis*, 10 vols. (Niort, 1883–1887).

Carruthers, Mary. *The Book of Memory: A Study of Memory in Medieval Culture* (Cambridge, 1990).

Casagrande, Carla and Vecchio, Silvana. *Les péchés de la langue: Discipline et éthique de la parole dans la culture médiévale*, trans. Philippe Baillet (Paris, 1991).

Bibliography

Cau, Ettore and Settia, Aldo A., eds. *San Maiolo e le influenze Cluniacensi nell'Italia del Nord: Atti del Convegno Internationale nel Millenario di San Maiolo (994–1994) Pavia-Novara, 23–24 settembre 1994* (Como, 1998).

Cauvin, Henri E. "Fateful Meeting Led to Founding of Cult in Uganda," *New York Times*, 27 March 2000, p. A3.

Chachuat, G. "L'érémitisme à Cluny sous l'abbatiat de Pierre le Vénérable," *Annales de l'Académie de Mâcon* 58 (1982): 89–96.

Chélini, Jean. *L'aube du moyen âge: Naissance de la chrétienté occidentale* (Paris, 1991).

Chenu, M.-D. "Monks, Canons, and Laymen in Search of the Apostolic Life," in *Nature, Man, and Society in the Twelfth Century: Essays on New Theological Perspectives in the Latin West*, ed. and trans. Jerome Taylor and Lester K. Little (Chicago, 1968), pp. 202–238.

Chibnall, Marjorie. *The World of Orderic Vitalis* (Oxford, 1984).

Chitty, Derwas J. *The Desert a City: An Introduction to the Study of Egyptian and Palestinian Monasticism Under the Christian Empire* (Oxford, 1966).

Christ, Karl. "In Caput Quadragesimae," *Zentralblatt für Bibliothekswesen* 60 (1943): 33–59.

Clanchy, Michael. *Abelard: A Medieval Life* (Oxford, 1997).

Claussen, M. A. *The Reform of the Frankish Church: Chrodegang of Metz and the Regula canonicorum in the Eighth Century* (Cambridge, 2004).

Cochelin, Isabelle. "Peut-on parler de noviciat à Cluny pour les Xe–XIe siècles?" *Revue Mabillon* n.s. 9 (1998): 17–52.

"Besides the Book: Using the Body to Mould the Mind – Cluny in the Tenth and Eleventh Centuries," in *Medieval Monastic Education*, ed. George Ferzoco and Carolyn Muessig (London and New York, 2000), pp. 21–34.

"Evolution des coutumiers monastiques dessinée à partir de l'étude de Bernard," in *From Dead of Night to End of Day*, ed. Boynton and Cochelin, pp. 29–66.

Committenti e produzione artistico-letteraria nell'alto medioevo occidentale, 4–10 aprile 1991, Settimane di studio del centro italiano di studi sull'alto medioevo 39, 2 vols. (Spoleto, 1992).

Conde-Silvestre, Juan C. "The Code and Context of *Monasteriales Indicia*: A Semiotic Analysis of Late Anglo-Saxon Monastic Sign Language," *Studia Anglica Posnaniensia* 36 (2001): 145–169.

Constable, Giles. *Monastic Tithes from their Origins to the Twelfth Century* (Cambridge, 1964).

"The Treatise 'Horatur nos' and Accompanying Canonical Texts on the Performance of Pastoral Work by Monks," in *Speculum Historiale: Geschichte im Spiegel von Geschichtsschreibung und Geschichtsdeutung (Festschrift Johannes Spörl)*, ed. Clemens Bauer, Laetitia Boehm and Max Müller (Freiburg and Munich, 1966), pp. 567–577.

"The Monastic Policy of Peter the Venerable," in *Pierre Abélard – Pierre le Vénérable: Les courants philosophiques, littéraires et artistiques en occident au milieu du XII siècle (Abbaye de Cluny, 2 au 9 juillet 1972)* (Paris, 1975), pp. 119–142.

Religious Life and Thought (11th–12th Centuries) (London, 1979).

Cluniac Studies (London, 1980).

"Eremitical Forms of Monastic Life," in *Istituzioni monastiche e istituzioni canonicali in occidente, 1123–1215: Atti della settima Settimana internazionale di studio (Mendola, 28 agosto–3 settembre 1977)* (Milan, 1980), pp. 239–264.

Bibliography

"Renewal and Reform in Religious Life: Concepts and Realities," in *Renaissance and Renewal in the Twelfth Century*, ed. Robert L. Benson and Giles Constable, with Carol D. Lanham (Cambridge, MA, 1982), pp. 37–67.

Review of Jarecki, *Signa Loquendi, Mittellateinisches Jahrbuch* 18 (1983): 331–333.

"Baume and Cluny in the Twelfth Century," in *Tradition and Change: Essays in Honour of Marjorie Chibnall*, ed. Diana Greenway, Christopher Holdsworth and Jane Sayers (Cambridge, 1985).

"The Ceremonies and Symbolism of Entering Religious Life and Taking the Monastic Habit, from the Fourth to the Twelfth Centuries," in *Segni e riti nella chiesa altomedievale occidentales, Spoleto, 11–17 aprile 1985* (Spoleto, 1987).

Monks, Hermits and Crusaders in Medieval Europe (London, 1988).

"Entrance to Cluny in the Eleventh and Twelfth Centuries According to the Cluniac Customaries and Statutes," in *Mediaevalia Christiana, XIe–XIIIe siècles: Hommages à Raymonde Foreville*, ed. Coloman Etienne Viola (Paris, 1989), pp. 335–354.

"Cluny in the Monastic World of the Tenth Century," in *Il secolo di ferro: Mito e realtà del secolo X (Spoleto, 19–25 aprile 1990)*, Settimane di studio del centro italiano di studi sull'alto medioevo 38 (Spoleto, 1991), pp. 391–437.

Culture and Spirituality in Medieval Europe (London, 1996).

The Reformation of the Twelfth Century (Cambridge, 1996).

Cluny from the Tenth to the Twelfth Centuries: Further Studies (Aldershot, 2000).

"Hildegard's Explanation of the Rule of St. Benedict," in *Hildegard von Bingen in ihrem historischen Umfeld: Internationaler wissenschaftlicher Kongreß zum 900jährigen Jubiläum, 13.–19. September 1998, Bingen am Rhein*, ed. Alfred Haverkamp (Mainz, 2000), pp. 163–187.

Cottineau, L. H. *Répertoire topo-bibliographique des abbayes et prieurés*, 2 vols. (Mâcon, 1939).

Coulton, G. G. *Five Centuries of Religion*, 4 vols. (Cambridge, 1923–1950).

Cowdrey, H. E. J. *The Cluniacs and the Gregorian Reform* (Oxford, 1970).

"Two Studies in Cluniac History 1049–1126," *Studi Gregoriani* 11 (1978): 5–298.

"The Gregorian Papacy and Eremitical Monasticism," in *San Bruno et la Certosa di Calabria: Atti del Convegno Internazionale di Studi per il IX Centenario della Certosa di Serra S. Bruno (Squillace, Serra S. Bruno 15–18 settembre 1991)*, ed. Pietro de Leo (Messina, 1991).

Popes and Church Reform in the Eleventh Century (Aldershot, 2000).

Craun, Edwin D. *Lies, Slander, and Obscenity in Medieval English Literature: Pastoral Rhetoric and the Deviant Speaker* (Cambridge, 1997).

Cristiani, Riccardo. *"Infirmus sum et non possum sequi conventum*: L'esperienza della malattia nelle consuetudini cluniacensi dell'XI secolo," *Studi Medievali* 41 (2000): 777–807.

"Integration and Marginalization: Dealing with the Sick in Eleventh-Century Cluny," *From Dead of Night to End of Day*, ed. Boynton and Cochelin, pp. 287–295.

Cuissard, Charles. *Inventaire des manuscrits de la Bibliothèque d'Orléans, fonds de Fleury* (Paris, 1885).

Cygler, Florent, Melville, Gert and Oberste, Jörg. "Aspekte zur Verbindung von Organisation und Schriftlichkeit im Ordenswesen: Ein Vergleich zwischen den

Bibliography

Zisterziensern und Cluniazensern des 12./13. Jahrhunderts," in *Viva Vox und Ratio Scripta: Mündliche und schriftliche Kommunikationsformen im Mönchtum des Mittelalters*, ed. Clemens Kasper and Klaus Schreiner (Münster, 1997), pp. 157–176.

Daniels, Marilyn. *Benedictine Roots in the Development of Deaf Education: Listening with the Heart* (Westport, CT and London, 1997).

Davidson, C. ed. *Gesture in Medieval Drama and Art* (Kalamazoo, 2001).

Davril, Anselme. "Un moine de Fleury aux environs de l'an mil: Thierry, dit d'Amorbach," in *Etudes ligériennes d'histoire et d'archéologie médiévales*, ed. René Louis (Auxerre, 1975), pp. 97–104.

"La langage par signes chez les moines: Un catalogue de signes de l'abbaye de Fleury," in *Sous la règle de saint Benoît: Structures monastiques et sociétés en France du moyen âge à l'époque moderne* (Geneva, 1982), pp. 51–74.

"Coutumiers directifs et coutumiers descriptifs: D'Ulrich à Bernard de Cluny," in *From Dead of Night to End of Day*, ed. Boynton and Cochelin, pp. 23–28.

Davril, Anselme and Palazzo, Eric. *La vie des moines au temps des grandes abbayes, Xe–XIIIe siècles* (Paris, 2000).

Davy, M. M. "La vie solitaire cartusienne d'après le *de quadripartito exercitio cellae* d'Adam le Chartreux," *Revue d'Ascétique et de Mystique* 14 (1933): 124–145.

Degler-Spengler, Brigitte. "The Incorporation of Cistercian Nuns into the Order in the Twelfth and Thirteenth Century," in *Hidden Springs: Cistercian Monastic Women*, ed. John A. Nichols and Lillian Thomas Shank, 2 vols. (Kalamazoo, 1995), vol. I, pp. 85–134.

Delisle, Léopold. *Inventaire des manuscrits de la Sorbonne* (Paris, 1870).

Inventaire des manuscrits de la Bibliothèque nationale: Fonds de Cluni (Paris, 1884).

Dereine, C. "Vie commune, règle de Saint Augustin et chanoines réguliers au XIe siècle," *Revue d'Histoire Ecclésiastique* 41 (1946): 365–406.

Deshman, Robert. "*Benedictus Monarcha et Monachus*: Early Medieval Ruler Theology and the Anglo-Saxon Reform," *Frühmittelalterliche Studien* 22 (1988): 204–240.

Devroey, Jean-Pierre. "The Economy," in *The Early Middle Ages: Europe 400–1000*, ed. Rosamond McKitterick (Oxford, 2001).

Dickinson, J. C. *The Origins of the Austin Canons and Their Introduction into England* (London, 1950).

Diem, Albrecht. *Das monastische Experiment: Die Rolle der Keuschheit bei der Entstehung des westlichen Klosterwesens* (Münster, 2005).

Dietz, Maribel. *Wandering Monks, Virgins, and Pilgrims: Ascetic Travel in the Mediterranean World, 300–800* (University Park, PA, 2005).

Donnat, Lin. "Recherches sur l'influence de Fleury au Xe siècle," *Etudes ligériennes d'histoire et d'archéologie médiévales*, ed. R. Louis (Auxerre, 1975), pp. 165–174.

"Les coutumiers monastiques: une nouvelle entreprise et un territoire nouveau," *Revue Mabillon*, n.s. 3 (1992): 5–21.

Donnelly, James S. *The Decline of the Cistercian Laybrotherhood* (New York, 1949).

Dumville, David. "Two Approaches to Dating the *Navigatio Sancti Brendani*," *Studi Medievali* 29 (1988): 87–102.

Dunn, Marilyn. "Mastering Benedict: Monastic Rules and Their Authors in the Early Medieval West," *English Historical Review* 105 (1990): 567–594.

"The Master and St. Benedict: A Rejoinder," *English Historical Review* 107 (1992): 104–111.

Bibliography

The Emergence of Monasticism: From the Desert Fathers to the Early Middle Ages (Oxford, 2000).

Dyer, Joseph. "Monastic Psalmody of the Middle Ages," *Revue bénédictine* 99 (1989): 41–73.

"The Psalms in Monastic Prayer," in *The Place of the Psalms in the Intellectual Culture of the Middle Ages*, ed. Nancy Van Deusen (Albany, 1999), pp. 59–90.

Edwards, Cyril. "German Vernacular Literature: A Survey," in *Carolingian Culture: Emulation and Innovation*, ed. Rosamond McKitterick (Cambridge, 1994), pp. 141–170.

Engelbert, Pius. "Bericht über den Stand des *Corpus Consuetudinum Monasticarum (CCM)*," *Studien und Mitteilungen zur Geschichte des Benediktinerordens und seiner Zweige* 102 (1991): 19–24.

Evans, Joan. *Monastic Life at Cluny, 910–1157* (London, 1931).

Farmer, Sharon. *Communities of Saint Martin: Legend and Ritual in Medieval Tours* (Ithaca and London, 1991).

Fassler, Margot. "The Office of the Cantor in Early Western Monastic Rules and Customaries: A Preliminary Investigation," *Early Music History* 5 (1985): 29–51.

Fichtenau, Heinrich. "Reisen und Reisende," in *Beiträge zur Mediävistik*, 3 vols. (Stuttgart, 1975–1986), vol. III, pp. 1–79.

Fishman, Joshua. *Sociolinguistics: A Brief Introduction* (Rowley, MA, 1970).

Folz, Robert. "Pierre le Vénérable et la liturgie," in *Pierre Abélard – Pierre le Vénérable: Les courants philosophiques, littéraires et artistiques en occident au milieu du XII siècle (Abbaye de Cluny, 2 au 9 juillet 1972)* (Paris, 1975), pp. 143–161.

Foot, Sarah. *Veiled Women I: The Disappearance of Nuns from Anglo-Saxon England* (Aldershot, 2000).

France, John. "Rodulphus Glaber and the Cluniacs," *Journal of Ecclesiastical History* 39 (1988): 497–508.

Frank, Suso. *ΑΓΓΕΛΙΚΟΣ ΒΙΟΣ: Begriffsanalytische und begriffsgeschichtliche Untersuchung zum "engelgleichen Leben" im frühen Mönchtum* (Münster, 1964).

Fried, Johannes. "Endzeiterwartung um die Jahrtausendwende," *Deutsches Archiv für Erforschung des Mittelalters* 45 (1989): 385–473; English trans.: "Awaiting the End of Time Around the Turn of the Year 1000," in *The Apocalyptic Year 1000: Religious Expectation and Social Change, 950–1050*, ed. Richard Landes, Andrew Gow and David C. Van Meter (Oxford, 2003), pp. 17–63.

Fuchs, Peter. "Die Weltflucht der Mönche: Anmerkungen zur Funktion des monastisch-ascetischen Schweigens," *Zeitschrift für Soziologie* 15 (1986): 393–405; repr. in *Reden und Schweigen*, ed. Niklas Luhmann and Peter Fuchs (Frankfurt, 1989), pp. 21–45.

Garand, Monique-Cécile. "Copistes de Cluny au temps de saint Maieul (948–994)," *Bibliothèque de l'Ecole des Chartes* 136 (1978): 5–36.

Garnier, François. *Le langage de l'image au moyen âge*, 2 vols. (Paris, 1982).

Geertz, Clifford. *Negara: The Theatre State in Nineteenth-Century Bali* (Princeton, 1980).

Gehl, Paul F. "*Competens Silentium*: Varieties of Monastic Silence in the Medieval West," *Viator* 18 (1987): 125–160.

Gindele, Corbinian. "Bienen-, Waben- und Honigvergleiche in der frühen monastischen Literatur," *Regulae Benedicti Studia* 6/7 (1981): 1–26.

Giuliani, Adelindo. *La formazione dell'identità certosina (1084–1155)* (Salzburg, 2002).

Bibliography

Gleason, Maud. "Visiting and News: Gossip and Reputation Management in the Desert," *Journal of Early Christian Studies* 6 (1998): 501–521.

Goehring, James E. *Ascetics, Society, and the Desert: Studies in Early Egyptian Monasticism* (Harrisburg, PA, 1999).

"The Dark Side of the Landscape: Ideology and Power in the Christian Myth of the Desert," *Journal of Medieval and Early Modern Studies* 33 (2003): 437–451.

Goffart, Walter. "Le Mans, St. Scholastica, and the Literary Tradition of the Translation of St. Benedict," *Revue bénédictine* 77 (1967): 107–141.

Gougaud, Louis. "Les relations de l'abbaye de Fleury-sur-Loire avec la Bretagne armoricaine et les Iles britanniques (Xe et XIe siècles)," *Mémoires de la Société d'Histoire de Bretagne* 4 (1923): 3–30.

"Le langage des silencieux," *Revue Mabillon* 19 (1929): 93–100.

Gould, Graham. *The Desert Fathers on Monastic Community* (Oxford, 1993).

Le gouvernement d'Hugues de Semur à Cluny: Actes du Colloque scientifique international (Cluny, septembre 1988) (Mâcon, 1990).

Gransden, Antonia. "Traditionalism and Continuity during the Last Century of Anglo-Saxon Monasticism," *Journal of Ecclesiastical History* 40 (1989): 159–207.

Green, Dennis. *Medieval Listening and Reading: The Primary Reception of German Literature 800–1300* (Cambridge, 1994).

Gremont, D. and Donnat, Lin. "Fleury, le Mont Saint-Michel et l'Angleterre à la fin du Xe et au début du XIe siècle à propos du manuscrit d'Orléans, no. 127 (105)," in *Millénaire monastique du Mont Saint-Michel*, ed. J. Laporte *et al.*, 5 vols. (Paris, 1966–1967), vol. I, pp. 751–793.

Gretsch, Mechthild. "Aethelwold's Translation of the *Regula Sancti Benedicti* and its Latin Exemplar," *Anglo-Saxon England* 3 (1974): 125–151.

Griesser, Bruno. "Ungedruckte Texte zur Zeichensprache in den Klöstern," *Analecta Sacri Ordinis Cisterciensis* 3 (1947): 111–137.

Groce, Nora Ellen. *Everyone Here Spoke Sign Language: Hereditary Deafness on Martha's Vineyard* (Cambridge, MA, 1985).

Guillaumont, Antoine. "La conception du désert chez les moines d'Egypte," *Revue de l'Histoire des Religions* 188 (1975): 3–21.

Gwara, Scott and Porter, David W. *Anglo-Saxon Conversations: The Colloquies of Aelfric Bata* (Woodbridge, 1997).

Guy, Jean-Claude, *Recherches sur la tradition grecque des Apophthegmata Patrum* (Brussels, 1962).

Hallinger, Kassius. *Gorze-Kluny: Studien zu den monastischen Lebensformen und Gegensätzen im Hochmittelalter*, Studia Anselmiana 22–25 (Rome, 1950).

"Zur geistigen Welt der Anfänge Klunys," *Deutsches Archiv für Erforschung des Mittelalters* 10 (1954): 417–445.

"Klunys Bräuche zur Zeit Hugos des Grossen (1049–1109)," *Zeitschrift der Savigny-Stiftung für Rechtsgeschichte: Kanonistische Abteilung* 45 (1959): 99–140.

"Das Phänomen der liturgischen Steigerungen Klunys (10./11. Jh.)," in *Studia historico-ecclesiastica: Festgabe für Prof. Luchesius G. Spätling O.F.M.*, ed. Isaac Vázquez (Rome, 1977), pp. 183–236.

"Überlieferung und Steigerung im Mönchtum des 8. bis 12. Jahrhunderts," in *Eulogia: Miscellanea Liturgica in onore di P. Burckhard Neunheuser O.S.B.*, Studia Anselmiana 68 (Rome, 1979), pp. 125–187.

Bibliography

"*Consuetudo*: Begriff, Formen, Forschungsgeschichte, Inhalt," in *Untersuchungen zu Kloster und Stift* (Göttingen, 1980), pp. 140–166.

Review of Jarecki, *Signa Loquendi*, *Zeitschrift für Kirchengeschichte* 44 (1983): 145–150.

Halsall, Guy, ed. *Humour, History and Politics in Late Antiquity and the Early Middle Ages* (Cambridge, 2002).

Hare, Michael. "Abbot Leofsige of Mettlach: An English Monk in Flanders and Upper Lotharingia in the Late Tenth Century," *Anglo-Saxon England* 33 (2004): 109–144.

Harlow, Mary and Smith, Wendy. "Between Fasting and Feasting: The Literary and Archaeobiological Evidence for Monastic Diet in Late Antique Egypt," *Antiquity* 75 (2001): 758–768.

Häussling, Angelus. *Mönchskonvent und Eucharistiefeier: Eine Studie über die Messe in der abendländischen Klosterliturgie des frühen Mittelalters und zur Geschichte der Messhäufigkeit* (Münster, 1973).

Hauviller, Ernst. *Ulrich von Cluny: Ein biographischer Beitrag zur Geschichte der Cluniacenser im 11. Jahrhundert* (Münster, 1896).

Haye, Thomas. *Das lateinische Lehrgedicht im Mittelalter: Analyse einer Gattung* (Leiden, 1997).

Head, Thomas. *Hagiography and the Cult of Saints: The Diocese of Orléans, 800–1200* (Cambridge, 1990).

Hildebrand, Stephen M. "*Oboedientia* and *oboedire* in the Rule of Benedict: A Study of Their Theological and Monastic Meanings," *American Benedictine Review* 52 (2001): 421–436.

Hiley, David. *Western Plainchant: A Handbook* (Oxford, 1993).

Hirsau St. Peter und Paul 1091–1991, 2 vols. (Stuttgart, 1991).

Hoffmann, Richard C. "Economic Development and Aquatic Ecosystems in Medieval Europe," *American Historical Review* 101 (1996): 631–669.

Hohler, C. E. "Some Service-Books of the Later Saxon Church," in *Tenth-Century Studies: Essays in Commemoration of the Millennium of the Council of Winchester and Regularis Concordia*, ed. David Parsons (London and Chichester, 1975), pp. 60–83.

Holze, Heinrich. "Schweigen und Gotteserfahrung bei den ägyptischen Mönchsvätern," *Erbe und Auftrag* 69 (1993): 314–321.

Horn, Walter and Born, Ernest. *The Plan of Saint Gall: A Study of the Architecture and Economy of and Life in a Paradigmatic Carolingian Monastery*, 3 vols. (Berkeley, Los Angeles and London, 1979).

Hourlier, J. "Cluny et la notion d'ordre religieux," in *A Cluny*, ed. Société des amis de Cluny, pp. 219–226.

Howe, John. "St. Benedict the Hermit as a Model for Italian Sanctity: Some Hagiographical Witnesses," *American Benedictine Review* 55 (2004): 42–54.

Huisman, J. A. "Die Pariser Gespräche," *Rheinischer Vierteljahrsblätter* 33 (1969): 272–296.

Hunt, Noreen. *Cluny Under Saint Hugh 1049–1109* (South Bend, IN, 1967).

Hunt, Noreen, ed. *Cluniac Monasticism in the Central Middle Ages* (Hamden, CT, 1971).

Innes, Matthew. "He Never Even Allowed His White Teeth to Be Bared in Laughter: The Politics of Humour in the Carolingian Renaissance," in *Humour, History and Politics in Late Antiquity and the Early Middle Ages*, ed. Halsall, pp. 131–156.

Bibliography

Iogna-Prat, Dominique. "Continence et virginité dans la conception clunisienne de l'ordre du monde autour de l'an mil," in *Académie des Inscriptions et Belles-Lettres: Comptes rendus, 1985* (Paris, 1985), pp. 127–146.

Agni Immaculati: Recherches sur les sources hagiographiques relatives à saint Maieul de Cluny (954–994) (Paris, 1988).

"Les morts dans la compatibilité céleste des moines clunisiens autour de l'an mil," in *Religion et culture autour de l'an mil: Royaume capétien et Lotharingie*, ed. Dominique Iogna-Prat and Jean-Charles Picard (Paris, 1990), pp. 55–69; English trans.: "The Dead in the Celestial Bookkeeping of the Cluniac Monks Around the Year 1000," in *Debating the Middle Ages*, ed. Lester Little and Barbara Rosenwein (Oxford, 1998), pp. 340–362.

"Panorama de l'hagiographie abbatiale clunisienne (v. 940–v. 1140)," in *Manuscrits hagiographiques et travail des hagiographes*, ed. Martin Heinzelmann (Sigmaringen, 1992), pp. 77–118.

"La confection des cartulaires et l'historiographie à Cluny (XIe–XIIe siècles)," in *Les cartulaires: Actes de la table ronde organisée par l'Ecole nationale des chartes, Paris 5–7 septembre 1991*, ed. Olivier Guyotjeannin, Laurent Morelle and Michel Parisse (Paris, 1993), pp. 27–44.

Etudes clunisiennes (Paris, 2002).

Order and Exclusion: Cluny and Christendom Face Heresy, Judaism, and Islam (1000–1150), trans. Graham Robert Edwards (Ithaca and London, 2002).

Iogna-Prat, Dominique and Rosenwein, Barbara. *Saint Maïeul, Cluny et la Provence: Expansion d'une abbaye à l'aube du moyen âge* (Mane, Haute Provence, 1994).

Isenhath, John O. *The Linguistics of American Sign Language* (London, 1990).

Jacobsen, Werner. *Der Klosterplan von St. Gallen und die karolingische Architektur: Entwicklung und Wandel von Form und Bedeutung im fränkischen Kirchenbau zwischen 751 und 840* (Berlin, 1992).

Jarecki, Walter. *Signa Loquendi: Die cluniacensischen Signa-Listen eingeleitet und herausgegeben* (Baden-Baden, 1981).

"Die 'Ars signorum Cisterciensium' im Rahmen der metrischen Signa-Listen," *Revue bénédictine* 99 (1989): 329–399.

John, Eric. "The Sources of the English Monastic Reformation: A Comment," *Revue bénédictine* 70 (1960): 197–203.

Johnson, Penelope. *Prayer, Patronage, and Power: The Abbey of La Trinité, Vendôme, 1032–1187* (New York and London, 1981).

Jones, Christopher A. "Monastic Identity and Sodomitic Danger in the *Occupatio* by Odo of Cluny," *Speculum* 82 (2007): 1–53.

de Jong, Mayke. "Power and Humility in Carolingian Society: The Public Penance of Louis the Pious," *Early Medieval Europe* 1 (1992): 29–52.

"Carolingian Monasticism: The Power of Prayer," in *The New Cambridge Medieval History*, Volume II, *c. 700–c. 900*, ed. Rosamond McKitterick (Cambridge, 1995).

In Samuel's Image: Child Oblation in the Early Medieval West (Leiden, 1996).

Joris, A. "On the Edge of Two Worlds in the Heart of the New Empire: The Romance Regions of Northern Gaul during the Merovingian Period," *Studies in Mediaeval and Renaissance History* 3 (1966): 1–52.

Kauffmann, C. M. *Romanesque Manuscripts 1066–1190*, A Survey of Manuscripts Illuminated in the British Isles III (London, 1975).

Bibliography

Ker, N. R. *Catalogue of Manuscripts Containing Anglo-Saxon* (Oxford, 1957).

Kershaw, Paul. "Laughter After Babel's Fall: Misunderstanding and Miscommunication in the Ninth-Century West," in *Humour, History and Politics in Late Antiquity and the Early Middle Ages*, ed. Halsall, pp. 179–202.

Kienzle, Beverly Mayne. *Cistercians, Heresy and Crusade in Occitania, 1145–1229: Preaching in the Lord's Vineyard* (York, 2001).

King, Leslie A. "*Surditas*: The Understandings of the Deaf and Deafness in the Writings of Augustine, Jerome, and Bede" (Ph.D. dissertation, Boston University, 1996).

Klima, Edward S. and Bellugi, Ursula. *The Signs of Language* (Cambridge, MA, 1979).

Knowles, David. *Cistercians and Cluniacs: The Controversy Between St. Bernard and Peter the Venerable* (London, New York and Toronto, 1955).

"The Reforming Decrees of Peter the Venerable," in *Petrus Venerabilis 1156–1956*, ed. Giles Constable and James Kritzeck, Studia Anselmiana 40 (Rome, 1956), pp. 1–20.

The Monastic Order in England: A History of its Development from the Times of Dunstan to the Fourth Lateran Council, 940–1216 (Cambridge, 1963).

Kornexl, Lucia. "The *Regularis Concordia* and its Old English Gloss," *Anglo-Saxon England* 24 (1995): 95–130.

Koziol, Geoffrey. *Begging Pardon and Favor: Ritual and Political Order in Early Medieval France* (Ithaca and London, 1992).

Ladner, Gerhart B. *The Idea of Reform: Its Impact on Christian Thought and Action in the Age of the Fathers* (Cambridge, MA, 1959).

Lambot, C. "Un *ordo officii* du 5e siècle," *Revue bénédictine* 42 (1930): 77–80.

Lane, Harlan. *When the Mind Hears: A History of the Deaf* (New York, 1984).

Lapidge, Michael. "The Study of Latin Texts in Late Anglo-Saxon England," in *Latin and the Vernacular Languages in Early Medieval Britain*, ed. N. P. Brooks (Leicester, 1984), pp. 99–140.

"A Frankish Scholar in Tenth-Century England: Frithegod of Canterbury/Fredegaud of Brioude," *Anglo-Saxon England* 17 (1988): 45–65.

"B. and the Vita S. Dunstani," in *St. Dunstan: His Life, Times and Cult*, ed. Ramsay, Sparks and Tatton-Brown, pp. 247–259.

Anglo-Latin Literature, 900–1066 (London and Rio Grande, 1993).

"Latin Learning in Ninth-Century England," in *Anglo-Latin Literature, 600–899* (London and Rio Grande, 1996), pp. 409–454.

Lapidge, Michael and Winterbottom, Michael, eds. and trans. *Wulfstan of Winchester: Life of St Æthelwold* (Oxford, 1991).

Laporte, J. "Saint Odon, disciple de saint Grégoire le grand," in *A Cluny*, ed. Société des Amis de Cluny, pp. 138–143.

Lawless, George. *Augustine of Hippo and His Monastic Rule* (Oxford, 1987).

Lawrence, C. H. *Medieval Monasticism: Forms of Religious Life in Western Europe in the Middle Ages*, 2nd edn (London and New York, 1989).

Le Goff, Jacques. *The Birth of Purgatory*, trans. Arthur Goldhammer (Chicago, 1984).

"Le rire dans les règles monastiques du haut moyen âge," in *Haut moyen âge: Culture, éducation et société. Etudes offertes à Pierre Riché*, ed. Claude Lepelley et al. (Nanterre, 1990), pp. 93–103.

Leclercq, Jean. "L'idéal monastique de saint Odon d'après ses oeuvres," in *A Cluny*, ed. Société des Amis de Cluny, pp. 227–232.

Bibliography

"Pierre le Vénérable et l'érémitisme clunisien," in *Petrus Venerabilis 1156–1956*, ed. Giles Constable and James Kritzeck, Studia Anselmiana 40 (Rome, 1956), pp. 99–120.

"Saint Antoine dans la tradition monastique médiévale," in *Antonius Magnus Eremita 356–1956: Studia ad antiquum monachismum spectantia*, ed. Basil Steidle, Studia Anselmiana 38 (Rome, 1956), pp. 229–247.

Etudes sur le vocabulaire monastique du moyen âge, Studia Anselmiana 48 (Rome, 1961).

The Life of Perfection: Points of View on the Essence of the Religious State, trans. Leonard J. Doyle (Collegeville, MN, 1961).

The Love of Learning and the Desire for God: A Study of Monastic Culture, trans. Catharine Misrahi (New York, 1961).

"L'érémitisme en occident jusqu'à l'an mil," in *L'eremitismo in occidente nei secoli XI e XII: Atti della seconda settimana internazionale di studio (Mendola, 30 agosto–6 settembre 1962)* (Milan, 1965), pp. 27–44.

"Religious Obedience According to the Rule of Benedict," *American Benedictine Review* 16 (1965): 183–193.

"Prayer at Cluny," *Journal of the American Academy of Religion* 51 (1983): 651–665.

Lekai, Louis. *The Cistercians: Ideals and Realities* (Kent, OH, 1977).

Lester, Anne E. "Cleaning House in 1399: Disobedience and the Demise of Cistercian Convents in Northern France at the End of the Middle Ages," in *Oboedientia: Zu Formen und Grenzen von Macht und Unterordnung im mittelalterlichen Religiosentum*, ed. Sébastien Barret and Gert Melville (Münster, 2005), pp. 423–444.

"Cares Beyond the Walls: Cistercian Nuns and the Care of Lepers in Twelfth- and Thirteenth-Century Northern France," in *Religious and Laity in Northern Europe, 1000–1400: Interaction, Negotiation and Power*, ed. E. Jamroziak and J. Burton (Turnhout, 2006), pp. 197–224.

Levison, Wilhelm. *England and the Continent in the Eighth Century* (Oxford, 1946).

Leyser, Conrad. *Authority and Asceticism from Augustine to Gregory the Great* (Oxford, 2000).

"Angels, Monks, and Demons in the Early Medieval West," in *Belief and Culture in the Middle Ages: Studies Presented to Henry Mayr-Harting*, ed. Richard Gameson and Henrietta Leyser (Oxford, 2001), pp. 9–22.

Leyser, Henrietta. *Hermits and the New Monasticism: A Study of Religious Communities in Western Europe 1000–1150* (New York, 1984).

Leyser, Karl. "The Ottonians and Wessex," in *Communications and Power in Medieval Europe: The Carolingian and Ottonian Centuries*, ed. Timothy Reuter (London and Rio Grande, 1994), pp. 73–104.

Liddell, Scott K. *American Sign Language Syntax* (New York, 1980).

Little, Lester. *Religious Poverty and the Profit Economy in Medieval Europe* (Ithaca, 1978).

Longo, Umberto. "Riti e agiografia: L'istituzione della *commemoratio omnium fidelium defunctorum* nelle *Vitae* di Odilone di Cluny," *Bullettino dell'Istituto Storico Italiano per il Medio Evo e Archivio Muratoriano* 103 (2002): 163–200.

Lorenz, R. "Die Anfänge des abendländischen Mönchtums im 4. Jahrhundert," *Zeitschrift für Kirchengeschichte* 77 (1966): 1–61.

Lutterbach, Hubertus. *Monachus factus est: Die Mönchwerdung im frühen Mittelalter, zugleich ein Beitrag zur Frömmigkeits- und Liturgiegeschichte* (Münster, 1995).

Lynch, Joseph H. "Hugh I of Cluny's Sponsorship of Henry IV: Its Context and Consequences," *Speculum* 60 (1985): 800–826.

Bibliography

McCluskey, Stephen C. *Astronomies and Cultures in Early Medieval Europe* (Cambridge, 1998).

McDougall, David and McDougall, Ian. "Evil Tongues: A Previously Unedited Old English Sermon," *Anglo-Saxon England* 26 (1997): 209–229.

McGuire, Brian Patrick. "The Cistercians and the Rise of the Exemplum in Early Thirteenth-Century France: A Reevaluation of Paris B.N. MS lat. 15912," *Classica et Medievalia* 34 (1983): 211–267.

Friendship and Faith: Cistercian Men, Women, and their Stories, 1100–1250 (Aldershot, 2002).

McKitterick, Rosamond. *The Frankish Kingdoms Under the Carolingians, 751–987* (London and New York, 1983).

The Carolingians and the Written Word (Cambridge, 1989).

McNulty, J. Bard. "The Lady Aelfgyva in the Bayeux Tapestry," *Speculum* 55 (1980): 659–668.

Manitius, Max. *Geschichte der lateinischen Literatur des Mittelalters*, 3 vols. (Munich, 1911–1931).

Martène, Edmond. *De antiquis ecclesiae ritibus libri*, 4 vols., 2nd edn (Antwerp, 1736; repr. Hildesheim, 1967–1969).

Martins, Mario. "Livros de Sinais dos Cistercienses Portugueses," *Boletin de Filologia* 17 (1958): 293–357.

Meens, Rob. "The Frequency and Nature of Early Medieval Penance," in *Handling Sin: Confession in the Middle Ages*, ed. Peter Biller and A. J. Minnis, York Studies in Medieval Theology II (Woodbridge, 1998), pp. 35–63.

Meissner, Martin and Philpott, Stuart B. "The Sign Language of Sawmill Workers in British Columbia," *Sign Language Studies* 9 (1975): 291–308.

Melville, Gert. "Action, Text and Validity: On Re-Examining Cluny's *Consuetudines* and Statutes," in *From Dead of Night to End of Day*, ed. Boynton and Cochelin, pp. 67–83.

Meyvaert, Paul. "Peter the Deacon and the Tomb of Saint Benedict: The Cassinese Tradition," *Revue bénédictine* 65 (1955): 3–70.

"Bede's Text of the *Libellus Responsionum* of Gregory the Great to Augustine of Canterbury," in *England Before the Conquest: Studies in Primary Sources Presented to Dorothy Whitelock*, ed. Peter Clemoes and Kathleen Hughes (Cambridge, 1971), pp. 15–33.

Benedict, Gregory, Bede and Others (London, 1977).

Milis, Ludo. "Ermites et chanoines réguliers au XIIe siècle," *Cahiers de Civilisation Médiévale* 22 (1979): 39–80.

Miller, Patricia Cox. "Jerome's Centaur: A Hyper-Icon of the Desert," *Journal of Early Christian Studies* 4 (1996): 209–233.

de Miramon, Charles. "Embrasser l'état monastique à l'âge adulte (1050–1200): Etude sur la conversion tardive," *Annales: Economies, Sociétés, Civilisations* 54 (1999): 825–849.

Molitor, Stephan. "*Ut fertur, sub Pippino rege*: Zur karolingerzeitlichen Gründung Hirsaus," in *Hirsau St. Peter und Paul*, vol. II, pp. 45–54.

Morghen, Raffaello. "Riforma monastica et spiritualità cluniacense," in *Spiritualità Cluniacense: Convegni del Centro di Studi sulla spiritualità medievale, 1958* (Todi, 1960), pp. 33–56.

Bibliography

Morrison, Karl F. "Know Thyself: Music in the Carolingian Renaissance," in *Committenti e produzione artistico-letteraria nell'alto medioevo occidentale*, vol. I, pp. 369–483.

Mostert, Marco. "Le séjour d'Abbon de Fleury à Ramsey," *Bibliothèque de l'Ecole des Chartes* 144 (1986): 199–208.

Mostert, Marco, ed. *New Approaches to Medieval Communication* (Turnhout, 1999).

Moyse, Gérard. "Monachisme et réglementation monastique en Gaule avant Benoît d'Aniane," in *Sous la règle de saint Benoît: Structures monastiques et sociétés en France du moyen âge à l'époque moderne* (Geneva, 1982), pp. 3–19.

Murray, Alexander. "Confession Before 1215," *Transactions of the Royal Historical Society*, 6th series, 3 (1993): 51–81.

Neiske, Franz. "Visionen und Totengedenken," *Frühmittelalterliche Studien* 20 (1986): 138–185.

Nelson, Axel. "Teckenspråket I Vadstena Kloster," *Nordisk Tidskrift för Bok- och Biblioteksväsen* 22 (1935): 25–43.

Nightingale, John. "Oswald, Fleury and Continental Reform," in *St. Oswald of Worcester: Life and Influence*, ed. Brooks and Cubitt, pp. 23–45.

Noble, Thomas F. X. "The Monastic Ideal as a Model for Empire: The Case of Louis the Pious," *Revue bénédictine* 86 (1976): 235–250.

"Louis the Pious and His Piety Reconsidered," *Revue Belge de Philologie et d'Histoire* 58 (1980): 297–316.

Nussbaum, Otto. *Kloster, Priestermönch und Privatmesse: Ihr Verhältnis im Westen von den Anfängen bis zum hohen Mittelalter* (Bonn, 1961).

Oexle, Otto Gerhard. "Les moines d'occident et la vie politique et sociale dans le haut moyen âge," *Revue bénédictine* 103 (1993): 255–272.

Ohlgren, Thomas H. "The Grumbling Monk in the Hereford Gospels," *Old English Newsletter* 24.3 (Spring, 1991): 22–24.

Ortenberg, Veronica. *The English Church and the Continent in the Tenth and Eleventh Centuries: Cultural, Spiritual, and Artistic Exchanges* (Oxford, 1992).

Othon, R. P. "De l'institution et des us des convers dans l'ordre de Cîteaux (XIIe et XIIIe siècles)," in *Saint Bernard et son temps*, 2 vols. (Dijon, 1928–1929), vol. II, pp. 139–201.

Paden, Jr., William D. "*De monachis rithmos facientibus*: Hélinant de Froidmont, Bertran of Born, and the Cistercian General Chapter of 1199," *Speculum* 55 (1980): 669–685.

Pearson, Kathy L. "Nutrition and the Early-Medieval Diet," *Speculum* 72 (1997): 1–32.

Plann, Susan. "Pedro Ponce de Leon: Myth and Reality," in *Deaf History Unveiled: Interpretations from the New Scholarship*, ed. J. V. Van Cleve (Washington, DC, 1993), pp. 1–12.

A Silent Minority: Deaf Education in Spain, 1550–1835 (Berkeley, Los Angeles and London, 1997).

Poncelet, A. "La vie et les oeuvres de Thierry de Fleury," *Analecta Bollandiana* 27 (1908): 5–27.

Porter, David W. "The Latin Syllabus in Anglo-Saxon Monastic Schools," *Neophilologus* 78 (1994): 463–482.

Power, Eileen. *Medieval People* (Boston and New York, 1924).

Bibliography

Prinz, Friedrich. *Frühes Mönchtum in Frankenreich: Kultur und Gesellschaft in Gallien, den Rheinlanden und Bayern am Beispiel der monastischen Entwicklung (4. bis 8. Jahrhundert)*, 2nd edn (Munich, 1988).

Proust, Bernard. "Essai historique sur les origines de l'abbaye de Baume-les-Moines," *Mémoires de la Société d'Emulation du Jura* (1871–1872): 23–132.

Quay, Suzanne. "Signs of Silence: Two Examples of Trappist Sign Language in the Far East," *Cîteaux: Commentarii Cistercienses* 52 (2001): 211–230.

Ramsay, Nigel, Sparks, Margaret and Tatton-Brown, Tim, eds. *St. Dunstan: His Life, Times and Cult* (Woodbridge, 1992).

Reimann, Norbert. "Die Konstitutionen des Abtes Wilhelm von Hirsau: Bermerkungen zur Überlieferungs- und Wirkungsgeschichte," in *Hirsau St. Peter und Paul*, vol. II, pp. 101–108.

Resnick, Irven M. "*Risus monasticus*: Laughter and Medieval Monastic Culture," *Revue bénédictine* 97 (1987): 90–100.

Riché, Pierre. "Le rôle de la mémoire dans l'enseignement médiéval," in *Jeux de mémoire: Aspects de la mnémotechnie médiévale*, ed. Bruno Roy and Paul Zumthor (Montréal and Paris, 1985), pp. 133–148.

Richter, Helmut. *Die Persönlichkeitsdarstellung in cluniazensischen Abtsviten* (Erlangen, 1972).

Rieche, Anita. "*Computatio Romana*: Fingerzählen auf provinzialrömischen Reliefs," *Bonner Jahrbücher* 186 (1986): 165–192.

van Rijnberk, Gérard. "De Gebarentaal in een Cisterciënserklooster der Nederlanden in de XVe eeuw," *Cîteaux in de Nederlanden* 2 (1951): 55–68.

Le langage par signes chez les moines (Amsterdam, 1953).

Rosenwein, Barbara. "St. Odo's St. Martin: The Uses of a Model," *Journal of Medieval History* 4 (1978): 317–331.

Rhinoceros Bound: Cluny in the Tenth Century (Philadelphia, 1982).

Negotiating Space: Power, Restraint, and Privileges of Immunity in Early Medieval Europe (Ithaca and London, 1999).

"Perennial Prayer at Agaune," in *Monks and Nuns, Saints and Outcasts: Religion in Medieval Society*, ed. Sharon Farmer and Barbara Rosenwein (Ithaca and London, 2000), pp. 37–56.

"Views from Afar: North American Perspectives on Medieval Monasticism," in *Dove va la storiografia monastica in Europa? Temi e metodi di ricerca per lo studio della vita monastica e regolare in età medievale alle soglie del terzo millennio*, ed. Giancarlo Andenna (Milan, 2001), pp. 67–84.

Rouche, Michel. "Miroirs des princes ou miroir du clergé?" in *Committenti e produzione artistico-letteraria nell'alto medioevo occidentale*, vol. I, pp. 341–367.

Rousseau, Philip. *Ascetics, Authority, and the Church in the Age of Jerome and Cassian* (Oxford, 1978).

Pachomius: The Making of a Community in Fourth-Century Egypt (Berkeley, Los Angeles and London, 1985).

Rubenstein, Jay. *Guibert of Nogent: Portrait of a Medieval Mind* (New York and London, 2002).

Rüffer, Jens. *Orbis Cisterciensis: Zur Geschichte der monastischen ästhetischen Kultur im 12. Jahrhundert*, Studien zur Geschichte, Kunst und Kultur der Zisterzienser VI (Berlin, 1999).

Bibliography

Sacks, Oliver. *Seeing Voices: A Journey into the World of the Deaf* (New York, 1989).

Sackur, Ernst. *Die Cluniacenser in ihrer kirchlichen und allgemeingeschichtlichen Wirksamkeit bis zur Mitte des elften Jahrhunderts*, 2 vols. (Halle an der Saale, 1892).

Saint Mayeul et son temps: Actes du congrès international de Valensole, 2–14 mai 1994 (Dignes-les-Bains, 1997).

Saurette, Marc. "Excavating and Renovating Ancient Texts: Seventeenth- and Eighteenth-Century Editions of Bernard of Cluny's *Consuetudines* and Early-Modern Monastic Scholarship," in *From Dead of Night to End of Day*, ed. Boynton and Cochelin, pp. 85–107.

Schmidt, Paul Gerhard. "*Ars loquendi et ars tacendi*: Zur monastischen Zeichensprache des Mittelalters," *Berichte zur Wissenschaftsgeschichte* 4 (1981): 13–19.

Schmitt, Jean-Claude. *La raison des gestes dans l'occident médiéval* (Paris, 1990).

Ghosts in the Middle Ages: The Living and the Dead in Medieval Society, trans. Teresa Lavender Fagan (Chicago, 1998).

Schmitz, G. "*Quod rident homo, plurandum est*: Der Unwert des Lachen im monastische geprägten Vorstellungen der spätantike und des frühen Mittelalters," in *Stadtverfassung, Verfassungsstaat, Pressepolitik: Festschrift E. Naujoks*, ed. F. Quarthal and W. Setzler (Sigmaringen, 1980), pp. 3–15.

Schreiner, Klaus. "Verschriftlichung als Faktor monastischer Reform: Funktionen von Schriftlichkeit im Ordenswesen des hohen und späten Mittelalters," in *Pragmatische Schriftlichkeit im Mittelalter: Erscheinungsformen und Entwicklungsstufen*, ed. Hagen Keller, Klaus Grubmüller and Nikolaus Staubach (Munich, 1992), pp. 37–75.

Selmer, Carl. "The Beginnings of the St. Brendan Legend on the Continent," *Catholic Historical Review* 29 (1943): 169–176.

"Israel, ein unbekannter Schotte des 10. Jahrhunderts," *Studien und Mitteilungen zur Geschichte des Benediktiner-Ordens und seiner Zweige* 62 (1949–1950): 69–86.

Semmler, Josef. "Die Beschlüsse des Aachener Konzils im Jahre 816," *Zeitschrift für Kirchengeschichte* 74 (1963): 15–82.

"Karl der Grosse und das fränkische Mönchtum," in *Karl der Grosse: Lebenswerk und Nachleben*, ed. Helmut Beumann *et al.*, 5 vols. (Düsseldorf, 1965–1968), vol. II, pp. 255–289.

"Pippin III. und die fränkischen Klöster," *Francia* 3 (1975): 88–146.

"Mönche und Kanoniker im Frankenreich Pippins III. und Karls des Grossen," in *Untersuchungen zu Kloster und Stift* (Göttingen, 1980), pp. 78–111.

"Benedictus II: Una regula, una consuetudo," in *Benedictine Culture, 750–1050*, ed. W. Lourdaux and D. Verhelst (Leuven, 1983), pp. 1–49.

Smith, Julia M. H. "The Problem of Female Sanctity in Carolingian Europe, c. 780–920," *Past and Present* 146 (1995): 3–37.

Société des Amis de Cluny, ed. *A Cluny, Congrès scientifique: Fêtes et cérémonies liturgiques en l'honneur des saints Abbés Odo et Odilon* (Dijon, 1950).

Southern, Richard. *Western Society and the Church in the Middle Ages* (London, 1970).

Squatriti, Paulo. *Water and Society in Early Medieval Italy, AD 400–1000* (Cambridge, 1998).

Stafford, Pauline. "Queens, Nunneries and Reforming Churchmen: Gender, Religious Status and Reform in Tenth- and Eleventh-Century England," *Past and Present* 163 (1999): 3–35.

Steidle, Basilius. "Das Lachen im alten Mönchtum," *Benediktinische Monatsschrift* 20 (1938): 271–280.

Bibliography

Stokoe, William. *Sign Language Structure* (Buffalo, 1960).

Stokoe, William, Casterline, Dorothy and Croneberg, Carl. *A Dictionary of American Sign Language on Linguistic Principles* (Washington, DC, 1965).

Sullivan, Richard E. "What Was Carolingian Monasticism? The Plan of Saint Gall and the History of Monasticism," in *After Rome's Fall: Narrators and Sources of Early Medieval History, Essays Presented to Walter Goffart*, ed. Alexander Callander Murray (Toronto, 1998), pp. 251–287.

Symons, Thomas. "The Sources of the *Regularis Concordia*," *Downside Review* 59 (1941): 14–36, 143–170 and 264–289.

"*Regularis Concordia*: History and Derivation," in *Tenth-Century Studies: Essays in Commemoration of the Millennium of the Council of Winchester and Regularis Concordia*, ed. David Parsons (London, 1975), pp. 37–59.

Taylor, Anna. "Just Like a Mother Bee: Reading and Writing *Vitae metricae* around the Year 1000," *Viator* 36 (2005): 119–148.

Tellenbach, Gerd. "Die Sturz des Abtes Pontius von Cluny," *Quellen und Forschungen aus italienischen Archiven und Bibliotheken* 42–43 (1963): 13–55.

Trichet, Louis. *La tonsure: vie et mort d'une pratique ecclésiastique* (Paris, 1990).

Tutsch, Burkhardt. *Studien zur Rezeptionsgeschichte der Consuetudines Ulrichs von Cluny* (Münster, 1998).

Umiker-Sebeok, Jean and Sebeok, Thomas A., eds. *Monastic Sign Languages* (Berlin, New York and Amsterdam, 1987).

Van Engen, John. "The 'Crisis of Cenobitism' Reconsidered: Benedictine Monasticism in the Years 1050–1150," *Speculum* 61 (1986): 269–304.

Religion in the History of the Medieval West (Aldershot, 2004).

Vezin, J. "Leofnoth: un scribe anglais à Saint-Benoît-sur-Loire," *Codices manuscripti* 4 (1977): 109–120.

de Vogüé, Adalbert. *Les règles monastiques anciennes (400–700)* (Turnhout, 1985).

"The Master and St. Benedict: A Reply to Marilyn Dunn," *English Historical Review* 107 (1992): 95–103.

"Obéissance et autorité dans le monachisme ancien jusqu'à Saint Benoît," in *Imaginer la théologie catholique: Permanence et transformations de la foi en attendant Jésus-Christ: Mélanges offerts à Ghislain Lafont*, ed. Jeremy Driscoll, Studia Anselmiana 129 (Rome, 2000), pp. 565–600.

Regards sur le monachisme des premiers siècles: Recueil d'articles, Studia Anselmiana 130 (Rome, 2000).

"Influence de sainte Basile sur le monachisme d'occident," *Revue bénédictine* 113 (2003): 5–17.

Waddell, Chrysogonus. "The Myth of Cistercian Origins: C. H. Berman and the Manuscript Sources," *Cîteaux: Commentarii Cistercienses* 51 (2000): 299–386.

Wallace-Hadrill, J. M. *Bede's Ecclesiastical History of the English People: An Historical Commentary* (Oxford, 1988).

Wathan, Ambrose G. *Silence: The Meaning of Silence in the Rule of Saint Benedict* (Washington, DC, 1973).

Weiss, Jean-Pierre. "Le statut du prédicateur et les instruments de la prédication dans la Provence du Ve siècle," in *La parole du prédicateur, Ve–XVe siècle* (Nice, 1997), pp. 23–47.

Bibliography

White, Hayden. "Pontius of Cluny, the Curia Romana, and the End of Gregorianism in Rome," *Church History* 27 (1958): 195–219.

Williams, Burma P. and Williams, Richard S. "Finger Numbers in the Greco-Roman World and the Early Middle Ages," *Isis* 86 (1995): 587–608.

Wischermann, Else Maria. *Marcigny-sur-Loire: Gründungs- und Frühgeschichte des ersten Cluniacenserinnenpriorates (1055–1150)* (Munich, 1986).

Wollasch, Joachim. "Königtum, Adel und Klöster im Berry während des 10. Jahrhunderts," in *Neue Forschungen über Cluny und die Cluniacenser*, ed. Gerd Tellenbach (Freiburg, 1959), pp. 17–165.

"Cluny und Deutschland," *Studien und Mitteilungen zur Geschichte des Benediktinerordens und seiner Zweige* 103 (1992): 7–32.

"Reformmönchtum und Schriftlichkeit," *Frühmittelalterliche Studien* 26 (1992): 274–286.

"Zur Verschriftlichung der klösterlichen Lebensgewohnheiten unter Abt Hugo von Cluny," *Frühmittelalterliche Studien* 27 (1993): 317–349.

Cluny, Licht der Welt: Aufstieg und Niedergang der klösterlichen Gemeinschaft (Düsseldorf and Zürich, 1996).

"Das Schisma des Abtes Pontius von Cluny," *Francia* 23 (1996): 31–52.

Wormald, Patrick. "Æthelwold and his Continental Counterparts: Contact, Comparison, Contrast," in *Bishop Æthelwold*, ed. Yorke, pp. 13–42.

The Times of Bede, 625–865: Studies in Early English Christian Society and its Historian (Oxford, 2006).

Wright, Roger. *Late Latin and Early Romance in Spain and Carolingian France* (Liverpool, 1982).

Wright, Roger, ed. *Latin and the Romance Languages in the Early Middle Ages* (University Park, PA, 1991).

Yorke, Barbara, ed. *Bishop Æthelwold: His Career and Influence* (Woodbridge, 1988).

Zimmermann, Gerd. *Ordensleben und Lebensstandard: Die Cura corporis in den Ordensvorschriften des abendländischen Hochmittelalters* (Münster, 1973).

INDEX

Index

Index

speech
  harmful, 31–33, 34–35
  useful, 30–31, 35
  see also Cluny, safeguards against harmful
    speech at; laughter, monastic attitudes
    toward; murmuring; slander

Thegan, *Deeds of Emperor Louis the Pious* (*Gesta
  Hludovici imperatoris*), 42–43
Thierry of Fleury, 104–105, 106

Ulrich of Zell, 9–10, 20, 22, 23, 26–27, 49, 63,
  66, 68, 70, 71, 78, 83, 87, 89, 104, 114,
  118–120, 173–174
Urban II, pope (1088–1099), 160

Valerian, bishop of Cimiez (d. *c.* 460), 31, 36
vernacular, translation of monastic texts into,
  115–116

Virgil, *Aeneid*, 23, 88–89
virtue, monastic, 3, 35–36
  see also humility; obedience; sexual purity;
    silence
Voyage of Saint Brendan (*Navigatio sancti
  Brendani*), 9, 53–54, 61

Waldebert, *Rule for Virgins* (*Regula ad virgines*), 34
William I, duke of Aquitaine and count of
  Auvergne, 15, 16, 17, 18, 24, 28
William IV, duke of Aquitaine (963–995), 99
William of Hirsau, 89, 118–123, 173
William of Malmesbury, 109
Winchester, Council of (*c.* 970), 110–112
Wollasch, Joachim, 9
women, religious, 146–147, 151, 164
  use of sign language among, 162
Wulfstan of Winchester, *Life of Saint Æthelwold*
  (*Vita sancti Æthelwoldi*), 112–113

209

Cambridge Studies in Medieval Life and Thought
Fourth Series